Problem Solving Therapy in the Clinical Practice

Problem Solving Therapy in the Clinical Practice

Mehmet Eskin
Adnan Menderes University,
Department of Psychiatry,
Turkey

ELSEVIER

AMSTERDAM • BOSTON • HEIDELBERG • LONDON • NEW YORK • OXFORD
PARIS • SAN DIEGO • SAN FRANCISCO • SINGAPORE • SYDNEY • TOKYO

Elsevier
32 Jamestown Road, London NW1 7BY
225 Wyman Street, Waltham, MA 02451, USA

First edition 2013

Notices
Knowledge and best practice in this field are constantly changing. As new research and experience broaden our understanding, changes in research methods, professional practices, or medical treatment may become necessary.

Practitioners and researchers must always rely on their own experience and knowledge in evaluating and using any information, methods, compounds, or experiments described herein. In using such information or methods they should be mindful of their own safety and the safety of others, including parties for whom they have a professional responsibility.

To the fullest extent of the law, neither the Publisher nor the authors, contributors, or editors, assume any liability for any injury and/or damage to persons or property as a matter of products liability, negligence or otherwise, or from any use or operation of any methods, products, instructions, or ideas contained in the material herein.

British Library Cataloguing-in-Publication Data
A catalogue record for this book is available from the British Library

Library of Congress Cataloging-in-Publication Data
A catalog record for this book is available from the Library of Congress

ISBN: 978-0-12-398455-5

This book has been manufactured using Print On Demand technology. Each copy is produced to order and is limited to black ink. The online version of this book will show color figures where appropriate.

Dedication

For my wife Zeliha and my daughters Berke and Ege

Contents

Introduction

Mental health problems are common and cause unnecessary human suffering. The reasons for this are the ups and downs of life that develop in conjunction with irregularities in biological and social structures. Mental health problems, like all the other health-related problems, have some negative consequences for individuals as well as for society. Personal pain and unhappiness caused by mental health problems can make life unbearable. Some people who have mental health problems may engage in harmful behaviors such as injuring themselves and others. Suicidal behavior and violence, growing in frequency within society, are incidents that have consequences both at the individual and at the societal levels. On the other hand, mental health problems lead to considerable workplace absences. Furthermore, mental health problems constitute an important burden to national health care systems.

In addition to the mental disorders that develop independently, those that develop as a consequence of physical illnesses take an important place in the health care system. Such problems lower the patients' quality of life and make it difficult for them to adapt to their medical treatment. Important to the treatment of many medical illnesses is whether or not the patient complies with the lifestyle changes suggested in the treatment plan. For instance, it is extremely important that patients comply with treatment plan suggestions for treatment of diabetes, hypertension, among other illnesses.

Mental health problems show different frequencies in different periods in a lifetime. The scientific studies conducted on the frequency of mental health problems show that mental health problems such as depression, suicide and anxiety, and behavioral problems such as substance abuse, self-injury, and aggression are frequent events. Depression and suicide are common among the elderly. Having the capability to solve the problems encountered in daily life decreases the probability of experiencing mental health problems significantly.

Diverse behavioral and pharmacological technologies can be used for the treatment of mental health problems today. The increase in the number of pharmacological agents available for the treatment of mental health problems and the fact that their effectiveness has scientifically been demonstrated within the last 40 years is an important development for the provision of modern psychiatric treatment services. Similarly, there has been a significant increase in the diversity of psychotherapeutic methods used in the treatment of mental health problems. The concept of *empirically supported psychotherapy* has been suggested for psychotherapies and the requirement of basing their effectiveness on scientific grounds came into prominence. According to the data obtained from scientific studies in relation to the effectiveness of psychotherapy, cognitive–behavioral psychotherapies demonstrate particular effectiveness.

Within the complex social structure of today's societies, people are running short of both the time and the social and individual resources for long-term psychotherapeutic practices. Basic tendency in the practice of psychotherapy has been toward the ones whose effectiveness was scientifically proven and that can be implemented in a relatively short period of time. These have been preferred both by those who receive psychotherapy services and by those who finance them.

A major problem related to psychotherapeutic services is their inability to reach large masses of people. And the major reason for this is the scarcity of the resources and facilities allocated to psychotherapy training. It is known that the training of empirically supported psychotherapies does not take place in the educational curriculum of those professions that provide psychotherapy services (Weissman et al., 2006). Most people with mental health problems apply to primary health care units instead of applying to psychiatry clinics because of a lack of knowledge and the fear of stigmatization. Although physicians who offer primary care services encounter patients with a variety of mental health problems, they normally do not have the necessary knowledge required to deal with such health problems with nonpharmacological means.

As a cognitive–behavioral mode of action, problem-solving therapy is a psychotherapy alternative that can overcome the aforementioned problems. Practicing and learning the problem-solving therapy is relatively easy. Due to its characteristics, problem-solving therapy, whose effectiveness in dealing with and treating various mental health problems has scientifically been demonstrated, can be considered as an alternative that has the ability to reach large masses of people. Problem-solving therapy—which is easy to learn and teach due to its structured nature—is an alternative that can meet the educational needs of the professional groups that provide the mental health services. For instance, Hegel, Dietrich, Seville, and Jordan (2004) indicate that problem-solving therapy is feasible in training residents in family medicine.

Who needs to learn the problem-solving therapy presented in this book? In other words, what is the target audience of this book? Because of the characteristics discussed in the previous paragraph, the professional groups that need to learn problem-solving therapy are those who provide mental health services at different levels in society, such as psychologists, physicians, counselors, nurses, and social workers. Since mental health problems are frequently encountered in primary care services, it is believed that teaching problem-solving therapy to nurses and physicians will make it easier to deal with such cases at this level and will make it possible to offer psychotherapy services to large masses of people.

This book—which includes topics in relation to the theories, research findings, and the practice itself—is organized into 11 chapters. Chapters 1–4 include the definition, concepts, and theoretical points of view in relation to problem solving and therapy. Chapter 1 discusses the basic definitions and concepts, while Chapter 2 relates the problem solving to resilience and coping. Chapter 3 discusses the cognitive, metacognitive, and motivational components of the problem solving, and Chapter 4 examines the theoretical views on problem-solving therapy. While Chapter 5 emphasizes the scientific findings on the relationship between problem-solving skills and mental health problems, Chapter 6 discusses the effectiveness of problem-solving therapy in the treatment of mental health problems in light of the scientific studies. Chapter 7 discusses the implementation of the problem-solving therapy and the patient groups to which it is being applied. Chapter 8 discusses the principles, the skills, the characteristics of the therapists, and the change processes in psychotherapeutic practices. Chapter 9 examines the assessment in problem-solving therapy. The process and the stages of problem-solving therapy are presented in Chapter 10. The eleventh chapter presents a complete implementation of problem-solving therapy applied to a 16-year-old female client.

Does problem-solving therapy solve all the problems? The answer to this question must undoubtedly be "No." Problem-solving therapy is an alternative just like other treatment approaches. Keeping in mind the increase in demand for mental health services, employing various treatment alternatives is useful for both the individuals and the society. Every therapeutic approach has its advantages and its disadvantages. What is important is having alternatives that can meet different demands. In light of the information just presented, it is true that problem-solving therapy has certain advantages. But one should not forget that problem-solving therapy, just like other treatment methods, may have certain limitations. It is thought that problem-solving therapy will meet the individual and social requirements to a great extent. The book that you are reading has been written in consideration of the potential individual and social contributions of the problem-solving therapy.

1 Definition and Concepts

Introduction

Before we can consider using a therapy, we need to be sure that we understand the basic definitions and concepts so that we all interpret and apply the information in the same way. The definitions draw the boundaries around the terms and the concepts of any scientific topic and introduce its relationship to and difference from other topics. A scientific topic or a clinical therapy needs to be viewed within a theoretical and conceptual framework. In order to facilitate understanding and provide a guideline for application, this chapter introduces the fundamental definitions and concepts of problem-solving therapy (PST). It begins with a definition of PST and then proceeds to define the concept of a problem and of a solution. Once this has been established, we can consider problem solving and the difference between coming up with a solution to the problem and applying the solution. The clarification of these concepts is necessary for both research and application.

What Is PST?

PST is a treatment method that can be used when people have developed emotional problems through enduring the hardship caused by the daily problems that they face. The goal of PST is to teach people how to approach their problems as well as strategies and other means they can develop to solve these problems. Thus, PST aims to treat the emotional difficulties caused by these problems as well as to prevent the emergence of psychological difficulties.

In general, the problem-solving approach can be used in two ways. The first is the standard therapy method, wherein PST is used to treat psychological problems caused by exposure to problem situations. The second is a preventive approach. People can be taught how to effectively handle daily problems before those problems have produced any emotional difficulties. It is assumed that training healthy individuals how to solve or handle problems of daily living prevent the development of psychopathology. This way, problem solving mainly aims to increase the resiliency of the person.

The PST approach can also be defined as the clinical application of the information on problem solving and decision making collected through academic psychology. PST is a cognitive–behavioral psychotherapy approach. Psychotherapies are considered to be empirically supported if their efficiency is shown scientifically

Problem Solving Therapy in the Clinical Practice. DOI: http://dx.doi.org/10.1016/B978-0-12-398455-5.00001-2

(Borkovec & Castonguay, 1998). As is known, cognitive–behavioral treatment approaches have come to occupy a very important place in the mental health field with good scientific evidence to support their use (Bandelow et al., 2007; Butler et al., 2006; DeRubeis et al., 2005; Hollon et al., 2005; Malhi et al., 2009; Steward & Chambless, 2009). Recent meta-analytic studies indicate that the efficacy of PST is shown empirically in the treatment of a wide range of health problems (Bell & D'Zurilla, 2009a; Cuijpers, van Straten, & Warmerdam, 2007; Malouff, Thorsteinsson, & Schutte, 2007).

So, where does PST take its place among cognitive–behavioral therapies? McGuire (2001) appraises cognitive and behavioral therapies on a scale that ranges from being "purely behavioral" to being "purely cognitive." On the purely behavioral end of the scale, behavioral modification takes place, and on the purely cognitive end of the scale, schema-focused therapy takes place. On this scale, PST sits between self-instructional training and cognitive therapy.

PST is being used more and more for the treatment of emotional problems. Scientific research shows that the absence of problem-solving skills in people causes the emergence of psychopathology and its endurance. For this reason, the PST approach is important for eliminating the negative effects that people face in their lives as well as making it easier for them to cope with these problems.

What Is a Problem?

One of the most important definitions of PST is the definition of the problem. What is a problem? How does PST define a problem? How can a problem be defined in a formal way?

A problem can be defined in many ways. Creating a formal definition that allows everyone to meet on common ground is crucial. The *Encyclopedia Britannica* defines a problem as "a question raised for inquiry, consideration, or solution." According to the extended definition offered by *Webster's Online Dictionary*, "a problem is an obstacle which makes it difficult to achieve a desired goal, objective, or purpose. It refers to a situation, condition or issue that is yet unresolved. In a broad sense, a problem exists when an individual becomes aware of a significant difference between what actually is and what is desired. Every problem requires an answer or solution."

These definitions consist of four aspects. The first aspect requires the problem to be inquired about and investigated. For example, a student who encounters a math problem should learn more about it. The student should collect and acquire more information about it and investigate what is required for solution. According to the second aspect, a problem is a situation that should be thought about and solved. The person who encounters the problem should think about it and find out what needs to be done. Third, a problem needs to be solved. One needs to solve the problem according to one's own personal goals. Last, a person should know his or her goal or objective with regard to the problem. This way, he or she will know what to do and where to go.

Aside from the formal definitions, how PST defines the problem is also important. D'Zurilla, Nezu, and Maydeau-Olivares (2004) define a problem as "any life situation or task (present or anticipated) that demands a response for adaptive functioning but no effective response is immediately apparent or available to the person or people confronted with the situation because of the presence of one or more obstacles" (pp. 12–13). According to this definition, a solution to a problem requires a reaction from the individual who faces the problem. However, the individual may not be able to give a reaction due to certain obstacles. According to the authors, these obstacles can be environmental as well as personal. For D'Zurilla et al. (2004), objective qualities of the problem are referred to as the environmental obstacles, whereas the characteristics of the individual such as personal goals, needs, and commitment constitute the personal obstacles. The authors emphasize that the novelty, ambiguity, and unpredictability of the problem, conflicting stimulus necessities, lack of skills, and lack of resources can also be considered as obstacles.

What kind of problems do people encounter? What kinds of situations require a reaction from an individual? Literature on the issue shows that the problems that people face in their daily lives can be grouped into four main categories. These are personal, interpersonal, impersonal, and social problems.

Personal Problems

Personal problems can be described as health-related, behavioral, and emotional problems. No one is exempt from experiencing physical or mental health difficulties or problems. Therefore, personal problems can be identified as the most common problems that people go through. In order to overcome these problems and reduce their possible negative effects, the individual should know how to approach and handle them. The adaptive functioning of the individual increases based on the success of these efforts. If these efforts are unsuccessful or insufficient, both the effects and the intensity of the individual's problems increase.

Interpersonal Problems

Most people find that what makes life beautiful is the time they share with loved ones. Yet, another thing that we learn in life is that those people who make our lives beautiful, livable, and meaningful can be the major source of our problems. Interpersonal relations can be the source of both happiness and unhappiness. Therefore, the most common problems that people have in life are likely to be caused by interpersonal relations. Interpersonal problems may have tremendous impact on people's emotional well-being.

In order to search for the scientific basis of interpersonal problems, Horowitz (1979) studied the interpersonal problems of 28 psychiatry patients who had just begun receiving psychotherapy. Using a multidimensional scaling technique, the researcher found that interpersonal problems have three fundamental cognitive characteristics. The first characteristic is the psychological closeness between two people. As the psychological closeness between two individuals increases, the likelihood of facing problems in their relationship increases. The second characteristic is the nature of the interpersonal relationship, such as whether it is friendly or hostile. Friendly interpersonal relationships enhance psychological well-being, whereas hostile interpersonal relationships deteriorate it. The third characteristic concerns one party's intention of effecting, controlling, or changing the other party. In a relationship between two people, problems are more likely to arise when one party realizes that the other party is trying to change or control him or her.

Impersonal Problems

The problems in this group are easier to solve because they are usually clearly defined—they are mundane problems that have mundane solutions (see Chapter 9) Examples include having your car break down or running out of groceries at home. These are well-defined problems and what is required from the individual is clear.

Social Problems

Everyone encounters social problems within the communities in which they live. The issues we face in our everyday lives such as heavy traffic, political problems, economic problems, and educational problems can be put in the social problems category. Even though these issues affect the individual both emotionally and socially, the discussion and the solution of social problems can take a long time. Naturally, the solutions for these problems are not personal. Individuals can contribute to the solution, but in order to solve the problem, different factions of society such as political, economical, social, and judicial should come together. Social problems can only be overcome by collective efforts and means. Different segments of the population should exert effort and make contributions in order to solve these problems.

What Is a Solution?

One of the concepts that should definitely be discussed within PST is the concept of a solution. What is a solution? How can we define it? What is considered an effective solution in PST? How can the therapist know that the problems of the client can be solved? According to what measures can it be said that a problem is resolved? Having answers to these questions is crucial for successful PST and the problem-solving therapist.

Webster's Online Dictionary defines solution as "a statement that solves a problem or explains how to solve the problem; a method for solving a problem; the successful action of solving a problem and the act of solving, or the state of being solved; the disentanglement of any intricate problem or difficult question." By solution, what is meant is the result of the attempts that one makes in order to solve a problem. The important point here is the quality of the result and its coherence with the aim. Is the result that is reached by the process consistent with one's aim regarding the problem? People can make attempts to solve a problem, but the result that they get may not be the one that they were aiming to reach. It may be consistent with one's aim, but it may not be satisfying in terms of its quality. In order to be named as a solution, one should have reached one's aim and one should be satisfied with the quality of the solution.

In the context of PST, D'Zurilla et al. (2004) define the solution as "a situation-specific coping response or response pattern (cognitive or behavioral) that is the product or outcome of the problem-solving process when it is applied to a specific problematic situation" (p. 13). Based on this definition, the individual who encounters a problem starts a problem-solving process, which serves as a cognitive or behavioral way of coping with it. In order for this process to lead to a solution, the coping behavior should lead the individual to a positive outcome.

The crucial point here is to determine if the coping behavior that is produced by the problem-solving process is effective or not. D'Zurilla et al. (2004) define the effective solution as "one that achieves the problem-solving goal (i.e., changing the situation for the better or reducing the emotional distress that it produces), while at the same time maximizing other positive consequences and minimizing negative consequences" (p. 13). The problems that are discussed and sought to be solved in PST are mostly interpersonal. D'Zurilla et al. define the effective solution to interpersonal problems as "an effective solution is one that resolves the conflict or dispute by providing an outcome that is acceptable or satisfactory to all parties involved" (p. 13).

What Is Problem Solving?

What is problem solving? What does problem solving refer to? Heppner and Krauskopf (1987) define problem solving as "a goal-directed sequence of cognitive and affective operations as well as behavioral responses for the purpose of adapting to internal or external demands or challenges" (p. 375). The authors describe problem solving as the organization of cognitive, emotional, and behavioral reactions. Problem solving is understood as the individual's adaptation to self-imposed demands and demands made by his or her environment.

Heppner and Krauskopf (1987) view problem solving as a coping process and as the interaction of three factors. Accordingly, problem solving is a result of an interaction of the characteristics of the problem, whether or not the individual applies problem-solving steps, and the individual's personal characteristics. This is, in a sense, identical to Lewin's (1939) $B = f(P,E)$ formula, the one he used to highlight the determinants of human behavior as a combination of the characteristics of the individual and the environment. In this formula, "P" represents the person and "E" represents the environment.

On the other hand, D'Zurilla et al. (2004) define problem solving as "the self-directed cognitive–behavioral process by which an individual, couple, or group attempts to identify or discover effective solutions for specific problems encountered in everyday living" (p. 12). The authors emphasize that the cognitive–behavioral problem-solving process has two important functions. Accordingly, the process first brings to light the effective possible solutions for a problem and secondly it increases the possibility of finding the most effective solution among these options. They view problem solving as a conscious, rational, and goal-directed activity that requires effort.

The Difference Between Finding a Solution and Applying It

In problem solving, there is an urgent need to distinguish between two processes and to follow the necessary strategies accordingly. The first thing for PST to determine is if the individual is having trouble with coming up with a solution to the problem or having trouble applying a solution. A problem-solving therapist should be able to distinguish between these two processes. The difference between finding a solution and applying the solution is crucially important both for the theory and the application.

The difference between finding a solution and applying it is especially important for assessment in PST. An assessment of whether a client has deficiencies in finding a solution or applying it is important for the treatment to be successful. If the client has deficiencies in finding a solution, then interventions aiming at teaching problem-solving skills should be implemented. For example, a client who has difficulty in seeing, perceiving, and distinguishing the problem should be taught skills on having a positive problem orientation. In a similar vein, a client who is not able to come up with enough number of solutions to a problem and who impulsively applies the first solution should be taught skills based on these issues. For a client who cannot foresee the consequences of his or her behaviors and who acts impulsively, cognitive and behavioral interventions aiming at decreasing the level of his or her impulsivity should be implemented.

On the other hand, a client may not have deficiency in problem-solving skills but he or she may still not be solving or handling problem situations effectively. In this situation, the person may have deficiency in applying the solution. The reasons for skill deficiencies for applying the solution may vary. A client may not know the skills required to apply the solution. In this case, the problem-solving therapist should teach the client the necessary skills to solve a problem. One may know these skills but might be held back by emotional obstacles such as anxiety. In these situations, the therapist should teach the client ways to cope effectively with the emotional difficulties and the skills to overcome any kind of obstacles preventing the client from applying the solution.

Conclusion

The definitions and concepts discussed in this chapter are important both at a conceptual level and in the application of PST. Without coverage of definition and concepts, understanding the rationale and scientific basis of PST would be incomplete. Doing psychotherapy involves translating a number of conceptual, theoretical, and definitional issues into practice. For this reason, it is helpful for the mental health professionals who apply this therapy approach to know these concepts and definitions.

2 Resilience, Coping, and Problem Solving

Introduction

People encounter different types of difficulties in their daily lives. This is the nature of life. The extent to which one is able to cope with difficulties is as important as the nature and the structure of the encountered difficulties. Difficulties can be taken as the motivating factors giving life its meaning. When we contemplate a life without difficulties, we realize that there is nothing to motivate an individual and to keep him or her alive in the pursuit of life. The point emphasized in the literature is not the individual's encounter with difficulties but the extent to which he or she is able to cope effectively with them. If an individual is able to cope actively and effectively with difficulties, then we cannot talk about the existence of a problem. The problem exists only when the individual does not possess skills and strategies required to overcome the difficulties he or she encounters. In this case, the individual's adaptive capacity and capability will show a sharp decline. Aside from the decline in the adaptive capacity and capability, the individual may develop some mental health problems requiring treatment.

Within the science of psychology, a source of curiosity is the fact that some people are able to maintain their psychological well-being despite being exposed to adverse conditions such as fire, flood, earthquake, terror, theft, traffic accidents, violence, abuse, and rape while others experience worsening in their psychological functioning. Some authors started emphasizing the need to investigate how people are able to maintain their psychological health but not why they get ill. One of the questions addressed in this context is: What are the characteristics that help people maintain their mental health despite the adverse conditions? Despite the devastations, the absence of love, the disappointments and disasters, which factors help an individual maintain his or her psychological well-being?

It is, of course, not easy to find the answer to this question. A different question was asked previously in the sciences of psychology, psychiatry, and allied disciplines. As is known, the questions being asked can determine and have an influence on the answers and their nature. In those areas, contrary to the aforementioned question, more questions were raised about the factors that contribute to the deterioration of individuals' mental health. Since the question was being asked in this direction, the findings obtained through the efforts and methods of answering it have been related to the factors that contribute to the deterioration of an

Problem Solving Therapy in the Clinical Practice. DOI: http://dx.doi.org/10.1016/B978-0-12-398455-5.00002-4

individual's mental health. But within the last 20 years, this trend has started to change in the fields of both psychology and medicine. Disease- or illness-oriented explanations and points of view led to adaptation-oriented explanations and points of view. Especially within the last 20 years, there has been a visible change in this respect in the science of psychology.

In recent years, looking at concepts about an individual's psychological functioning within the science of psychology, we see that two general concepts—coping and resilience—have stood out. What, then, are coping and resilience? What is the conceptual relationship between the two? How is problem solving situated as a concept beside the concepts of coping and resilience? Resilience is a metaconcept including both coping and problem solving on a conceptual level. Coping, however, is an indicator of resilience and is its subconcept. Problem solving, the subject of this book, constitutes the subgroup of coping skills. Problem-solving skills are in fact a form of coping. In this chapter, resilience, then coping, and finally problem solving are discussed.

Resilience

Everyone has their share of life's ups and downs. Life, in this sense, treats people equally. Some experience more and some experience less than others, but everyone withstands hardship. Generally speaking, most people do not get affected by the events and processes caused by these ups and downs. The majority of people are in question is able to use life's difficulties as a means for strengthening in the future. An important phenomenon observed here is that every individual shows a different reaction to the difficulties that we described as ups and downs. While some people are able to cope effectively with difficulties and even grow stronger as a result, some become completely devastated. Some are able to surmount major difficulties in a healthy way; others are distressed by minor events that have lesser impacts. Why?

This situation in question led the researchers working in the science of psychology to investigate the personal characteristics of those individuals who are able to keep functioning despite the life's ups and downs (Klohnen, 1996). As a result, in the early 1970s, a group of psychologists and psychiatrists came up with the concept of "resiliency," an important concept in the field of developmental psychopathology (Chambers & Belicki, 1998; Klohnen, 1996). These pioneers investigated the characteristics of children experiencing similar amounts of difficulties without developing psychopathological or behavioral problems. As a result of these investigations, they called attention to the fact that resilient children are not vulnerable to risk. In those years, these children were named as "super kids" (Masten, 2001).

What, then, is resilience? Many researchers and theoreticians defined the concept of resilience in different ways. For example, resilience is characterized by Rutter (1991) as the outcome and the process of adaptation to negative life events and difficult conditions. As can be seen, the concept of resilience is closely related to maintaining a positive attitude toward stress. Resilience is defined by Klohnen (1996) as the capacity to adapt successfully and flexibly to internal and external stressors. On the other hand, Beardslee and Gladstone (2001) emphasized that adaptation to life events increases with an increased level of resilience.

What are the necessary and sufficient conditions for resilience? How can we understand whether a person is resilient or not? Who can we name as resilient? In their explanations about the structure of resilience in adolescents, Smokowski, Reynolds, and Bezruczko (1999) referred to the presence of two steps. First, the individual should be exposed to an important or difficult life event or should be under threat. At this stage, the individual is under high risk or is faced with a risky situation. Second, the individual adapts to the risky situation and continues his or her normal development. People who go through these two stages are named as resilient. From another perspective, neither being exposed to negative life events nor a high level of functioning are solely sufficient conditions for resilience.

What are the personal characteristics of resilient individuals? The results of empirical studies identified the presence of certain personal characteristics differentiating resilient individuals from others. Accordingly, compared to nonresilient individuals, resilient persons were found

- to be more optimistic (Folkman & Lazarus, 1985; Scheier & Carver, 1987);
- to possess better social skills (Olsson, Bond, & Burns, 2003; Rouse, Ingersoll, & Orr, 1998; Smokowski et al., 1999);
- to have better problem-solving skills (Dumont & Provost, 1999; Rouse et al., 1998; Smokowski et al., 1999);
- to have higher self-esteem and self-efficacy (Bandura, 1986; Dekovic, 1999; Kinard, 1998; Luthar, Cicchetti, & Becker, 2000);
- to have better academic standing (Dekovic, 1999; Smokowski et al., 1999);
- to be more intelligent (Kinard, 1998; Klohnen, 1996; Smokowski et al., 1999);
- to have more positive future orientation (Maluccio, 2002; Smokowski et al., 1999);
- to display higher interpersonal sensitivity (Rouse et al., 1998);
- to be more androgynous (a term used to refer to people displaying both feminine and masculine traits)—resilient women are found to be more adventurous and show initiative while resilient men are more socially receptive and emotionally responsive (Rouse et al., 1998);
- to have more social support (Masten, 2001).

What should a person do in order to be resilient? What should one do to build and flourish such an important personal trait? Which methods are helpful? What should we do as health care professionals to better serve our clients and to help them build resilience? Listed below are 11 ways to build resilience as published in the American Psychological Association's website (www.APAHelpCenter.org/resilience, retrieved May 12, 2007). The suggested ways to build resilience are as follows:

1. *Establishing interpersonal relationships*: Maintaining good relationships with family members and friends is an important indicator of resilience. That is why it is important to help people establish good relationships in order to increase their resilience level.

2. *Not to see crises situations as insurmountable*: As has been stated earlier, life's ups and downs are unavoidable. Everyone may experience some difficult moments. We cannot change this fact as individuals. However, we can change the way we perceive, interpret, and respond to such situations. The moment we start seeing adverse life situations as insurmountable problems, the positive steps we are able to make will be restricted or inhibited.
3. *Accepting that change is unavoidable in life*: The only reality in life is that everything constantly changes. Sometimes a person may not be able to reach or attain the goals he or she set for him- or herself due to some adverse life situations. Accepting the situations that one cannot change and focusing on circumstances that can be altered is an important step toward building one's own resilience.
4. *Setting goals*: Having goals in life and being able to set goals is an important indicator of resilience. A person who sets goals gets attached to life, his or her future orientation increases, and he or she can structure personal time. A person who sets goals will work for the realization of his or her goals. Striving for this, and the attainments themselves, will be a source of happiness and satisfaction for the person.
5. *Taking decisive actions*: As will be discussed in the subsequent chapters, some people may stay passive when faced with problems and wait for problems to resolve themselves. This kind of approach to problems is an indication of nonresilience. To be able to act assertively within adverse situations in order to solve the problem is an indicator of resilience.
6. *Accepting that problems are ways for self-discovery*: A person who has not encountered any problems in life, leading a protected life, is a person who has not found the opportunity to know him- or herself. Problems are opportunities for self-discovery. People who see problems as chances for self-discovery are resilient individuals.
7. *Nurturing a positive view of self*: Possessing self-confidence and trust in one's own capabilities for problem solving is an indicator of resilience. Before trying to solve problems successfully, one has to believe in his or her ability to do so. A person without this belief cannot take the steps necessary to solve the problems.
8. *Keeping things in perspective*: If a person facing adverse life situations evaluates them in a short-term perspective, these difficult situations may look bigger than they actually are. That is why evaluating problem situations in a broader context is an important indicator of resilience. People who can accomplish this may perceive the problem more realistically without carrying the immediate emotional burden of it. Keeping a long-term perspective on problem situations and dealing with them in a broader context will lessen the negative effects that the problem has on the person.
9. *Being optimistic*: Maintaining an optimistic outlook is considered an important indicator of resilience. Optimistic people expect that good things will happen, while pessimistic people fear that bad things will happen.
10. *Taking care of oneself*: Taking care of oneself is an important indicator of resilience. This can be characterized as being sensitive toward one's own needs and emotions, making time for oneself, maintaining physical health, and participating in activities one enjoys. A person who can keep him- or herself physically and psychologically fit will show more effort and willingness to solve the problem situations.
11. *Additional ways of strengthening resilience*: The 10 ways of building resilience cited above are the ones suggested by the American Psychological Association. People may use different strategies in order to strengthen their resilience. For example, writing down the views, the feelings, and the thoughts about the stressful events are considered as one useful method to strengthen the person's resilience. Some people may also strengthen their resilience through meditation and some religious and spiritual practices.

Coping

As was mentioned earlier, problem solving is a coping skill. Coping is basically a psychological process and it relates to how people deal with problems and difficulties they encounter, and what they do with them. Difficulties are inevitable in life. Life gains meaning not only with its beauties with its problems but with difficulties as well. Wishing a life without problems is wishing a dead life. Stress is a concept of modern life. The question of "what needs to be done" has to be addressed here after accepting that life and stress are part of a whole. Life gains meaning not only with its beauties but also with its problems and difficulties (Frese, 1986; Trumbull & Appley, 1986). In recent years, the question of how an individual deals with stress started to gain importance in stress literature.

According to the cognitive model, the way an individual perceives a problem situation is more important than the situation itself. The perception of stress results from the interaction of personal and environmental factors. More precisely, an individual's perception of the situation as stressful is the result of the mutual interaction of personal and environmental factors (Folkman & Lazarus, 1985). According to Folkman and Lazarus, the individual makes two kinds of appraisal when faced with a stressful situation. When an individual encounters a stressful event, he or she first goes through the primary appraisal stage, during which he or she reviews the seriousness of the event. Then, during the secondary appraisal stage, the person evaluates whether or not he or she possesses the necessary personal resources to cope with the situation (Coyne, Aldwin, & Lazarus, 1981; Lazarus, 1993). The individual experiences stress when he or she believes that the demands of the situation exceed the resources he or she possesses to cope with the problem.

Roughly speaking, coping is the combination of cognitive and behavioral strategies adopted to solve a negative incident or to minimize its effects on the individual (Folkman & Lazarus, 1986). Personal coping resources include behavioral skills, cognitive flexibility, sense of general self-efficacy, feelings of control, and social support. According to this definition, coping is defined very broadly. Many define coping as a goal-directed behavior. Taking into consideration the difficulties of defining coping, Krohne (1986) identified commonalities between different definitions of coping. According to Krohne, the common features of these definitions are as follows:

- Coping is not a goal but a process. Coping is not a target point to be reached immediately. In order to cope successfully with a difficult situation, an individual starts and completes a process encompassing a series of behavioral, emotional, and cognitive skills. Whereas a person is constantly coping or striving to cope in life, only the outcome of this process becomes prominent.
- The process of coping includes cognitive as well as behavioral acts. In the process of coping, an individual makes use of a series of complicated cognitive skills and capabilities in an effort to accomplish something. In other words, behavioral and cognitive skills and capabilities are used simultaneously in the process of coping.
- In coping, a person focuses on a situation perceived as difficult. By definition, coping presumes some level of difficulty. If a situation does not present a difficulty, the person does not need to cope with the situation in question.

- The goal of coping is to eliminate the imbalance between the resources the person possesses and the necessary resources to overcome the difficulties and resolve the problems. The problem arises when there is an imbalance between the person's own resources—meaning his or her efforts, ability, and skills to overcome the problem—and the ability, skills, and efforts that the situation demands. In other words, if the individual's personal resources fall behind the demands of the situation, then difficulties arise.
- There is an important relationship between coping strategies and personal characteristics of the individuals. The techniques and strategies that the person utilizes in his or her efforts to resolve and deal with the problem situation are congruent with his or her personal characteristics. For example, a hasty person will demonstrate an impulsive style when faced with a problem.

According to Folkman and Lazarus (1984) there are two kinds of coping. The first one is problem-focused coping. Here, the individual focuses on the problem in a rational way and concentrates on the usage of his or her own resources for the resolution of the problem. This is, in fact, similar to the problem-solving behavior that we discussed earlier. This kind of approach to problem solving is more effective in generating solutions and coping with the problem. Emotion-focused coping, on the other hand, emphasizes the emotional reactions when dealing with problems. In this type of coping, the individual displays an effort to balance his or her emotional reactions. Here the individual tries to deal with the effective outcomes of the source of stress. While the individual tries to resolve and deal with the problem or the source of stress in problem-focused coping, he or she tries to alleviate the negative effects that the problem or the source of stress has on him or her in emotion-focused coping. The emotion-focused coping has proved to be less effective than problem-focused coping in reducing the negative effects of stress.

Despite the fact that stress is a brand new term in the science of psychology, it nevertheless occupies an important place in everyday life. Stress results from deprivation, losses, noises, illnesses, workload, personal difficulties, etc. A single event may not by itself be the source of stress. What is important is whether or not the event or situation gets perceived as stressful by the individual. What, then, indicates whether or not a person will perceive the situation as stressful? Appley and Trumbull (1986) draw attention to five factors that will influence people's perception of an event as stressful or nonstressful. These are:

1. *Personal coping resources*: Perceiving a situation as stressful is directly related to coping resources. If an individual has good amount of personal coping resources, then he or she will not perceive a given situation as stressful. An individual's coping resources may include social, behavioral, cognitive, and emotional skills. The material and economic resources are also important coping resources.
2. *The person's attitude toward the source of stress*: If the person has a positive view of the source of the event, he or she is more likely not perceiving the event as stressful. The person's way of looking at the source of stress and his or her perception of it determine whether or not he or she feels stress. For example, an academic exam will not create stress for a student who perceives the exam as an opportunity to display his or her academic ability and skills.

3. *Familiarity with the source of stress from a previous encounter*: If the person has met the source of stress before, the probability that he or she perceives the situation as stressful decreases. If the source of stress is familiar to the individual, it may not present itself as stressful. That is the reason why individuals feel less discomfort in familiar circumstances.
4. *Perceiving the incident or event as risky or dangerous*: The incidents perceived as risky and dangerous constitute a source of stress for people. If the person sees the incident risky and dangerous, he or she perceives it as stressful. Those incidents and situations that are perceived as dangerous, risky, and important are potential stressors for the individual.
5. *The person's vulnerability for stress*: Some people are more vulnerable to perceive stress than others. The vulnerability factors may be cognitive, behavioral, and emotional in nature. Due to certain cognitive, behavioral, and emotional characteristics, some people are more prone to stress. For instance, people who are anxious by nature have a higher tendency for stress than nonanxious people. They have a higher tendency to attend to negative cues in their lives than nonanxious people, and they also have a tendency to exaggerate their perception.

Every human being encounters difficult situations. What matters is not whether or not the individual faces difficulties but how he or she copes with them. For the person who cannot cope with difficulties, both their physical and psychological well-being fall into danger. In this sense, deficiencies in coping skills are predisposing factors for the emergence of mental problems. A person who does not know how to cope with the encountered problems and difficulties easily surrenders to hopelessness and helplessness. As is known, these two feelings lead to the emergence of psychological problems such as anxiety and mood disorders.

Problem Solving

Following the discussion of coping and resilience, one may wonder about the place of problem solving in this picture. What is problem solving? Being a goal-directed, cognitive–behavioral skill and ability, problem solving is without any doubt an indicator of coping. A person who can handle and resolve the problems effectively is a resilient person. Within the context of coping, problem solving is an important personal coping resource. People who can resolve the problems they encounter in their daily lives have high levels of coping and psychological adaptation.

In our daily lives, coming face-to-face with problems is inevitable. Individuals face different kinds of problems, big or small, at different periods in their lives. In such circumstances people display different reactions. Each individual attempts to resolve the same problem in very different ways, some of which are successful and some unsuccessful. Although people follow different ways to resolve the same problem, they end up with solutions that are congruent with their goals. At this point, problem-solving skills of an individual are of central importance. A number of studies found that people who are good at problem solving are also good in resilience (Dumont & Provost, 1999; Klohnen, 1996; Rouse et al., 1998; Smokowski et al., 1999). Problem-solving skills are in this regard an important indicator of resilience.

Problem solving is a process. For Westen (1999), problem solving is the transformation of one situation to another in order to achieve a goal. The individual tries to reach a goal starting from an initial state. The initial state is consisted of the individual's wills, wishes, and desires about the situation he or she wishes to alter or transform. In order to reach the goal, the individual needs to perform a series of actions. Problem solving is a process going from the person's initial encounter with the problem through the resolution of the problem. Westen defines this process in three stages. These three stages can be summarized as follows:

1. *Initial stage (encounter with the problem)*: At this stage, the individual encounters a problem and shows specific reactions. He or she evaluates whether the problem is easy or difficult. At this initial stage, the individual has only faced the problem. Here, whether or not the person recognizes the problem is crucial. Some people may not recognize the problem when they face it. Some people may not see the problem. Even if they see it, they may not consciously accept its existence. The ability of the person to recognize the problem at the initial encounter and to say "I have a problem" is important.
2. *Operation stage (taking action for problem solving)*: The individual takes some actions to eliminate the problem or to find a desired solution to the problem. His or her way of fighting with the problem may take him or her to a solution or to chaos. The person goes through a series of actions here to solve the problem, to eliminate the problem situation, or to reach the desired goal. The nature and type of these actions depend on the type and the nature of the problem and constitutes the main subject of this book.
3. *Reaching the desired goal (elimination of the problem)*: The individual succeeds in resolving the problem using the right techniques and strategies. The problem does not exist anymore. Here the person followed the actions that he or she believed would eliminate the problem situation. Whether the person will reach the desired goal depends on whether he or she makes the right action choices or not. The individual is now ready to resolve new problem situations. This process will go on throughout the individual's entire life. The life cycle of humankind can be outlined by these three stages in question.

Conclusion

Problem-solving therapists and researchers need to take into consideration the clarification of and the interrelationships among the aforementioned three concepts. From a purely theoretical point of view, defining concepts such as resilience, coping, and problem solving is an important task. Basically, these are psychological constructs. To know the contents and boundaries of these constructs is a significant issue for theory building and conducting research. Knowing these concepts and constructs, the problem-solving therapist or trainer will provide clarity and power when offering their services to those in need.

3 Components of Problem Solving

Introduction

As a complex human behavior process, developing problem-solving skills requires a series of mental processes. What are the components of human problem solving? What are the mental and psychological processes involved in problem solving? What are the processes or the components of processes that help us understand problem solving? Problem solving consists of three important components: These are cognitive, metacognitive, and motivational in nature.

The term "problem-solving components" refers to the nature of skills and abilities the individual is able to use during problem solving. For example, the cognitive component of problem solving refers to the skills and abilities that belong to the cognitive domain. Similarly, the motivational component refers to the motivational aspects of skills and abilities an individual can employ during problem solving. The cognitive, metacognitive, and motivational components of problem solving will be discussed in this chapter.

Cognitive Components of Problem Solving

The cognitive component of problem solving is related to whether or not the individual perceives the problems correctly. In order to be able to solve the problem, the individual needs to perceive it correctly in the first place. This perception is closely related to the way the individual processes information.

Founded on the knowledge base within the field of academic psychology, Mayer (1998) categorizes cognitive skills in problem solving into three groups. The first group is comprised of the skills needed for the resolution of the instructional objectives. The second group of skills is related to the learning hierarchy. Here the individual needs to learn a skill in a lower level of the hierarchy and move to the next level in order to reach the targeted skill at the top. What is important here is the person's ability to create the steps of the hierarchy and learn the necessary skills ranging from lower to higher levels in the hierarchy. The third group is related to learning the problem-solving skills as components in the information-processing procedure. During information processing, an individual first encodes the information, then makes an inference about it, then applies it, and, finally, responds with it.

Problem Solving Therapy in the Clinical Practice. DOI: http://dx.doi.org/10.1016/B978-0-12-398455-5.00003-6

The focus of this book is problem solving within the context of interpersonal relations. PST is interested mainly in interpersonal problems as they relate to everyday living. This may be the reason why some authors like D'Zurilla, Nezu, and Maydeu-Olivares (2004) refer to PST as "social problem-solving therapy." That is why the cognitive skills and abilities used in the context of interpersonal relations are important. Knowledge of cognitive skills and abilities is important for teaching problem solving and planning the PST interventions.

Interpersonal cognitive skills and abilities within the context of problem solving have been discussed by Spivack, Platt, and Shure (1976). These authors indicate five cognitive skills in this area. Within the context of this approach, which they call "interpersonal problem solving," the skills in question are important for the development of interpersonal skills and harmony. These cognitive skills are summarized as follows.

Ability to Think About Alternative Solutions

An individual who encounters a problem should be able to think about alternative solutions to the problem in order to be able to solve the problem in a way he or she desires. The individual should be able to think about these alternative solutions and should be able to choose the solution that best fits the personal and situational demands. In order to be able to make this choice, the individual should be able to think about different aspects of the problem and be able to generate alternative solutions.

An issue related to the consideration of alternative solutions is the concept of cognitive rigidity. People who possess cognitive rigidity see things within a limited framework and are not able to see other aspects of the situation and, consequently, cannot generate alternative solutions. PST contributes to the loosening of these individuals' rigid characteristics. The characteristics that make them prone to psychological problems get eliminated in this way. This is one of the mechanisms of PST that leads to change and improvement.

Ability to Conceptualize Step-by-Step Means to Reach the Target

The ability to conceptualize a step-by-step means necessary to reach the goal is a complicated cognitive process. Here, the individual should be able to think about the steps that will take him or her to the target. In order to be able to develop and use such a skill, the individual needs to contemplate the whole process. The person who succeeds at it is able to organize in his or her imagination all the necessary steps to achieve the target.

The individual possessing this skill should be able to engage in cognitive activities of both analysis and synthesis. First, he or she should be able to imagine the task as a whole and then divide it into small components by analyzing it. Finally, based on the small components, he or she should be able to cognitively design the task as a whole and engage in the necessary cognitive, motor, and emotional reactions and actions to reach the goal.

Ability to Think About Consequences

One of the most important characteristics of human beings is the ability to think about the consequences of his or her actions. The responsibility of the actions belongs to the person. This causes the person to take on the burden of responsibility. Responsibility is the guarantee of our personal freedom in life, but it is at the same time a personal attainment difficult to carry. It is difficult to bear responsibility because the person cannot put the responsibility for the consequences of his or her actions on somebody else's shoulders. This hands over the person the key for her or his personal freedom.

In order to assume such a responsibility, the individual should be able to assess the gains and losses of his or her actions or inactions for both the self and his or her environment. One of the cognitive skills one should possess for the successful resolution of life's problems is the ability to think beforehand about the consequences of one's actions with regard to both the self and the environment. One who can think about the consequences of the steps one takes is able to solve the problems encountered in life in a healthy way.

Ability to Think About Cause and Effect in Social Situations

Social events contain complex cause-and-effect relationships. One event may be both the cause and the result of another event. Therefore, one should be able to associate the consequences with the correct causes and should be able to think about the nature of the complex relationships in a flexible manner. People who are successful in problem solving are able to consider the cause-and-effect relationships within social events despite their complex nature.

This complex cognitive ability is important for the development of interpersonal problem-solving skills. People who can identify the interrelated causes and effects concerning social events are successful at solving social problems in real life. As one can imagine, the ability to think about cause and effect in social relationships renders an individual able to anticipate possible positive and negative consequences.

Ability to Take Perspective

According to Selman's (1971, 1977) social cognitive theory of role taking, the ability to take perspective is one of the most important characteristics that distinguish humans from other species. Selman defines perspective taking as the ability to perceive oneself and the other as distinct subjects, to see others as oneself and to see oneself as the others. This being the case, taking perspective is apparently the key social cognitive ability or skill base for the resolution of interpersonal problems.

The main characteristic of people who are deficient in problem solving is their lack of flexibility in their efforts to deal effectively with problem situations. If an individual who experiences interpersonal difficulties is not able to look at the events from another person's perspective and insists on his or her own point of view, he or she will show cognitive rigidity which will make it difficult or impossible to resolve conflicts. A person who is able to take perspective, on the contrary, will be able to look at the event from another person's perspective and thus will display cognitive flexibility, which is necessary for the resolution of the problem situation.

An important condition for establishing and maintaining harmony in interpersonal relationships is the ability to see the events and problems from the other party's perspective. The roots of all communication problems lie in people's insistence on their own points of view and their inability to look at events from another's standpoint. Thus social cognitive ability defined as perspective taking plays a crucial role in both the resolution and the prevention of problems in interpersonal relationships.

Metacognitive Components of Problem Solving

Problem solving involves cognitive, emotional, behavioral, and cultural aspects. It is a behavioral endpoint in which a number of skills are used simultaneously. The individual needs to blend all of these skills simultaneously in order to reach the goal of problem solving. Not only does the individual need to make use of a variety of skills, he or she has to manage these skills, too, so that the process develops in line with the desired outcome.

The metacognitive aspect of problem solving is defined as the ability to control and review the problem-solving strategies. This can also be named as management of one's own problem-solving ability. The individual needs to check every step he or she makes in relation to problem solving and analyze what he or she has done right and wrong at each step. Mayer (1998) defines metacognitive knowledge about problem solving as the knowledge of when to use, how to coordinate, and how to monitor various skills in problem solving. In addition, the individual needs to be able to transfer the knowledge of when to use, how to coordinate, and how to monitor skills for the resolution of new problems. Here we can talk about the transfer of problem solving. For example, a student who learns about how to solve a problem about sets in mathematics should be able to use this knowledge to solve more of the same.

The individual needs to retain information about when to use skills for problem solving, as well as how to coordinate and monitor them. In other words, the individual stores the skills and the strategies he or she used during the process of problem solving in his or her memory. Later on, he or she can retrieve this information and apply it to the resolution of a new problem. The information in question is in fact personal information. Storing such personal information and retrieving it are necessary for the development of the adjustment skills of an individual. Retention of the self-related metacognitive information in memory is called *autobiographical memory*.

The fact that metacognitive knowledge about problem solving gets stored in the autobiographical memory leads us to think that people who experience difficulties in problem solving do experience it in the autobiographical memory. The literature emphasizes the need to investigate the psychological processes involved in problem solving in order to better understand it.

The scientific evidence shows that suicidal individuals are less skilled in problem solving than nonsuicidal ones (Cheng, 2001; Dixon, Heppner, & Rudd, 1994; Pollock & Williams, 1998, 2004; Weishaar, 1996). The research findings suggest that compared to nonsuicidal individuals, suicidal people have difficulties in autobiographical memory (Williams & Broadbent, 1986). For instance, while retrieving information from their autobiographical memory, suicide attempters were found to make overgeneralizations and experience problems retrieving information (Williams & Dritschel 1988). One should bear in mind that cognitive rigidity is the main characteristic of depressed and suicidal individuals. Thus, the aforementioned findings suggest that autobiographical memory problems may be the reasons behind the display of inefficient problem-solving skills in suicidal individuals.

Autobiographical memory problems may result from either problems in the storage of metacognitive knowledge and skills in memory or the retrieval of information from memory. But further scientific efforts are needed to clarify these issues. Consequently, metacognitive skills are important in the transfer and monitoring of problem solving. The use of this information requires the ability to successfully store the related skills in the autobiographical memory and to retrieve them from the memory when needed.

Motivational Components of Problem Solving

In order to understand the motivational aspect of problem solving, one needs to understand the concept of motivation itself. What is motivation? How is it defined? It is defined by Smith (1993) as an internal process affecting the direction, the power, and the maintenance of the goal-directed behavior. In other words, motivation is the process of displaying goal-directed behavior and orientation toward a goal with an inner driving force. In short, as an internal process, motivation is goal directed and the individual acts in accordance with these goals. Thus, motivation plays a key role in the initiation and maintenance of human behaviors. The motivational aspect of problem solving is related to the reasons why an individual attempts or does not attempt to solve a problem. This can be interpreted as whether the individual wants or does not want to deal with the problem.

Problem solving is a behavioral concept referring to the individual's engagement in some cognitive, behavioral, and emotional activities about the problem situation. In short, it designates the changes an individual wants to make in a problem situation. The motivational aspect of problem solving is related to whether or not the individual is interested in the problem situation. Because interest is the primary driving force that will lead the individual to take action about the problem situation, whether or not the individual gets interested in the problem situation is of critical importance.

There may be several reasons why an individual may or may not get interested in the problem situation. How the individual interprets the problem situation forms the basis of his interest or disinterest. The person's encounter with a problem may not necessarily result in the person's perception of it as a problem or doing something with it; therefore, no actions can be taken toward the resolution of it. For Mayer (1998), motivational aspect of process of problem solving can be analyzed under three headings.

Interest in the Problem Situation

An individual faces a number of situations in daily life which require a response. Every situation an individual encounters is in fact a problem. The individual does not try to solve all of them. He or she may not even perceive some of them as problems. On the other hand, he or she may exaggerate the importance of some. Does the person want to solve it? Or does he or she ignore it? For example, a father's willingness to solve a problem he is experiencing with his children is very effective as to whether or not the problem gets resolved. Whether or not one is interested in a problem situation indicates whether or not one will do something with it.

A person encountering a problem may react in three ways. First, the individual may show a positive interest in the problem situation and may want to solve it in line with his or her wishes and goals. Positive interest helps the individual to structure his or her efforts constructively and to take the necessary positive steps for the resolution of the problem and act accordingly. Second, the individual may be uninterested in the problem situation and harbor negative feelings toward the problem situation. The person harboring negative attitudes cannot be expected to act constructively toward the resolution of the problem. The problem situation infuriates the person so much so that the person engages in negative actions in relation to the situation or chooses to avoid it. Third, the individual may stay indifferent to the problem situation. A person who stays indifferent to a situation cannot be expected to act in neither positive nor negative manner. For some reason, the individual does not get connected to the situation or completely disconnects him- or herself from it.

The person's interest or disinterest toward a problem situation is related to the personal needs, will, and other characteristics of the individual. The development of a positive and negative interest in a problem will be possible if and only if the characteristics of the problem overlap with the individual's personal characteristics. Think about a student who is not very enthusiastic about academic subjects and is not ready to devote him- or herself in this direction. Most probably, this student thinks that his or her personal skills and abilities are inadequate in the academic field; or perhaps, even if the individual thinks that he or she has adequate skills and abilities, his or her personal interests and life plans lie outside the academic realm. Such a student is not expected to be interested in academic success or failure. In short, the possibility that a person becomes interested in a problem depends on the overlap of his or her own personal characteristics with that of the characteristics of the problem situation.

The person's interest in a problem is also related to the perception that the problem is relevant to his or her personal situation. People get interested in the problems that they consider personally important, whereas they remain indifferent toward the unimportant ones. Being interested in a problem is directly related to the belief that the distress and difficulties one experiences are caused by that problem. For example, the student who identifies work ethic as the reason for his or her academic failure will be interested in the problem he or she experiences. Such an interest will not be present in an individual who does not think in this way.

From a clinical perspective, knowledge of a client's quality and degree of interest toward problem situations can have an effect on the treatment process. A client who is not interested in the problem he or she experiences will be unwilling to take the necessary steps toward the resolution of the problem. For example, a client who has not been convinced that his depression is caused by wrong or distorted cognitions will not be willing to make the effort to accomplish the changes necessary to replace maladaptive cognitions with adaptive ones. Let us consider a patient presenting to a health care center due to an illness as another example. If the physician has not been able to convince this patient about the use of the prescribed drugs or medical procedures by explaining him or her the nature of the illness and the treatment rationale, the patient will not develop an interest in the connection between the illness and the prescribed drugs or medical procedures. In such a situation, the patient may be unwilling to take the prescribed medicine or follow the prescribed medical procedures.

Perception of Self-Efficacy

Self-efficacy is defined by Bandura (1977, 1986) as the degree of one's feelings about one's ability to accomplish goals. Self-efficacy expectancy is one's anticipation of whether or not one will be able to realize certain behavior. People's self-efficacy beliefs about a task or a job are important for the accomplishment of the task or job. For example, individuals assess their own abilities with regard to the assignments and exercises given during psychotherapy in different ways. Let us say that between psychotherapy sessions, patients are assigned to keep records in order to show the interaction between thoughts and emotions. While some patients find this assignment easy and say "I can do it," others may find it difficult and say "I cannot do it."

Given the preceding explanation, the possible outcomes within the individual–problem relationship matrix are a function of the characteristics of both the problem and the individual. As a personal factor, people's feelings of self-efficacy may result in the perception of a problem as easy or difficult or impossible to solve, but problems themselves may also be responsible for creating feelings of inadequacy at solving them. As is the case with motivation, feelings of self-efficacy are the result of the interaction between people's personal characteristics and the characteristics of the problem. Bandura (1977) calls this interaction as the *principle of reciprocal determinism.*

Within the context of problem solving, the perception of self-efficacy is related to a person's subjective beliefs about his or her capabilities with respect to the problems encountered. When faced with a problem situation, how one perceives oneself in relation to the problem is important. One engages in an action if he or she perceives him- or herself as self-efficient. For example, a male client experiencing difficulties connecting with female peers is given the assignment of greeting women by making eye contact at least once a week. If he feels self-efficient, he will try to accomplish this the moment he believes himself capable of doing it. If he does not feel self-efficient, he will display a nonconstructive attitude toward the problem.

A person's degree of self-perceived efficacy also determines whether or not he or she will be successful at a job. This effect is empirically demonstrated by Wood and Bandura (1989). During a simulation experiment conducted with graduate students of management, researchers gave one group the feedback that they could improve their self-efficacy, while they gave another group the feedback that their self-efficacy was constant and should not change. As a result of these studies, researchers were able to demonstrate that people would achieve success they believed they could.

What are the sources and types of self-efficacy within the context of problem solving? Based on the observations in academic settings, Mayer (1998) refers to the existence of four important sources of self-efficacy. These four sources of self-efficacy are as follows:

1. *Self-efficacy based on the interpretation of the person's own performance*: People assess their own performance when they accomplish or learn a task. Based on these assessments, their long-term motivation and efficiency will be enhanced when they think they are making progress in performing or learning something. When successfully completing homework assignments, clients recognize their own capability.
2. *Self-efficacy based on the interpretation of the performance of others*: People can judge their own state by observing the performance of others in similar situations. For example, the individual may think, "If others are able to do it, I can do it as well." This kind of observation and assessment helps people by enhancing their own feelings of self-efficacy.
3. *Self-efficacy based on others' assessment of one's own capability*: People around us observe and evaluate our own performance. For example, teachers evaluate students' performance and offer feedback. Based on the nature of this feedback, the students' judgment of self-efficacy increases or decreases. Wood and Bandura (1989) demonstrated empirically that others' assessment of people's own performance has an effect on their motivation. Providing feedback to clients in or between PST sessions enhances their sense of self-efficacy.
4. *Self-efficacy based on the assessment of physiological states*: People's feelings of self-efficacy may develop from the interpretation of their physiological state. For instance, a gentleman may interpret his physiological changes like sweating or voice trembling during interactions with women as a proof of his inefficacy and incompetency. Or, if these changes are absent, he will evaluate himself as efficient and competent. In the first case, his view of self-efficacy will be low while in the second case it will be high. The level of self-efficacy will be a determining factor in the behavioral outcomes, i.e., whether or not the client is comfortable initiating a relationship with a woman.

Attribution Style

The kind of causal attributions that people make about a situation will have an effect on efforts toward the behavioral performances in relation to that situation.

What is attribution and what kind of process is it? In what way do attributions influence people's efforts and willingness to solve or deal with a problem? How do attributions about a problem situation affect the problem-solving process itself?

Attribution is defined by Westen (1999) as the process of making an inference about the causes of people's mental states or behaviors. In daily life, people meditate on and explore the causes of their own and other people's behaviors and psychological states. Generally, when people make an inference about the causes of their own and other people's behaviors, they attribute the causes to external factors (state focused, e.g., the client behaved angrily because today the weather was very hot) or to internal factors (person focused, e.g., the client behaved angrily because he is an impulsive person). The attributions people make may directly affect their performances on a task or behaviors.

According to the attribution theory of Weiner (1986), the attributions students make to their academic failures or successes are directly related to academic performance. According to the theory, students who attribute academic success or failure to effort work harder on academic tasks than students who attribute success and failure to ability. Research findings from the theory also show that students infer that they lack ability when teachers offer sympathy or pity in case of a failure, whereas they infer the need to work harder when teachers tell them to be more persistent on a subject.

Another theory related to attribution theory is the theory of explanatory style (Peterson, Buchanan, & Seligman, 1995; Peterson & Seligma, 1984). According to this theory, people's explanatory style of negative events has an effect on their psychological health. People who use pessimistic explanatory style for negative life events are more likely to suffer from depression. When people who display pessimistic explanatory style are faced with a negative event, they explain it in a way that adversely affects their emotional states. For this theory, when confronted with negative life events, depression-prone individuals make internal, stable, and global attributions. For example, a person who experiences an academic failure may attribute it to internal/personal factors (i.e., inability and low intelligence) rather than to external factors. And they see these reasons as stable and unchangeable. Furthermore, these individuals perceive the failure as an overall characteristic of themselves.

The attribution style and the explanatory style theories encompass a series of effects giving direction to and shaping human behavior in the process of problem solving. A person's attribution and explanatory styles following their efforts to solve the problems they encounter will have an effect on their psychological condition. They will also determine whether the problems will get resolved and whether the efforts to solve the problem will be maintained or not. The knowledge of people's causal attributions and explanations about an issue may be taken as a possible predictive factor for the success or the failure of the problem-solving process. In other words, within the context of problem solving, attributes contain judgments and inferences that people make in relation to whether or not they will be successful in solving the problem.

Attribution and explanatory styles are important during two stages in the problem-solving process. They are important first during the individual's initial encounter with the problem and second after the individual's attempts to solve it. When one encounters the problem for the first time, one appraises both the problem and one's skills and abilities in relation to the problem. As a result of this appraisal, the individual will arrive at a judgment. For instance, the individual who thinks that the problem he or she encounters is impossible to solve will not even attempt to solve it. Such an attribution will lower the person's self-esteem and will make it impossible to solve the problem. The person with a low self-esteem will stay away from any attempt to solve the problem. On the other hand, the individual may perceive the problem situation as difficult but his or her skills and abilities as adequate. In that case, this person will be able to make an attempt to solve the problem.

In the second, let us assume that after the first assessment the person decided to make an attempt to solve the problem, that this attempt did not result in the resolution of the problem, and that the situation got even worse. In this case, the assumptions and the explanatory styles of the person will have an effect on the possible solution and the person's emotional state. For instance, if a problem-solving process results in a failure and the individual reaches the judgment that the failure was caused by his or her stupidity, the feeling of self-efficacy will show a sharp decline. The person with this kind of explanatory style will easily fall into depression. With a lowered self-esteem, a depressed mood, and a pessimistic way of explaining personal failures, this person may not engage in new problem-solving attempts in the future.

People's attributions about the problems they encounter play an important role in whether or not they will attempt to solve a problem. The attributions in question will be able to motivate and activate the individual facing a problem. What are then the attribution styles of people who can and cannot solve the problems effectively? Baumgardner, Heppner, and Arkin (1986) investigated this subject. The results of their study showed that people who thought that they could effectively solve their problems were more likely to think that the problem situation was under their control and that the problem situation was the result of their lack of effort.

The attributions people make of the problem situation and of their skills and abilities may have a determining effect on the problem-solving process. For this reason, the knowledge of the client's attributions of the problem situation and his or her skills will have an effect on the result of the PST. Therefore, there is a need for the assessment of attribution and explanatory styles of clients during PST. One of the covert goals of PST is to enable the clients use functional or adaptive attributions.

Conclusion

It is important that researchers and practitioners interested in problem solving know about the components of problem solving. Theorists and researchers need to know about the components of the phenomenon they wish to explain. And from the practitioners' point of view, knowledge of the components of problem solving is important so that they can be incorporated and developed during practice. For example, knowledge of cognitive features and functioning in problem solving helps the practitioner understand the client better, assess the deficits in basic cognitive faculties, and use the appropriate helping strategies.

4 Theoretical Approaches to Problem Solving

Introduction

As an indicator of resilience, problem solving is important not only for humans but for all the living species. All living beings encounter different problem situations at every stage in their lives and are able to survive as long as they can meet the demands of problem situations they encounter. If one cannot overcome problems in the way one wishes, he or she loses the chances for survival and to lead a happy life. There is a survival value to problem-solving skills.

It is important to know what problem solving is and what kinds of processes it includes. The conceptualization of problem solving and understanding its meaning is important for studying it in a scientific way. In order to be able to get studied in a scientific way, problem solving needs different levels of conceptualization. Theoretical approaches lying behind the problem-solving treatment are important for both scientific and application purposes.

Theoretical Approaches to Problem Solving

There are three theoretical approaches to problem solving. The first one is the social problem-solving process model (D'Zurilla & Goldfried, 1971; D'Zurilla, et al., 2004). This model is important for describing the problem-solving process and is an approach shaping today's practice of PST. It presents a detailed framework for how people solve problems they encounter in daily living and the factors taking part in the process. The second approach is PST used in the treatment of psychological disorders in primary health care settings (Gath & Mynors-Wallis, 2000). This pragmatic approach describes the problem-solving process in different steps and defines the directions for use during treatment. This approach differs from the social problem-solving process model in that it does not include the "problem orientation component." The third one is the information-processing approach to problem solving. This approach defines problem solving in terms of the stages of information processing and describes what is happening during the process of problem solving in cognitive terms.

The three models are presented as follows in an outline. First, the social problem-solving process model is described in detail with the consideration of its

Problem Solving Therapy in the Clinical Practice. DOI: http://dx.doi.org/10.1016/B978-0-12-398455-5.00004-8

practice and the researches it has generated. Then, the problem-solving model used in the treatment of psychological problems in primary care is presented. Finally, the information-processing approach to problem solving will be detailed. As one can contemplate, the three approaches have much in common.

Social Problem-Solving Process Model

The social problem-solving approach originally introduced by the seminal work of D'Zurilla and Goldfried (1971) and expanded later by D'Zurilla and Nezu (1982, 1999) is concerned with the resolution of problems and difficulties people encounter in daily living. D'Zurilla et al. (2004) have further advanced this approach as the "*problem-solving process model.*" The model assumes five distinct but related dimensions underlying the problem-solving process.

According to the social problem-solving model, the person's first encounter with the problem and his or her reactions are important. The social problem-solving model characterizes the cognitive, emotional, and motivational reactions of the individuals when faced with a problem as *problem orientation*. The model assumes that the reactions of the individuals when they face a problem situation can be characterized as constructive reactions and dysfunctional reactions. Constructive reactions are defined as *positive problem orientation*, whereas dysfunctional reactions are defined as *negative problem orientation*. The definitions of the positive and negative problem orientations and their effects on the problem-solving process are explained in detail as follows.

The model also assumes that individuals display three kinds of problem-solving styles. These are (1) impulsive-carelessness, (2) avoidance, and (3) rational problem-solving styles. Individuals who display dysfunctional impulsive-carelessness problem-solving styles are likely to solve the problems in a hurry, in the direction of the first idea that comes to their mind, without thinking through the problem; thus, they act impulsively. The avoidant problem solving is also a dysfunctional style. People possessing avoidant problem-solving style ignore problems when they arise or are unable to act even if they are aware of them. Rational problem solving is a functional problem-solving style. Individuals who employ the rational problem-solving style perceive the problems clearly and accurately when they emerge and are able to take the rational steps for their resolution in a systematic way. People who use rational problem solving have a high likelihood of solving their problems.

The social problem-solving process model assumes that the three problem-solving styles lead to certain outcomes. Depending on the individual's goals, the obtained result or outcome may be positive or negative. Problem solving reaches its aim if the outcomes are in line with the individual's goals and if they satisfy the individual's expectations in relation to the resolution of the problem. If the outcomes are positive, the process of problem solving may be terminated and the individual may deal with the resolution of another problem if it exists. If the obtained results are negative, the individual may quit the problem-solving process or may go back and start the problem solving cycle from a stage he or she feels may have failed. Some people may terminate the problem-solving process and stop solving the problem when they face negative outcomes. An individual who is faced with a negative outcome can go back to the problem orientation stage or the problem-solving style stage of the problem-solving process.

The point to emphasize here is that rational problem solving has a relatively higher likelihood of resulting in positive outcomes than the impulsive-careless and avoidant problem-solving styles. The dimensions of the social problem-solving model are presented in detail as follows.

Problem Orientation

People's cognitive, emotional, and behavioral attitudes toward a given problem situation are important and are called problem orientation. When people encounter a problem, they generally display two kinds of reactions. A person's constructive attitudes toward a problem are called *positive problem orientation.* Some people on the other hand display dysfunctional or negative attitudes when faced with a problem and are called *negative problem orientation.*

Problem orientation is defined by Nezu and Nezu (2001) as "*the motivational process including the individual's cognitive and emotional reactions when confronted with a problem*" (p. 188). D'Zurilla et al. (2004) define problem orientation as "*relatively stable cognitive–affective schemas that represent a person's beliefs, attitudes, and emotional reactions about problems in living and one's ability to cope with such problems*" (p. 14). The commonality between these two definitions is that they both include in problem orientation the cognitions, emotions, and beliefs about problems that a person has developed throughout life.

In problem orientation, the individual acts in a certain way based on his or her cognitions, emotions, and beliefs related to the problem situation. Thus the content and the nature of her or his cognitions, emotions, and beliefs determine the way in which the process of problem solving will develop and terminate. For instance, a person possessing a constructive orientation and attitude will be successful at displaying the skills and efforts necessary for problem solving. People possessing a dysfunctional style of approaching problems on the other hand get either demoralized or refrain from displaying the patience, the perseverance, the effort, and the skills necessary to solve the problems and at the end they are unsuccessful at problem solving.

The problem-solving process model presented here indicates that when people encounter problems, they behave in different ways depending on their attitudes, beliefs, and values. The main point is that people behave in two ways when they face problems, one way being positive or functional and the other being negative or dysfunctional.

Positive Problem Orientation

The positive problem orientation includes individual's cognitions, behaviors, emotions, attitudes, and beliefs in relation to the problem situation and to him- or herself. As noted, positive problem orientation represents a constructive attitude toward problems. Research has indicated that people who approach problems positively possess some common characteristics. These people view problems as opportunities to display their abilities instead of considering them as unwanted elements in life. When faced with problems, these individuals trust their own abilities and believe that they can surmount the problems. People who approach the problems positively evaluate the consequences of the problems positively. They believe that positive outcomes will be obtained when problems get solved (Robichaud & Dugas, 2005a).

What are the cognitive or emotional characteristics of people who approach problems positively? Nezu and Nezu (2001) and D'Zurilla et al. (2004) indicate that people who employ positive orientation toward a problem show some common characteristics, which are as follows:

- They are able to perceive the problems when they emerge in an accurate way and do not ignore them. When problems occur, they are willing to and ready to see them. Some people with psychological problems do not and cannot see the problems and prefer not to see them due to some psychological reasons. Some pretend that a problem does not exist at all.
- They see problems as part of life. They do not get easily demoralized when faced with problems. This increases their psychological resilience and their likelihood of solving the problems.
- They attribute the causes of the problems to the right sources. These people do not only perceive the problems accurately but also understand and perceive their dynamics correctly. They identify the causes of the problems and are able to see accurately the factors from which they are derived.
- They perceive the problems as positive occurrences that can be taken advantage of. Instead of perceiving and seeing problems as threats and undesired situations, they see them as opportunities. For those people, every problem is an opportunity for self-discovery and improvement. Most probably, this is the reason why they are optimistic in facing life and its problems.
- They believe that problems can be solved. People who approach problems positively display an optimistic attitude toward problems. As is known, optimism is related to various signs of adaptation and health. When faced with problems, optimistic individuals use all the possible resources, efforts, and strategies for the resolution of the problem without lowering their mood. Being able to maintain optimism often guarantees the resolution of the problem.
- They believe that their skills and abilities to solve life's problems are adequate. As part of their optimism, these people are positive about their skills in relation to problem solving. Such people trust their abilities to solve problems.
- They are aware of the fact that solving problems takes time and effort. People who possess positive problem orientation know that problems do not get solved automatically and that time and effort are necessary for their resolution, and they act accordingly.
- They show perseverance about the resolution of problems. Such people are determined and patient about solving problems instead of ignoring them and getting away from them. They do not easily quit but they push for resolution.

Negative Problem Orientation

As a motivational dimension, negative problem orientation results from generalized past experiences. Some people display certain dysfunctional behavioral and motivational characteristics when facing problems. What are the cognitive, behavioral, and motivational characteristics of the individuals who approach problems in a negative way? What kind of attitudes do people with negative problem orientation display? It is important to know the behavioral, cognitive, and motivational characteristics of persons with negative problem orientation in terms of both theory and practice.

Negative problem orientation is not an effective way of approaching problems. Contrary to positive problem orientation, negative problem orientation evokes psychological processes which impede the individual to take effective actions when faced with problems. What are the common characteristics of people who approach problems negatively? Nezu and Nezu (2001) and D'Zurilla et al. (2004) indicate that people employing negative problem orientation show some common characteristics, which are as follows:

- They falsely attribute the causes of problems to either themselves or to the others. They cannot attribute the causes of the problems to the right sources. As was pointed out in the section on attributions, to have a correct knowledge about problems and to perceive the role of the causal mechanisms involved in the emergence of problem situations are important for the process of problem solving. For instance, such people may hold themselves responsible for the emergence of a problem and may think that everything is their fault or may hold other people responsible and think that they experience problems because of other people's faults. The real cause of the problem may or may not be themselves or others. Rather than seeking the real causes and acting accordingly, people with negative orientation attribute the causes of problems to wrong sources.
- When problems arise, they do not see them or ignore them. People with negative problem orientation for some reason do not see the problems and ignore them even if problems affect them. Problems they encounter are left unresolved since they do not make the necessary attempts to solve the problems. As a result, the problems accumulate and the person's life becomes negatively affected.
- They perceive problems as threats. People with a negative problem orientation have a tendency to perceive problems as threats to their well-being. Since they see problems as threats, they tend to either ignore or avoid them, which leads to inaction or omission. Avoiding and ignoring problems result in the accumulation of problems. Perceiving problems as threats drag the person into a state of inertia.
- They expect that solving problems is difficult. People who perceive problems as threats to their well-being have pessimistic expectations about the resolution of the problems. Because of this pessimistic expectation, the person cannot take necessary actions to solve the problems. The expectation that the resolution of the problems is very difficult may inhibit the attempts that might possibly solve the problems.
- They doubt their own personal skills and abilities to solve problems. People who approach problems negatively are not confident about their personal skills and abilities. Lack of confidence in one's skills and abilities may result in panic and giving up. People's appraisal of their own skills and abilities affect their attitudes. For instance, a person not trusting his or her abilities will show an unwillingness to see problems, will perceive the problems as threats, will hold pessimistic expectations about their resolutions, and will be worried when faced with a problem. The worry means cognitive, emotional, and behavioral inhibitions for the person.
- They get frustrated and worried when problems arise. People with a negative problem orientation may feel disappointed, worried, and frustrated when they encounter problems.

Since such people do not perceive the problems as opportunities for self-discovery and improvement, they get devastated when facing them. Even if they do not get devastated, they feel bad and helpless. D'Zurilla et al. (2004) indicate that people who have a negative problem orientation have a low threshold for frustration.

When the characteristics of people with negative problem orientation are taken into account, the importance of cognitions, emotions, attitudes, and behaviors is apparent. One can say that cognitions, emotions, attitudes, and behaviors of a person facing a problem situation are a sign of how the problem-solving process will end. In other words, the nature of the first reaction of the individual to the problem situation gives information about its result. For instance, expecting that people who ignore problems or who rush into the problem-solving process will reach their aim in relation to the problem situation will not be realistic.

Research show that negative problem orientation is strongly related to various forms of conditions and psychopathology including academic failure, depression, suicide, stress, worry, and anxiety (Elliott & Shewchuk, 2003; Grant et al., 2006; Jeglic et al., 2005; Robichaud & Dugas, 2005b). A meta-analysis of studies investigating the efficacy of PST in decreasing mental and physical health problems by Malouff, Thorteinsson, and Schutte (2007) pointed out that the success of PST depended to a large extent on diminishing negative problem orientation.

Problem-Solving Styles

Attitudes and problem-solving endeavors of the individuals when faced with problems are important for the outcomes. We may then ask the following question: What kind of attitudes and behaviors do individuals display when they face a problem? The social problem-solving model assumes that people make use of three problem-solving styles when handling problems (D'Zurilla et al., 2004). They are as follows:

- Avoidant problem-solving style
- Impulsive-careless problem-solving style
- Rational problem-solving style.

Problem-solving styles are the behavioral characteristics of individuals when faced with problem situations. The knowledge of these behavioral styles is important for both research and practice. Understanding the problem-solving style of an individual helps the practitioner design and implement intervention strategies to reduce dysfunctional problem-solving styles and increase the functional ones. Indeed, this is the main goal of PST.

Avoidant Problem-Solving Style

The avoidant problem-solving style is a dysfunctional one. Some people do nothing when they face problem situations. They act as if a problem does not exist or they are not concerned about the problem situation. Such people display passive, inactive, dependent, and procrastinating behaviors. Instead of facing the situation and doing what the situation requires, people with an avoidant problem-solving style prefer to ignore. It would be appropriate to say that such people bury their heads in the ground.

People who employ the avoidant problem-solving style possess some common characteristics. Such people are unwilling to take and escape responsibility. Therefore, they avoid taking responsibility to solve the problem. They wait until the last minute to handle, deal with, and solve problems. They expect problems to get solved by themselves.

The point to reflect on is the reason why individuals with avoidant problem-solving styles act the way they do. Why do people ignore the problems they face? Do they really ignore the problems or do they not see them? It is the clinician's job to find the answers to these questions. We can think about the existence of conscious and unconscious motivational mechanisms if the client ignores the problems. For instance, when an individual ignores problems, defense mechanisms or some cognitive distortions may be operating.

From another perspective, a person who does not see problems may be acting realistically. One who does not believe in his or her skills to solve problems may ignore those problems, thinking that he or she will not be able to do something about it. In other words, his or her avoidance may lie on realistic grounds. It is the clinician's job to reveal the valid reasons for avoiding problems and the way they work. Only a good clinical assessment may reveal the underlying causes of avoidance. The clinical assessment may help the client develop an insight about him- or herself and his or her behaviors. To increase one's consciousness about oneself, the events and about the environment is an important mechanism of change in psychotherapy.

Impulsive-Careless Problem-Solving Style

The impulsive-careless problem-solving style is also a dysfunctional one. Although it is an active style, this type of problem solving has been indicated to be of an impulsive, careless, and hasty in nature. Such people are aware of only a few problem-solving techniques. They verify the alternatives and the solutions in a nonsystematic way. They try to solve the problems with very few data. The impulsive-careless problem-solving style is an effort to solve the problems in a hasty manner (D'Zurilla et al., 2004). This is the reason that the outcome of such efforts will not result in outcomes desired by the individual. The impulsive-careless problem-solving style carries the risk of giving way to the development of further new problems. In other words, when problems are handled this way, the solutions themselves will become further problems.

Nezu and Nezu (2001) indicate that individuals employing the impulsive-careless problem-solving style possess some common behavioral characteristics. According to this research, people employing this style of problem-solving strategy focus on one or more solutions and act with the first thought that comes to their mind. They evaluate the solutions and the possible consequences in a reckless and nonsystematic manner. These people do not follow and verify the solutions carefully. In other words, because they are not aware of their mistakes, such people seem to be doomed to use this dysfunctional problem-solving style all the time. Moreover, individuals who employ the impulsive-careless problem-solving style have been described as having a low threshold of tolerance for ambiguity, recklessness, or negative emotions.

As can be guessed, "impulsivity" has the key role in the impulsive-careless problem-solving style. What is impulsivity and what are the characteristics of impulsive persons? How can we understand impulsivity as a characteristic of people using such a style for problem solving? Understanding impulsivity on a conceptual level is important both for understanding the individuals employing this problem-solving style and for designing and applying helping strategies. For that reason, information on impulsivity and the relationship of the extent of impulsiveness with impulsive-careless problem-solving style will be explained in detail as follows.

We can roughly define impulsivity as *acting without thinking*. The term *impulsive* implies the inability of such a person to control his or her impulses or a significant difficulty in doing so. It should not be hard to imagine the kinds of problems individuals may experience when they act without thinking. Impulsive individuals have been shown to experience some psychological and interpersonal problems. The impulse-control problem has causal implications on the emergence of psychological problems. For example, the Diagnostic and Statistical Manual of Mental Disorders (DSM-IV) of the American Psychiatric Association (1994) classifies psychological disorders like intermittent explosive disorder, pathological gambling, kleptomania (stealing disorder), pyromania (fire-starting disorder), and trichotillomania (hair-pulling disorder) as impulse-control disorders. Also, the impulse-control disorder is known to be an important characteristic of psychological disorders like borderline and histrionic personality disorders.

What, then, are the behavioral characteristics of individuals who cannot control their impulses? A person with an impulse-control problem cannot control his or her anger and rage. A person who is not able to control such strong emotions will undoubtedly experience problems in social situations. A person with an impulse-control problem loses control over his or her behaviors. A healthy behavior under normal circumstances requires a judgment of the costs and the benefits and the consequences of one's actions. A person acting impulsively cannot think of the negative consequences that his or her actions might have for him- or herself or for others.

Impulsive persons share some common behavioral characteristics. The literature on impulsivity has identified four main characteristics of impulsive individuals (Carlton & Goldstein, 1987; Carlton & Manowitz, 1987; White et al., 1994). These are detailed in the following sections.

Impatience

People who behave impulsively are sensitive to rewards and have difficulty in delaying gratification. Such people want to obtain the reward instantly and do not resign from it. These people want to obtain what they want the moment they want it. Since they cannot delay gratification, impulsive people pay the price of this.

Delay of gratification is one of the main features of healthy human functioning. It is not hard to think of the consequences this kind of behavior would carry for the individual.

Hastiness

Impulsive persons have a tendency to act without thinking about negative consequences. They experience difficulty delaying their desires and act as if they have been enslaved by their impulses.

Indifference to Punishment

Since impulsive individual acts only for the reward without thinking about the consequences of his or her actions, he or she is indifferent to punishment. Punishments do not mean much to these individuals. They are in the pursuit of the things they wish to obtain. They do not think about the punishment and its consequences. Such conduct creates more problems to the individual. The problem-solving training aims to decrease such personal characteristics and improve people's ability to take into account the effects their choices, behaviors, and decisions have on themselves and on others.

Lack of Control

Impulsive people are not able to control their tendency to act in accordance with their impulses. They have no control over their wishes and behaviors. That is why they make decisions in a hurry and engage in certain activities without clear thinking. This behavioral style causes adaptation difficulties and new problems for individuals and their environment.

Rational Problem-Solving Style

It is difficult for individuals who employ impulsive-careless and avoidant problem-solving styles to reach the goals they are trying to achieve. Both styles are ineffective ways of solving problems. People employing rational problem-solving styles possess the ability to judge the problem-solving steps accurately and design, implement, and verify the strategy that will lead to the solution. Compared to the other two styles, individuals with rational problem-solving style solve their problems in an easier and healthier way. An individual with a rational problem-solving style goes through a series of problem-solving steps.

People engaging in rational problem-solving style prefer solving the problems they encounter in a systematic and goal-directed way. People who display a rational style in problem solving employ a functional style that gets results. This increases their functionality. As was noted earlier, problem-solving skills and abilities are important indicators of resilience.

According to the social problem-solving process model suggested by D'Zurilla et al. (2004), people make use of four main problem-solving skill sets in order to solve their problems in a rational way. The four problem-solving steps will be presented in detail in the following chapters; therefore, they will be described in this chapter only briefly. The four problem-solving steps, according to the social problem-solving theory, are as follows.

Problem Definition and Formulation

Here the individual tries to understand and define the problem. The definition and the formulation of the problem is one of the main steps leading the individual to the solution. For this reason, the first step in rational problem solving as described in the social problem-solving model is the definition of the problem.

Solution Generation

When faced with a specific problem, an individual needs to generate alternative solutions for a satisfactory problem resolution. This step, characterized by generation and identification of possible solutions for the resolution of the problem, is a crucial part of the problem-solving process.

Decision Making

After the definition of the problem and the generation of possible solutions comes the step of identifying the most effective solution. The decision to be made here is vital and can have an effect on the whole process of problem solving. A healthy decision at this stage may have a positive effect on the process and contribute to the successful resolution of the problem while an unhealthy decision may decrease the success of the problem-solving process and make it impossible to solve the problem.

Solution Implementation and Verification

The individual at this stage has already made the decision and picked up the most effective solution from among the possible alternatives. In this final stage, the individual makes an effort to implement the chosen solution, while at the same time verifying the outcomes against his or her own goals. As a result of this verification, the individual either terminates the problem-solving process or if the problem solving has been unsuccessful, the individual tries to find the reasons for its failure and starts the process from an appropriate stage. This process restarts when necessary for the resolution of other important problems for the individual.

Problem-Solving Treatment Model Used in Primary Care

This approach to problem solving was suggested by Gath and Mynors-Wallis (2000) for the treatment of the psychological problems in primary health care. The model shows a great resemblance to the social problem-solving model, but it differs in that it does not contain the problem orientation component. It is not a theoretical model in the usual sense but describes the stages of the problem-solving treatment rather than being a model for understanding the process of problem solving. This approach to PST defines the therapeutic process in seven steps. The steps described as follows are approximately the same as the rational problem-solving steps of the social problem-solving model. They are as follows.

Explanation of the Treatment and Its Rationale

Here the problem-solving therapist explains the treatment and its rationale to the client. Informing the client about the PST and its rationale is important in terms of client rights, the development of a therapeutic collaboration, and the adaptation of the client to the therapy.

Defining and Clarifying the Problems

This stage is the same as the problem definition and formulation stage defined by D'Zurilla et al. (2004). The main goal is to understand and clarify the client's problem. The aim of this stage is to identify the problem that causes distress and discomfort to the client.

Establishing Realistic Goals

Different from the process of social problem solving defined by D'Zurilla et al. (2004) where goal setting is considered in problem definition, Gath and Mynors-Wallis (2000) consider goal setting as a separate stage in PST. Here, the problem-solving therapist and the client work together on the identification of the goals to be achieved during and at the end of the treatment. How to identify the goals is described in detail in the following chapters.

Generating Alternative Solutions

This stage is also an essential part of the problem-solving process. At this stage, different alternative solutions for a problem need to be generated. The criteria according to which and the way the solution alternatives are generated will be described in more detail in the following chapters.

Choosing the Most Effective Solution

The most basic stage in the problem-solving process is the selection of the most effective solution among the solution alternatives generated by the patient. Choosing the effective solution is called decision making in the social problem-solving model. The rule here is the capacity of the chosen solution both to solve the problem and to satisfy the goal.

Evaluation

At the final stage, the client evaluates the outcomes of his or her implementation and in case the implementation got successful in reaching the goal, the process either terminates or restarts to solve other problems. If the implementation was unsuccessful, one goes back to the beginning of the process and the process starts from the stage at which it became unsuccessful.

Information-Processing Model of Problem Solving

The third theoretical approach to problem solving is the information-processing approach. According to the information-processing model suggested by Heppner and Krauskopf (1987), people receive information about the problems they encounter, form an action plan about the solution of the problem based on this information, and implement their action plan. Information-processing models assume that individuals constantly receive and process information and operate on the internal and the external world as a result of this process. In other words, people formulate their action plans as a result of information processing and in this way they reach their goals.

Heppner and Krauskopf (1987) indicate that what the information is and the way it is processed is important within the framework of information processing. According to Anderson (1982, 1983), three memory systems are important for the information processing. These are: (1) working, (2) declarative, and (3) operational memories. The working memory is the information in use—actively used information. Information in the working memory is stored for long-term use. Declarative memory is people's knowledge of the things, the events, and the phenomena—in other words, their representations about them. Operational memory is the knowledge of how to do something. Using the terminology of the cognitive psychology, the process of transforming the declarative knowledge to operational knowledge is called knowledge compilation.

Eventually, the process of solving problems is the act of retrieving and compiling information from memory. One will first gather information about the problem, next the information will be stored in memory, and then the stored information will be used in relation to the information in the working memory and the problem will get solved. In problem solving, the individual will make use of his or her past experiences and at the same time he or she will store the information related to the process of problem solving. This is nothing but the metacognitive aspect of problem solving. The impact of memory on the process of problem solving explains the fact that people lacking in their problem-solving skills experience problems in the autobiographic memory. Persons with deficient problem-solving skills may experience difficulties storing their behavioral experiences and acquisitions in relation to problem solving in the autobiographic memory.

In the information-processing model that they outlined, Heppner and Krauskopf (1987) talk about four basic information-processing stages in problem solving. For them, problem solving is a complex cognitive process accomplished by the use of the information based on the individual's past experiences. The four information-processing stages constituting the complex cognitive process are the following:

- Encoding
- Goal setting
- Pattern matching
- Problem solving.

Encoding

The process of encoding is related to the way information entering the individual's perceptual system is processed and structured. The way information is organized and structured by the information-processing system is important here. An individual facing a problem situation perceives the situation initially when the input enters the main system through the perceptual channels. Problems not perceived at this stage may constitute a source of discomfort for the individual. The inability to perceive the problem may result from a variety of reasons. The individual may not perceive the situation with the thought that he or she will not be able to do anything about it, or the perception may not be occurring because of some unconscious processes.

For Heppner and Krauskopf (1987), encoding is accomplished in two ways: (1) perceiving cues about a problem or the problem situation and (2) appraisal of the meaning and the importance of the problem. They emphasize that encoding is subjective and that every individual sees the problem situations through lenses or filters formed as a result of their life experiences and skills, and that the nature of these filters and lenses has a great impact on perception. Individuals see the events and their environment through the color of the lenses of their spectacles, so to speak. Past experiences, thought patterns, and psychological dispositions are the determining factors for whether or not individuals will be able to perceive the problems and also for the way they will perceive them.

Perceiving the Cues About Problems

Reference is made here to the individual's initial perceptions of the problem. As was pointed out, the perception of the problem or the problem situation is an important endeavor. When perception does not occur, there will not be a problem in the individual's perceptual world. A problem that does not exist need not be solved. From the awareness of the problem to its definition, the perception of the problem comprises a series of activities such as studying the problem, information gathering about it, differentiation of the problem from other problems, and classification of the problem.

From the information-processing perspective, the perception of the problem is important for processing and solving it. For this reason, initially the problem needs to be perceived by the individual. Three important characteristics are indicated in relation to the perception of the problem. These are *the speed*, *the accuracy*, and *the wholeness* of perception.

- *Speed of perception*: The ability of an individual to perceive problems when they occur at a maximum speed is important for planning and thinking though the activities in relation to the problem. Perceiving problems accurately and responding to them at a maximum speed is important not only for problem solving but also has an evolutionary importance for the individual by having an impact on his or her survival.
- *Accuracy of perception*: Perceiving the problem accurately is equally important as perceiving it at a maximum speed. The characteristics of the problem need to be perceived

accurately by the individual. It is vitally important for an individual to determine accurately whether or not he or she experiences problems with the person he or she is in relationship with. Solving an accurately defined and perceived relational problem is an important opportunity for the individual. Inaccurately perceived problem may be worse than a problem not perceived. Trying to solve an inaccurately perceived problem may lead to the emergence of more complex relationship problems.

- *Wholeness of perception*: A fast and accurate perception of a problem is not sufficient. The problem needs to be perceived as a whole. Working on a problem that is partly perceived accurately but not perceived wholly may bring about other problems.

Heppner and Krauskopf (1987) refer to two cognitive abilities that they think are important for information processing. One is the *causal thinking*. In order for the individual to successfully overcome a problem situation, he or she needs to be able to perceive the causal chain of events in relation to the problems. In other words, the individual needs to be able to establish the causal relationships between events. Otherwise, the individual will express the difficulty but will not be able to see the causal chain of events that lead to the problem situation. The second cognitive ability is the *interpersonal sensitivity*. Individuals who are sensitive to the clues that could possibly be the onset of a problem experience fewer problems with other people and are able to solve their problems in an easier way. Interpersonal sensitivity will help the individual perceive the interpersonal problems that have been experienced or may possibly be experienced, at the right time. Perceiving the problem at the right time will make it easier to solve it.

Appraisal of the Personal Importance of the Problem

A critical stage in the perception of the problem is the evaluation of its importance for the individual. In previous chapters, the individual's assessment of the problem is defined by Lazarus and Folkman (1984) as *primary* and *secondary appraisals*. In the primary appraisal, the individual makes an initial judgment about whether or not a problem or difficulty exists. In the secondary appraisal, the individual thinks about what to do with the difficulty and judges whether or not he or she possesses adequate coping skills.

How do people appraise the problems they encounter? Heppner and Krauskopf (1987) indicate that problems get appraised in five dimensions. As it was explained in the previous paragraph, the individual engages initially in the primary appraisal and comes to a judgment about whether or not a difficulty or problem exists. After the first appraisal, the individual makes four more appraisals. They are as follows: (1) the cost of the perceived problem, (2) the difficulty of the perceived problem, (3) the cause of the perceived problem, and (4) the perceived coping skill. These dimensions are described below:

- *The perceived cost of the problem*: It is the perception of personal, social, and short- and long-term consequences of the problem situation. The cost of a problem for the individual will appear as the combination of these elements. When the individual faces a problem situation, he or she makes evaluations about the consequences of the problem and its costs.

A problem that may have a high personal cost may be motivating for some individuals and discouraging for others.

- *The perceived difficulty of the problem*: The individual when faced with a problem situation makes an assessment of its difficulty. A difficult and complex problem may appear to the individual at a level above his or her capability for solving it. In such circumstance, the individual may see the efforts to solve the problem as a useless and unnecessary activity. This kind of perception will lower the motivation of the individual in relation to problem solving.
- *The perceived causes of the problem*: The individual's perception of the causes of the problem is important. The person shows a willingness to make the effort for solving a problem only if he or she sees that he or she can control, change, or influence the situation. Otherwise, he or she may remain passive thinking that he or she will not be able to change it anyway.
- *The perceived coping skill*: Following the primary appraisal where the difficulty level, the consequences, and the causes of the problem are appraised, the individual assesses his or her own coping skills too. The individual's assessment of whether or not he or she will be able to cope effectively with the problem and whether or not he or she has the necessary skills and resources is a determining factor for the resolution of the problem. If the individual assesses that he or she has adequate coping skills, then the individual may attempt to solve the problem. Otherwise he or she will stay inactive.

What are the criteria for successful encoding/perception of problems? What a successful encoding or perception is made up of? For Heppner and Krauskopf (1987), four factors play a role in the successful perception of a problem. Accordingly, a successful perception of a problem depends on

- the person's ability to gather information about him- or herself (thoughts, emotions, and behaviors), the environment (social norms and expectations), and characteristics of the problem (obstacles, goals), and synthesize this information;
- accurate and objective perception of the problem;
- an accurate assessment of the meaning and the importance of the problem;
- an accurate assessment of the individual's coping skills.

Goal Setting

Problem solving is a goal-directed human behavior. To resolve the problem, the individual sets a goal and tries to achieve it. To be able to engage in a problem-solving activity and to be successful at it, the individual needs to set the goals thoroughly. A human deed without a goal is doomed to disappear in space. By providing the individual with an orientation, goals prevent the behaviors from getting lost in space. In other words, a goal shows the individual the way and the direction.

For Heppner and Krauskopf (1987), there are two basic ways of processing information in goal setting: top-down and bottom-up processes. In top-down information processing, the individual first sets a general goal and in order to reach that goal, he or she sets smaller goals. The top-down processing is also described as goal-directed planning. On the other hand, in the bottom-up processing, the person reacts to the characteristics of the problem situation. An individual immediately reacting to the behavior of a friend may be taken as an example for bottom-up processing.

How should the goals be and what should be their features? The goals identified for a resolution of a problem some common features. The first is the *complexity* of the goal, the second is the *objectivity*, and the third is its *functionality*. *Complex* goals carry more than one objective. Such goals are hard to achieve and work on. The second feature is whether or not the goals are *objective*. Objective goals are more convenient to work on. The third feature of the goals is their ability to fulfill a certain function. The most important function of a goal is its ability to organize the human behavior and to make it purposeful. The behaviors of an individual without a goal may be considered as the collection of random activities. The behaviors of an individual with a goal will be organized around a purpose and his or her activities will be carried out to fulfill that purpose.

How should goals be set successfully? According to Heppner and Krauskopf (1987), in order for an individual to successfully identify goals in relation to the problem situation, some conditions should be present. According to this, the person should (a) perceive or encode the problem accurately and (b) identify clear and concrete goals.

The goal identified by the individual should be able to organize the problem-solving process by providing short-term, long-term, and compatible solutions. Taking into account the problem and the individual's skills and capabilities, the goal identified should be realistic and should set the time limits for the completion of the problem-solving process. Said another way, the organizing characteristic of the goal is important within the context of problem solving, which is a goal-directed human behavior.

Planning and Pattern Matching

An individual facing a problem situation thinks about what can be done in such situation, what he or she has done previously in similar situations, and what the consequences of his or her actions were and tries to match the problem with the information in his or her memory. As a result of this matching, the individual acts for the resolution of the problem. This matching is defined as pattern matching in cognitive psychology. The individual sometimes acts before matching has been finalized. Such people make use of bottom-up information processing and act impulsively. This is not an effective method for the resolution of a problem.

In order for an individual to cope with problem situations in daily living and to resolve the problems in line with the goals, the first step is the perception of the situations as problems. In order to resolve a perceived problem, the individual needs to have information about the situation. The individual may think about solution alternatives by matching the characteristics of the problem situation with what he or she has done in similar situations in the past. In other words, pattern matching combines the requirements of the problem with the knowledge and goals and wishes in the individual's mind. The goal identified by the individual will ease this matching process.

An ill-identified goal will make it difficult for the individual to develop an action plan and to match patterns. As it was emphasized in the previous paragraph, if the goals are not well defined (e.g., simple or objective), they will have a negative impact on problem-solving process. Ill-defined and subjective goals are the sources of ambiguity for the individual and the ambiguity constitute a source of anxiety for an individual. A study by Kizilbash, Vanderploeg, and Curtiss (2002) found compounded anxiety and depression had an adverse effect on the retrieval of information from memory. If pattern matching includes the retrieval of information from memory, then ambiguous situations will have a negative impact on pattern-matching process.

What are the necessary cognitive skills for pattern matching? Which cognitive abilities can ease this process? As in the case of problem solving, there are some cognitive skills that are important for planning and pattern matching. These are: (1) ability to think about the solution, (2) ability to conceptualize a step-by-step means to reach the goal, and (3) ability to think about consequences. These cognitive skills were explained in detail in the previous chapters.

The process of pattern matching that we can define as the matching of the characteristics and requirements of a problem situation with the requirements of the problem solving is the most important process in information processing. The most important feature of this process is the individual's generation of possible solution alternatives. When faced with a problem situation, the individual should be able to think about the alternative solutions in order to be able to make the necessary steps to solve the problem.

The individual should be able to select one of the solution alternatives and develop an action plan. This requires complex mental process and is a decision-making process. In this process, the individual makes two major decisions. The first one is about choosing the best solution alternative from among others. The second is the identification of the action plan in relation to the chosen solution. How does a person make decisions? How does the decision-making process work?

Heppner and Krauskopf (1987) indicate that individuals make use of some automatic processes of information processing in decision making and judging. These are:

- *According to the current situation*: Individuals make judgments and decisions according to the current situation. The individual makes decisions based on the situational demands.
- *According to its typicality*: When selecting an alternative solution from among others, the individual makes comparisons with the solutions that have previously been successful. Here the individual, based on his or her own experiences, selects the solutions that he or she thinks worked well in the resolution of the previous problems.
- *Acting according to the first belief*: It is difficult for people to change their first beliefs even though data supports the opposite. Despite the evidence in the opposite direction, some people base their decision on their first beliefs.

According to the authors, in order for planning and pattern matching to be successful, the following conditions are necessary: (a) the perception of the problem and goal setting, (b) carefully reviewed and screened information base of the individual related to problem solving, (c) evaluation of alternative solutions in relation to the problem, (d) preconsideration of the necessary steps to reach the goal, (e) comparison and assessment of the possible effects and the consequences of the alternative solutions, (f) accurate selection of the alternative solution that best suites the purpose, and (g) the individual's knowledge and skill level and the nature of the problem have been taken into account during the cognitive processes cited.

Problem Solving

An individual who perceives the problem keeps it in memory, defines it, and then sets goals and makes plans for the resolutions of the problem. At the final stage, the individual acts in accordance with the specified goals and plans. Heppner and Krauskopf (1987) consider problem solving as the last step in information processing and see it as the combination of a series of cognitive, emotional, and behavioral activities. For a successful problem-solving process, the cognitive, emotional, and behavioral activities should be executed in coordination and harmony.

Heppner and Krauskopf (1987) emphasize a series of cognitive, affective, and behavioral acts that they consider are important in problem-solving process. These behaviors are those having a function in the resolution of a problem. Cognitive and affective behaviors for the resolution of the problem are as follows:

- *Problem-solving behaviors*: All human behaviors relevant to problem solving are considered here, for instance, coping behaviors. Authors underline four points that they believe are relevant to problem solving. These are: (1) the problem-solving behaviors that have been tried before, (2) the reasons for why some behaviors are ineffective, (3) the functional outcome of the behavior, and (4) the client's perseverance in problem solving. The behaviors that the patient had previously engaged in are important. If he or she had been unsuccessful, why had these problem-solving behaviors been unsuccessful? The point to be considered here is whether effective behaviors have been inhibited by the feelings of sadness, fear, and anxiety or whether there is a deficiency in the client's problem-solving behavior. What have the functional outcomes of the client's previous problem-solving behaviors been? Has the client's level of perseverance been effective in the resolution or nonresolution of the problem?
- *Cognitive behaviors related to problem solving*: An individual's cognitions or cognitive processes are important in the process of problem solving. The cognitive features that the individual displays when faced with a problem called personal coping techniques, for example, belong to this category. Problem orientation is partly a cognitive behavior.
- *Affective behaviors related to problem solving*: Individuals' emotional reactions are effective in the problem-solving behaviors. Individuals' emotions and emotional reactions are extremely effective not only on problem-solving behavior but also on their behaviors in general. While reactions such as sadness, fear, anxiety, and sorrow may inhibit some effective problem-solving behaviors, emotional reactions like happiness and good mood may have a positive effect on the problem-solving process.

According to the information-processing model, what does a successful problem solving depend on? Under what circumstances can we say that the problem has been successfully solved? According to Heppner and Krauskopf (1987), a successful problem solving depends on: (a) adequate perception, appropriate goal setting, and pattern matching; (b) the resolution of the problem in a desired way; (c) effective cognitive organization of the solution actions; (d) factors influencing problem solving positively and providing feedback; (e) taking individual's skills and abilities into account; (f) making use of behavioral, cognitive, and affective coping strategies that result in the successful resolution of the problem.

According to the information-processing model, a successful problem-solving process depends on a series of cognitive processes of the individual. What is important here is the knowledge, the assessment, and the teaching of these cognitive processes. The problem-solving therapist's job is to know about these cognitive processes and abilities. For a successful problem-solving treatment, the problem-solving therapists need to assess these skills/abilities and if deficiencies are diagnosed to teach them to their clients.

Conclusion

Human problem solving is a complex endeavor involving cognitive, affective, and behavioral characteristics. As mental representations, theoretical approaches help us understand this complex process. Three main theoretical approaches to PST are given in this chapter. They help us better understand a phenomenon and discuss it in scientific terms. They also guide the application of scientific knowledge as in the case of PST.

5 Problem-Solving and Psychological Problems

Introduction

Mental health problems are common worldwide and cause tremendous suffering for the afflicted individual, their loved ones, and society. In addition, these problems also constitute economic loss and burden. Therefore, understanding the causal mechanisms involved in the development and maintenance of psychological problems is important and has implications for treatment. As a psychological construct, *problem-solving* offers an important conceptual framework for the understanding of the etiology of psychological problems. The framework offered by problem solving is helpful for an understanding of psychological problems and allows us to draw causal inference. In addition to the etiological conceptual framework, the concept of problem solving presents itself as an instrumental method that can be used in the resolution of psychological problems.

This chapter reviews and discusses the relationship between problem solving and various forms of psychological problems. Scientific studies show that people who have been hospitalized for psychiatric disorders display deficiencies in problem solving (Coche & Flick, 1975; Platt, Siegel, & Spivack, 1975; Platt & Spivack, 1972). Studies also show that people who are able to solve or feel that they are be able to solve their problems experience fewer difficulties in life than people who do not think or feel that way. For instance, in one study, Nezu (1985) compared effective problem solvers with ineffective problem solvers and found that effective problem solvers experience fewer psychological problems than ineffective problem solvers.

The relationship between problem solving and psychological disorders will be examined as follows. In this chapter, the relationship between problem solving and depression, suicide, anxiety disorders, schizophrenia, aggression, and psychological problems secondary to medical conditions are examined. Here, the role of the problem-solving skills in the development and the maintenance of psychological problems is dealt with in the light of the results from empirical scientific investigations.

Problem Solving and Depression

According to the World Health Organization (WHO, 2004), depression is the most prevalent mental health problem and affects 340 million people worldwide. For the

Problem Solving Therapy in the Clinical Practice. DOI: http://dx.doi.org/10.1016/B978-0-12-398455-5.00005-X

WHO, only unipolar depression is expected to become the second-ranked cause of disease burden, constituting a 5.7% disability rate, just behind ischemic heart disease, by the year 2020. Any person can become depressed at any time. Biological, psychological, family, social, and societal factors contribute to the onset and maintenance of depression.

Depression should be taken seriously. If untreated, depression, the cause of extreme unhappiness and pessimism, may lead an individual to suicide. That is why depression is a psychological problem that needs to be taken seriously and be treated with the current available technologies. For this reason, it is important that the signs of depression be known to health care workers and the general population.

Major depression and dysthymic disorders are defined as unipolar mood disorders by the DSM-IV (APA, 1994) developed by the American Psychiatric Association. Sad mood, loss of interest or pleasure, loss of energy, change in sleep and appetite, difficulty in concentration, feelings of worthlessness, and accompanying thoughts of suicide are considered as common signs of these disorders.

It should be noted that not every sadness or pessimism is clinical depression. Depressive mood and clinical depression are two separate but related phenomena. According to the diagnostic criteria of DSM-IV, what is important is not whether or not an individual carries signs of depression, but the fact that he or she has been experiencing a number of signs for the previous 2-week period. Therefore, clinical depression causing a deep sadness, pessimism, and loss of energy and interest in the individual is different from the term commonly used in everyday language and from the state of sadness that anybody may fall into from time to time. Clinical depression is an illness just like other physical illnesses and may put the individual to bed.

Causing an extreme unhappiness and pessimism, depression makes the individual feel hopeless, helpless, and pessimistic. As stated, hopelessness plays a key role in the relationship between depression and suicide. What is leading the individual to consider suicide is not depression but the feelings of hopelessness and choicelessness caused by the depressive mood. In such a situation, the individual feels pressured by either personal-intrapsychic or the socio-environmental events and feels like there is no way out. This mood prevents the individual from getting away from pessimism and hopelessness and from seeing alternative ways out. Therefore, the individual with depression thinks the only solution is ending his and her own life and may act on this belief. Dying is perceived as salvation.

Today depression is one of the most important mental health problems affecting modern societies. Taking into consideration the personal unhappiness and losses caused by depression, it is important to understand the causal mechanisms involved in the onset, development, and maintenance of depression. This involves more than one domain of human functioning to consider. The scope of psychosocial interventions is limited to psychological and behavioral domains. Therefore, this book on problem solving is concerned with the psychological level of functioning. This chapter reviews the findings from scientific investigations examining the role of problem-solving skills in the development of depression.

From a problem-solving and life-events perspective, Nezu (1987) proposed a model that considers depression a state caused by a lack of problem-solving skills.

Starting with the fact that not everyone who faces difficult life situations falls into depression, the model indicates that the basic factor in the development of depression in people is their inability to solve problems or manage negative life events effectively. If the individual possesses effective coping or problem-solving skills, he or she will not develop depression when faced with problems or adverse life situations.

The literature containing empirical studies analyzing the relationship between problem-solving skills and depression is continuously growing. For instance, in a study conducted with university students, Gotlib and Asarnow (1979) compared the problem-solving skills of students with high and low depression scores. They found that the interpersonal problem-solving skill levels of students with high depression scores were lower than those with lower depression scores. In another study, Nezu (1987) identified a strong relationship between depression and problem-solving skills in adolescents. Thus, studies indicate that when the problem-solving skill level of the individual increases, the probability of being depressed decreases.

Studies analyzing the relationship between depression and problem-solving skills are numerous with respect to the methodological approaches and the measurement tools. In addition to the ordinary measurement tools, some researchers made use of tools used in the assessment of personality. In one such study, Heppner and Anderson (1985) used the depression subscale scores of the Minnesota Multiphasic Personality Inventory (MMPI). Their findings revealed that people with ineffective problem-solving skills had higher scores on the MMPI depression subscale than those with effective problem-solving skills. Working with clinical samples, Nezu (1986) identified a strong relationship between depression and inadequacies in problem solving.

In order for a successful adjustment, the individuals should be able to cope with the demands of life stages and environment. Problem-solving skills are the best coping strategies meeting the necessary demands for the adjustment of the individuals. Individuals who possess effective problem-solving skills are more successful in coping with the problem situations of daily living than those with ineffective problem-solving skills. Having adequate problem-solving skills allows the person to generate alternative solutions for problem situations which in turn leads to the maintenance of general social skills at an adequate level (Nezu, 1987). As one can anticipate, persons who possess effective problem-solving skills have a lower likelihood of falling into depression than those with ineffective problem-solving skills.

It is no surprise that stressful life situations with subsequent ups and downs negatively affect the individual. These events, defined in the literature as negative or adverse life events, cause stress and discomfort to the individual who may then develop psychological problems. Divorce, academic or commercial failure, death of a loved one, exposure to maltreatment, having been involved in a serious accident, unemployment, separations, witnessing or experiencing violence, surviving a natural disaster, and the like are defined as adverse life situations. The individuals' problem-solving skill levels have the capability of lowering the effects of stressful life situations. For instance, D'Zurilla and Nezu (1982) emphasized the buffering effect of the problem-solving skills in adverse life situations. In a study conducted with university students, Nezu and Nezu (1986) found that individuals with inadequate problem-solving skills and who experienced stressful life events were more depressed than those with adequate problem-solving skills and who experienced negative life events.

The rates of depression in children are low but show an increase with the onset of adolescence (Collishaw, Maughan, Goodman, & Pickles, 2004; Hamrin & Pachler, 2005; Kim, 2003). The frequency of its occurrence in childhood is less than 3%, but with the onset of adolescence, depression is observed in 14 out of 100 young people (Lewinsohn, Rohde, & Seeley, 1998). In a study conducted with 966 adolescents in the United States, Schichor, Bernstein, and King (1994) found that 22 out of 100 young people frequently feel depressed. In one study with Turkish adolescents, Eskin, Ertekin, Harlak, and Dereboy (2008) found that about 18% of 805 adolescents attending high school had depression.

Against this background, studies are being conducted to investigate the role of problem-solving skills in depression. For instance, Printz and Shermis (1999) conducted a study with university students in order to explore the role of social problem solving and social support on their adjustments to stressful life situations. Their findings showed that students with effective problem-solving skills had a lower likelihood of falling into depression than those with ineffective problem-solving skills. In a similar fashion, in a study conducted with high school students, Marcotte and Alain (1999) demonstrated that young people possessing adequate problem-solving skills got low scores on the Beck Depression Inventory and those with inadequate problem-solving skills got high scores. In still another study conducted with university students, Dixon and Heppner (1993) showed that among students with ineffective problem-solving skills, depressive symptoms were both more severe and more frequent. Gotlib and Asarnow (1979) compared university students with and without depression and showed that the problem-solving skills of students with depression were less adequate than those of the students without depression. In a study carried out with young people from Hong Kong, Siu and Shek (2005) demonstrated that students with high problem-solving skills were psychologically healthier and experienced less conflicts with their parents than students with low levels of problem-solving skills. In a study conducted with adolescents in Turkey, Eskin et al. (2008) identified that deficiencies in problem solving constituted a risk factor for depression.

Psychological problems are common among those individuals who care for a family member who is seriously ill. Both the fatigue brought about by caregiving and the emotional burden of having an ill loved one create a difficult situation with which to cope. It is not surprising that depression is common among those individuals. However, it is also known that not all the individuals who care for a family member fall into depression. In this context, Kurylo, Elliott, DeVivo, and Deer (2004) investigated the relationship between social problem-solving skills and depression among persons who care for a family member recovering from a heart attack. Investigators showed that depression and low life satisfaction were common in those caregivers who possessed a negative problem orientation. In still another study, Elliot and Shewchuk (2003) documented that negative problem orientation was an important factor in caregiver stress and depression levels.

In line with the aforementioned findings, studies indicate that, rather than rational problem solving, motivational aspects of problem solving seem to be strongly associated with depression, stress, and problems in adjustment. In a study with 439 clinically depressed adolescents enrolled in an adolescent depression study, Becker-Weidman et al. (2010) showed that high negative problem orientation, low positive problem orientation, and high avoidant problem-solving style were risk factors for depression severity. Findings from another study with 259 college students demonstrated that negative problem orientation was the most consistent moderator or a mediator of the relationship between daily stress and adjustment (Bell & D'Zurilla, 2009b).

As indicated in the beginning of this chapter, ineffective problem-solving skills are common among psychiatric patients. In a study conducted with psychiatric inpatients with major depression, Fossati and Ergis (2001) found that these patients' levels of problem-solving skill were inadequate. Similarly, a study conducted with 20 depression patients undergoing antidepressant treatment revealed that inadequacies existed in the patients' problem-solving skill levels (Garland & Harrington, 2000).

In a study carried out with 138 individuals in outpatient treatment, Cannon and Mulroy (1999) investigated the relationship between hopelessness and problem solving. They identified an inverse relationship between problem solving and hopelessness. Accordingly, as the problem-solving skill decreases, hopelessness increases. Watkins and Baracaia (2002) compared the problem-solving skills of 32 patients with depression, 26 individuals in remission, and 26 individuals who never suffered from depression. They found that individuals who were suffering from depression possessed a lower problem-solving skill level than those who were never depressed or who were remitted.

Depression is also common among individuals in prison or penitentiaries. Biggam and Power (1999), in a study that they conducted with Scottish prisoners, found that those who possessed inadequate problem-solving skills experienced high levels of psychological problems and that their hopelessness levels were high. The irony here is that if the problem-solving skill levels of these individuals were adequate, they would be able to prevent the occurrence of the conditions that brought them to the prison anyway.

The studies reviewed and discussed in this chapter do not, of course, encompass all investigations analyzing the relationship between depression and problem-solving skills. That was not the objective. The studies discussed in this chapter provide information about the scientific research in relation to the subject. The results of these studies demonstrate a robust relationship between problem solving and depression. The question we should ask here is whether the depression level of the individuals who suffer from depression can be increased or decreased with an improvement in their problem-solving skills. The answer to this question will be provided in Chapter 6, in which the effectiveness of PST is reviewed and discussed.

Problem Solving and Suicide

Today suicidal behavior is as a major public health problem affecting all societies in varying degrees (Eskin, 2012). The term suicidal behavior is used here to address both the deaths caused by suicide and thoughts and attempts about killing oneself.

According to the WHO's estimates, approximately 1.53 million people commit suicide annually worldwide and 10–20 times more people will attempt to kill themselves by the year 2020 (Bertolote & Fleischmann, 2002). Suicidal behavior is widespread especially among young people (Evans, Hawton, Rodham, & Deeks, 2005; Johnson, Krug, & Potter, 2000; Langhinrichsen-Rohling, Friend, & Powell, 2009). The cross-cultural studies suggest that suicidal behavior is becoming a problem for societies with low suicide rates as well. For instance, suicide ideation and attempts are as frequent among young people in Turkey as in Sweden (Eskin, 1995, 1996, 1999). A study carried out with Turkish university students has shown that 42% of students thought about killing themselves, and that 7% has made at least one attempt to kill themselves (Eskin, Kaynak-Demir, & Demir, 2005).

An individual resorts to suicide when he or she perceives the situation as unsolvable and sees killing him- or herself as the only solution. The common finding of studies conducted in this area is that individuals who display suicidal behavior have deficiencies in problem-solving skills (Levenson & Neuringer, 1971; Rotheram-Borus et al., 1990; Schotte & Clum, 1987; Weishaar, 1996). Evidence indicates that in addition to displays of suicidal behavior, its recurrence is an important issue. In one study, McAuliffe, Keeley, and Corcoran (2002) indicated that individuals who have had many attempts to commit suicide possessed a lower problem-solving skill level than individuals who have had only one attempt.

The resolution of a problem requires the consideration of many different solutions for a problem, the ability to generate creative solutions, and to make the necessary cognitive transitions between different alternatives. Scientific investigations show that individuals who attempt suicide are not able to generate alternative solutions to the problems they face (Platt et al., 1975). Suicidal persons are stuck with one view of a problem and they cannot change their views. In other words, they cannot see different solution alternatives when faced with problems.

Cognitive rigidity is the common cognitive trait of the individuals who display suicidal behavior (Ellis & Rutherford, 2008). Individuals who show cognitive rigidity do not possess the flexibility required for the solution of a problem. The individual in this case stays without a choice and therefore feels hopeless. Mraz and Runco (1994) analyzing the relationship between suicidal thoughts and creative problem solving have pointed out the importance of creativity and flexibility in problem solving. The problem-solving view holds an important place in the explanation of the suicidal behaviors. The starting point of this view is the concept of cognitive rigidity. Accordingly, there is an interaction between cognitive rigidity and the inefficiencies in problem solving.

An individual who displays inefficient problem-solving skills cannot generate alternative solutions for the resolution of a problem. A person who cannot generate alternative solutions falls into despair. As the level of hopelessness increases, the individual becomes more prone to depression and in the end may attempt to end his or her own life (Clum, Patsiokas, & Luscomb, 1979; Schotte & Clum, 1982, 1987). An ineffective problem-solving skill resulting from the cognitive rigidity is a factor making the individual prone to suicide. The ineffectiveness of the problem-solving skills or the encounter with a problem alone does not have an effect on the risk for suicide. What is important here is that the individual possesses a low level of problem-solving skill coupled with the fact that he or she is faced with a problem situation. This view is called the diathesis-stress model of suicide (Clum et al., 1979). In such a situation, the individual may fall in to despair. As stated earlier, the basic common characteristic of individuals who kill themselves or who attempt to do so is their experience of hopelessness.

The empirical tests of the diathesis-stress model provide support for the validity of this view. A study conducted by Schotte and Clum (1982) with US university students found that individuals who displayed ineffective problem-solving skills were found to display a higher tendency to commit suicide when their stress levels were high. Another study conducted with psychiatric patients by Dixon et al. (1994) has shown that ineffective problem-solving skills predicted suicidal thoughts and that this prediction increased when combined with the stress factor. In another study, Priester and Clum (1993) empirically demonstrated that problem solving was an important factor for psychological health and adjustment of the individual under stressful life situations. Esposito and Clum (2002) investigated the effects of social problem solving on the psychological well-being of individuals who might have been affected by sexual or physical abuse in childhood. The study compared the suicidal thoughts and attempts of individuals possessing high and low levels of problem-solving skills. The results have shown that fewer individuals with high problem-solving skills thought about suicide and made suicide attempts compared to the group with low problem-solving skills.

It may seem very restrictive that the majority of the studies testing the model are being conducted with American participants. In a study conducted with Asian students in the United States, Yang and Clum (1994) examined the relationship between problem solving, life stress, social support, hopelessness, and depression and suicidal thoughts. The results from a path analysis were found to support the diathesis-stress model. The study has shown that individuals with low life stress did not think about suicide even though their problem-solving skills were inadequate; however, when inadequate problem solving was coupled with high life stress, the risk for suicidal ideation was high.

In still another study, Eskin, Akoglu, and Uygur (2006) tested the diathesis-stress model with 121 Turkish psychiatric outpatients. In line with findings from earlier studies, both the suicidal thoughts and attempts were more common among patients with inadequate problem solving and who experienced stressful life situations. In another study, Eskin, Ertekin, Dereboy, and Demirkiran (2007) have demonstrated that inadequate problem-solving skills were predictive of both the thoughts and the attempts of suicide among high school adolescents.

As mentioned in preceding paragraphs, those individuals who displayed suicidal behaviors possessed cognitive rigidity. Also mentioned was the fact that as a result of cognitive rigidity, individuals were not able to generate different solution alternatives; therefore, they fell into despair and they saw suicide as the only way out. Some of the studies suggest that suicidal behavior may be associated not with cognitive rigidity or ability to generate alternative solutions but with the inability to make use of alternative solutions. In one study, Wilson et al. (1995) compared

20 adolescent psychiatric patients who had attempted suicide with a control group of 20 nonpsychiatric patients. Contrary to other studies, this study indicated that adolescents who had suicidal attempts did not display cognitive rigidity. Those who attempted suicide were able to generate solution alternatives as much as those who did not have suicidal attempts; however, this group was able to use very few of the solution alternatives they generated to cope with their problems.

Problems experienced in interpersonal relations by individuals who engage in suicidal behavior are the most common reasons for fatal and nonfatal suicidal behavior. Relationships with others can be the source of both problems and happiness. The perception of the problem encountered as unsolvable is important in the case of suicide. Suicides are generally the only way out the individual can determine when faced with an unsolvable situation. In adolescent suicides, the perception of family problems as unsolvable is a primary reason. The perception of intrafamilial problems as unsolvable is thought to affect the family dynamic and to give the adolescent individual the feeling that he or she has lost control over his or her own life. Orbach (1986, 1989) and Orbach et al. (1999) indicate that unsolvable problems within family pushing adolescents to suicidal behaviors have four main characteristics. These characteristics are:

1. *The problem is not a kind of problem that an adolescent can solve*: The problem encountered by the adolescent is independent from his or her skills and abilities. For instance, parents placing high standards that the adolescent cannot achieve.
2. *Solution alternatives being restricted*: Parents structure the solution alternatives in ways that are not appealing to the adolescent. For example, the belief that a hardworking student is able to solve every problem. Parents may have placed restrictions on freedom of choice and behavior.
3. *Solution creates a new problem*: This is a series of problems created by groupings within the family. For example, a father telling his daughter that he is having an affair and asking her to hide this from her mother. The problem will lead to other problems and nasty situations will take place as a result.
4. *Presenting a family problem as the problem of the adolescent*: Such problems are rooted in the family dynamics. This is a hidden problem that is not clearly manifested as a family problem. However, the problem is shown as the adolescent's problem and he or she is expected to make the effort to solve the problem. The adolescent here is in a way a scapegoat.

Beside the inadequacies in the generation of solution alternatives and in the application of these solutions, the individuals displaying suicidal behaviors when faced with problems are known to view suicide as a solution to the problems. Even the individuals who do not display any suicidal behaviors see suicide as a solution to the problems encountered. For example, adolescents believe that their peers who killed themselves by committing suicide solved their problems by doing so (Eskin, 1997). Orbach, Rosenheim, and Hary (1987) indicated that children who displayed suicidal behaviors saw the act of suicide as a desired alternative. Linehan et al. (1987), in a study carried out with suicide attempters and nonsuicidal psychiatric patients, revealed that suicide attempters believed that suicide would solve their problems.

Pollock and Williams (1998) in their review of studies on the relationship between problem solving and suicide pointed out to the need for further explanations in the field. Is problem solving an active or passive skill? The data at hand shows that individuals displaying suicidal behaviors acted passively to solve their problems. The second question is whether the deficiency in problem-solving skills is a state or a trait. The findings from Schotte, Cools, and Payvar (1990) suggest that problem-solving skills are state related. The third point is the necessity of further studying the psychological processes in problem solving. Studies on memory gain importance in this respect. For instance, Williams and Broadbent (1986) indicated that the problem of suicide was related to problems in the autobiographical memory. Suicide attempters were found to make overgeneralizations in recalling past events and were experiencing problems in recalling specific information from memory (Arie et al., 2008; Williams & Dritschel, 1988).

Thus, inadequate problem solving is an important risk factor for suicide. To understand this risk factor and to design treatment and prevention strategies by taking the necessary precautions is an important endeavor for a serious public health problem such as suicide. The research findings on the problem-solving deficiencies in persons with suicidal behavior provide an important field of study for the treatment and the prevention of suicidal behavior.

Problem Solving and Anxiety Disorders

Anxiety is a normal human feeling. That is why it is not a feeling that we should remove from our lives. The absence of this feeling does not define health or normality. On the contrary, it is one of the feelings essential to the survival of the individual. Anxiety pushes the individual to fight against difficulties and problems encountered under normal life circumstances and to flight from the difficulties he or she cannot fight back. The survival of the individual depends on his or her ability to fight when necessary. In evolutionary terms, fight or flight reaction is one of the behaviors easing the survival (Bateson, Brilot, & Nettle, 2011).

Anxiety has a motivating power on human behavior. In other words, if an individual gets anxious he or she can engage in actions related to the issue he or she feels anxious about. Otherwise, the individual may be in lethargy and be the victim of inactivity. Why is then such a useful feeling involved in psychiatric conditions? In order to understand the relationship of the feeling of anxiety with healthiness and unhealthiness, it is necessary to remember the golden rule about the difference between psychopathology and normality. The golden rule is "neither too much nor too little." For example, being too anxious or being not anxious at all disrupts normal human functioning. Certain amount of anxiety motivates the individual against difficulties in life and encourages the person to fight back. According to the law of Yerkes–Dodson (Yerkes & Dodson, 1908), one of the basic findings in psychology: The absence of anxiety, too little anxiety, or too much anxiety have a negative effect on an individual's performance. Thus, an optimum level of anxiety has a positive effect on the individual's performance.

The major characteristic of anxiety disorders is the presence of worry for no apparent reason. Anxious individuals are commonly worried, skeptical, suspicious, and apprehensive people. The common characteristic of individuals with anxiety disorders is their focus on negative thoughts and expectations. They constantly have the expectation that bad things and disastrous events will happen. Individuals with anxiety disorders focus only on negative events and act as if only negative events will happen in the future. They are constantly in worry. Every individual has worries in life. These worries are in fact compatible with life, because the individual increases his or her chance of survival by worrying about certain things in life. It would be scary even to think of an individual who has no fear of creating a traffic accident. Compared to individuals with no anxiety disorders, people who have such disorders either do not know what they are afraid of or the anxiety they feel is not congruent with the situation they are in (Morris & Maisto, 1996). Anxiety disorders are one of the most prevalent mental health problems (Stanley & Beck, 2000).

DSM-IV (APA, 1994) categorizes the anxiety disorders into seven. These are:

1. *Panic disorder*: In panic disorder, the individual experiences recurring panic attacks. During panic attacks, the individual feels sudden, unexpected, and intense feelings of terror without a valid reason. During a panic attack, the individual feels a disaster is about to come and may start feeling some or all of the symptoms such as chest pains, trembling, dizziness, shortness of breath, fear of losing control, or fear of death.
2. *Generalized anxiety disorders*: The most explicit characteristic of the generalized anxiety disorder is the persistent sense of intense and continuous fears or worries without an identifiable reason. Individuals with generalized anxiety disorders experience tension, uneasiness, and agitation, insomnia, and negative expectations about the future all the time.
3. *Posttraumatic stress disorder*: The individual experiences fearful attacks a certain amount of time after being exposed to traumatic experiences such as fire, flood, war, accident, earthquake, maltreatment, torture, and rape. If the individual experiences the fearful attacks right after the incident, the diagnosis is defined as acute stress disorder.
4. *Obsessive–compulsive disorder*: Obsessions are uncontrollable and unwanted thoughts and ideas. For example, an individual thinking about engaging in sexual relations with family members or an individual imagines the death of a loved one. Compulsions generally are ritualistic. For instance, washing the body following a specific order of tasks in the bathroom or counting the number of individuals that one comes across. While the individual is aware that obsessions and compulsions are irrational, he or she cannot stop them.
5. *Social phobias*: An individual with social phobia feels an extreme and inappropriate fear in social settings or public places. When these individuals' fear of being evaluated is combined with their desire to be perfect and precise, the life becomes unmanageable.
6. *Specific phobias*: The intense, extreme, and irrational fear that an individual feels about certain objects. For instance, extreme fear of spiders, planes, knives, or blood may restrict the lives of individuals with specific phobias.

The most important characteristic of anxious individuals is their cognitive focus on the negative. The characteristics of individuals with a negative problem orientation and avoidant problem-solving styles have been discussed in previous chapters and they overlap with the characteristics of persons with anxiety disorders.

The individual believes he or she will not be able to solve the problems encountered in living. The individual, who thinks he or she will not be able to cope effectively with difficulties and will not solve problems in a desirable way, expects that bad things will happen. As is known, problem solving is composed of two basic processes: problem orientation and rational problem solving. The relationship between problem solving and anxiety disorders may take two forms. The individual may display a motivational deficiency thinking that he or she will not be able to solve the problems. The individual may also stay without a choice in the face of the problems because of the deficiencies in rational problem-solving skills.

There is a meaningful relationship between the individual's approach to the problem and his or her levels of anxiety. A number of studies support this relationship. They show that when people approach problems in a negative way, their anxiety level increases. Individuals who have anxiety disorders of any kind negatively approach their problems. For instance, a study conducted by Robichaud and Dugas (2005b) with university students of an average age of 23.6 years revealed that negative problem orientation was related to high levels of anxiety. Similarly, in another study conducted with university students, Dugas, Letarte, Rhéaume, Freeston, and Ladouceur (1995) showed that negative problem orientation was related to high levels of anxiety but that rational problem-solving skills and anxiety were not related. It is logical to expect people with worry to use avoidant problem-solving styles. In a study with 57 children aged 6–10 years, Wilson and Hughes (2011) found children with higher levels of worry and anxiety used more avoidant problem solutions in social-problem situations. On the other hand, in a study conducted with university students, Belzer, D'Zurilla, and Maydeu-Olivares (2002) implied that both negative problem orientation and rational problem-solving skills were related to the students' anxiety levels.

Both the problem orientations and the individuals' problem-solving skill levels are found to be related to anxiety disorders. Nezu and Carnevale (1987) explored the relationship between problem-solving skills and posttraumatic stress syndrome among Vietnam veterans. According to the results, those veterans with posttraumatic stress disorder possessed ineffective problem-solving skills compared to those without such disorders. Furthermore, Ladouceur, Blais, Freeston, and Dugas (1998) in their studies showed that problem orientation was related to anxiety levels of individuals with generalized anxiety disorders. Problem orientation that is composed of individuals' cognitive, emotional, and behavioral characteristics when faced with a problem situation is found to be strongly related to anxiety and anxiety disorders.

The analysis of the literature shows that compared to depression and suicide, the number of scientific studies investigating the relationship of problem-solving skills and anxiety disorders is limited. Though limited, evidence suggests that problem-solving skill may have an important role in the onset and maintenance of anxiety disorders, which together constitute one of the most widespread mental health problems today. For this reason, future studies should aim to make up for the deficiencies of the scientific information in this area. There is a need especially for longitudinal studies to make inferences about cause and effect. The relationship between problem solving and anxiety disorders may be seen in two ways. In the one, deficits in problem-solving skills can cause anxiety disorders, and in the second, individuals' anxiety levels can influence their perceptions of their problem-solving skills. Caselli et al. (2004) indicated that chronic anxiety negatively affected the problem-solving skills of individuals.

Problem Solving and Schizophrenia

Schizophrenia is one of the most serious mental illnesses. The general characteristic of schizophrenia is the distorted perception of reality and the deterioration of the functional capacity. The individual, disconnected from outer realities, tries to keep functioning despite the complexities created by the inner world. The schizophrenic individual cannot differentiate between the realities he or she generates in his or her inner world and the reality of the outer world. Schizophrenia being a severe mental health problem covered under the title of "schizophrenia and other psychotic disorders" in DSM-IV (APA, 1994). According to DSM-IV, schizophrenia is characterized by delusions, hallucinations, disturbed speech and behaviors, catatonic behaviors, blunted affect, and the loss in the ability to perceive reality. It is the most severe of all psychiatric disorders. To be diagnosed as schizophrenic, the individual must display two of the aforementioned characteristics for a period of at least 6 months and the social and work-related functioning of the individual must be impaired.

Schizophrenia causes impairments in basic human functioning such as thoughts, affects, language, perception, and sense of identity. It is an illness with multiple causes and the mechanisms involved in its development are poorly or not understood at all. Affecting men and women equally, both researchers and medical professionals, the illness follows a chronic trend. This section will discuss its relationship with problem-solving skills; however, the relationship should not be thought in terms of causality. Because of the effects on the human functioning cited earlier, schizophrenia may affect problem-solving skills, but the deficiencies in problem-solving skills may just as well lay the causal foundation for the development of schizophrenic spectrum disorders. This situation makes it impossible to make causal inferences between problem solving and schizophrenia. The relationship may be causal in both ways.

The grouping of the symptoms has been one of the conceptualizations in the literature on schizophrenia in recent years. For instance, Andreasen (1985) suggested that the symptoms of schizophrenia be clustered in two groups: positive and negative symptoms. Positive symptoms are delusions, hallucinations, confusion in speech, and overt behaviors. Negative symptoms include blunted affect, social withdrawal, and a decline in the initiation of the goal-directed behaviors.

Social problem-solving skills are important for schizophrenic patients as much as they are for nonschizophrenics (Morris, Bellack & Tenhula, 2004). In order to solve a problem situation, the individual should materialize a number of cognitive activities such as discrimination, generalization, retention in memory, and retrieval of information from memory. As was pointed out, schizophrenia causes important deficits in cognitive functioning. Impairments in cognitive functioning and problem-solving skills have been observed in individuals with schizophrenia (Bedell, Lennox, Smith, & Rabinowicz, 1998; Blanchard, Sayers, Collins, & Bellack, 2004; Bustini, Stratta, Daneluzzo, & Pollice, 1999; Medalia, Revheim, & Casey, 2002; Revheim & Medalia, 2004). For instance, it was found that the abilities of goal directedness and activity planning were impaired in schizophrenic patients (Medalia et al., 2002). Research indicates that impairments in cognitive functioning are related to the negative symptoms of schizophrenia (Bustini et al., 1999; Halder & Mahato, 2009; Rushe, Morris, & Miotto, 1999).

In order to solve problems in life, the individual should be able to display the skills necessary for the resolution of the problem. Studies show that schizophrenic patients are less likely than nonschizophrenics to define problems, generate solution alternatives, and reach the right solutions. The problems experienced in this area may lead them to make faulty assumptions in interpersonal relations. Relational problems that have not accurately been identified may lead to the development of interpersonal problems (Bedell et al., 1998). Cognitive rigidity is a situation preventing the individual from perceiving and evaluating the problem situations in a flexible way. Cognitive flexibility, on the other hand, may help the individual perceive the problem situations encountered in an accurate way and generate alternative solutions. Hatashita-Wong, Smith, Silverstein, Hull, and Willson (2002) explored this subject with 44 schizophrenic outpatients. They found that patients displaying cognitive flexibility were more likely than those possessing cognitive rigidity to generate accurate, appropriate, and problem-related solutions. Similarly, in a study conducted with 49 schizophrenic patients and a control group of 28 healthy individuals, Yamashita, Mizuno, Nemoto, and Kashmina (2005) showed that cognitive flexibility was important in problem-solving ability.

The relationship between cognitive functioning and problem solving has been the subject matter of many scientific studies. Zanello, Perrig, and Huguelet (2006) carried out a comparative study with 20 chronic schizophrenic patients and a control group of 20 healthy individuals. Their findings showed that inefficiencies in cognitive performance had a negative effect on the problem-solving skills. According to the researchers, programs designed to improve the cognitive abilities of schizophrenic patients may help them improve their skills such as problem solving.

Research shows that components of interpersonal problem-solving skills of persons with schizophrenia are unrelated to one another and related to some neuropsychological processes. Vaskinn et al. (2009) compared the social problem-solving skills of 26 high-functioning schizophrenic patients to that of a group of 10 healthy controls. The schizophrenia group showed significantly more deficits in all aspects of problem-solving skill than the control group. The results also showed that social problem solving was associated with psychomotor speed, verbal learning, semantic fluency, and cognitive flexibility. Moreover, the findings from this study demonstrated that receiving, processing, and sending components of problem-solving skills of schizophrenic patients are not related to one another.

Though biological factors are important for an understanding of schizophrenia, family and environmental factors play an important role in the course of this illness (Hooley, 2007). In a study with 60 Mexican American caregivers and their ill relatives, Aguilera et al. (2010) showed that emotional overinvolvement was associated with increased relapse and criticism was associated with increased symptomatology. Thus, family interactions are important in the course of schizophrenia. In longitudinal study with 33 adolescents and their primary caregivers, O'Brien et al. (2009) investigated whether family problem-solving interactions play a role in social functioning of youth at ultra-high risk for psychosis and recent onset psychotic symptoms. Controlling for social functioning at baseline, researchers found that participants' skillful problem-solving and constructive communication and parents' constructive communication were related to adolescents' enhanced social functioning at 6 months later. Controlling for symptom severity at baseline, participants' conflictual communications were related to an increase in positive symptoms 6 months later.

The causes of the inefficiencies or deterioration in the problem-solving skills of the schizophrenic patients are important for the planning and the development of the scientific interventions geared toward the treatment and the rehabilitation of the patient groups in question. One of the scientific thoughts emerging in relation to this problem is whether or not the observed deterioration in the problem-solving skills in schizophrenia is linked with some structural deterioration in the brain. Chan et al. (2004) conducted a study with 51 schizophrenic patients, 51 patients with a brain damage, and 51 healthy individuals. Their findings showed that deficiencies in problem-solving skills in schizophrenic patients were worse than that of the other groups. Accordingly, the investigators suggested that damages in the frontal or the temporal cortex were not sufficient in explaining the deficiencies in problem-solving skills.

Problem Solving and Personality Disorders

DSM-IV (APA, 1994) defines personality disorders as behaviors that deviate from the expectations of the society the individual lives in, and the enduring patterns developed in their inner world. These behavioral patterns are made up of the individuals' thoughts about themselves, the events, and their environment, as well as emotional instability, difficulties in interpersonal functioning, and control of impulses. Personality disorders are inflexible across situations and lead to personal and interpersonal problems and impairments in social functioning. Individuals with personality disorders are often seen as "difficult patients." Most personality disorder patients do not see themselves as needing help and hence do not seek help. They most often seek help for distress caused by DSM-IV Axis I disorders such as depression, anxiety, and suicidal behavior, but not for personality maladjustment.

Personality disorders are clustered around three main groups by DSM-IV. The first group is the Cluster A personality disorders, also named *odd personality disorders.*

These are: (a) *paranoid personality disorder*, (b) *schizoid personality disorder*, and (c) *schizotypal personality disorder*. Cluster B personality disorders are: (a) *antisocial personality disorder*, (b) *borderline personality disorder*, (c) *histrionic personality disorder*, and (d) *narcissistic personality disorders*. The third and the last group is the Cluster C personality disorders, which are: (a) *avoidant personality disorder*, (b) *dependent personality disorder*, and (c) *obsessive–compulsive personality disorder*.

In addition to the personal characteristics of the individual, personality disorders are closely related to the norms and expectations of the society in which the individual lives. What behavioral patterns under which conditions are considered as personality disorder is as important here as the behaviors and behavioral patterns that are considered disorders. In other words, societal norms and values are important in the personality disorders. The characteristics of the diagnostic categories accepted by DSM-IV as personality disorders are listed as follows.

Cluster A personality disorders: Distrust and suspicion of others' motives interpreted as malevolent are salient in the paranoid personality disorder. Individuals having schizoid personality disorder are detached in the social relationships and have restricted range of emotions in interpersonal settings. Individuals with schizotypal personality disorders feel discomfort in close relationships and display odd behaviors accompanied by cognitive and perceptual distortions.

Cluster B personality disorders: Individuals with antisocial personality disorder display behavioral patterns of disregarding and violating the rights of others in social relationships. Individuals with borderline personality disorder display instability in self-image and affects and difficulty in impulse control. People with histrionic personality disorder are extremely emotional and they seek for attention. In narcissistic personality disorder, the individual displays grandiosity, need for admiration, and lack of empathy.

Cluster C personality disorders: Individuals with avoidant personality disorder display social inhibition, feelings of inadequacy, and hypersensitivity to negative evaluation. People with dependent personality disorder display excessive need to be taken care of and submissive and clinging characteristics. People with obsessive–compulsive personality disorders display an extreme need for orderliness, perfectionism, and control.

The prevalence of personality disorders both in community populations and psychiatric patient groups is higher than what it was predicted to be (Coid, 2003). In their review of studies on the epidemiology of personality disorders, Klonsky, Oltmanns, and Turkheimer (2002) indicated that depending on the kind of the measurement tools used and the samples, the prevalence of any personality disorder can vary from 6% to 14%. In another review, Lenzenweger (2008) concluded that the median prevalence of any personality disorder to be 10.56% and the mean prevalence rate to be 11.39%. In a community sample in the United Kingdom, Coid et al. (2006) found the weighted prevalence rate of any personality disorder to be 4.4%. Some studies found even higher prevalence rates for personality disorders. For instance, a study by Dereboy, Eskin, and Senyuva (2007) with 528 community participants selected by a stratified random sampling procedure found the prevalence of any personality disorder to be 25.6% and that of more than one personality disorder to be 21.4%. The prevalence rates of personality disorders in psychiatric populations seem to be even higher. In one study with 2528 psychiatric patients in the United Kingdom, Newton-Howes et al. (2010) found that 40% of all patients suffered from at least one personality disorder.

The treatment of personality disorders is relatively difficult. The disorder causes serious impairment in the individual's personal and social functioning. The psychosocial approaches are indispensable for a scientific understanding of personality disorders since biological approaches are often insufficient. The problem-solving approach may present an important conceptual framework to explain personality disorders in a scientific way. In addition, an empirical demonstration of the relationship between problem solving and personality disorders may have implications for the treatment of personality disorders.

The studies conducted to explain the role of problem solving in relation to personality disorders are very recent and insufficient in number. In a study researching the role of problem-solving skills in personality disorders, Bray, Barrowclough, and Lobban (2007) compared a group of patients with borderline personality disorder with a control group. The results of the study showed that individuals with borderline personality disorders generated vague solutions to the problems they encountered, had negative problem orientation, and displayed more impulsive/careless problem-solving style compared to the control group.

The majority of the studies examining the relationship between problem-solving skills and personality disorders have been conducted with individuals with borderline personality disorders. Berk et al. (2007) investigated the relationship between problem solving and personality disorders with 180 suicidal patients admitted to hospitals' emergency departments. They compared the patients diagnosed and not diagnosed with borderline personality disorders. They found that the suicidal patients diagnosed with borderline personality disorders displayed more serious psychopathology and had more inadequate levels of problem-solving skills than patients not diagnosed with borderline personality disorders. In another study conducted with 312 major depression patients under medication, Harley et al. (2006) found that individuals with at least one personality disorder displayed a more inadequate problem-solving level than individuals with no personality disorders.

Some of the diagnostic features of borderline personality disorders overlap with the characteristics of persons displaying impulsive/careless problem-solving style suggested by the social problem-solving model. For instance, impulsiveness is a characteristic observed among patients with borderline personality disorders (Dowson et al., 2004) and this is one of the diagnostic criteria of the disorder. That is the reason why individuals with borderline personality disorders will display an impulsive/careless style in dealing with their problems.

In one study with 705 Turkish university students, Yetis (2010) investigated the prevalence of personality disorders and their relationship with social problem solving. Using DSM-IV and the ICD-10 Personality Disorder Questionnaire and Social Problem Solving Inventory Revised, the researcher found that 13% of the sample had at least one personality disorder. Comparisons of students with a diagnosis of personality disorder to students without a diagnosis of personality disorder showed that those with personality disorders displayed poorer social problem-solving skills than those without personality disorders across social problem-solving dimensions and across personality disorder clusters. A logistic regression analysis for the prediction of whether or not an individual has a personality disorder showed that among social problem-solving dimensions, negative problem orientation was the only dimension with a significant association with personality disorder diagnosis.

Personality disorders are mental health problems that affect large segments of the population and cause significant impairments in psychological and social functioning of the afflicted individuals. The review of scientific work on the role of problem solving in personality disorders shows that structured cognitive–behavioral treatment approaches such as PST may have important contribution to the treatment of persons with personality disorders. However, this short overview shows that the numbers of scientific investigations exploring the role of problem-solving skills in the course of personality disorder are too small to reach conclusive inferences. Therefore, well-designed and possibly longitudinal investigations are needed to better understand this issue.

Problem Solving and Aggression

Aggression and aggressive behaviors are a significant social issue in society today. News stories about aggression and violence in interpersonal relations are reported in the mass media every day. Aggression is associated with personal and social costs. Persons with aggressive behavior have difficulties in social relationships and hence face social exclusion. Social exclusion leads to depressive affect and diminished capacity for positive mood which in turn lead to more aggression and the cycle goes on. The individual as well as society pays a high price for the damages that the aggressive behaviors cause. Therefore, understanding the course and the consequences of aggression is of a high priority. The problem-solving approach provides a valuable conceptual framework for a scientific understanding of aggression and aggressive behavior. The scholarly work conducted on the role of problem solving in the development and expression of aggression is reviewed in the following.

How is aggression defined within the field of psychology? What are the characteristics that differentiate aggressive behavior from other behaviors? How is aggression acquired? Is the individual aggressive by nature or is aggression a learned behavior? Aggression is defined in psychology as "behaviors that have the intention of harming other people physically or psychologically" (Morris & Maisto, 1996, p. 421). The most important characteristic differentiating aggression from other behaviors is its intentionality. For a behavior to be taken as aggressive, it should aim at harming others. If a behavior harms other people but is not intentional it is not seen as aggression. Such behaviors are seen as accidents. Within the science of modern psychology, aggression is viewed both as an inborn trait and a learned behavior.

Various theoretical views have been proposed as to the source and the causes of aggression. Historically, there have been three basic theoretical views on human aggression. The first one is the psychodynamic view, the second one is the social learning theory, and the third one is the frustration–aggression view. The psychodynamic theory traditionally views aggression as a behavior emerging as a result of the individual's inborn impulses, whereas the social learning theory views it as a learned behavior (Atkinson et al. 1999). The oldest view on aggression is the frustration–aggression theory. According to this theory, a human being shows aggression when he gets frustrated. However, the social learning theory sees aggression as only one of the behaviors displayed during frustrating situations. The individual's perception about frustration and past experiences is important in this process (Atkinson et al., 1999).

Aggression is a behavior that an individual displays as a result of his or her perceptions of a situation. One should pay attention that the situation itself or the external stimuli are not sufficient conditions to produce aggression. How the individual perceives the situation and which information about the stimuli he or she pays attention to have critical importance in this process. This is the social information-processing view on aggression. Social information processing has been important in understanding aggression (Dodge & Crick, 1990). The individual's social information-processing skills and the characteristics of their social information processing are important here. According to the social information-processing approach, the individual encounters a situation, and encodes the information, stimuli, and the cues in relation to the situation in the information-processing mechanism. Depending on both the structural and the functional characteristics of the information-processing mechanism, the individual reaches a judgment on or an assessment of the situation at the end of the process. As a result of this judgment and evaluation, the individual reacts to the situation. How the individual processes the situational cues and the stimuli and what judgments he or she reached are important here.

We can consider the aforementioned situation as a problem for the individual. The way in which the individual interprets the problem and reacts to the situation stands out here. The reaction of the individual to the situation as a result of his or her interpretations and perceptions is in fact the problem-solving behavior in relation to the situation. In other words, the individual does something about a situation that he or she deems as a problem. This is a problem-solving process. The nature of an individual's responses depends on his or her interpretations of the situation. The aggressive behavior results when the person interprets the situation in a way that elicits aggressive acts. The individual displaying aggressive behavior as a result of his or her perceptions and interpretations of the situation is defined as "aggressive problem solving" by Pakaslahti (2000).

Emphasizing the social information-processing steps in problem solving, Pakaslahti (2000) defines the information-processing and the problem-solving steps concurrently. According to this research, an individual who encounters a social problem situation displays an orientation to the situation. The orientation is the individual's emotional, cognitive, and behavioral tendencies. As has been mentioned earlier, these tendencies may be positive or negative. Aggressive people are individuals displaying negative problem orientation. Then, the individual interprets the situation. The most important characteristic of a human being is his or her ability to interpret the situation. The nature of interpretations directs an individual's behaviors in a certain way. At the next step, the individual sets a goal in relation to the situation. Based on the interpretations, the goal will determine where and in which direction the individual will go. For Pakaslahti, the individual generates strategies about how to reach the goal or the aim. The strategy or the action plan will take the individual to the goal or the target. In the final step of social information processing, the individual selects one or two strategies and implements them.

Pakaslahti (2000) tried to determine the information-processing characteristics of aggressive and nonaggressive individuals in light of the studies conducted with adolescents. Accordingly, some information-processing characteristics differentiate aggressive adolescents from nonaggressive adolescents. Compared to nonaggressive individuals, aggressive individuals pay more attention to the aggression-related stimuli in their environment. Such stimuli capture easily the attention of aggressive individuals. Aggressive individuals seek less concrete information in social relationships than nonaggressive individuals. Aggressive individuals interpret a social situation according to a speculation in their own minds and react accordingly. In other words, these individuals have metaphorical lenses in their eyes through which they perceive the events in an aggressive way.

One of the important characteristics of aggressive individuals is their interpretation of other people's intentions and motivations in a hostile way. In their interaction with others, aggressive individuals have the tendency to perceive other people's unintentional behaviors as deliberate acts directed to them. That is why they think that other people want to harm them on purpose. We mentioned earlier that one of the characteristics of aggressive behaviors differentiating them from other behaviors was their intentional nature. Otherwise we would have defined them as accidents. Since aggressive individuals think that other people deliberately want to harm them, they display intentional behaviors such as bullying and conspiracy.

An important component of problem solving is the ability to think of alternative solutions, interpretations, and alternative behaviors for a problematic situation. Alternative thinking skills play a key role in the problem-solving process. Since aggressive individuals cannot think of alternative solutions, interpretations, and behaviors for a problematic situation, they are stuck with only aggressive solutions, interpretations, and behaviors when confronted with a problem situation. A study by Takahashi, Koseki, and Shimada (2009) with 1100 Japanese elementary and junior high school students found inadequate alternative thinking skills to be predictive of children's aggressive behavior across all grades.

In our discussion about the cognitive components of problem solving, we emphasized that the individual needs to be able to make inferences about his or her own actions and make predictions about the possible outcomes of these actions. Compared to nonaggressive individuals, aggressive individuals are not able to make valid inferences about their own actions. For instance, an individual who attacks another person with a sudden rage cannot see what the results of this behavior can be in the long run. And this behavior can ruin his or her whole life or his or her relationships as a result.

As has been previously stated in this book, goal setting is an important stage in problem solving. Successful problem solvers are people who can set goals when faced with problem situations. The quality of the goal is as important as the ability to set the goal. Aggressive individuals usually set hostile goals. They establish the goal of superiority and vengeance in relation to the social situations they encounter. Since individuals move in the direction of the goals they set, hostile goals lead the individuals into aggressive directions. When the goals are hostile, aggressive individuals make use of hostile problem-solving strategies in order to reach the aggressive goals.

Another characteristic of aggressive individuals is their perception of the aggressive behaviors. These individuals interpret the aggressive behaviors in a more positive way. Aggressive individuals' perception of the victims of their behaviors is also noteworthy. They think that the victims deserve such behaviors and that they do not suffer. Studies conducted in this area demonstrate that aggressive adolescents and children are not able to show empathy (Lovett & Sheffield, 2006). What the other person deserves or does not deserve or may feel is certainly closely related with the individual's level of empathy.

When we look at the other characteristics of aggressive individuals, we can see that they look at events from a narrow perspective and that they cannot anticipate the possible outcomes of their behaviors. Such individuals experience difficulty in suppressing their aggressive impulses. Research shows that, compared to other people, aggressive individuals are more easily aroused physiologically (Lochman & Lenhart, 1993). Since they get easily aroused, the hostile feelings they possess influence negatively their information-processing and problem-solving processes.

As stated earlier, individuals lacking in problem-solving skills have a higher likelihood of engaging in aggressive behaviors. Individuals who do not know what to do or how to solve the problem when faced with problem situations may see aggressive behaviors as possible solutions for the problem situation. For instance, Keltigangas-Jarvinen (2002) conducted a study with 1655 Finnish adolescents with an age range of 11–17 years showing that aggressive problem-solving strategies are related to aggressive behaviors. In other words, adolescents who employed aggressive problem-solving strategies had a higher likelihood of displaying aggressive behaviors than those who employed nonaggressive problem-solving strategies.

Aggression, especially during adolescent years, is an important social problem, and scientific studies show that aggressive behaviors are developmentally stable. Keltigangas-Jarvinen and Pakaslahti (1999) and Keltigangas-Jarvinen (2001) stated that aggressive behaviors are chronic behaviors and that aggressive children very rarely turn out to be nonaggressive adolescents. Other studies conducted with children with conduct disorders show that problem-solving skills are important in the development of aggressive behaviors. In a study of 53 children with an age range of 7–12 years, Wasbusch, Walsh, Andrade, King, and Carrey (2007) indicated that the signs of conduct disorders are related to inadequate problem-solving skills.

One of the groups showing a high risk of displaying aggressive behaviors is comprised of children with conduct, hyperactivity–attention deficit, and oppositional defiant disorders. The possibility of such children to experience deficiencies in problem-solving skills was explored in a study conducted by Matthys, Cuperus, and Engeland (1999). Researchers compared a group of children with an age range of 7–12 years possessing attention-deficit/hyperactivity, oppositional defiant, and conduct disorders with a healthy control group and a depressive psychiatric group. The findings from study demonstrated that compared to the control group, children with conduct, hyperactivity–attention deficit, and oppositional defiant disorders showed serious deficiencies in their problem-solving skills.

The individuals' self-esteem is an important indication for the generation of healthy solutions to problem situations they encounter. Individuals who try to resolve their problems in an aggressive way may have low self-esteem. How do low self-esteem and problem-solving skills interact in aggression? D'Zurilla, Chang, and Sanna (2003) explored this question with 205 American university students. According to the findings from this investigation, the individuals with inadequate problem-solving skills and low self-esteem were found to have a higher likelihood of displaying aggressive behaviors. Researchers emphasized that this relationship is stronger for those individuals possessing a negative problem orientation and low self-esteem.

Problem Solving and Psychological Problems Secondary to Medical Conditions

Problem-solving skill deficits are not only limited to persons suffering from psychological disorders, the results of empirical investigations show that individuals suffering from a wide variety of medical problems also experience emotional and behavioral problems. In this section, the emphasis will be on a short review of findings from scientific studies examining the relationship between problem solving and emotional and behavioral problems secondary to some medical conditions. The nature of this relationship, however, should not be taken as implying one-directional causality. Problem-solving skill deficits of an individual may be a risk factor for the onset and the maintenance of emotional or behavioral problems secondary to medical conditions or, once started, emotional and behavioral problems may negatively influence the perception and use of problem-solving skills. The following review shows that problem solving is related to emotional and behavioral problems in individuals with various medical conditions.

Persons with spinal cord injuries are known to be at risk for preventable complications. For this reason, the prevention of secondary complications such as fatigue, immobility, pain, social isolation, anxiety, depression, and weight problems are the major issues for the care of this patient group (Hughes et al., 2003). That is why the problem-solving skill levels of patients with spinal cord injuries may have an effect not only on their health but also on certain behaviors that affect their health. In a study with 43 male and 13 female patients with spinal cord injuries, Dreer, Elliott, and Tucker (2004) found that patients with a positive problem orientation displayed more adaptive wellness and accident prevention behaviors. Patients with negative orientation toward problem solving and avoidant and impulsive/careless problem-solving styles displayed increased traffic and substance risk taking.

Deficiencies in problem-solving skills are also common among individuals possessing health problems classified by DSM-IV (APA, 1994) as pervasive developmental disorders. One of these problems is Asperger's syndrome, accepted as high-functioning autism, characterized by difficulties in social interactions and in understanding other people's intentions, motives, and emotions. The most distinctive feature of individuals with Asperger's syndrome is the difficulty they experience in communication and social interactions. Channon et al. (2001) compared a group of 13 male and 2 female adolescents with Asperger's syndrome ranging in age from 11 to 19 years with a control group of matched 15 normal developing adolescents. Researchers indicated that the problem-solving skills of the group with Asperger's syndrome were worse than that of the control group. The solution alternatives suggested by the Asperger's patients were found to be socially inappropriate.

Providing care to individuals with acute or chronic health problems is one of the most stressful jobs. Such care is usually provided within family by family members. The problem-solving skill levels of the families with respect to health care problems have an effect on family members' mental health. In a study of 11 male and 49 female caretakers of family members with spinal cord injuries, Elliott and Shewchuk (2003) examined the relationship between social problem-solving skills and distress experienced by caregivers. According to the research findings, a negative problem orientation of caregivers constituted a risk factor for the development of both psychological and physical health problems.

The problem-solving skill deficiencies of caregivers appear as a risk factor not only for themselves but also for the psychological and physical well-being of the individuals being cared for. For instance, in one study, Kurylo et al. (2004) analyzed the problem-solving skills of caregivers and health-related problems of the individuals with congestive heart failure. The results showed that the problem-solving skill levels of family members providing care were related to the depression and life satisfaction of the individuals with congestive heart failure. If the caregivers had efficient problem-solving skills, the depression level of the individuals with congestive heart failure was low and their life satisfaction was high.

Being diagnosed with a fatal disease such as cancer is a highly stressful situation for both the individual and their relatives. It is very difficult for the individual and the family members to cope with such a situation. The emotional, mental, and behavioral resources of the individuals involved must be adequate to deal with it. Recently, the problem-solving approach was studied in the field of psychosocial oncology with regard to the psychological difficulties cancer patients and their relatives cope with. The literature on psychosocial oncology indicates that problem-solving skills of the individuals are related to the psychological difficulties they may possibly experience. If the problem-solving skill levels of the individuals are high, their probability of experiencing psychological distress is low.

Nezu et al. (1999), in a study they conducted with patients suffering from different types of cancer, revealed that compared to the patients with adequate problem-solving levels, individuals with inadequate problem-solving skills experienced psychological problems. In a study they conducted with the spouses of 32 prostate cancer patients, Malcarne et al. (2002) found out that spouses possessing proactive problem-solving skills experienced less psychological problems compared to those with nonproactive problem-solving skills.

Diabetes is a chronic disease and requires good behavioral management skills. Persons with diabetes should be able to follow the procedures prescribed by their physicians. Adhering to medical and behavioral procedures requires good problem-solving skills. For instance, Wang et al. (2012) reported that diabetes patients demonstrate poor problem-solving skills when detecting hyperglycemia and hypoglycemia via self-monitoring of blood glucose. The work of King et al. (2010) indicated that self-efficacy, problem solving, and social-environmental support were associated with compliance with diet and exercise in diabetes patients. Self-management glycemic control skills are important in the disease management in diabetes patients (Zoffmann & Kirkevold, 2005). Hill-Briggs et al. (2006) studied 65 African-Americans with type 2 diabetes and found that an increase in avoidant problem-solving style was associated with an increase in blood glucose levels. Further, ineffective social problem-solving skills in a group of diabetes patients were found to be related to higher depression and lower life satisfaction (Elliott, Schewchuk, Miller, & Richards, 2001).

Conclusion

The review of findings from scientific studies on the relationship between problem solving and psychological problems suggests that problem solving is an important indicator of resiliency factor against a wide array of mental health problems. The evidence shows that problem-solving skills are involved in varying degrees in the onset and the course of depressive disorders, suicidal behaviors, anxiety disorders, personality disorders, aggression, and emotional–behavioral problems secondary to medical conditions.

The literature reveals that one needs to take into account a number of methodological issues in evaluating the results from the scientific studies investigating the relationship between problem solving and psychological problems. The first methodological issue is related to causality. Almost all of the research makes use of cross-sectional designs. Although studies utilizing cross-sectional methodologies show us that a relationship exists between the two phenomena, this, however, does not allow us to infer cause and effect. In order to be able to make a causal inference about two events, there is a need for longitudinal studies. The second methodological issue is the need to consider causality on a conceptual level. For instance, even if the longitudinal studies show that problem-solving skills of schizophrenic patients are inadequate, it will not be realistic to accept that schizophrenia is caused by a lack of or inefficiency in problem-solving skills. The third methodological issue is related to the generalizations made between diagnostic groups. For example, it is not possible to think about a single and homogenous disease category like schizophrenia. If we think of diseases on a spectrum, it is not scientifically correct to generalize the findings obtained in one section of the spectrum over others.

Taking the methodological issues into consideration, the findings obtained so far should be approached with caution. The contribution of the data obtained from the longitudinal studies meeting the causality criteria on a conceptual level is indisputable. For this reason, there is a need for scientific studies designed according to the methodological requirements for examining the causal role of the deficiencies in problem solving in the onset and the course of psychological problems.

Anxiety disorders, in particular, constitute one area in which the role of problem solving is relatively less often investigated. There is a need for more systematic and extensive scientific investigations in this diagnostic group of conditions. The scientific knowledge about the role of problem solving in anxiety disorders may contribute to the treatment of persons with anxiety disorders. Personality disorders constitute another such group. The etiology of personality disorders is understood poorly. A better understanding of the relationship between problem solving and personality disorders is important in terms of both theory and practice. It is known that pharmacological treatment options are symptomatic and have relatively poor success in the treatment of individuals with personality disorders. Therefore, PST may play an important role in the treatment of this difficult patient group.

6 Efficacy of Problem-Solving Therapy in Treating Mental Health Problems

Introduction

Mental health problems are prevalent and cause unnecessary human suffering and economic loss. Therefore, their treatment and prevention is of utmost importance. Important developments took place within the past 40 years in the treatment of the psychological problems. One such development is the expansion of pharmacological treatment methods. Second, important steps have been taken to establish and assess the efficacy of psychosocial interventions for the treatment of psychological problems. Despite these developments, psychotherapy has been irreplaceable in the treatment of the psychological disorders. Evidence-based psychological treatments with shorter duration and ease of teaching and practicing are needed.

There are some advantages of using psychotherapy either by itself or together with pharmacological treatment methods in the treatment of psychological disorders. First of all, it is known that combining biological treatments with psychosocial approaches increases the chances of recovery. Second, in some cases, psychotherapy continues to be the only solution. For example, during certain periods of pregnancy, the use of medication is not recommended for medical reasons. Third, the use of antidepressants contains some safety risks. Tricyclic antidepressants are very toxic in overdose and the use of selective serotonin reuptake inhibitors (SSRIs) in children and adolescents is related to an increased risk in suicidal behavior. Empirical evidence suggests that the use of antidepressants by that age group may increase the risk of suicide (Newman, 2004; Richmond & Rosen, 2005; Wohlfarth et al., 2006). For this reason, the types of methods to be used in the treatment of psychological problems in children and adolescents are still being debated (Ryan, 2005). Fourth, psychological treatment methods do not have side effects such as dry mouth, weight gain, and disruption of sexual functioning.

For the aforementioned reasons and many others, psychosocial interventions are important in the treatment of psychological problems. In short, brief, structured, and empirically supported psychotherapy methods are needed. PST is a cognitive–behavioral treatment method that fulfills this need. Its structured nature makes it easier to learn and practice. Compared with other kinds of psychotherapy, the shortness and flexibility of its practice make PST one of the most important

Problem Solving Therapy in the Clinical Practice. DOI: http://dx.doi.org/10.1016/B978-0-12-398455-5.00006-1

advancements in the area. Is PST an empirically supported method? In other words, is PST effective in the treatment of psychological problems? The following sections discuss the results of the empirical studies in relation to the efficacy of PST in the treatment of various forms of psychological disorders.

Efficacy of PST for Depression

As it has been indicated in the previous chapters, depression is the disease of our time. It affects large numbers of people and causes serious disability. Therefore, the treatment of depression needs to be dealt with urgently. Depression may at the same time be the onset of important social and health-related problems such as suicide and aggression. That is why effective treatment methods are urgently needed.

Evidence shows that psychotherapy and pharmacotherapy are effective in the treatment of depression, but that psychotherapy has some advantages over pharmacotherapy. Maat, Dekker, Schoevers, and De Jonghe (2006) conducted a meta-analysis reviewing the randomized clinical trials assessing the efficacy of treatment methods for depression. They showed that both pharmacotherapy and psychotherapy were equally efficacious. However, the dropout rates are larger in pharmacotherapy. According to the findings from the reviews conducted by Maat et al. (2006) and Paykel (2007), the relapse in psychotherapy is lower than that of the pharmacotherapy.

As a cognitive–behavioral treatment mode of action, the efficacy of PST in treating depression has been proven. Indeed, cognitive–behavioral therapy includes a problem-solving module. An important question that comes to mind is this: Are changes in a client's problem-solving skills and perceptions related to the efficacy of the cognitive–behavioral treatment for depression? Chen, Jordan, and Thompson (2006) investigated this question with 30 depressed patients using antidepressant drugs. They provided patients with cognitive–behavioral therapy in a group format for 2.5 hours a day for a week. The pre- and posttreatment measurements showed that depression of the patients decreased as their problem-solving skills increased. Researchers reached the conclusion that patients' training on problem-solving skills played a key role in the treatment of depression via cognitive–behavioral therapy. A recent study by Ghahramanlou-Holloway et al. (2012) found that persons receiving cognitive therapy who had previously attempted suicide demonstrated faster improvement in negative problem orientation and impulsive/careless problem-solving style compared to those in the control condition. A study by Warmerdam et al. (2010) with 263 participants randomized to online cognitive–behavioral therapy, online PST, or a waiting list control group found that both treatments were equally successful in reducing dysfunctional attitudes, worry, negative problem orientation, and enhancing feelings of control.

The scientific evidence for the relationship between problem solving and depression renders PST a viable option for the treatment of depression. Is PST effective in the treatment of depression? What does empirical evidence say? Does the evidence support the efficacy of PST in the treatment of depression? In what ways can we assess whether PST is an effective method of treatment? The efficacy of PST in the treatment of psychological problems in general and depression in particular can be assessed in three ways: First, people undergoing treatment should show improvements at posttreatment compared to pretreatment. Second, the group receiving treatment should show more improvements compared to the group not receiving treatment. And third, PST should provide at least as much recovery as other treatment methods do (i.e., different psychotherapy methods and pharmacotherapy).

Nezu (1986) tested the efficacy of the PST with 26 patients with unipolar depression with nonpsychotic features. Eleven patients received PST, nine patients received a problem-focused therapy, and six patients were in the waiting list control group. In problem-focused therapy, the problems of the patient are being discussed; however, a systematic problem-solving skill is not being provided. No therapy is implemented to the control group. Measurements right after the treatment and at a 6-month follow-up indicated that patients undergoing problem-solving treatment showed more improvements than those receiving problem-focused treatment or those in the waiting list control group.

In another study, Nezu and Perri (1989) randomly assigned 39 patients with depression to PST, problem orientation training, and the waiting list group conditions. The group receiving problem orientation training was provided only with positive problem orientation training and rational problem-solving stages were not taught. Their findings showed that 85% of the patients in the PST group, 50% of problem orientation training group, and only 9% of the waiting list group recovered. The improvements were maintained at a 6-month follow-up.

Another way to assess the efficacy of the problem solving therapy is to compare cases for whom psychoeducation is provided with controls. Dowrick et al. (2000) randomly assigned 452 people diagnosed with major depression in Finland, Ireland, Norway, Spain, and England to PST, group psychoeducation, and control groups. In this study, 128 patients were provided with six sessions of PST, 108 patients were provided with eight sessions of group psychoeducation, and 189 patients were assigned to the control group. At the end of the study it was observed that 63% of the patients receiving PST and 44% of the patients receiving psychoeducation completed the study. Findings showed that both PST and psychoeducation decreased the levels of depression, but patients indicated greater satisfaction with PST.

One of the life stages in which depression is frequently seen in is late adulthood. Geriatric depression, like depression in all other age groups, is also an important risk factor for suicide (Beautrais, 2002; Yang at al., 2001). That is why the treatment of depression in the elderly is an important health priority. Findings in this direction are encouraging. Haverkamp, Arean, Hegel, and Unutzer (2004) presented a case of a 60-year-old woman who benefited from PST. Alexopoulos et al. (2011) compared the efficacy of PST with that of supportive therapy in older adults with major depression and executive dysfunction. They randomized 221 eligible older adult patients to either PST or supportive therapy conditions and provided 12 sessions of PST or supportive therapy. The results from this study suggest that PST is superior to supportive therapy in reducing disability.

In another study, 75 patients with major depression aged 65 and older were randomly assigned to PST, reminiscence therapy, and control group conditions (Arean et al., 1993). Patients in the two treatment conditions received 12 sessions of problem-solving and reminiscence therapy in group format. At the end of the treatment, patients receiving PST showed more improvement compared to those in the reminiscence and control groups. In still another study, Alexopoulos, Raue, and Arean (2003) randomly assigned 25 patients with major depression aged 66–88 years old to PST and supportive therapy conditions and provided therapy once a week for 12 weeks. Findings indicated that PST was more effective in the treatment of the geriatric depression than supportive therapy. Thus, evidence points to the fact that PST may be an important alternative in the treatment of depression in the elderly.

Depression is common in patients applying to primary health care services. For instance, prevalence studies conducted in the Netherlands showed that 10% of patients applying for primary care facilities had depression (Bijl, Ravelli, & van Zessen, 1998). For this reason, an increase is being observed in scientific studies carried out for effective treatment of depression in primary care. Due to the advantages of learning and implementing problem solving therapy for the treatment of depression in primary care (Pierce & Gunn, 2011), many research efforts are being done to assess its effectiveness and many others in diverse settings and populations are being planned within the past 20 years (Ackerman & Williams, 2002; Barret et al., 1999; Hoek, Schuurmans, Koor, & Cuijpers, 2009). Based on registrar's views, Hassink-Franke et al. (2011) have voiced a recommendation that PST training be offered in residency programs for general practice.

Reviewing the scientific studies on the effectiveness of psychosocial and pharmacological interventions in the treatment of depression in primary care, Wolf and Hopko (2008) reached the conclusion that both treatment approaches were similarly effective. The authors indicated that in the treatment of adult depression in primary care, PST, interpersonal therapy, and pharmacotherapy could be considered effective treatment methods. On the other hand, Ijff et al. (2007) announced that they had started a multicenter study in order to study cost-effectiveness of PST in the treatment of depression in primary care in Holland. All these point to the possibility for important advancements and accumulation of knowledge in relation to the role of PST in the treatment of depression in primary care.

Scientific investigations show that PST is an effective method in the treatment of depression among both psychiatric patient groups and patients in primary care. Another question is related to the way in which the effectiveness of PST and pharmacological treatment methods can be compared in the treatment of depression. Gath and Mynors-Wallis (2000) referring to the effectiveness of PST in the treatment of depression in primary care indicated that PST was as effective as pharmacological treatment methods or even more effective than antidepressant drug treatments.

In one study, Mynors-Wallis, Gath, Lloyd-Thomas, and Tomlinson (1995) comparatively investigated the effectiveness of PST and antidepressants in the treatment of depression in primary care. In the study, 91 depression patients were randomly assigned to PST, drug treatment (amitriptyline), and placebo drug conditions. PST sessions applied in the study lasted for 30–60 minutes for six to seven sessions. Measurements taken 6 and 12 weeks following the therapy indicated that PST was more effective than placebo, and no difference had been observed between PST and drug treatment.

As mentioned earlier, psychosocial treatment methods were labor-intensive interventions. Beside labor intensiveness, a major problem with psychosocial treatments is the scarcity of trained professionals to implement them. This problem is important especially in primary care. Physicians either have a heavy workload or do not get training on such interventions. Who, then, will be able to implement such interventions? As previously emphasized, PST is relatively easy to learn and implement due to its short and structured nature. Studies conducted in the United Kingdom (Mynors-Wallis et al., 1997; Mynors-Wallis, Gath, Day, & Baker, 2000) besides showing the effectiveness of PST in the treatment of depression in primary care indicated that PST could be effectively administered by trained nurses. The results from these studies showed that administration of PST by nurses was not different from that of physicians in terms of efficacy.

The scarcity of both financial resources and trained professionals for implementing psychosocial interventions for the treatment of mental health problems is especially important in the developing parts of the world. The studies indicate that the PST approach suits the needs for the treatment of mental problems in these settings. A pilot study done by Hof et al. (2011) implemented PST in booklet/workshop format for common mental disorders in deprived communities in South Africa. The findings from this pilot study showed that psychological distress of participants declined significantly after the completion of the treatment. Moreover, their results further showed that PST in this implementation format was received positively by the participants. Another study by Chibanda et al. (2011) applied PST for depression and common mental disorders in Zimbabwe, Africa. PST was delivered by trained and supervised female lay health workers. Their findings showed that participants experienced a clinically meaningful improvement in common mental disorders upon the completion of the treatment.

Depression is frequently seen in young people, such that its frequency increases with the onset of adolescence. For instance, Eskin et al. (2008) in a study with high school adolescents found that almost 18% of 805 ninth graders were depressed. The treatment of depression in young people remains a challenge for the mental health delivery systems. Both SSRIs and tricyclic antidepressants, widely used for treating depression, include serious safety concerns. It has been advised that prescribing SSRIs in children and youth be closely monitored since they may cause an increase in the risk of suicide. Tricyclic antidepressants are risky because individuals can commit suicide by overdose. For this reason, treating depression in youth with more secure methods is a mental health priority. Considering the developmental characteristics of the youth, PST can be thought of as a viable treatment option. Is PST effective in the treatment of depression in youth?

Eskin, Ertekin, and Demir (2008) tested the efficacy of PST with adolescents and young adults with major depression. A total of 27 participants (13 high school students and 14 university students) with a diagnosis of major depression were randomly assigned to PST and a waiting list control conditions. Six sessions of individual manualized PST were provided to the participants in the PST group. According to the results, PST was an effective method for the treatment of major depression in adolescent and young adults. Statistical analyses conducted demonstrated that the pretreatment depression scores of participants within the treatment group significantly decreased after the treatment while no difference was found in the pre- and postwaiting depression scores in the control condition. According to Beck Depression Inventory scores, 77.8% of the participants within the PST condition but only 15.8% of the participants within the control group achieved full or partial remission. According to Hamilton Depression Rating Scale scores, 96.3% of the participants within the PST condition but only 21.1% of the participants within the control condition achieved full or partial remission. Their findings further showed that improvements achieved by participants within the PST condition were maintained after 1 year.

It was noted in previous sections that PST suits well to the developmental needs of young people. In the study by Eskin et al. (2008), not only depression but also assertiveness and self-esteem had been measured. Findings supported the expectation that PST could have an effect on both the developmental indicators. The pretreatment assertiveness and self-esteem scores of the individuals within the PST group increased significantly after the treatment, but the pre- and postwaiting assertiveness and self-esteem scores of participants within the control group were unchanged.

Reviews of the scientific studies testing the effectiveness of PST have been emerging within recent years. Two reviews have shown that PST is being applied more and more frequently. Cuijpers et al. (2007) conducted a meta-analysis study including 13 scientific studies using PST in the treatment of depression, with a total of 1133 participants. The findings from this meta-analysis indicate that the results from the individual studies show considerable variation, the magnitude of effect sizes differs from one study to the other, and there is a need to further investigate the causes of these differences. The authors concluded that PST was an effective method in the treatment of depression; however that there was a need for more controlled scientific studies. In another meta-analysis, Bell and D'Zurilla (2009a) reviewed 21 independent studies testing the efficacy of PST for depression. The results from this meta-analysis showed that PST was equally effective as other psychosocial therapies and medication treatments and significantly more effective than no treatment and support/attention control conditions.

On the other hand, Gellis and Kenaley (2008) reviewed 22 scientific studies assessing the efficacy of PST in the treatment of adult depression. The authors point out a number of issues in the studies covered in their review. They note that studies differ in scope and methodological rigor, sample sizes vary widely, and there is vagueness of the methods by which participants are assigned to conditions. Despite these methodological shortcomings, the authors concluded in their reviews that PST may be an effective method in the treatment of depression in adults and that it may be more effective when combined with pharmacological treatments.

Efficacy of PST for Suicide

Suicidal behavior is a serious public health issue. As indicated in earlier chapters, depression plays a causal role in suicidal behavior. Therefore, assessing the effectiveness of PST is of vital importance. As addressed, suicidal behavior is the individual's search for a solution for situations perceived as unsolvable. PST is an important treatment method that can be used to increase the resiliency of individuals against suicidal behaviors (Eskin, 2007). For this reason, a number of study protocols aiming at assessing the efficacy of PST for suicide are being published (Hatcher et al. 2011; Spijker, Straten, & Kerkhof, 2010).

Cognitive–behavioral treatments are approaches that can be used in the treatment of suicide-prone individuals just as they can be used in the treatment of other mental health problems and they are successfully implemented in the treatment of suicide (Tarrier, Taylor, & Gooding, 2008). PST, being a cognitive–behavioral approach, is a suitable method for the treatment of individuals displaying suicidal behaviors, because individuals displaying suicidal behaviors perceive killing themselves as the only solution (Weishaar, 1996) and in general suicide is perceived as a problem-solving act (Eskin, 1997). Researchers who investigate the efficacy of PST in individuals who are at risk for suicide indicate that the approach is an effective one (Clum & Febbraro, 2004; Hawton, 2000).

In a study conducted in India with 40 psychiatric patients aged 16–30 years who had survived suicide attempts, Raj, Kumaraiah, and Bhide (2001) delivered 10 sessions of cognitive–behavioral therapy including PST to half of the patients, and routine medical treatment to the other half. Patients diagnosed with anxiety, depression, and adjustment disorder were included in the study. The results of the comparisons of the pre- and posttreatment measures demonstrated that the suicidal tendencies and depression of the patients in the treatment group decreased, and that of their problem-solving skill levels increased.

In another study, Salkovskis, Atha, and Storer (1990) provided problem-solving training to 10 of the 20 depression patients with an age range of 16–65, carrying high suicide risk, and assigned 10 of them to the waiting list control condition. The measurements after the intervention indicated that there had been a decrease in the depression, hopelessness, and suicidal ideation in patients receiving problem-solving training compared to the control group. In a 6-month follow-up, a decrease in the suicide attempts has been observed in the group receiving problem-solving training.

Negative problem orientation being the combination of emotional, behavioral, and cognitive characteristics the individuals display when they face problem situations is related to an elevated risk for suicide. Based on this fact, Fitzpatrick, Witte, and Schmidt (2005) conducted a study with 110 university students experiencing suicidal ideations. They randomly assigned half of the students to a short problem orientation training condition and half of them to the control condition. A 35-minute video displaying problem orientation and coping skills was shown to the problem orientation group. The aim of this training was to decrease the negative problem orientation and increase the positive problem orientation of the students when faced with problem situations. A decrease in the suicidal ideation has been expected as a result. The pre- and posttraining measurements demonstrated that the suicidal ideation and depression levels of participants in the experimental group decreased while no change was identified in their problem orientation levels.

In a study testing the efficacy of PST in individuals with suicidal ideation, Lerner and Clum (1990) demonstrated that PST was a systematic approach that could be used in individuals displaying suicidal problems. In this study, researchers assigned half of the 18 students with suicidal ideation to PST and half of them to supportive therapy conditions. The average age of the participants was 19 years. Research findings demonstrated that PST was more effective than supportive therapy in reducing the feelings of depression, hopelessness, and loneliness. However, no difference was found between the two interventions in reducing the suicidal ideation.

In the study of Eskin et al. (2008), suicide risk levels of participants were also obtained. The results of the study demonstrated that posttreatment suicide risk scores of participants were significantly lower than the pretreatment scores within the PST group. However, the pre- and postwaiting suicide risk scores within the control group were unchanged. These findings show that PST can be an effective method to reduce the risk for suicide among adolescents and young adults.

In a recent pilot study, Bannan (2010) assessed the efficacy of group-based PST in self-poisoning suicidal Irish females. In this study, a total of 18 patients were equally randomized to problem-solving treatment and a control condition. The PST group received eight sessions of group PST and the participants in the control condition were provided treatment as usual in the form of standard individual therapy. The results from this pilot study showed that the treatment group experienced significant reductions in levels of depression, hopelessness, suicidal ideation, and improvements in social problem-solving skills. The improvements achieved by the treatment group were maintained at 2-months follow-up.

The review of results from scientific investigations assessing the efficacy of PST for suicide problem points to some important shortcomings. One of them is the small sample sizes. Thus, investigations using larger samples sizes are needed to test the efficacy of the PST in the treatment of suicidal patients. Although studies using small samples yield to promising results, the need for larger samples is apparent. A practical way to overcome this is to make systematic reviews of the studies using the same treatment method with relatively small number of participants. The problem of small numbers of subjects, being a shortcoming in most of the studies, will be eliminated in this way.

In the review of 20 scientific studies testing the efficacy of treatments in preventing the recurrence of suicidal or self-destructive behaviors, Hawton et al. (1998) concluded that PST was a more promising approach compared to other treatment methods. In a meta-analysis study evaluating the results of six clinical trials conducted to determine the efficacy of the PST, Townsend et al. (2001) indicated that PST was an appropriate and effective method to deal with self-destructive behaviors. Authors concluded that PST was a more effective method than no intervention in obtaining a decrease in depression and hopelessness levels and an increase in coping with problems in individuals engaging in self-destructive behaviors.

Efficacy of PST for Anxiety Disorders

Anxiety disorders are the most common psychological problems. That is why it is important to test the efficacy of the psychosocial treatment approaches for the treatment of anxiety disorders. As it is seen in the previous chapter, deficiencies in the individuals' problem-solving skills are related to feelings of anxiety and the diagnosis of anxiety disorders. For this reason, PST may play an important role in the treatment of anxiety disorders. The empirical findings related to the efficacy of the PST in the treatment of such disorders are reviewed and discussed as follows.

The common characteristic of persons with anxiety disorders is the intolerance for worry and ambiguity. Patients with anxiety disorders are constantly in a state of worry for no real reasons and they cannot tolerate ambiguity. It was previously demonstrated that PST increases people's feelings of control (Warmerdam et al., 2010) and self-esteem (Eskin et al., 2008). Thus, teaching problem-solving skills to individuals with anxiety disorders may reduce their feelings of ambiguity and provide comfort. Conceptually, there is a considerable overlap between negative problem orientation and anxiety.

Lang (2004) indicated that the treatment of generalized anxiety disorders (GADs) characterized by worries for no reason and intolerance for ambiguity is possible through cognitive–behavioral treatment methods including problem-solving skills. In a study, Dugas et al. (2003) implemented a 14-session cognitive–behavioral therapy including problem-solving skills to GAD patients in groups of four to six individuals. Researchers indicated that the treatment group showed more improvement in the signs of GAD, intolerance for ambiguity, anxiety, depression, and social adjustments compared to the control group. A 2-year follow-up showed that the gains of the therapy were still maintained.

GADs are commonly seen among the elderly. That is why the treatment of GAD is important in the elderly population. Conducted studies show that the GAD can be dealt effectively with PST. In a study, Ladouceur, Léger, Dugas, and Freeston (2004) scientifically tested the efficacy of the cognitive–behavioral therapy including problem-solving skills training in the treatment of GAD in the elderly, with eight patients with an age range of 60–70 years. The results demonstrated that cognitive-behavioral treatment targeting the intolerance for ambiguity, distorted thoughts about anxiety, negative problem orientation and cognitive avoidance, is effective in the treatment of GADs in the elderly.

Posttraumatic stress disorder (PTSD) is seen in some individuals who are exposed to traumatic experiences. Earthquakes are one of the most devastating traumatic experiences and the prevalence of PTSD is high among the individuals experiencing an earthquake. Determining the effectiveness of treatment methods that can be used for the treatment of psychiatric disorders occurring after disasters such as earthquakes is important. In one study, Oflaz, Hatipoglu, and Aydin (2008) conducted a study with 51 individuals diagnosed with PTSD after the 1999 Marmara earthquake in Turkey. They assigned these individuals to three groups, such as the psychoeducation only, psychoeducation and pharmacotherapy, and pharmacotherapy groups. In psychoeducation, coping strategies including the problem-solving skills were taught to the patients. Research findings demonstrated that the group receiving both psychoeducation and pharmacotherapy showed the most improvement.

As a man-made disaster, war is one of the most devastating human experiences. It affects not only the persons involved but also the whole social fabric of the communities involved. The scientific evidence shows that the prevalence of PTSD is high in individuals involved in war (Hoge et al., 2004). In a study, Bass et al. (2012) provided group problem-solving counseling for a group of members of communities involved in armed conflict in Aceh, Indonesia, and another group served as a control group. They found no impact of problem-solving intervention on mental health functioning but they observed an increase in the use of positive coping strategies.

Efficacy of PST for Schizophrenia

Schizophrenia is a chronic psychiatric disorder that results in cognitive, social, and emotional impairment. In addition to blunted affect, schizophrenic patients experience a tremendous amount of cognitive and behavioral impairment. With the progression of illness, impairment takes place in the general functioning of the individual. The impairment in the functioning is mostly felt in the cognitive domain. As a result, some schizophrenic patients display poor insight or awareness about the neurocognitive deficits the illness caused (Medalia & Tysen, 2008).

Standard psychoeducation programs designed for schizophrenic patients need to be formulated to make up for the impairment in the functioning resultant of the illness. Psychoeducation programs are being used to compensate for the impairments and to teach new skills. The goal of the psychoeducation programs is to help both the patients and their significant others accept the illness and to increase their coping resources. Problem solving, assertiveness, communication, and related cognitive–behavioral skills form the backbone of such programs. For instance, a multicenter randomized study in Germany showed that psychoeducation reduced the rehospitalization rates of the schizophrenic patients from 58% to 41% and the time spent at the hospital from 78 to 39 days (Bauml et al., 2006).

Taking into account the deficits caused by the illness, one can infer the importance of the cognitive–behavioral approaches in the treatment and rehabilitation of schizophrenic patients (Kingdon & Turkington, 2005). Scientifically controlled studies show that the cognitive–behavioral therapy is effective in the treatment and the rehabilitation of schizophrenic patients. In such a study, cognitive–behavioral therapy was provided to 10 schizophrenic patients and 9 patients were assigned to the control group (Temple & Ho, 2005). Results empirically demonstrated that compared to the patients in the control group, general symptoms and hallucinations of patients receiving cognitive–behavioral therapy decreased and their psychosocial functioning increased. In another study, Granholm et al. (2005) randomly assigned half of the 76 chronic schizophrenic patients with an age range of 42–74 to cognitive–behavioral therapy and half of them to treatment as usual. They implemented a cognitive–behavioral social skills training including social skills and problem-solving skills training in a group format on a weekly basis for 24 weeks to the cognitive–behavioral therapy group. As a result, compared to the group receiving pharmacotherapy, a decrease in the positive symptoms and an improvement in the psychosocial functioning and the cognitive deficits in the patients receiving cognitive–behavioral therapy occurred. Granholm et al. (2007) indicated that these gains were maintained at a 1-year follow-up.

Healthy or sick, one of the necessary human conditions is the ability to solve the problems encountered and to cope effectively with such situations. Taking the impairments caused by the illness into consideration, the situation is even more important and urgent for schizophrenic patients. Even though medication can be effective in eliminating the positive or negative symptoms in the treatment of schizophrenia, drugs are of no help for the deficits/impairments in the cognitive, emotional, and behavioral functioning. In a multicenter study, Bellack et al. (2004) investigated the effects of clozapine and risperidone, two neuroleptics commonly used in the treatment of schizophrenia, on the social competence and problem-solving skill levels of schizophrenic patients. Researchers found out that even though both the drugs lead to clinical improvements, they did not result in an increase in the social competence or problem-solving skill levels in the patients. Thus psychosocial interventions methods are irreplaceable for the rehabilitation and regaining functional capacity. Indeed, psychosocial interventions are recommended for the treatment of persons with schizophrenia by the schizophrenic patient outcomes research team (Dixon et al., 2010).

PST is a method that fulfills the treatment and rehabilitation needs of the schizophrenic patients (Falloon, Barbieri, Boggian, & Lamonaca, 2007). Medalia et al. (2002) indicated that PST was an appropriate and effective method in the elimination of the neuropsychological deficits or inadequacies observed in schizophrenia. They asserted that the PST approach is useful in providing intrinsic motivation and problem-solving strategies to the patients. This being the case, methods that will increase the problem-solving skill levels in schizophrenic patients are gaining importance. Kern et al. (2005) tested whether the errorless learning method used in the teaching of entry-level jobs will be useful in the elimination of the neurocognitive deficiencies observed in the schizophrenic patients. Researchers assigned 60 outpatients having schizophrenia or schizoaffective disorders, randomly to one of the errorless learning or symptom management conditions. Findings showed that compared to the symptom management group, patients in the errorless learning group showed improvements in their social problem-solving skills and the gains were maintained at a 3-month follow-up.

The effectiveness of the methods and the kinds of cognitive factors affecting the problem-solving skills during the treatment and rehabilitation of schizophrenic patients by PST are important for both theory and practice. In a study, Ucok et al. (2006) investigated the cognitive factors playing a role in the acquisition of problem-solving skills by schizophrenic patients. Researchers randomly assigned 32 of the 63 schizophrenic patients to problem-solving training and 31 of them to the control group conditions. The first group received problem-solving skills training as a group once a week for 6 weeks, and the second group received usual drug treatment. The pre- and postevaluations demonstrated that there were improvements in the problem-solving skills of the patients receiving PST and that such improvements did not take place in the control group. While improvements happened in the perception of the problem and the processing capacity of the problem-solving training group, no changes have been observed in their implementation skills. Research findings demonstrate that acquiring a skill gets affected by cognitive flexibility and sustained attention.

Impairments in neuropsychological functioning in persons with schizophrenia spectrum disorders are common. The impairments are more salient on cognitive and social functioning. Problem-solving training along with other interventions seems to make improvements on the functional capacity of schizophrenic patients. In one study, Rodewald et al. (2011) tested whether planning and problem-solving training was more effective in improving functional capacity of individuals with schizophrenia than a training program addressing basic cognitive functions. By randomly assigning 89 patients to either planning and problem-solving training or a training of basic cognition the researchers found that both interventions led to improvements in functional capacity, but they had no differential effect on specific cognitive functions. In another study, Veltro et al. (2011) randomly assigned 24 schizophrenic patients to either group problem-solving training or group cognitive emotional rehabilitation conditions. Both interventions were effective in reducing psychopathology and improving social functioning. In this study, problem-solving training improved capacities for planning and memory while cognitive emotional rehabilitation improved social cognition.

The preventive approach, with roots in the field of public health and recent adaptations in the field of mental health, is also being applied in schizophrenia. Trainings on problem solving to cope with stress and on the nature of mental disorders have been combined in the educational programs designed for early intervention in the field of mental health (Falloon, 2000). Problem-solving training is conducted with an experiential education approach. Individuals first receive a structured problem-solving training and then they apply it to the stressful, problem situations in their lives.

Determining whether or not PST is effective in the treatment of schizophrenia and its level of effectiveness is important in the development of health care services designed for individuals having this illness. Xia and Li (2007) reviewed the scientific studies conducted to determine the efficacy of PST. A study needs to be randomized controlled and needs to compare PST with other similar methods in the treatment of schizophrenia in order to be included in the review. Due to the scarcity of the controlled studies, researchers could only find three studies including a total of 52 subjects to be included in their review. They could not identify whether PST was effective or ineffective. Some limitations appeared in the studies such as inadequate number of participants and insufficient description of the methods. Consequently, researchers determined that there was a need for methodologically solid, valid, reliable, clinically meaningful studies with a sufficient number of participants.

Efficacy of PST for Personality Disorders

Personality disorders are prevalent in community samples and the pharmacological treatments to be provided to the individuals with such disorders is limited compared to other disorders. Although pharmacological treatment approaches play a role in the control and the organization of the clinical states such as depression, anxiety, and emotional instability in patients with personality disorders, they cannot help the patients learn the appropriate and functional behaviors to deal with the intricacies of life. PST may be useful in helping patients with personality disorders acquire functional attitudes, thoughts, and behaviors in facing life's demands. The scientific evidence pertaining to the efficacy of PST in the treatment of patients with personality disorders is reviewed as follows.

Patients with personality disorders are usually considered as difficult patients. They do not seek treatment. For this reason, it is critically important that they seek and accept treatment, find it useful, and appreciate it in order for them to comply. McMurran and Wilmington (2007) investigated this with 12 adult patients with personality disorders in the personality disorders treatment unit at a hospital in England. Using the Delfi method, personality disorder patients were asked about their opinions on the PST and the psychoeducation treatment approaches. According to their findings, patients indicated that they found both PST and the psychoeducation useful. Patients determined that problem solving had some advantages by frequently reviewing the developments, being consistent in its presentation, effectively displaying the problems, and constituting a landmark in approaching the difficulties. This means that when personality disorder patients are provided with PST, they will comply with the treatment.

Upon the analysis of the literature on personality disorders and problem solving, it has been identified that personality disordered patients had important deficiencies in their problem-solving skills. Crawford (2007), who investigated whether or not problem-solving deficiencies could be eliminated in personality disordered patients, determined that positive answers to this question are constantly growing in number. The PST is relatively easy to learn. The structured nature of it allows a variety of professionals (psychologists, psychiatrists, nurses, counselors, social workers etc) to offer this treatment to large masses of patients.

Huband, McMurran, Evans, and Duggan (2007), based on the view that PST was an appropriate method in the treatment of personality disorders, tested the efficacy of PST in the treatment of personality disorders. Researchers randomly assigned 87 of the 176 personality disorder patients to psychoeducation plus PST condition and 89 of them to the control condition. After a brief psychoeducation, 16 sessions of group PST were provided to the intervention group. The results demonstrated that PST was effective in the treatment of individuals with personality disorders. Comparisons using the intention to treat analysis method showed that problem-solving skill levels and the general functioning of the psychoeducation plus PST group were higher and their anger expressions were lower than the control group.

Determining the efficiency level of the psychosocial approaches in the treatment of patients with personality disorders is important for both the practice and the theory. Two Scandinavian researchers, Karterud and Urnes (2004), determined that a 10-hour per week treatment program was sufficient to treat the individuals with personality disorders. Based on the related literature, they suggested that small group therapy, art group therapy, large group therapy, cognitive group therapy, and problem-solving group therapy could be effective in the treatment of patients with anxiety and eating disorders in addition to personality disorders.

It was mentioned earlier that individuals with the diagnosis of personality disorders are difficult patients. It is hard for these patients to realize and accept their health problems and apply to an institution for treatment. Dropping out of the treatment is another obstacle preventing these patients from taking advantage of the help. Therefore, knowing the difference between the treatment completers and non-completers is important to design interventions necessary for the treatment of personality disordered patients. Based on this, McMurran, Huband, and Duggan (2008) investigated the characteristics of the personality disordered patients completing and not completing the treatment. They divided the personality disordered patients into three groups: (a) treatment completers, (b) those expelled for rule breaking, and (c) those that dropped out. They explored the differences between the three groups in the process of PST. Their findings showed that completers' problem-solving levels were higher than those in the other two groups. Researchers suggest that teaching rational problem-solving skills to impulsive patients will ease their compliance to the treatment.

Aggressive behaviors are common among offenders with personality disorders. In one study, McMurran et al. (2001) provided the problem-solving treatment to 14 offenders diagnosed with personality disorders and who were in the secure forensic psychiatric unit. The problem-solving treatment consisted of problem orientation, problem definition, goal setting, generation of alternatives, decision making, solution implementation, and evaluation. Social Problem Solving Inventory Revised was used as an assessment tool. According to the authors, after the treatment, patients showed improvements in all the subscales except the positive problem orientation subscale and changes were maintained at 15 months for 8 out of the 14 patients. In this study, as a situational constraint, the results were obtained through self-reports only. The basic limitation of the study was its failure to take into account the behavioral outcomes.

Efficacy of PST for Aggression

Aggression in modern societies is both a personal and a social problem that needs to be prevented by available behavioral technologies and sociopolitical means. Aggressive behavior is often perceived as an individual's reaction to problem situations. The person faces a problem situation and tries to overcome it by what he or she has in his or her behavioral repertoire. The problem-solving approach to the prevention of this costly phenomenon suits well. But, does the problem-solving approach or therapy play a role in the prevention of aggressive behaviors? If it does, is it effective? According to the social information processing theories, aggression is defined as aggressive problem-solving strategy. Scientific investigations on the use of the problem-solving approach for prevention purposes in offenders and the efforts to prevent subsequent crime episodes have shown a significant increase in the recent past years (Bourke & Hasselt, 2001; McGuire & Hatcher, 2001).

Anger is an emotion that precedes aggression. The analysis of the scientific literature shows that cognitive–behavioral approaches are frequently used in the prevention of aggressive behaviors and that they are effective. Sukhodolsky, Kassinove, and Gorman (2004) conducted a meta-analysis comparing 21 published and 19 unpublished scientific studies investigating the effectiveness of cognitive–behavioral approaches in reducing the feelings of anger in children and adolescents. A total of 1953 children and adolescents participated in these studies. Four cognitive–behavioral treatment approaches were compared in the meta-analysis study. These were skills training, problem-solving training, affective education, and multimodal interventions. According to the results, the overall effect size for the cognitive–behavioral approaches was found to be 0.67 (Cohen's *d*). This shows that the cognitive–behavioral approaches are effective in the medium range in reducing anger in children and adolescents. The results of the comparisons of the approaches showed that skills training and multimodal interventions were more effective than the others in reducing aggressive behavior and increasing social skills; however, the problem-solving approach was found to be the most effective approach in reducing subjective anger.

Aggressive behaviors constitute a major problem in schools, and they can be permanent if they are not prevented or if no attempts are made to prevent them. Therefore, the prevention of aggression in schools is an urgent social need. Some of the implementation of the problem-solving approach in schools produced mixed results. In a study, Lochman and Curry (1986) administered 18 sessions of problem-solving skills training to half of the 20 aggressive boys with an average age of 10 years, and 18 sessions of self-instructional training to the other half. Both the methods produced significant increases in on-task classroom behavior, reductions in parents' ratings of boys' aggression, and increases in boys' self-esteem. In another study, Hay, Byrne, and Buttler (2000) randomly assigned 20 male and female students with an average age of 15.8 years having low self-esteem and social relationship difficulties to a treatment or a control group conditions.

A 12-session problem solving and conflict resolutions treatment program was administered to the treatment group. At the end of the program, compared to the control group, a significant increase was observed in the self-esteem level of the students in the treatment group. In another study, Olexa and Forman (1984) randomly assigned 64, fourth- and fifth-grade urban disadvantaged students to social problem-solving training, response cost, social problem-solving training plus response cost, and no treatment control conditions. They found that students receiving social problem-solving training improved on measures of alternative thinking and consequential thinking skills. The social problem-solving skills of students in the response cost condition were not improved. However, this improvement was not reflected in the teacher evaluations.

Child and adolescent delinquency is an important social problem in today's modern societies. Therefore, the treatment and the prevention of juvenile delinquency is a pressing social need. Irreparable consequences may result from the delinquent acts both for the children engaging in the act and for the victims of delinquent acts. What can be done after it happens? Can problem-solving training be used to reduce aggressive behavior of juvenile offenders? Ang (2003) tried to answer this question by a study with 105 juvenile offenders with a mean age of 14.71 years. Fifty-eight of the children were assigned to social problem-solving skills training and 47 to a waiting list or control group. Social problem-solving skills training was provided once a week for 8 weeks in a group format. At the end of the study, the aggressive behaviors of the children in the problem-solving skills training group decreased significantly compared to the control group. The work of Lindsay et al. (2011) has shown that the problem-solving approach could be used in offenders with intellectual disability as well.

Aggressive children and youth are at a heightened risk for experiencing interpersonal difficulties and are unable to make use of appropriate conflict management skills. These children and youth experience isolation and loneliness. In a study, Webster-Stratton, Reid, and Hammond (2001) randomly assigned 99 children with early-onset conduct problems, ranging in age from 4 to 8 years, to a social skills and problem-solving treatment or to a waiting list. Compared to the waiting list control group, children in the treatment group had fewer externalizing behaviors at home, displayed less aggression at school, more ordinary behavior with peers, and more positive conflict management strategies. In another study, Vaughn, Ridley, and Bullock (1984) assigned 13 aggressive children to a problem-solving training and 11 to control conditions. Children in the treatment condition received 50 sessions of interpersonal problem-solving training and children in the control condition participated in reading-story sessions for an equivalent period of time. Results showed that aggressive behavior in children in the treatment condition decreased from pretest to posttest, but no change in aggressive behavior in children in the control condition took place.

Most intervention studies are designed for and carried out with aggressive boys. In one study, Leff et al. (2009) were interested in whether or not problem-solving would be an effective method of preventing aggression in relationally aggressive girls. For this purpose, they assigned 32 inner-city third- to fifth-grade African-American girls with relational aggression to problem-solving group and 11 to control conditions. The findings of the study suggested that girls' at-risk relational and physical aggressive behaviors, hostile attributions, and feelings of loneliness tended to decrease compared to the control condition. The investigators also noted that the problem-solving program was well accepted by the girls.

Aggression is a common feature of persons with antisocial behaviors. Therefore, the scientific evidence for effectiveness of intervention programs designed for reducing aggressive behavior of antisocial individuals is important. In a study, Kazdin, Siegel, and Bass (1992) randomly assigned 97 children (7–13 years) displaying serious antisocial behaviors into three groups. They provided one group with problem-solving skills training, one group with family management, and a third group with problem-solving skills training plus parent management conditions. As the investigators anticipated, both problem-solving skills training and parent management methods improved child functioning, and the combination of problem-solving and parent management was more effective than the individual interventions. At posttreatment and 1-year follow-up, children in the combined problem-solving skills training and family management conditions displayed less antisocial and aggressive behaviors than children in the control condition.

Efficacy of PST for Psychological Problems Secondary to Medical Conditions

Problem-solving treatment is successfully implemented for the amelioration of a wide range of mental health and behavioral problems. As is known, emotional and behavioral problems are restricted only to psychological or psychiatric conditions. These are also common in persons and their caregivers with medical illnesses. Taking into consideration the brief, structured, and relatively easy-to-learn and teach nature of PST, it can be said that PST will become an important method in the treatment of emotional and behavioral problems secondary to some medical conditions. Scientific investigations conducted so far indicate that PST is also an effective method in dealing with emotional and behavioral problems mostly secondary to some medical conditions. What follows is a short review of scholarly work testing the efficacy of problem-solving treatment for emotional and behavioral problems secondary to medical conditions.

A diagnosis of cancer is a situation difficult to cope with. It causes tremendous emotional distress for both the individual and his or her relatives. Therefore, reducing mental distress that may arise with the diagnosis of cancer is as important as curing the cancer itself. Taking care of and knowing that someone you love has a cancer presents a coping challenge both physically and psychologically. The scientific evidence indicates that the problem-solving approach can be successful in reducing emotional distress in the significant others of cancer patients. The findings from scientific studies indicate that PST is an effective method of reducing depression and distress in persons taking care of individuals diagnosed with cancer. The results from studies with the caregivers of cancer patients by Cameron, Shin,

Williams, and Stewart (2004), Nezu et al. (2003), Sahler et al. (2005), and Sahler et al. (2002) demonstrated that problem-solving training was an effective method in reducing their depression and mental distress.

Caregivers and cancer patients alike are at a heightened risk for depression and emotional distress. The results of studies show that problem-solving treatment is an effective method in reducing the mental distress of cancer patients themselves (Nezu et al., 2003; Sherwood et al., 2005). Allen et al. (2002) conducted a study of 149 women aged 50 and younger with breast cancer in which a 12-week problem-solving training was implemented. The study shows that PST was effective in reducing the stress caused by being diagnosed with cancer and being treated, among middle-aged women undergoing breast cancer treatment. In another study, Hopko et al. (2011) randomly assigned 80 patients (mean age of 55.4 years) diagnosed with breast cancer and depression to either a PST or a behavioral activation treatment for depression treatment conditions. The results from this study showed that 75% of patients exhibited clinically significant improvement and the gains were maintained at 12-month follow-up.

Patients with somatization disorders frequently visit a doctor without any physical reason. Because no medical reason can be found for their illnesses, they never get satisfied. That is why they change doctors frequently and they become a burden for the health care system. Such patients typically refer to general practitioners or family physicians. That is why taking care of these patients in primary care is important. PST can be an effective method in the care and management of these patients in primary care. Wilkinson and Mynors-Wallis (1994) provided PST to 11 patients (aged between 18 and 65 years) with unexplained physical symptoms. Researchers observed a decrease and a reduction in the patients' hypochondriac dealings, mental distress, and number of doctor visits after the completion of the study. As a result, it is indicated that PST is both effective and feasible for this patient group.

Hypertension is a serious public health problem. Untreated high blood pressure causes important damages to several bodily systems. Biopsychosocial factors play a role in essential hypertension. There is scientific evidence that problem-solving approach may be a feasible way of helping persons control their blood pressure. In one study, Garcia-Vera, Sanz, and Labrador (1998) investigated the efficacy of PST in reducing high blood pressure with a study where 21 male hypertensive patients were assigned to a stress-management training group, including problem-solving training, and 21 male hypertensive patients were assigned to the waiting list control conditions. Patients with diastolic blood pressure of 90 and over and a systolic blood pressure of 140 and over were included in the study. According to the results of the study, problem-solving skills of the patients in the treatment group improved and a decrease was observed in their systolic and diastolic blood pressures.

Caregiving to persons with disabilities is a highly stressful issue. Most often it is family members who provide care for their afflicted individual. Caregivers are expected to function as extensions of the health care system. Thus, there is a heavy burden both physically and emotionally on family caregivers of persons with disabilities. It is unsurprising that depression and emotional distress are common in such persons. In one study, Elliott, Berry, and Grant (2009) tested the effectiveness of problem-solving training provided to family caregivers of women with disabilities. The investigators randomly assigned 64 women and 17 men from a total of 81 community residing family caregivers to either problem-solving or education-only control conditions. According to the results, caregivers who received problem-solving training reported a linear decrease in depression and an increase in constructive problem-solving styles over time, but for caregivers in the control condition the reverse was true.

Diabetes is a chronic illness that requires disease management and adherence to a regimen over the course of life. Problem solving is deemed an essential skill for successful diabetes management (Hill-Briggs, 2003) and PST approach is seen as an evidence-based behavioral treatment for diabetes patients (Schumann, Sutherlan, Majid, and Hill-Briggs, 2011). In a study, Hill-Brigs et al. (2011) randomized 56 urban African-American patients with type 2 diabetes into either an intensive-standard problem-solving training or a condensed-current practice in diabetes with necessary components of PST conditions. Results showed that average blood glucose levels (A1C) of patients within the intensive condition and A1C reduction were partially mediated by problem-solving skills at follow-up. Also patients in this condition demonstrated improvements in knowledge, problem-solving, and self-management skills. In another study, Allen, Whittemore, and Melkus (2011) randomly assigned 29 women with a mean age of 53 years and with type 2 diabetes to either continuous glucose monitoring with problem-solving skills or continuous glucose monitoring with general diabetes education conditions. Findings from the study revealed that women in the continuous glucose monitoring plus problem-solving condition had significantly greater problem-solving skills and they tended to have greater dietary adherence, moderate activity minutes, weight loss, and higher satisfaction with the intervention.

Illness management and regimen adherence are even more important for child and adolescent diabetes patients. For young diabetes patients, it is of a critical importance to motivate them in their care. The work of Chisholm et al. (2010) suggests that adherence and health of children are optimized when they are given opportunities to participate in their care. Scientific work indicates that problem solving is also an effective method for adolescent diabetes patients. In a study, Cook, Herold, Edidin, and Briars (2002) randomly assigned 53 adolescents with type 1 diabetes to either a 6-week problem-solving diabetes education program or to usual care control conditions. From baseline to 6 months, participants in the problem-solving condition compared to those in the control condition had improved problem-solving skills and blood glucose levels (A1C). At 6 months, they were doing blood glucose testing more often than those in the control condition.

Alcohol addiction is the most common addiction among individuals with substance abuse. Relapse is a serious problem for the treatment of alcohol dependency. A study by Demirbas, Ilhan, and Dogan (2012) suggests that effective problem-solving skills may help prevent relapse in patients after alcohol dependency treatment. After the treatment of alcohol addiction, patients undergo methadone maintenance treatment. For Rosen, Morse, and Reynolds (2010), PST is a viable treatment option for clients undergoing methadone treatment with comorbid depressive disorders. The most important problem of individuals in the methadone maintenance treatment is unemployment. Zanis, Coviello, Alterman, and Appling (2001) tested the efficacy of vocational problem-solving skills program in unemployed methadone patients. For this purpose, they randomly assigned 109 unemployed patients in methadone maintenance treatment either to a vocational problem-solving skills training or to an interpersonal problem-solving training conditions. Measurements obtained after a 10-session problem-solving training demonstrated that vocational problem-solving training was no more effective than interpersonal problem-solving training in finding a job; however, that vocational problem-solving training tended to have a positive effect on the vocational functionality.

The application of problem-solving treatment is not limited to the aforementioned conditions. A number of other investigations tested the efficacy of PST for emotional and behavioral problems in other medical conditions as well. For instance, Boeschoten et al. (2012) tested the efficacy of web-based PST for depression in multiple sclerosis patients and Silverstein et al. (2011) tested its efficacy for depression in low-income mothers of preterm infants. Moreover, Gellis and Bruce (2010) tested the efficacy of PST for subthreshold depression in home health care patients with cardiovascular disease and Seid et al. (2010) examined the efficacy of PST for health-related quality-of-life outcomes in families of children with persistent asthma. All of these applications have shown that PST was an efficacious treatment method for reducing depression and increasing health-related quality-of-life outcomes. In one study, Robinson et al. (2008) compared the efficacy of PST to escitalopram and placebo for prevention of depression in 176 nondepressed post-stroke patients. Results showed that both PST and escitalopram treatments resulted in lower incidence of depression over 12 months of treatment over placebo. But an intention-to-treat analysis showed that PST was not superior to placebo.

Conclusion

Psychological problems are widespread and cause not only personal suffering but also loss of work days and a heavy burden to health care systems. Therefore, effective treatment methods should be at the top of the priority list. PST has some advantages over other treatment approaches. Research indicates that problem-solving treatments promote some psychological characteristics such as problem-solving skills, improved self-esteem, interpersonal effectiveness, and feelings of self-efficacy and agency that are considered protective against diverse psychopathological situations. This is an important advantage that goes beyond the traditional treatment approach. One can assert that the problem-solving treatment, among others, suits well to the developmental needs of young people.

The review of research findings assessing the efficacy of the PST shows that there is reliable evidence in the literature supporting the effectiveness of the approach in dealing with problems such as depression, suicidal behavior, and aggression. In light of these research findings, PST appears to be an empirically supported treatment approach. There is also scientific evidence supporting the use of PST in the treatment of depression among primary care patient groups. The empirical evidence also demonstrates that PST meets the treatment and rehabilitation needs of patients with schizophrenia spectrum disorders. Moreover, this review shows that problem-solving approach is an effective method of treatment for emotional and behavioral problems secondary to a wide range of medical conditions. The number of research done on the efficacy of problem-solving treatment for anxiety disorders, however, is not sufficient to arrive at a valid conclusion yet.

There are some methodological limitations of the scientific investigations designed to assess the efficacy of PST in the treatment of psychological problems. The first methodological limitation is the insufficiency of the number of participants in individual studies. This limits the possibility for arriving at valid results and generalization of the findings. Another methodological limitation is about the insufficient description of the intervention conditions. What exactly do the treatment approaches include and what kind of standardized precautionary measures are taken during the implementation are usually not fully explained. For instance, what does treatment as usual mean, and what kinds of procedures are being carried out during research are not fully explained or they are insufficiently explained. Third, the procedures followed in the treatments being compared are not manualized and mentioning the name only is not methodologically sufficient.

In closing, there is evidence supporting the view that PST is an effective psychosocial intervention method with some advantages in the treatment of various psychopathologies. For future reference, it is important that scientific studies conducted in order to assess the efficacy of the problem-solving treatment be well designed and free from methodological limitations. The number of participants should be determined by power analysis, the treatment conditions should be well defined, and the implementation should be standardized in a manual format. Methodologically not standardized research conditions will have a negative effect on the comparison and the generalization of the results. The comparison of the results obtained from studies with nonstandardized conditions will be as meaningful as comparing apples to oranges.

7 The Practice of Problem-Solving Therapy and the Applied Patient Groups

Introduction

PST is based on the assumption that individuals experiencing psychological problems have deficiencies in effective problem-solving skills. In other words, it is presumed that the inadequacy and the inefficiency of the problem-solving skills lead to the experience of mental health problems. Based on the cognitive models, PST aims at making changes in the individuals' cognitions and helps them develop some cognitive–behavioral skills. Being a structured-treatment method, just like other cognitive–behavioral treatment methods, it provides convenience and a structure to the practitioners.

The way PST is practiced and the patient groups it is practiced with are presented in this chapter. Nezu (2004) pointed out three general research questions that are being discussed in the literature on PST. These research questions are as follows:

1. The first question is about whether or not a statistically significant inverse relationship exists between problem solving and mental health problems. Whether problem-solving skill levels of the individuals have a positive effect on their mental health is being researched with this question. As is discussed throughout this book, individuals' inadequacies in dealing with the problems they encounter and their inabilities to resolve problems in the way they desire lead to the experience of psychological problems.
2. The second question addresses whether or not effective problem-solving skills reduce the psychological distress caused by stressful life events. According to the view in this question, what is important is not the individuals' experience of problems in life but their inability to cope effectively with the problems and their inability to resolve them in the way they desire. In other words, problem solving is a protective factor against the problems individuals encounter in life. Possessing problem-solving skills or abilities is an important indicator of resilience.
3. The third and the last question is related to whether or not treatment initiatives based on the principles of PST significantly decrease the psychological problems of the individuals. PST, being a cognitive–behavioral psychotherapy, is currently one of the psychotherapies that are being empirically supported. This means that the efficacy of the PST has been empirically proven. The scientific literature on the effectiveness of PST in psychiatry and psychology and allied disciplines shows that PST is efficacious in the treatment of a wide array of psychological problems.

Problem Solving Therapy in the Clinical Practice. DOI: http://dx.doi.org/10.1016/B978-0-12-398455-5.00007-3

The Way PST Is Practiced

Today, PST is basically implemented in four ways. These are individual, group, telephone, and Internet practices.

Individual Practice

The individual practice of PST is the standard way of practicing, as in other psychotherapies. In this way of practice, the problem-solving therapist conducts therapy face-to-face with the client. This is a common practice in clinical settings and in settings where psychological counseling services are provided. Individual practice is the collaboration of the client and the therapist for the resolution of a problem. It is intended to help individuals deal with the problems they encounter in living and to reduce the negative impact of problem situations on the individual.

Another example of the individual practice is the self-help practice. In the self-help practice, all the problem-solving stages and procedures are presented to the individual. Individuals may practice the problem-solving process by following the structured stages in the text. Such practice has some advantages. The medium of self-help may take two forms. In the first, self-help problem solving can be given to the individual in a manual form such as pamphlets, in the form of bibliotherapy. In the second, procedures of problem solving can be given in a written form via the Internet. The self-help practice will be convenient especially for individuals who cannot afford to get an expert's help or to those who are not in the vicinity of such help.

Group Practice

The flexible characteristic of PST makes the individual as well as group practice possible. The group implementation may have advantages in certain situations. For instance, it makes it possible to offer help to a large number of clients in situations where the resources in terms of time and the number of therapists are limited. One of the major problems preventing psychotherapy services from reaching needy groups is the insufficient number of trained therapists. This is especially valid in countries where resources for providing psychotherapy services are limited or nonexistent. The second problem is the limited time of the therapists. Psychotherapy is a labor-intensive treatment method and it is important that the therapists serve as many people as possible. One way to accomplish this is by implementing the therapy in a group format. PST is suitable for group practice. Apart from treatment purposes, group practice is a convenient way of practicing problem-solving training for preventive purposes.

Telephone Practice

Face-to-face practice, either in individual or in group format, is not the only way to offer PST. The constraints cited in the previous paragraph and many more reasons necessitate the use of PST in different ways. Attainability and resource sufficiency are in the key position here. In situations where the therapist and the client cannot come together, it is possible to make use of the technology. Telephone practice provides an important flexibility and advantage in delivering psychotherapy services. For instance, Allen et al. (2002) implemented PST over the phone to a group of women with breast cancer in order to help them cope with the negative emotional impact of the illness. In another study, Grant et al. (2002) implemented PST over the phone to the caregivers of stroke survivors. In another study, Hegel et al. (2011) tested the feasibility of a randomized control trial of a telephone-delivered problem-solving occupational therapy for breast cancer survivors undergoing chemotherapy. The obtained results demonstrate that the telephone implementation of PST is an efficient way of providing help.

Internet Practice

The Internet is an important aspect of modern life. Internet technologies may be used to deliver PST or training. Internet practice is important for several reasons. First, it is a suitable medium for offering problem-solving training to persons who cannot meet a therapist face-to-face. For instance, if Internet is available, providing problem-solving training for individuals living in the remote parts of a country where psychotherapy services are unavailable may be a feasible way of reaching persons in need. Second, developmental characteristics of a client render individual or group practice limited. Adolescents and young adults, for instance, are reluctant to participate in individual practice. It has also been established that these age groups are extremely skilled in the use Internet. In the third, some adults, for various reasons such as fear of stigmatization, lack of financial resources, etc., may be reluctant to receive psychotherapy services on a face-to-face basis. Taking these issues together, the use of Internet technology is a powerful means of providing problem-solving skills training to adolescents and young adults.

Thus, delivering problem-solving treatment via the Internet is a feasible and convenient way of providing such services. The structured nature of problem-solving treatment makes the Internet a suitable medium for providing problem-solving skills training. As evidenced in Strecher (2007), the Internet is a suitable medium for delivering behavioral and health-related interventions. The number of scientific investigations testing the effectiveness of PST via the Internet is flourishing. For instance, Boeschoten et al. (2012), Hoek et al. (2009), Mulvaney et al. (2011), Spijker et al. (2010), and Warmerdam et al. (2010) all have either conducted or planned web-based studies testing the efficacy of PST for depression, anxiety, suicidal behavior, and diabetes.

Patient Groups Receiving PST

There are three patient groups to whom PST is commonly applied. They are: (1) psychiatric patients, (2) primary health care patients, and (3) individuals with other medical conditions. The practice of PST for each of the three patient groups is discussed as follows.

Psychiatric Patients

As has previously been indicated, individuals applying for psychiatric services show deficiencies in problem-solving skills. Therefore, PST is mostly practiced with psychiatric patients. In the previous chapter, we saw that problem-solving treatment is an effective method for alleviating psychological problems or distress.

Individuals seeking psychological care are incapable of solving or overcoming effectively the problems they face in living. Unresolved problems are both the triggering and maintaining factors for psychiatric problems. Szasz (1961), based on the differentiation he made between "diseases of the brain" and "diseases of the mind," identified that *problems in living* lie beneath mental health problems. Individuals applying for psychiatric services bring out a problem they were not able to solve effectively. For instance, Eskin et al. (2006) demonstrated that negative life events were widespread among psychiatric outpatients. From this perspective, a problem-solving approach is extremely important for the treatment of individuals with psychiatric problems.

Primary Health Care Patients

A good percentage of individuals applying for primary health care services are patients with mental health problems such as depression and anxiety. The literature shows that PST is being successfully implemented among these patients.

Recognizing and treating these patients in primary health care facilities has some advantages. The most important advantage is preventing unnecessary suffering by directly treating these patients in the health care unit that the patients refer to. Another advantage is the preventive characteristic of such treatment. Depression, as is known, is the most important cause of self-destructive tendencies and behaviors such as suicide. Behaviors with destructive results like suicide can be prevented with the treatment of such mental problems right in the primary health care system. Another advantage is that the treatment of the patients in primary health care will keep patients away from the psychiatric units and hence prevent being labeled as mentally ill. This in turn will prevent stigmatization that most individuals with mental health problems fear, stigmatization that is also the reason for reluctance for receiving treatment.

The advantages provided by PST are important for the effective treatment of patients applying to primary health care. PST is an important treatment method for primary care patients who do not prefer or cannot tolerate medical treatment. That is why providing problem-solving training for family physicians or general practitioners is important (Pierce & Gunn, 2007a). For instance, Hegel, Barret, and Oxman (2000) indicated that training family physicians or general practitioners on PST for the treatment of depression in primary health care was important. On the other hand, Hegel, Dietrich, Seville, and Jordan (2004) stated that PST needed to be incorporated in the training of residents seeking to become family physicians. In relation to the training of family physicians in Australia, Pierce and Gunn (2007b) indicated that physicians had a positive appreciation of PST and they thought that the presentation of PST to the patients by family physicians and practitioners was important.

Patients with Psychological Problems Secondary to Medical Conditions

It is important to motivate the patients in relation to the treatment in both mental and somatic therapies. Motivation is an important factor in the treatment. Motivating the patients will help them comply with the procedures of the treatment. This is possible if and only if the treatment proposed makes sense to the patient. Complying with the procedures and knowing the expected behaviors within a therapy plays an important role in the success of the treatment. Noncompliance is an important issue in any treatment and side effects of drugs constitute a major source of noncompliance. Psychological treatment methods are important tools for dealing with these issues.

Psychological problems are not only seen in psychiatric patients. They are also common in individuals suffering from a wide range of medical diseases or illnesses. As was discussed in the previous chapter, problem-solving treatment is successfully applied to emotional and behavioral problems secondary to medical conditions. The review in Chapter 6 shows that problem-solving treatment is effectively implemented for the treatment of psychological problems in individuals diagnosed with cancer, alcohol dependency, diabetes, multiple sclerosis, and hypertension, among other conditions. The review has also shown that PST is an effective mode of action for reducing caregiving stress.

Conclusion

An important issue about psychotherapy is that its provision is limited. The most important reason for this is the scarcity of trained psychotherapists. It can be inferred from this and the previous chapters that PST is a suitable method that can meet the needs of patients with diverse health problems. Brief and structured problem-solving treatment can be delivered by different professional groups such as psychologists, psychiatrists, physicians, social workers, and nurses. The most important point to consider here is that training family physicians or general practitioners will make it possible to deal with mental health problems seen in the primary health care setting. This will reduce the burden on mental health professionals and can cure mental health problems before they can become chronic and more serious. The problem-solving treatment can be implemented on an individual or group basis. It can also be delivered via telephone or Internet. The literature shows that Internet practice is increasing in numbers.

8 Psychotherapy

Principles, Skills, Characteristics, Difficulties, and Change Processes

Introduction

Etymologically, psychotherapy means the psychological treatment of the mind. A general definition of psychotherapy is the treatment of mental or emotional problems by using psychological methods. When used in a technical sense, it should be noted that psychotherapy is a process that is carried out systematically in the treatment of mental health problems by making use of the scientific knowledge based on theories of psychotherapy and psychopathology.

PST presumes that lack of or deficiency in problem-solving skills lies beneath the onset and the maintenance of psychopathology and predicts that psychological problems will be resolved through the teaching of these skills to afflicted individuals. An important issue is: Under what conditions should clients be taught problem-solving skills? Under what conditions and in what format can this be done most effectively? The answer to these questions is that the teaching of problem-solving skills will be realized within a therapeutic relationship that facilitates this learning or teaching process. The nature of and the skills used in this relationship determine whether or not the teaching of problem-solving skills to clients will be effective.

The practice of psychotherapy requires complex and advanced personal and interpersonal relationship skills. In order to accomplish the goals of psychological treatment, the psychotherapist should possess the ability to manage the therapeutic relationship and the therapeutic process. The ability to manage the therapeutic process includes not only the therapist's skills to run the process but also the meta-skills to manage the therapeutic process. During the process of psychotherapy, the therapist should sit with the client, start the educational and experiential psychotherapeutic processes, and complete them, all the while observing the process from an external point of view. This task necessitates the possession of meta-skills for management as well as implementation.

It was mentioned in previous chapters that psychotherapy is a labor-intensive professional activity. The conditions under which the practice of psychotherapy will take place are important. In this chapter, the emphasis is on the professional requirements of the practice. What principles should the therapist follow in

Problem Solving Therapy in the Clinical Practice. DOI: http://dx.doi.org/10.1016/B978-0-12-398455-5.00008-5

accomplishing the psychotherapeutic task? Which skills are necessary for a therapeutic process to be an effective one? Which professional characteristics should a problem-solving therapist possess in order to be effective? What difficulties do beginning psychotherapists face? Through which change processes does psychotherapy in general and PST in particular achieve treatment goals? The answers to these questions are covered in this chapter.

Basic Principles and Skills in Psychotherapy

What should the characteristics of the therapeutic environment be if the PST aims to teach the requisite skills to individuals with mental health problems? What should the guiding principles and the therapeutic skills be in teaching these skills? What are the principles a therapist should follow? These ought to be the basic principles of psychotherapy.

Another way to ask this question is: Under what conditions should teaching take place if PST aims to teach problem-solving skills to clients? Under what conditions is an individual able to learn and internalize information provided by another person? As it is known, in the process of learning, there is a trainer, a trainee, and a subject of training. Psychological treatment includes, in a way, the learning processes. The basic question is: Under what conditions and with which skills is this process most effective?

For the problem-solving treatment of a person with emotional difficulties to be successful, the client should be able to learn, adopt, internalize, and value the therapeutic material. On the part of the therapist, there are some basic principles to be followed and skills utilized to facilitate this process. Some of the therapeutic skills to be used and principles to be followed in PST are summarized as follows.

Ability to Listen

Most of the time, talking to someone is assumed to be the only way to communicate. However, a true communication is a gradual process taking place between the sender and the receiver of a message; and listening is as important as talking when it comes to providing the necessary response to the sender of the message. In the process of communication, the message is sent in two ways or through two channels, such as verbal and nonverbal. It is vitally important to receive and decode both of the messages in the same way they were conveyed. Listening is important for a successful decoding of a message.

Listening is not a passive activity in which we only hear what is being said. Listening is the ability of the therapist to feel the client with all the senses, because the most important feature of listening is not the words used but the meanings behind the words. That is why empathy, being another important skill in psychotherapy, is the basic requisite in the practice of psychotherapy. If the therapist listens well to the client, he or she can differentiate the style, the tone, and the speed of voice, and the emotive features behind the words and decode or understand the real message the client is trying to convey. Listening in the process of psychotherapy means understanding, decoding, and interpreting both the verbal and nonverbal clues. What is meant here is that the therapist's ability to interpret the client's nonverbal messages displayed by the body language and the tone of voice is as important as listening to the verbal messages.

If the PST includes the teaching of the skills in relation to the problems that the client encounters in living but is unable to resolve them effectively, the therapist needs to listen well to understand the source of the client's problems. The therapist can infer the real problem by effectively listening to what the client is telling. Finding the real problem is one of the basic skills taught in the PST. For this reason, as it is the case in other types of psychotherapies, effective listening by the problem-solving therapist is important.

Ability to Show Empathy

An important point in psychotherapy is the clients' perception of being understood by their therapists. The feeling of being understood has a positive therapeutic effect and it facilitates the clients' inclination to learn, adopt, internalize, and value the therapeutic material. As an affective–cognitive skill, it allows the therapist to better understand his or her client. Acquiring this skill is a necessary condition for a psychotherapist. As we pointed out earlier under the section "Ability to Listen," the most important act in the process of psychotherapy is to understand accurately the client's living conditions and emotional difficulties. Empathy is one of the basic therapeutic skills the psychotherapist can use to realize this goal.

Empathy is the therapist's putting him- or herself in the client's shoes for a brief moment, and understanding the client's feelings, wishes, and thoughts. It is an important step toward discovering the individual's inner life. However, the most important point to consider with regard to empathy is the amount of time the therapist puts him- or herself in the client's shoes. This time should not be so long as to turn empathy into sympathy. If the therapist experiences clients' experiences continually and intensely, he or she can lose identity as a therapist. It will be difficult for the therapist to help clients under this condition. In this case, the client–therapist relationship will lose its identity and will turn into a friendship, love, or parental relationship.

Empathy may seem as a difficult concept to grasp for some people. Empathy is a cognitive as well as an affective skill. Contrary to the common belief, empathy is a learned skill. For instance, a study by Dereboy et al. (2005) with medical students indicates that empathy can be learned. Empathy can be achieved in three steps. In the first step, the therapist puts him- or herself in the other person's shoes, then he or she has to identify the social and emotional state of the individual he or she empathizes with. In this step, the therapist should identify the feelings a situation creates in the individual. In the second, the therapist goes back to his or her own spot. At the third and the last step, the therapist gives feedback about the contents and the kinds of thoughts and feelings of the individual empathized without making any judgments.

Ability to Pay Attention

Psychotherapy, in a broad sense, consists of being able to pay attention to the patient. Like in all other relationships, the client–therapist relationship grows with reciprocal attention. This is valid especially for the client, and also, within professional boundaries, for the therapist. The attention of the therapist helps the clients continue the treatment, motivates them to do what is expected of them, and encourages them to make the necessary changes in order to get treated. None of these features can be realized without the attention of the therapist.

Paying attention, in psychotherapy, means trying to know and understand the client. The attention of the therapist is limited to understanding the patient with all the positive and negative characteristics, and to provide help in this direction. Professional attention from the problem-solving therapist encourages the patient to investigate, find, and identify the problems causing distress and to work on them.

The client–therapist relationship is a professional relationship. As it is the case in all human relationships, there are some limitations to the reciprocal attention. During the process of psychotherapy, different kinds of interests may emerge, such as sexual attraction or friendship. This situation will make the process difficult. The therapist will establish a professional relationship with the client to the extent that he or she is able to identify his or her own impulses and needs, by providing the client with the necessary attention and care. From a professional perspective, the therapist should know him- or herself well and should be able to acknowledge his or her strengths and weaknesses. If the therapist is not able to meet these professional requirements, the client needs to be referred to another qualified and competent therapist.

Being Nonjudgmental

Judging is not the therapist's task. Judging is the job of the judiciary. Evaluating the behaviors of a person asking for professional help as good–bad, right–wrong, moral–immoral is not compatible with the pursuit of psychotherapy. The prerequisite for psychological treatment is a good client–therapist relationship. Judgmental attitudes and behaviors decrease the treatment's likelihood of success by preventing the development of a good relationship.

Being judged brings about certain fears in the individual. Patients may be reluctant to disclose themselves because they are afraid to be judged and blamed. That is why it is important for the therapist to provide a secure environment and to accept the patient impartially without being carried away by prejudices. A therapist judging and blaming the client can definitely be of no help. Taking into account the fact that therapists are also human beings, one should not expect that they are absolutely free of prejudices and values. The therapist should acknowledge his or her own values and prejudices, and should refer the patient to another therapist if he or she is unable to escape them.

Accepting that his or her task is not about judging, the psychotherapist should not judge the lives of others he or she encounters. The therapist should embrace all sorts of different colors and styles in life, and should keep him- or herself at an equal distance to all of them. For instance, the judgmental attitude of the therapist toward the individuals who have sexual practices or preferences that are not socially acceptable in a specific community will not contribute to the therapeutic process; by contrast, this attitude will deteriorate clients' compliance to their treatment.

Expecting that a therapist is purified from all values may not be a realistic expectation. Having values makes the therapist a living individual. The authenticity of the therapist is important for the success of the psychotherapy. A realistic requirement to increase the success of the treatment is not to expect that a therapist is free of values but to expect that the therapist is aware of them. The dictum "to know oneself" is also valid in this case. The therapists who know themselves well refer their clients to another therapist or colleague in situations in which they will not be able to control their feelings. This is one of the ethical principles to follow during the practice of psychotherapy including PST.

Being Flexible

One of the important characteristics of people working in the service sector is the ability to behave flexibly both personally and professionally. As a person, the therapist should behave flexibly. In psychotherapy, being flexible means two things. One regards his or her attitude toward all the different colors and shapes of life. This requires that the individual does not see him- or herself continuously in the approving position.

Second, being flexible means the ability of the therapist to display a flexible attitude in his or her professional practices. Therapists have certain practical and theoretical knowledge. Attitudes and behaviors of therapists toward clients manifest themselves in the light of this knowledge. On the other hand, each client is unique with special characteristics and problems. For this reason, the therapist should not get stuck with stereotypic views and information in trying to understand the client and his or her problems. The therapist should make the necessary adjustments in the methods and practices in order to meet the patient's needs, because different theories and practices are appropriate for different patients.

Flexibility described here coincides with the practices that already exist in the practice of psychotherapy. For instance, an eclectic approach to psychotherapy means blending different types and techniques of therapy. The therapist may blend various techniques from different schools of psychotherapy. Another kind of practice is the consideration of the client's needs above theoretical requirements. The concept of *tailoring*, which means making changes in line with the patient's needs, is an accepted practice in psychotherapy. These practices show that the therapist possesses a certain degree of theoretical flexibility.

Ability to Give Time

Practicing psychotherapy is often akin to "digging a well with a needle." As can be understood from this Turkish saying, psychotherapy is a time-consuming activity. Thus, it is necessary to view "giving time" from the client's and the therapist's perspective. From the standpoint of the client, "giving time" is accepting that the resolution of the problems may take time.

Giving time concerns mostly the therapist. The therapist, during the gradual process of psychotherapy, should be willing and ready to give the necessary time to the client and to him- or herself. Because, when the necessary time is not allocated, psychotherapy may create new problems rather than solving the client's problems. The therapist should know how to keep up with the client's pace. This is one of the most basic things taught during psychotherapy training. In cases in which the therapist wants more rapid change, the feelings of anxiety and insecurity of the client will increase.

The therapist should accept the client's pace of producing changes and learning therapeutic material. If the therapist insists that his or her own pace and tempo be adopted, a more complicated situation will be created and in turn this situation creates more problems rather than resolving them. In PST, especially during training on the problem-solving stages, the therapist should keep up with the client's tempo. Otherwise, he or she may be faced with the conscious or unconscious resistance from the client. These obstacles will make resolution of problems difficult.

Being Trained in Psychotherapy

Psychotherapy is conceived as a process where clients open their heart and the therapist listens attentively and makes certain recommendations. The specifications made here are certainly part of psychotherapy, but only just a part. If psychotherapy consisted of this interaction only, our friends and family listening to our problems and supporting us in daily living would be sufficient and we would not need a time-consuming and demanding activity such as psychotherapy. Being relieved during psychotherapy may be important; however, it is not a sufficient condition for being cured. Comforting the individual is not the sole aim of psychotherapy. As in the exposure treatment, some situations should be confronted even if they are painful and clients should learn them in a therapeutic atmosphere.

The psychotherapist is different from other people comforting the client. This difference is created by the therapist's training on psychotherapy. Psychotherapy is not a process of listening and sharing only; it is an active process containing certain dynamics, a process in which different techniques are used. Psychotherapy's effectiveness is continually scientifically scrutinized. A therapist should know which techniques to implement with which patients and when to implement them. This is only possible through psychotherapy education. How this education is to be pursued is an important issue for the training of therapists. For Weissman et al. (2006), a combination of a didactic education and supervised clinical work is the gold standard for learning a new treatment. These researchers conducted a national survey of psychotherapy training in psychiatry, psychology, and social work in the United States. Their findings showed that the majority of programs in the three disciplines did not require didactic education together with supervised clinical work for learning a new treatment. A person cannot practice something that he or she has not been trained for. Psychotherapy is not exempt from this.

Ability to Clarify

One of the reasons individuals seek psychotherapy is that they are confused about the difficulties created by internal (or supposed) and external realities they have been exposed to. Sometimes clients seeking psychotherapy have difficulties expressing themselves for reasons related to their psychopathologies. In the practice of psychotherapy, therapists' skills for clarification are of utmost importance. What exactly is it that a client is suffering from? What causal mechanism is involved in a client's reasons for seeking professional help?

In PST, the therapist tries to help the patient clarify the confusions resulting from the difficulties and understand exactly what the patient experiences. The therapist's ability to clarify is of great importance here. The ability to clarify is the skill used in understanding exactly what the patient is trying to say and in mirroring what the patient means in essence. A good example of the ability to clarify is to explore exactly what the patient means by saying that his or her "situation is bad at home," what is bad, who is responsible for it, what others think about it, how this situation affects the patient, and if the patient can give an example.

Characteristics of an Effective Psychotherapist

What are the characteristics of an effective therapist? What are the characteristics of a therapist who can help the client resolve the problems, and who can achieve clinical improvements? Such characteristics are discussed in this section. It is accepted that in the healing process, the characteristics of a psychotherapist are as important as the quality and the procedural characteristics of the psychotherapy. In the previous section, we considered psychotherapy as an educational process. Whether or not the therapeutic material to be taught during psychotherapy will be adopted, valued, and put into practice by the person being trained depends to large extent on the personal characteristics of the trainer. Knowing these characteristics will contribute to growing as an effective psychotherapist.

What should the characteristics of a problem-solving therapist be? Which characteristics of the problem-solving therapist ease this learning process? Corey (1996, pp. 16–18) discusses the characteristics of an effective therapist and indicates that certain characteristics may define the effective therapist. Corey points out that it is not necessary that a therapist possesses all of these characteristics and suggests that one should not forget that other characteristics may be added to the list. The author also emphasizes that these are merely suggestions. Characteristics of effective therapists are summarized in the following sections.

Effective Therapists Have an Identity

An effective psychotherapist has an identity and is aware of this identity. They know who they are and know their professional boundaries. For instance, they know what they are capable and incapable of doing. Such individuals know which problems they will be able to handle themselves and which problems they should refer to another therapist. Since they know themselves well, the therapists with a clear identity are aware of their strengths and weaknesses. A therapist who knows his or her own characteristics is able to figure out the difficulties he or she may experience with a specific kind of clients and problems. Effective therapists know what they want out of life. Rather than reacting to external reality, effective therapists act on the external reality. Such individuals display an active stand in life.

Identity eventually brings about some spatial and societal limitations. A psychotherapist with a clear identity, who can draw his or her limitations in the therapy office and in society, constitutes a good role model for clients experiencing problems with their boundaries. The majority of the clients applying for psychotherapy are individuals experiencing problems with their personal boundaries. Psychotherapy, in its broad sense, is an educational activity. From this perspective, the psychotherapist using him- or herself as a role model in his or her efforts to cure the client is of great importance.

Effective Therapists Respect and Appreciate Themselves

Besides knowing themselves, effective psychotherapists appreciate and respect who they are and what they know about themselves. Such therapists can give love, help, and support to others. The respect and love they have for themselves do not result from narcissistic tendencies such as considering themselves superior to others. They are realistic about themselves. Based on a realistic evaluation, they can respect and appreciate themselves. They do not exclude themselves from the external world and others.

A distinction should be made here between feeling respect and appreciation for oneself and the egocentric approach of seeing oneself superior to others. Contrary to the first approach, the second approach is not helpful for the treatment of the client. Being egocentric and feeling superior to others hinders the development of a collaborative relationship between therapist and client. As emphasized earlier, a therapist puts some therapeutic mechanisms into action by being a role model for the client. A psychotherapist who does not show respect and appreciation for him- or herself as a person has a very low likelihood of constituting a positive role model for the client.

Effective Therapists Are Aware of Their Own Power

Based on his or her education on psychopathology and theories of psychotherapy, a therapist possesses a high level of knowledge on human behavior. For this reason, the psychotherapist has professional power. Due to a psychotherapist's expertise, the client completely confides in him or her. What is important here for the therapist is accepting his or her own professional power without abusing it and using this power in the best possible way to help the patient.

The scientific knowledge about human nature and the psychic world is the most important characteristic differentiating the psychotherapist from others. This characteristic also provides certain power to the therapist. The therapist must use this power to help the patient. The use of this power in any other way is against the professional ethical codes and personal ethics. This situation is among the professional ethical codes to follow in both psychological and psychiatric practices.

The attitude of the individual toward power is at the same time a moral issue. The individual may act submissively toward the individuals or institutions holding the power and may have the tendency to use it for his or her own benefit whenever he or she gets hold of it. This situation is a moral problem that individuals are faced with in today's societies. These professional and personal concerns are even more important for psychotherapists; that is why they must adhere to the ethical codes and be careful about this issue.

Effective Therapists Are Open to Change

What does being open to change mean for a psychotherapist? Which changes should a psychotherapist be open to? What are the advantages of being open to change as a professional and as an individual? The openness of the psychotherapist as a professional practitioner implies two things. The first implication is being open to professional change and innovations. The second is appreciating openness and reflecting it in his or her behaviors.

The openness to change in the professional field means being open to the scientific changes and innovations in the practice of psychotherapy and being able to follow them. The therapist, based on his or her education in psychopathology and theories of psychotherapy, starts her or his career with certain knowledge and skill. However, the skills and knowledge of the therapist may become outdated due to the rapid changes in the fields of psychology, psychiatry, and allied disciplines. Therapists must follow the changes and developments in the field and to be open to changes in order to be an effective therapist.

Another point implied by "being open to change" is the openness of the therapist in his or her own personal world. As indicated, psychotherapy, in a general sense, is process in which psychotherapists are trained. In order for the training to be successful, the trainee has to be willing to receive and value contents of the training. The willingness of the client will motivate him or her to change. In this dynamic process, the psychotherapist will constitute a role model for the client. A psychotherapist who is not open to change in his or her own personal world will not be able to motivate the client to change. In this dynamic process, a defensive therapist who is not open to change may trigger a similar mental state.

Effective Therapists Are Willing to Increase Their Awareness

Psychotherapy can be considered a liberating process. This process possesses characteristics that contribute to the liberation of the psychotherapist and the client. An individual who becomes free in his or her inner world and in his or her behavioral choices will become ready to change. In order to become free, the individual has to be aware of the changes occurring in his or her inner world and his or her environment.

Awareness about oneself and the people around increases the freedom of the individual. Effective therapists are aware and are willing to be aware of themselves and others. Instead of displaying a defensive attitude, effective therapists adopt an open and active role in life. Effective therapists are willing to learn about themselves and others and are willing to make an effort in this direction.

Effective Therapists Tolerate Ambiguity and Confusion

Every stage of life contains ambiguity. But psychotherapy is a process containing even more ambiguity. A psychotherapist should be able to tolerate ambiguity in his or her personal and professional life. Otherwise, the therapist will be confused and this will be detrimental to the process of helping the client. In cases where one is unable to tolerate confusion and ambiguity, his or her level of anxiety will increase. A person will be of no help for a client whose external and internal world is full of confusion and ambiguity.

Asking for psychological help means that the person carries with it confusion and ambiguity. Things are complicated enough for the client to seek psychotherapy. The individual seeks psychotherapy because he or she has been unable to deal with a problem. Psychotherapy in its broad sense can be defined as the reorganization or restructuring of the inner world. This means that the individual's inner world is complicated and this complication contains ambiguity. The client applies for professional help because of this confusion and ambiguity. The confusion and ambiguity are challenges for the therapist. The question of "Am I going to be able to deal successfully with the problem?" includes both confusion and ambiguity. Effective therapists are willing to tolerate the confusion and ambiguity resulting from professional requirements or personal characteristics, and they are able to do it.

Effective Therapists Develop Their Own Therapeutic Style

Every one of us has different ways of doing things. Every therapist uses his or her own style and personal characteristics. Personal differences exist because therapists show different characteristics as human beings. An important asset of the psychotherapist lies in the personal characteristics differentiating him or her from others and in his or her ability to use this in developing his or her own therapeutic style. However, this is a trait that is only acquired over time by individuals who know their strengths and weaknesses such as the ability to tolerate ambiguity, being aware of surrounding events, and being open to change.

Therapists with same theoretical framework go through similar psychotherapy education. However, when the issue is communication, even though each and every therapist goes through the same training with similar technical and theoretical framework, the therapist's own communication style, attitude, mimics, personal characteristics, and orientation toward people play an important role in developing a personal therapeutic style. For this reason, developing a personal therapeutic style without giving up on the basic principles and skills of psychotherapy is an important trait differentiating the therapist from others. One should not also forget that psychotherapy is an art. As art requires creativity, so does psychotherapy. The way the therapist conveys the knowledge and skills to the patient will be a reflection of his or her creativity.

Effective Therapists Are Able to Understand Clients Without Taking Them into Their Possession

During the psychotherapy practice, the client is vulnerable and can easily be exploited. They can easily be possessed and limited. The boundaries can be unclear depending on the degree of the patient's disorder and the therapist's power. That is why therapists must show professional competency to help clients by protecting both individuals' boundaries despite their vagueness. This situation depends on the ability of the therapist to see the client as a distinct individual.

The ability to show empathy for a patient is important for the therapist to understand and help the client. However, the intensity and the duration of empathy are of critical value here. If the therapist exaggerates the empathy, it transforms into sympathy. In this case, he or she may do a disservice to the client rather than helping the client. By doing so, the therapist loses his or her objectivity by prioritizing feelings in the relationship with the client. A true and healthy understanding of the client depends on the ability of both the client and the therapist to maintain the boundaries related to their roles.

Effective Therapists Are Lively

The educational characteristic of psychotherapy has been emphasized previously in this chapter. Because of the educational characteristic of the psychotherapy, the psychotherapist in this process is both a trainer and the subject of training. It has been emphasized that as a subject of training, the psychotherapist would constitute a model, a standard for the client. A psychotherapist who is lively and at peace with life can satisfy the functions stated above.

Many patients come to psychotherapy with a complete disinterest in life, having lost all expectations. Life has exhausted them, so to speak. A therapist who has lost his or her energy in life cannot be expected to reorient the patient toward life. Only a therapist full of energy can be successful at showing the client the beauty of life.

Effective Therapists Are Authentic

The most important point for a person, no matter what profession he or she is in, is whether or not he or she behaves authentically in life. An individual who cannot act authentically and who imprisons him- or herself into some preconceived forms is considered to have closed the doors to happiness. Psychotherapists are not exempt from this rule. Not being able to act authentically or being forced to behave contrary to his or her nature forms the basis of the problems of individuals seeking psychological treatment.

One should not forget that therapists are human beings. They can establish a healthy relationship with their patients as long as they can combine their knowledge and skills with their own self. Psychotherapy is a relationship between two individuals and a healthy communication requires being natural. A therapist who does not act as him- or herself will be unsuccessful in creating a sincere and confident environment for the patient. Patients often idolize the therapists and perceive them as supernatural beings; spontaneity plays an important role here in helping them see the therapists as human beings and taking them as role models. This is calling the patient for authenticity and rationality within the complexities he or she experiences.

Effective Therapists Have a Sense of Humor

It is true that life is a serious business. However, taking life too seriously will result in a rigidity that creates problems. In some psychopathologies, individuals experience difficulties because they are not capable of displaying the flexibility that will comfort them during the ups and downs of life. This rigidity may be the reason for or the precursor of the psychopathologies. The therapist's use of humor when necessary will help the patient see the rigid situations from a different perspective. However, the use of humor in psychotherapy requires skill and attention. The inattentive use of humor may result in more harm than good.

Effective therapists are individuals who have developed a sense of humor. Humor is considered a factor leading to therapeutic change, and its use in psychotherapy has the power to make patients perceive various situations in different ways. The client is stuck in a certain situation in life and his or her perspective has lost its flexibility. He or she is enslaved by some self-assigned cognitive, behavioral, and emotional rules. The client applies to the therapist because of the discomfort caused by these rules. An effective therapist who uses humor in treatment is able to soften these rigid rules. By using humor an effective psychotherapist may make the client see the situations in different ways, the ways he or she has never thought of before. The therapist succeeds at doing this by using humor as a therapeutic tool.

Effective Therapists Make Mistakes and Are Willing to Admit Them

Making mistakes is part of being human. People are able to prevent further mistakes as long as they can learn from their past mistakes and see them as an opportunity to make fewer mistakes in the future. The individual approaching their mistakes in this way obtains the possibility to learn from their mistakes. If the ability to make mistakes is strength, admitting and confessing them is a virtue. Individuals should deprive themselves neither from the new learning opportunities nor from displaying virtuous behaviors in life.

Therapists are not exempt from this case. As mentioned before, patients idolize their therapists. They consider or wish that their therapist's skills, knowledge, and power are limitless. However, therapists are human beings and are far from being perfect. They can be devastated by the ups and downs of life. In such a case, therapists should not forget that they have a dual responsibility. The first is the responsibility toward themselves. They have to create for themselves the opportunity to display virtuous behaviors and learn from their mistakes. The second is the responsibility of the therapist toward the client. In some psychopathologies, clients confine themselves into a narrow space in order to be perfect and not to make mistakes in life. The psychotherapists' ability to admit and confess their mistakes, and perceive such situations as a learning opportunity will constitute a good role model for the clients during the practice of PST.

Effective Therapists Live in the Present

The past no longer exists, and the future has yet to occur. The only reality is the present. Effective psychotherapists are not riveted to the past nor are they fixated on the future. Effective therapists live in the present. They can share the joy and the sorrow of the patients "in the here and now." This does not mean that the past and the future are unimportant. Being in the present and living the present make the therapy more effective.

Being stuck in the past or leading future-oriented lives may be both the cause and the consequence of some psychopathologies. A psychotherapist who lives in the present without ignoring the past or the future constitutes a role model for the patient, while at the same time increasing the chances of ridding patients of the rigid attitudes that diminish their freedom of action.

Effective Therapists Appreciate the Influence of Culture

A fish does not know water exists until it jumps out of water. Similarly, all individuals live in a culture; however, they are not aware of it until they are out of their cultural milieu. The behaviors of individuals are shaped by the culture they are born into and grow up in. The culture in which we grow up marks all our behaviors. This is true for both the client and the therapist. Culture affects the way individuals feel, behave, and think; in sum, culture shapes them.

One cannot undermine the influence the culture has on our eating habits, our perspectives in life, attitudes and behaviors toward our parents, the way we express our feelings, and cope with difficulties. Such an important influence in the lives of human beings will certainly play an important role in the onset and the expression of psychopathologies. The therapist is expected to know the characteristics of the culture the patient lives in and to help the patient within that framework. This way the therapist can make helping process successful.

The psychotherapists should be aware of the influence of the culture not only on their patients but also on their own behaviors and ways of thinking and feeling. This is an important part of knowing oneself. A psychotherapist who is able to know him- or herself acknowledges that culture affects his or her own behaviors and ways of thinking and feeling, as well those of the patient. This is important and necessary for the therapist to be able to help the patient effectively.

Effective Therapists Have the Tendency to Discover Themselves

Most cultures on our planet acknowledge that knowing oneself is an important virtue. An important Turkish poet and Sufist from the thirteenth century AD called Yunus Emre stated: "Knowledge means to know yourself. If you don't know who you are what's the use of learning?" Shakespeare expressed the same idea by saying "Know thyself." Eagerness and inclination to discover oneself is a virtuous personal trait. Psychotherapists' tendency to know and discover themselves is essential to effective treatment of the client.

Psychotherapists are human beings. They have negative and positive characteristics just like their patients. They should be ready to discover themselves over and over again. They should know about their strengths and know how to use them in the best possible way for their patients, or know their weaknesses and know how to control them in order not to hurt the patients.

Psychotherapy is in general an activity where two people embark together on a journey of discovery and learning. In this journey, discovery and learning take place for both the therapist and the client. The psychotherapist assumes here the role of guidance for a successful learning and discovery on behalf of the patient. In this journey, the therapist, having gone through the necessary steps, should set a good example of discovering and knowing oneself and the world.

Effective Therapists Make Choices That Affect Their Lives

Life is about making choices. The individual starts each day by making choices: Whether or not to wash one's face, have breakfast, what to eat, what to wear, to go to work or not, to do housework or not, to obey the societal rules or not, etc. Making choices is both a necessity and an existential issue. The individual proves his or her existence by making choices. Making choices involves responsibilities. This is true for both the client and the therapist.

Like all human beings, therapists make choices and decisions about themselves, the future, and other people. Effective therapists are people who can take responsibility for these choices and decisions. Effective therapists can review these decisions and choices, can change them, and know that they can change them if they want to. Being realistic individuals, therapists accept that the decisions and choices they make can be mistaken and they are able to express that. A therapist who can make vital decisions and who can take responsibility for these decisions constitutes a good role model for the client. Thus, the therapist can guide the client effectively in the journey of discovery and learning.

Effective Therapists Have Interest in the Welfare of Others

The practice of psychotherapy requires being a caregiver. Being interested in the welfare of others makes it easier for therapists to do their job effectively. This attitude combined with the professional skills and knowledge base helps the therapist provide the client with an effective treatment. A client applying for psychotherapy is a person who is deprived of the relational characteristics that support him or her developmentally, psychologically, or intellectually. An attitude wishing for the welfare of others helps the therapist create a secure therapeutic environment for the client. This secure environment is similar to Winnicott's (1986) concept of a "*holding environment*," i.e., the environment a mother creates for her baby. In this secure environment, the client can accomplish the tasks of change and learning. The initiatives designed to create change in the client contain threats and insecurities at the perceptual level. The client can cope with these threats and insecurities only in a secure environment created during treatment by the therapist.

Psychotherapy includes, by nature, a caring and a sincere interest toward others. Even though professionalism requires that psychotherapy be compensated, it is difficult to set a value for the effort and the attention invested in psychotherapy. That is why a therapist works for the maximum well-being of the patient. The therapist uses all the knowledge and skills he or she possesses to make the client happier, better, and more functional. A psychotherapist strives to equip the client with the necessary skills to deal effectively with the problems and difficulties encountered in living. Meanwhile, the psychotherapist uses his or her professional and personal skills to keep appropriate personal distance from the client.

Effective Therapists Are Deeply Involved in Their Work and Derive Meaning from It

Psychotherapy is a professional job. There are two choices that deeply affect the life of an individual. The first is the choice of a spouse and the second is the choice of a profession. It is difficult to get separated from both of them. That is why a person who chooses to be a psychotherapist has to be careful about not regretting it in the future. A poorly thought-out choice of profession brings with it some difficulties. One should not forget that psychotherapy involves creating and construing meaning for both the therapist and the client. During this therapeutic process, two individuals create meaning for their own personal world and for therapeutic goals.

It was mentioned earlier that psychotherapy was as difficult as digging a well with a needle. Such a profession cannot be exercised without love and interest. That is why effective therapists love their job. In addition, they derive meaning from their job. Human beings have a tendency to make an effort to do the work they find meaningful. Therapists who cannot derive meaning from their work are faced with the danger of being exhausted.

Effective Therapists Are Able to Maintain Healthy Boundaries

Psychotherapists work in an environment in which emotional intensity is high. Contextual factors inherent in the psychotherapeutic environment may render the boundaries vague and make boundary violations possible. In such an environment, keeping the boundaries between the therapist and the patient, the patient and family members, and other institutions is an important therapeutic and professional skill for the creation of a healthy and effective treatment process. The therapist's training helps him or her maintain healthy boundaries and creates new ones when necessary.

As the client opens up to the therapist in the secure and nonjudgmental therapeutic environment created by the therapist, the development of an emotional bond between the therapist and client is inevitable. However, this emotional bond has to stay within certain boundaries. If this bond carries the therapist–client relationship to a different level, the treatment process gets difficult. The therapist needs to keep the warm relationship he or she establishes with the client without adjusting their identities as a therapist and patient; otherwise, he or she may hurt the patient. In situations where boundaries are vague, both the therapist and the client will get confused and the recovery will not take place or the therapeutic process will not be healthy.

Effective Therapists Are Culturally Sensitive

Today's societies show complex cultural characteristics. The most important reason for this is the fact that people move from one place to another due to economic difficulties or disasters. Individuals who move to new settings try to keep their past cultural characteristics and social ties. In providing psychological help or service, psychotherapists are faced with individuals of different cultural heritage and characteristics.

Culture is the sum of tangible or intangible goods and values generated in a society. It was mentioned earlier that culture has a great impact on peoples' attitudes and behaviors. A behavior considered as normal, expected, and approved in one cultural setting may not be appropriate in another. That is why it will be meaningless to keep the cultural characteristics with great impact on the individual outside the domain of psychological illnesses. The therapist needs to be informed about the cultural environment the client lives in. The more the therapist learns about different cultures, the more he or she will be able to work with individuals from diverse cultural backgrounds. On the other hand, the therapist also comes from a culture, and it will not be realistic to expect that he or she frees him- or herself of those cultural characteristics or codes. However, therapists should welcome diverse cultural characteristics. They need to form and implement the therapy by taking into account the cultural characteristics of the patient.

In order for the treatment to be effective and be accepted by the clients, the psychotherapists have to know and be sensitive about the cultural characteristics of the individuals they provide help for. This is not only a therapeutic requirement, it is also one of the ethical codes in the practice of psychotherapy today. Following the ethical codes and principles in providing psychological services are the rights for service users, but they are also the professional rights for the therapists to produce and provide psychotherapy services.

Difficulties Faced by Beginning Therapists

Psychotherapy is not easy for beginners. As it is the case with all professions, there are some difficulties awaiting the beginning therapists. One of the difficulties involves not knowing what to do with oneself, how to do things and how to do the right thing. How can a person be a good psychotherapist after he or she completes psychotherapy training? Psychotherapists may experience various difficulties depending on his or her personal characteristics. The ones discussed here are common difficulties and not everybody needs to face them. It is also not necessary that beginning problem-solving therapists face all of these issues. What are the difficulties beginning problem-solving therapists are likely to experience? Corey (1996, pp. 31–34) lists some examples. Experienced problem-solving therapists are not exempt from these. Such difficulties are discussed below.

Dealing with Anxiety

Most individuals starting a new career feel anxious about whether or not they will do their job right. When therapists begin practicing psychotherapy, they feel anxious about whether or not they will be able to establish a good relationship with their patients, whether or not they will be able to apply the appropriate techniques in the right way, whether or not they will be helpful to their clients; in short, whether or not they will be able to display a good performance. This is a feeling expected of all individuals who wish to perform well in their career. What is important here is the ability of the therapist to accept this anxiety, to explore the causes of the problems when they arise instead of dramatizing them, to try to eliminate the professional deficiencies, and to see them as opportunities for self-improvement.

The difficulties beginning therapists face are not limited to professional competencies. Beginning therapists experience difficulties in relation to time management. New therapists generally exceed the time limit of their sessions in order to be able to help the client, or perhaps they experience difficulty in structuring and finding material to discuss during a session. Long sessions challenge the professional principles and give the unconscious message to the client that he or she has to get better immediately. The therapist does this out of his or her anxiety and hastiness. Under such conditions, the client feels pressure and hopelessness about whether or not he or she will be able to accomplish the desired changes.

On the other hand, therapists experiencing difficulties in time management hold on to their notebooks and try to write down everything the client says. In such situations, the therapists may miss what the client tells out of concern for filling the time, structuring the time, and writing everything down. In other words, therapists may forget what their clients tell while they struggle with their own anxieties. It may be helpful for beginning therapists to accept such anxieties as normal and to share them with their clients. If this is not possible, asking for support from an experienced therapist about these difficulties may be appropriate.

Being Oneself and Self-Disclosure

It is important for people to be and act like themselves. In the process of intense interaction taking place, during psychotherapy, between two individuals, it is crucial that therapists provide a role model and a learning opportunity to the client by being themselves. As it is known, the client applies for psychotherapy because he or she is not able to be like him or her and gets alienated from his or her own self. If the therapist acts in the same way, things get complicated. In that situation, the therapist cannot be a good role model for the client.

As emphasized earlier, being oneself was a characteristic of an effective therapist. Beginning therapists may get caught in their anxieties so much so that they may get away from being themselves. They may make the process more difficult by being overconcerned with the professional knowledge and skills such as how to talk, which questions to ask, how they should react, and even where and how to put their hands and legs.

One of the difficulties beginning therapists may possibly experience is self-disclosure. Self-disclosure means for the therapists to open themselves up to the client about their personal lives, values, and thoughts. When and about which subjects should the therapists open themselves up to their clients? In order for a sincere interaction to take place during psychotherapy, the therapist can offer self-disclosing explanations to their clients. However, this has to take place within some limits. The unnecessary self-disclosure affects negatively the treatment process and some unethical situations may arise. An explanation on behalf of the therapist such as "I do and behave in this way, you should also do the same" transforms the process of psychotherapy into giving advice. Self-disclosure during psychotherapy, if it should be done, needs to be done carefully.

Avoiding Perfectionism

Nobody and nothing is perfect in life. Individuals striving for perfectionism put themselves under high pressure. Individuals providing psychological services know quite well that a perfectionist attitude is the main problem of some clients. This situation creates problems for the individual. Attitudes such as *everything has to be perfect, I have to cure all the clients* put pressure on the psychotherapist. The goal should be to try one's best to make progress instead of being perfect.

Beginning therapists act with the motivation of doing everything in the best possible way because they believe that only then can they be an effective therapist. Of course, therapists need to do their best for their clients. However, therapists are also human beings and they can have some deficiencies and limitations. What is important is to know about one's limitations and deficiencies and try to compensate for them.

Being Honest About Their Limitations

Not everybody can do and know everything, and there is no need for it. One person can know a subject well and know another subject not so well; others can do and know other things well. Specialized expertise in many areas is a growing trend in psychotherapy. A therapist can gain mastery of a specific treatment method, with a specific disorder, while another therapist may be an expert in other methods. That is why a psychotherapist needs to know the personal and professional limitations and act accordingly. This point is related to the concept of knowing oneself. Being aware of the professional and personal limitations and putting this awareness into practice develops over time.

Beginning therapists can think that they ought to help their clients in every way. They may be incompetent at some point and have difficulty conveying it to their patients. Therapists have to accept their limitations when necessary and share this without hesitation with their patients. Therapists may fear that the patients perceive them as incompetent when they share such information. However, one should not forget that it is not natural for a therapist to be knowledgeable and skilled in all methods and all psychological problems. Such an expectation will put both the therapist and the professional practices into trouble. What is natural is the ability of the therapist to ask for help from an experienced colleague in those areas he or she feels less competent.

Understanding and Tolerating Silence

The most difficult thing for a beginning therapist to understand and tolerate during therapy sessions is silence. Why does a person keep quiet? Why do two people suddenly stay quiet? What do silent moments mean? What should a therapist do in such situations? Those silent moments may seem like endless hours of torture to the beginning therapist. However, in human interactions, silent moments are as meaningful as lively speeches, tears, and laughter. For beginning therapists, those meaningful moments are seen as difficult moments to tolerate.

Silence during therapeutic sessions can have several meanings: The client may be organizing his or her thoughts; the therapist may be assimilating and deeply feeling the intense life of the patient; the patient may be surprised in relation to the subject discussed, or may show resistance and the like. Beginning therapists might perceive such silent moments as intimidating and threatening; therefore, the therapist may try to break the silence as soon as possible. However, knowing that silence is meaningful, that it is a normal function of the process and is helpful, should relieve this anxiety.

The best approach is to understand that silent moments have a function and can be used for further therapeutic goals. Furthermore, experienced therapists use silent moments to increase communication with their clients and to understand them better. While silence is a difficult situation to grasp and tolerate for beginning therapists, experienced therapists treat it as an opportunity to learn new things and understand clients better. However, one should not forget that this transition takes time. Being aware is the first step toward improvement. An expectation in the opposite direction puts the therapist into a difficult situation both individually and professionally.

Dealing with an Extremely Demanding Client

Setting boundaries and being aware of the personal limitations were seen as characteristics of an effective psychotherapist. Extremely demanding clients can challenge the therapist's professional and personal boundaries. Because of their personal characteristics or as part of their psychopathologies, these clients may expect that therapists have to solve their problems immediately. In such situations, boundaries should be explained to the client in an easily understandable way.

Some patients may challenge their therapists with endless wishes. Experienced therapists do not experience difficulties in drawing the boundaries and in preventing the patients from crossing those boundaries. However, beginning therapists may feel they have to fulfill all the demands and fear that they will seem to be incompetent otherwise. A therapist does not have to fulfill every demand made by the patient and should be able to stop the patient when necessary. To make the expectations clear from the beginning may dissipate the confusion of such clients.

Another type of client that may challenge a beginning therapist is the reluctant or resistant client. The reluctance or the resistance of a client may present itself in different ways during the course of therapy. Some may be late for their appointments; some may prefer to talk about unrelated subjects. Egan (1998) discusses various reasons for clients that may be reluctant and resistant. Accordingly, the reasons for reluctance and resistance are: (1) fear of intensity, (2) lack of trust, (3) fear of decompensation, (4) feeling of embarrassment, and (5) fear of change. The author offers the therapists some suggestions in dealing with resistant clients. These are:

- Reluctance and resistance can be accepted up to a certain point. The therapist helps the client see the positive aspects of his or her reluctance by stressing the possibility that reluctance is the patient's way of expressing him- or herself.
- The client's reluctance and resistance needs to be worked on. Reluctance and resistance should not be ignored; they need to be revealed to the client.
- Assuming that reluctance and resistance do not result from the patient's bad intentions, the therapist should see reluctance and resistance as avoidance. The therapist works on the reasons for the client's avoidance and emphasizes that it can be prevented.

- The therapist should explore his or her own reluctance and resistance. The client's resistance and reluctance can be a reflection of those of the therapist.
- The quality of the interventions should be monitored. The interventions the therapist is trying to implement may not be of good quality or the patient may not be convinced about their necessity and quality.
- The therapist needs to be realistic and flexible. A therapist should see that the help offered to the client has a limit.
- The therapist needs to include the client into the therapeutic process and encourage his or her cooperation. One should not forget that the client will be more enthusiastic in engaging in cooperative behaviors when he or she is part of the process.

Accepting Slow Results

The most important point therapists, especially beginning therapists, should keep in mind is the fact that slow results are inevitable in psychotherapy. We mentioned earlier that the process of psychotherapy was as slow as "digging a well with a needle." A psychotherapist who rushes into the solution puts the client under unnecessary pressure. Accepting slow results is an important therapeutic skill necessary for an appropriate implementation of psychotherapy.

Beginning therapists want to proceed quickly in psychotherapy. Every step in the positive direction will be proof and an indication of their success. The therapist may attribute the slow change to his or her incompetence and he or she may become concerned. However, not each patient is alike. While it is very easy to proceed with some clients, even the slightest changes may be of great value with others.

The most important instruction beginning therapists should follow is the ability to use the skills and abilities they acquired during their training at the right time without rushing. Another point to remember is that the clients need to make certain changes in their feelings, thoughts, and behaviors and that these changes will not be easy. These changes may be intimidating and threatening for the client. It is difficult for people to make changes in themselves and changes may take place only in secure environments, free of time pressure. The therapist has to create this environment for the client. Beginning therapists will prevent the unnecessary injustice by not placing themselves and the client under the time pressure.

Staying Away from Fooling Oneself

One of the most important stands an individual may take in life is not diverging from reality. A realistic attitude of the therapist during therapy sessions means he or she will be engaged in a professional practice based on scientific knowledge and ethical codes. Providing the client with unrealistic information and hope will only fool the therapist. The most important point for the beginning therapists to keep in mind is that the basis of all the practices is scientific knowledge and professional ethical principles.

It is not possible for the therapist to see improvement in each and every client. There may be improvements in some patients and slow or no developments in some others. At this point, the therapist should accept it, should stop the therapy if necessary, or should refer the client to another colleague he or she thinks will be more helpful. An effective therapist does not hesitate to consult another colleague or to get supervision when necessary. This is true especially for beginning therapists.

Processes of Change in Psychotherapy

What are the processes of change in psychotherapy? In other words, how and through what processes does treatment work? These questions are of practical and theoretical value for the research and the practice of psychotherapy. Today the effectiveness of psychotherapy for the treatment of mental health problems has scientifically been proven; however, the search for identifying the processes through which change comes continues. Knowing the processes leading to change, treatment, and recovery is important for the scientific investigation of psychotherapy.

Mechanisms leading to change in psychotherapy in general and in PST in particular are discussed in this section. A discussion of the factors leading to change and recovery in PST is important for both the practitioners and the theoreticians of the treatment method in question. The factors leading to change in psychotherapy are usually designated as common and specific factors. Common factors are general and are not related to any specific psychotherapy. Specific factors are those specific to a psychotherapy method.

Prochaska and Norcross (1984), in a book discussing the factors of change from a transtheoretical perspective, indicate the presence of common factors that work with all forms of psychotherapy. These include positive expectation, therapeutic relationship, and Hawthorne effect. A client's expectation that psychotherapy will work and result in recovery has an important role in the success of the treatment. Today the impact of the placebo effect on the psychological treatment is a known fact. Therapeutic relationship is the major ingredient in all forms of psychotherapy. Therefore, a mutually trusting relationship between a client and the therapist is a prerequisite for recovery. The Hawthorne effect states that individuals' behaviors change simply in response to the fact that they are being observed. In psychotherapy, individuals are being monitored by their therapists and even by themselves. Accordingly, in PST, a client needs to review his or her old ways of handling the problems in order to improve them.

In addition to these factors, Prochaska and Norcross (1984) indicate that there are common factors or processes that lead to change and that can be observed in all of the theories on psychotherapy. They talk about five basic change processes that they think are present in all forms of psychotherapies. These are: (1) consciousness raising, (2) catharsis, (3) choosing, (4) conditional stimuli, and (5) contingency control. The authors indicate that these change processes work in every psychotherapy system and the comparison of the systems is possible by a discussion of these processes.

Accordingly, change processes work at two levels such as experiential and environmental. The change referred to as change processes at the experiential level is the result of the processes on the individual's behaviors, emotions, and cognitions. Change processes at the environmental level occur as a result of processes on environmental events. In all kinds of psychotherapies, the therapist aims to make changes in the client's affective world or his or her environment. The change processes in question are discussed as follows, in addition to emphasis on the way the processes work in PST. The processes of change in psychotherapies described by Prochaska and Norcross (1984) are described with special reference to PST.

Consciousness Raising

Consciousness raising is a change process specific to all forms of psychotherapies. Roughly defined, consciousness raising is increasing one's knowledge and experience of oneself, others, the environment, and societal norms and rules. Almost every therapy aims to increase the patient's knowledge of these issues and to create changes in the patient's attitudes and behaviors toward them. To state it more clearly, one of the main goals of psychotherapy is to increase the client's awareness of him- or herself and his or her environment. Prochaska and Norcross (1984) wrote: "Therapies that involve increasing consciousness are assumed to increase the information available to individuals so they can make the most effective responses to the stimuli impinging on them" (p. 6).

Consciousness Raising at the Experiential Level

If the information given to a client is about his or her behaviors and feelings, this is called *feedback*. Consciousness raising at this level is the development of the individual's awareness about his or her behavioral and affective world. In the practice of psychotherapy, the use of confrontation techniques provides the client information about his or her own behaviors, feelings, attitudes, and cognitions. In PST, individuals are informed about their own skills, reactions to problems, and the way they deal with problems. The problem-solving training a client receives on how they will overcome the difficulties they experience indicates that they will experience consciousness raising at the experiential level. In addition to problem-solving skills, the client becomes informed during this therapy about his or her own skills and the affective reactions they give to problems. Problem orientation training provided to clients in PST aims partly at changing his or her reactions to her or his problem-solving skills, affective reactions, behaviors, and cognitions.

Consciousness Raising at the Environmental Level

If information given to the client concerns environmental events, this is called *education*. Education includes factors such as understanding, interpreting, handling, and reacting to environmental events. We mentioned earlier that psychotherapy in its broad sense is an educational activity. In PST, the individual gets information about the environmental events, about the nature of relationships, difficulties, and skills on how to overcome these difficulties. During the course of PST, clients receive information on problem situations that require a response from him or her. In PST, the client decides on the most appropriate solution alternative, taking into consideration his or her behavioral, affective, cognitive, and moral and other societal characteristics.

Catharsis

Catharsis is one of the most important change processes in psychotherapy. Traditionally in a hydraulic model of emotions, unacceptable affects are blocked from direct expression. Releasing unacceptable emotions in psychotherapy eliminates the negative consequences of emotions. During psychotherapy, the client is freed from the emotional inhibitions and can experience his or her emotions. In order for catharsis to take place during therapy, the therapist should create a secure environment for the client. The critical point is liberating oneself from the psychological inhibitions. This is possible only in an environment as secure as a mother's arms.

Catharsis at the Experiential Level

If cathartic reactions come directly from within the client, such as his or her own feelings, thoughts, and behaviors, it is called *corrective emotional experience*. What is important here is that the individual's own subjective experiences start the catharsis. During PST, when the client sees his or her attitudes toward problems and his or her strengths or weaknesses in dealing with them, he or she may experience feelings like happiness, pleasure, anger, rage, or disappointment. The therapeutic skills of the problem-solving therapist will determine whether or not catharsis will take place, in which way it will take place, and whether or not he or she will be able to create a secure environment for the client.

Catharsis at the Environmental Level

If cathartic reactions are evoked by observing emotional scenes and processes in the environment, this is called *dramatic relief*. The individual's experience of catharsis by observing the scenes in the external environment and feeling a great relief as a result is as old as the history of humanity and it is very common. For instance, the individual will experience complex emotional reactions while watching a movie or a play in a theater and feel great relief leaving the theater. The reasons for watching the movie or play may partly be due to catharsis. The identification with the characters in the films is important here. During PST, the client with the new skills and perspectives he or she has recently acquired observes the reactions of the individuals to problems and may feel relief as a result of some feelings he or she experiences within the affective context of his or her own past. Or, he or she may experience catharsis by observing the way others deal with and solve their problems.

Choosing

Choosing or making choices is one of the most important existential conditions of being human. Human beings make choices at every moment in their lives. Whether or not the choices made are rational is beyond the domain of this book. If psychotherapy is defined, in the general sense of the term, as the reorganization of the individual's inner world, this reorganization will bring about new choices. By choosing, the individual makes choices between behavioral alternatives in both the external and the internal world. Choosing and making choices is an important process that facilitates change in psychotherapy. It should be noted that every choice will include some ethical and esthetic preferences. Preferences or choices bring with them responsibility.

Choosing at the Experiential Level

Choosing at the experiential level involves the individual becoming aware of new alternatives. Being aware of new alternatives involves being responsible and being aware of the anxiety and the tension inherent in the responsibility. The ability of the individual to be aware of the new alternatives and to make choices is called *self-liberation*. It should be noted here that changes in the individual may create new alternatives and this in turn may increase the individual's self-liberation. The critical point in self-liberation is that changes in the individual's inner world lead to liberation. In PST, especially during problem orientation training and while generating new alternatives, the client overcomes his or her inner obstacles and becomes aware of alternatives. Overcoming the psychological inhibitions and becoming aware of the new alternatives are important means for self-liberation during PST.

Choosing at the Environmental Level

The external world and its impositions limit the individuals as much as their inner lives. Therefore, self-liberation is dependent on getting over the internal and external inhibitions. Self-liberation was defined as the individual's access to more alternatives. When changes in the external world and the environment make more alternatives available to individuals, this is called *social liberation*. The important point here is the fact that alternatives allowing for *social liberation* happen as a result of changes in the environment. For instance, making the necessary legal changes to increase the quota for female representatives in parliament represents social liberation for women, who constitute half of the population. In PST, the client increases the alternatives by initiating the changes in the physical and social environment based on the knowledge and skills he or she acquires. For instance, a homosexual individual who works for societal change in order to establish values that will help other gay individuals live comfortably will increase his or her alternatives to a great extent.

Conditional Stimuli

Instead of changing through choosing and making choices, therapeutic change is sometimes possible through changing the conditional stimuli that directly affect the client's behaviors and the conditional stimuli that shape and direct those behaviors. Alterations in conditional stimuli are necessary when the individual's behaviors are elicited by classical conditioning or operant conditioning. The changes in question form the basis of all the psychological treatment methods, especially the behavioral ones. Behavioral treatments work with stimuli that have a direct influence on behaviors.

Changing Conditional Stimuli at the Experiential Level

Changing the individual's behaviors to the stimuli is called *counter-conditioning*. In other words, counter-conditioning is changing the client's reactions and attitudes to the stimuli that are thought to direct and change the behaviors. For instance, in behavioral therapies such as systematic desensitization or exposure therapies, the clients' reactions to stimuli that control and shape their anxiety are being modified. Similarly, in cognitive therapies, the individuals' cognitive reactions to stimuli that control their behaviors are modified through methods such as cognitive restructuring. In PST, during the problem orientation stage, the aim is to change the dysfunctional attitudes and behaviors of the client in dealing with the problems he or she encountered in living into a more positive direction.

Changing Conditional Stimuli at the Environmental Level

Change in psychotherapy takes place not only through changing the client's reactions to conditional stimuli but also through changing the client's environment. Making changes in the individual's environment is called *stimulus control*. Stimulus control involves restructuring and redesigning the conditions that control the client's behaviors in the desired way. Especially the restructuring accomplished through cooperation with the family during child psychotherapy, or restructuring the rules and regulations in the class environment at schools and token economy methods are good examples of stimulus control. In PST, the client learns to identify the environmental problems causing distress and discomfort and to restructure the environment with the help of skills he or she acquires during the treatment. The goal to be set in PST may sometimes consist of making changes in the environment.

Contingency Control

Psychology of learning gives us important clues about the conditions under which a behavior gets or does not get repeated. One of the clues is that the consequences of human behaviors are within their own control. For instance, if a reinforcer desired by the organism is given right after a particular behavior, the probability that the behavior will be repeated increases. Similarly, if an event that may be perceived as a punishment follows a particular behavior, the probability of that behavior decreases. As a general rule, we can say that a behavior can be changed by changing the contingencies following that behavior. This situation forms the basis of behavioral treatments and to some extent that of the cognitive–behavioral treatment methods.

Contingency Control at the Experiential Level

Changing the individual's responses to consequences without modifying the contingencies is called *reevaluation*. Here the client's responses to the consequences of the behavior are being modified. An example of contingency control at the experiential level, provided by Prochaska and Norcross (1984), is a man who is not able to ask anyone from the opposite sex out on a date because of his anticipation that he will be rejected. This male client thinks in essence that he will be turned down because he is not liked by women. That is why he is not asking women for dates. During therapy, the client will learn that when a woman turns down a date it is a statement about her and not about him; and this will lead to a reevaluation of the situation by the client. In PST, the client learns about the consequences of his or her own behaviors and looks at them from a different perspective. In PST, the client may reevaluate the consequences of his or her behaviors with the skills and abilities that he or she acquires during the stages of problem orientation and problem definition.

Contingency Control at the Environmental Level

If changes in the individual are made by modifying or restructuring the contingencies in the environment, this is called *contingency management*. Here the contingencies following the behavior are being modified. Prochaska and Norcross (1984) give the example of a male student who is ashamed of using public restrooms. With a contingency contract made during therapy, the client earns $2 from the therapist each time he uses a public restroom. This is an important situation for the client who wants to earn extra money. In this situation, the inability to use public restrooms is prevented by modifying a contingency in the environment that affects the client's behavior. Similar contracts can be made with the client in PST. In PST, the problem can sometimes be defined as changing the contingencies in the environment, or goals can be set in that direction.

Conclusion

Professional psychotherapy practices involve the implementation of certain principles, no matter at what level, by whom they are implemented, and which psychotherapy techniques are being used. For this reason, this chapter has discussed certain basic principles to be followed during the practice of psychotherapy in general. Today, psychotherapy is thought of as the practice of evidence-based or empirically supported techniques and methods. Psychotherapy practices are not activities taking place behind closed doors between a client and a therapist; they are activities carried out in the light of scientific advancements and findings. It is imperative that the practices be carried out within certain rules and principles. It is thought that knowing the basic principles of psychotherapy will guide the practice and the practitioners of PST.

The question asked in scientific investigations about is: Which psychotherapy method will be effective when practiced by whom, to which client, for what kind of problems, and under what conditions? A psychotherapist should possess certain characteristics in order to display effective practices. For this reason, the characteristics of an effective psychotherapist were discussed in this chapter. These characteristics will provide important insights for both the training of problem-solving therapists and the effective practices of PST.

To become a psychotherapist, a long and intensive training is required. This being the case, beginning psychotherapists have a high likelihood of experiencing certain difficulties. The most logical thing to do after accepting that difficulties are inevitable is to identify these difficulties. Based on this thought, this chapter introduced the difficulties beginning therapists are likely to experience and some suggestions as to how they can deal with them. The difficulties and problems presented in this chapter concern experienced problem-solving therapists as well. Beginning problem-solving therapists can benefit from the suggestions discussed in this chapter.

Finally, this chapter discussed the processes leading to change in psychotherapy. Scientific evidence shows that clients receiving psychotherapy more frequently recover compared to those who do not receive it. A legitimate question to be asked here is: Which processes make this possible? The process with which change occurs in psychotherapy is situated at the center of the efforts to understand psychological practice. With these thoughts, change processes in psychotherapy as described by Prochaska and Norcross (1984) are discussed shortly in this chapter with a special reference to PST.

9 Assessment in Problem-Solving Therapy

Introduction

Assessment is an important and inseparable part of the practice of psychotherapy. Without a good assessment, one cannot have the chance to assess in an objective way the situation the client is in, or whether or not therapeutic goals have been reached. What are the complaints of the clients? What are the causal mechanisms leading to the clients' complaints? What are the therapeutic goals? Is the client suitable for psychotherapy? What are the strengths and weaknesses of the client? These and other questions in PST can only be dealt with through an assessment based on scientific grounds.

The problem-solving skills and other characteristics of the individual should be assessed for the effective practice of PST. Assessment is one of the essential conditions not only for PST but also for all treatment methods. A good assessment is one of the prerequisites for a successful treatment. For this reason, individuals going through PST need to be assessed from different perspectives. For a problem-solving therapist, knowing the psychological characteristics predisposing the individuals to experience emotional problems, and the personal and social resources the individual can to resolve problems, will be important factors carrying the treatment to success.

As indicated earlier, assessment is important for the practice of PST. We can talk about two types of assessment in PST or in a psychological treatment in general. The first method is assessment through clinical interview. The second method is assessment based on self-report measures. The two assessment approaches are discussed here within the context of problem solving therapy.

An important point in PST is the assessment of the way in which the client applies for therapy. Through which channels and with what problem did the client come to the PST? Here it is necessary to gather as much information as possible about why and how the client applies to therapy. What is the client's scenario on why he or she came in? Why did the client come? At this stage the reason why the client came into the therapy and whether or not it overlaps with the service the therapist provides needs to be evaluated. In other words, the question of "Is the individual a good candidate for PST?" needs to be answered.

Assessment in PST, as is the case in other psychotherapeutic approaches, can be done in two ways. One is assessment through clinical interviews; the second is

Problem Solving Therapy in the Clinical Practice. DOI: http://dx.doi.org/10.1016/B978-0-12-398455-5.00009-7

assessment using standardized measurement instruments, i.e., measurement instruments based on self-reports. During the assessment through clinical methods, the therapist, through a face-to-face interview, gathers information that will form the basis for assessment. In gathering information, the therapist makes use of the skills and abilities he or she acquired during his or her professional training. During the assessment with self-report measuring instruments, standard tests and scales are used to gather information.

Assessment with Clinical Interview

It is important to evaluate the problem-solving skills of individuals through clinical interviews. As will be indicated below, although standardized measurement instruments based on self-reports are used in the assessment of individuals' problem-solving skills, clinical interviews have some advantages over self-reports. The most important advantage of this approach to assessment is its ability to obtain the necessary information directly from the client. Information obtained through self-report measures can be affected by the client's psychopathology. For this reason, the information obtained through self-reports can be distorted to some extent in the direction of the client's psychopathology.

Since the therapist is face-to-face with a client during the assessment through clinical interview, he or she has the opportunity to observe the nonverbal behaviors of the client. The therapist does not have to rely solely on the information the client presents, he or she also has the chance to make observations. During the assessment through clinical interviews, the problem-solving therapist is able to plan and effectively execute the PST and to evaluate at the same time the individual's skills and the difficulties caused by his or her life circumstances. In addition to the observations he or she makes, the problem-solving therapist gathers information firsthand about the characteristics of the client's problems, their resources, and their behavioral characteristics.

Problems

PST focuses primarily on the problems causing the client distress and on the implementation of the effective techniques to resolve them. That is why one of the most important points the therapist needs to consider is to gather as detailed information about the problems the client faces as possible. Knowing the characteristics of the problems the client encounters is important for planning the problem-solving treatment. The characteristics of the problems can be discussed both during the assessment stage and during the course of the treatment. The problems that cause distress and make the client seek help are defined in problem-definition stage of PST. However, an in-depth exploration of the objective and subjective characteristics of problem situations a particular client encounters during the course of PST provides a means of clarification for both the client and the therapist. The characteristics of the problems the therapist will gather information on are discussed as follows.

The Objective Characteristics of the Problems

Detailed information about the problem situations the client encounters needs to be gathered here. What are the objective characteristics of the problem the individual encounters and has difficulty in resolving? At this stage, the problem-solving therapist needs to have detailed information about the problems encountered in order to be able to evaluate the efficiency and the functionality of the individual's problem-solving skills. Having detailed information on the client's problems and their characteristics will give the therapist the opportunity to define and formulate the problems clearly. Otherwise the chances of obtaining success in developing and implementing a treatment plan will diminish.

The reasons why the client sought or was referred to treatment gains importance here. What are the situations that brought the client to therapy? What are the characteristics of that situation? Unquestionably, the answer is: the problem situations they encounter in living. The question here is the following: *What is the problem and what are its characteristics?* The individual searched for solutions to these problems; however, since their efforts were inefficient, they decided to get professional help. Consequently, understanding and identifying the current situation means understanding the individual's problems. That is why understanding the main characteristics of the problem is important. Simply hoping that the PST will be successful without having knowledge of the characteristics of the problem situations will produce nothing but extreme optimism.

How can we understand the characteristics of the problem situations that clients are faced with? What are these characteristics in question? Which characteristics of the problems should we handle so that we can better understand them and help the client resolve them? The characteristics of the problems the individuals encounter can be grouped into four main categories.

Ordinary Problems Versus Problems That Require Creativity

Ordinary and routine problems are problems that the individuals already know how to resolve. An example would be that of an individual who knows he or she has to go to a shop and buy a new pair of shoes if he or she needs a new pair of shoes. However, for certain kinds of problems, different from routine problems, the individual needs to engage in a more creative activity. For instance, an individual who has to solve a mathematical problem needs to behave creatively. Similarly, to be able to win a chess competition, both of the players need to see and make moves that the other does not see. There are different levels of creativity required to solve these problems. Some problems require a moderate level of creativity. The solutions to these kinds of problems necessitate both routine and creative conduct.

Are the problems routine problems, or are they problems that require creativity? As indicated earlier, solving routine problems is relatively easier. Solving problems that require creativity is more difficult and demands a certain level of skill from the individual. PST is an appropriate therapeutic method that can be used in handling this type of problem. Problems that drive clients to seek professional help are not routine problems and their resolution requires creativity. Interpersonal problems are a good example. Their resolution requires a different kind of creativity for each and every situation.

Formal Versus Informal Problems

Formal problems are like mathematical problems. Such problems have operational steps and an answer to be found guided by the data. Formal problems are situations that will be solved when certain operations are executed. In order to reach the solution, one has to follow a limited number of methods and go through the operational steps. For instance, the operational steps required to calculate the area of an equilateral triangle are explicit. It is possible to find the solution within certain rules and specific methods and to reach a single result. A number of different methods can help reach the same result.

Informal problems, however, are more personal problems, such as problems concerning the decisions to be made in daily living. These problems cannot be defined exactly, and their solution is not as easy as that of the formal problems. For instance the difficulty a medical school graduate experiences in deciding upon a field of specialization does not have a specific solution. The decision to be made here is a personal one. It is difficult to state that a particular field has to be chosen given the specific data. Formal problems are easy to solve, just like routine problems. Since they are related to daily living, informal problems are problems that are difficult to define and solve. They include personal preferences, characteristics, and decisions. That is why solving informal problems can be more difficult and require extra effort and skills compared to solving formal and routine problems.

Well-Defined Versus Ill-Defined Problems

Some problems are well defined. Well-defined problems are in a sense like formal problems because they are easier to handle. For instance, the necessary steps to be followed and operations to be done for the resolution of well-defined problems can be easily found and implemented. As will be indicated in the following chapters, defining a problem moves the person toward the solution.

However, the steps to follow in resolving ill-defined problems cannot be easily detected. Although the things to do or the steps to follow for the resolution of well-defined problems are clear, those of ill-defined problems are not. That is why solving these problems is not easy for the client. Complex cognitive, behavioral, and affective strategies are necessary for the resolution of ill-defined problems. The individual has to make use of different kinds of strategies for the resolution of well-defined versus ill-defined problems. The ability to transform an ill-defined problem into a well-defined problem has to do with the professional skill of the problem-solving therapist.

Real-Life Problems Versus Hypothetical Problems

The problems that interest the majority of people are real-life problems. People try to solve certain problems every day. Some of them are personal, some are family related, some are interpersonal, and some are work related. The problems that create difficulties for individuals are generally personal and interpersonal problems.

Hypothetical problems may be academic or scientific problems that need to be solved. Solving these problems is easier and less complicated than solving real-life problems. Compared to real-life problems, hypothetical ones are mostly well-defined and formal problems.

As discussed earlier, problems that worsen psychological health are real-life problems. The skills required for the resolution of the well-defined, formal, and hypothetical problems are generally taught in the curriculum. The skills required for the resolution of real-life problems, unfortunately, are not taught in training and educational programs, or if so, they are not sufficiently covered.

The Subjective Characteristics of the Problems

Besides objective characteristics, problems contain certain subjective characteristics. The preceding sections explore objective characteristics of clients' problems. The subjective characteristics of their problems are important in the individual's perceptual world. What is the meaning of the problem for the client? How does the individual perceive the problem? The subjective characteristics are what makes a problem or situation difficult for the client; these are briefly discussed as follows.

The Source of the Problems

Problems can be evaluated according to their sources. Some problems originate from the individual's environment, so they are external. For instance, a rape victim's depression has an external source. Some problems, however, may arise as a result of some processes and deficiencies in the individual. An individual who experiences an unfortunate event may experience depression because he or she does not possess the effective coping skills or because of a deficiency of a neurotransmitter in the central nervous system called serotonin. In these cases, the source of the problem is internal. The individual may not see the source of the problems accurately. For instance, the rape victim who develops depression may see him- or herself as the source of the problem and blame him- or herself for it.

The ability of the client to accurately see the problem during PST will help the client be motivated and turn toward the right source for resolution. Within the context of PST, the client's perception of the source of the problem will provide important information for the assessment.

The Way Problems Start

Some problems are acute, i.e., they start suddenly. And some others are chronic problems that develop over time. Sudden problems generally start with an event. For instance, the problem of an individual who undergoes depression because he or she has lost his or her job or because he or she has been raped is an acute problem. The problem here started after the job loss or the rape. However, the individual starting to lose his or her joy of life may be facing a chronic situation. Or the individual may undergo depression at the end of a slow and long-standing process because of accumulated stress resulting from cognitive distortions or behavioral inefficiencies.

The Cost of the Problem

The loss the problem causes to the individual or his or her environment, in other words, its cost varies from one problem to another. Some problems have high costs and some have low costs to the individual or his or her environment. The short-term cost of some problems is high, while their long-term cost is low. What is important here is the perceived cost of the problem more than its absolute cost.

The Individual's Assessment of the Problem

Some problems may be perceived as a threat, a challenge, or a loss. The way the individual perceives and evaluates the problem is important. If the individual evaluates the distressing situation as a problem that needs to be solved, he or she may start the necessary processes to cope with and eliminate the problem. If the individual interprets the problem as a challenge, then the problem may be perceived as an opportunity for self-exploration and improvement. In this case, the individual will feel motivated to cope with the problem and to do his or her best to solve it.

The Types of Plans

The behaviors, decisions, etc. for the solution of a problem may be routine for some and complex for some others. What needs to be done for a problem may be a single behavior for some but multiple behaviors for some others. For example, problems require defined or undefined conducts, problems having vague or ill-defined goals, and problems having countable or uncountable goals. Some problems require long-term planning in some situations and short-term planning in other situations.

Things That Should Be Done

Things that should be done may be postponed for some problems or need to be fulfilled immediately for some others. Things that should be done may be routine or complicated. What needs to be done for a problem may be a single behavior or multiple behaviors.

Perceived Difficulty of Problems

The individual may perceive different problems at varying levels of difficulty. A problem's difficulty level is closely related to the individual's characteristics. For an individual who possesses effective personal coping skills, problems may be perceived as easier to solve. There are two kinds of problem difficulty: objective problem difficulty and subjective problem difficulty. Just like the cost of the problem, the perceived level of difficulty is important here. What is important is the individual's perception. An individual's assessment of his or her coping resources as inadequate in relation to a situation makes a problem more difficult.

Identifying the Client's Resources

Knowing the resources the individual can make use of to cope with problems is as vital as the actual resolution of problems. Identifying and assessing the resources the client will be able to use to handle problems increases the chances of successful PST. If one does not take the individual's resources into account, one will not have the opportunity to realize the chosen alternatives. The resources the client can use in solving problems can roughly be grouped into three main categories: (a) personal resources, (b) social resources, and (c) economic resources.

Personal Resources

As indicated, determining the effectiveness of a client's personal resources for handling problems is important. Problems are part of living and they will always exist. And it is good that they exist. In the practice of psychotherapy, the therapist will not solve the client's problems. However the problem-solving therapist will help the client learn skills for solving problems. In other words, instead of giving the client a fish, the problem-solving therapist will teach the client how to fish. In this context, identifying the client's problem-solving skills is of crucial importance for the successful implementation of PST.

Personal characteristics are equally important to consider during assessment. The problematic aspects of the clients' personal styles are emphasized in assessment; this includes their personality characteristics. One should not forget that personal characteristics are resources for both the individual and his or her therapy. Considering these characteristics within the scope of assessment will increase the success of the PST. For instance, individuals who are open to change will be more successful in learning new skills and adapting to new circumstances. Any kind of personal characteristics, not just the positive ones, should be considered as a personal resource.

The Level of Insight in Relation to the Ability to See the Problems

Is the individual aware of the distress or problems he or she experiences? The ability of the individual to see the problems will help him or her solve the problems. Individuals with the courage or the ability to see the problems are halfway through their resolution. However, some people are either unaware of the problems or unwilling to accept the fact that they have problems. Here, the therapist asks questions to help the client see the problems and explores the factors preventing him or her from seeing them. The problem-solving therapist gathers as much information on the client's level of knowledge about the problems creating distress for the individual and his or her willingness to obtain this information. This will be an indication of a client's motivation.

There may be various reasons as to why individuals do not see or are unwilling to see the distressful situations they encounter. Some of them can be explained by automatic or unconscious processes. For example, defense mechanisms may keep the individual from seeing or being aware of the problems. A problem-solving therapist should consider these issues during the assessment of a client. Usually, people are unwilling to see or realize things in their lives that they regard as threats. Seeing or being consciously aware of threats implies a necessity for making changes about these threats. Change, in turn, means risk for the majority of people. The perceived risk may lower the motivation of some clients in therapy. The problem-solving therapist should collect as much data as possible about a client's perception of risks in assessment and encourage the client to take risks.

Being Free from Cognitive Distortions

People perceive certain phenomena that may threaten their inner world by distorting them in such a way that will decrease or eliminate their fears. In other words, they perceive the events and the phenomena by distorting them. It is important to know the client's cognitive distortions in order to implement the PST in a successful way. The problems themselves may be related to or may result from these distortions. At this stage, the therapist gathers information on the client's distortions. The point to keep in mind here is that these cannot be obtained from the client. The cognitive distortions can only be obtained during clinical interviews. The individual's ability to see and perceive the events and the problems he or she encounters in an objective way is an important personal resource. The therapist tries to increase this personal resource by decreasing a client's level of cognitive distortions.

Social Resources

Humans are social beings. They are not isolated like islands. They are born into a network of social relationships and continue to develop relationships throughout their lives. A person becomes affected by the characteristics of the network of relationships. The network of relationships and the societal background where the network takes place influence the individual's development and functioning. The qualitative and quantitative characteristics of the societal background and the network affecting the individual are important resources for the individual. For this reason, social resources are as important as personal resources. These resources not only enhance the individual's personal development but also provide the individual with the power to face the problems.

The assessment of the client's social resources during PST will be helpful in implementing the stages of problem solving. The client's social resources that the problem-solving therapist can discuss during the course of the treatment or during the assessment stage are presented in the following sections.

Social Support

An important social resource is the support the client receives from others. Social support, as it is known, contributes directly to the psychological well-being, and in addition, it prevents the development of mental health problems by buffering people against stress. For this reason, it is important to know which individuals will provide social support to the client throughout PST. The obstacles preventing the individual from getting social support may result from the individual's low levels of social skills. Therefore, the problem may be the inability of the individual to get support. All these issues may constitute the main subject of the PST. For this reason, the social support that the client can or cannot rely upon should be assessed during the course of the treatment.

Support Groups

Awareness of the support groups that the patient can refer to in trying to cope with the problems will increase the success of the PST. For instance, it is important to know the contact information of support groups for persons with schizophrenia, or that of Alcoholics Anonymous for people with alcohol problems.

Economic Resources

Economic Situation

Knowing the client's economic situation will provide a clarification for important aspects of the client's life. The absence of financial resources is an important source of stress and trouble. Knowledge on the financial situation of a client may give the therapist clues about a client's source of stress.

The Way the Client Approaches the Problems

It is important to assess the way a client who undergoes problem-solving treatment approaches the problems he or she encounters in living. What was the individual's style in the face of previous problems? Was the individual able to notice the causal connections as soon as the problems emerged and make the effort to carefully engage in activities to resolve them? Or did the client pretend problems did not exist? Or, on the contrary, has the client rushed into the first solution that came to his or her mind, without thinking through the problems and without obtaining the necessary information? It is necessary to make an assessment in detail about the individual's attitude and approach toward problem situations.

Identifying a client's attitude and style of approaching problems will undoubtedly increase the quality and the effectiveness of the problem-solving treatment that will be provided to him or her. When assessing a patient's way of approaching problems, it is important to obtain information not only from the client but also from his or her significant others. The client may be asked here to think about hypothetical problem situations and how he or she will behave and think in those situations. In short, the client may be asked, "Assume that you were faced with such and such situation or problem, what would you do, how would you feel and behave?" Such information will provide the therapist with important clues about the way he or she approaches and solves the problems.

Knowing the ways the client approaches problems may give the therapist an opportunity to use them during the practice of PST. According to the social problem-solving model proposed by D'Zurilla et al. (2004), people may approach problems in three ways. These are: (a) avoidant way of approaching problems, (b) impulsive/careless way of approaching problems, and (c) rational way of approaching problems. These were mentioned in Chapter 4; however, here they will be reviewed in the context of assessment.

The Avoidant Style of Approaching Problems

Procrastination, passivity, inactivity, and dependency are the dominant characteristics of people approaching problems in this way. The individual places the responsibility to solve the problems on somebody else's shoulders. Avoiding the problem is the basic characteristic. Individuals who approach problems in this way have the tendency to consciously or unconsciously ignore the problems or to distort them. That is why, assessing this style of approach by interviewing the PST client is important for the success of the treatment. The following questions can be used during the assessment to understand and evaluate whether or not the individual displays an avoidant style of approaching problems:

- What kind of attitude do you display in the face of the problems or distress in your life?
- Are you aware of the problems and distresses in your life, or do others remind you of them?
- Some people prefer to stay unresponsive to the problems they face rather than acting on them. Do you behave in a similar way when you are faced with problems?

Impulsive/Careless Way of Approaching Problems

Even though this is an active way of approaching problems, the impulsive/careless problem-solving style is of hasty nature. Individuals who approach and handle problems they encounter in an impulsive/careless way know only a few problem-solving strategies. They do not review the alternatives and the solutions in a systematic way. An important characteristic of the individuals with a hasty way of approaching problem situations is their inability to show the perseverance to solve the problems. These people can act impulsively and suddenly stop the problem-solving process instead of showing the necessary determination. Even if they possess effective problem-solving skills, these people either jump into an action without considering alternatives and thinking about the consequences or show a lack of determination.

From a problem-solving perspective, it is clear that such an approach to problem solving will complicate the issues further, rather than solving them. Making problem-solving attempts without thinking about the alternatives and the outcomes will make the individual face even more difficult problems and dilemmas. The basic approach of the PST is to make people think about possible solutions to the problems and help them choose the best alternatives from among these solutions. The following questions can be used to determine the existence of an impulsive/careless way of approaching the problems of a client.

- How do you behave when you are faced with problems in your life?
- Do you think you rush into the solution to the problems?
- Some people have the tendency to act without thinking when they are faced with a problem. How do you behave in this respect?
- The solutions found create new problems for some people instead of comforting them. How is your situation?

Rational Way of Approaching Problems

People who effectively handle problem situations in their lives do not avoid problems and they do not act impulsively when approaching problems. They make use of systematic ways of handling problems. These people perceive the problems accurately, define them, set a goal, generate alternative solutions, select a best possible solution from among them, implement that solution, and evaluate the outcome and the process. As addressed in previous chapters, people who handle problems in this way resolve them effectively. The whole purpose of PST is to teach people these problem-solving skills. The problem-solving therapist should inquire about whether or not a client has these skills during the assessment phase of the treatment.

Inability to Solve the Problem or to Implement the Solution

Identifying where during the process of problem solving the individual has a deficiency is an important point to consider during assessment. Does the individual display deficiency in problem orientation, problem-solving skills, or implementing the solution? Knowledge on these will be of vital importance for the success of the help provided to the client.

The important point here is to identify whether the client experiences problems in generating solution alternatives or in implementing them. Some people are unable to generate the solution alternatives that are necessary for the resolution of problems. Some clients are mentally or psychologically unable to generate the solution alternatives that are necessary to solve the problems. Perhaps if they are able to generate the solution alternatives, they will not experience problems in implementing them. The problem some people face is their inability to see the problems because of certain mental (cognitive distortions) and psychological (defense mechanisms) characteristics. Identification and clarification of these issues are important for helping the individual. Accordingly, deficient skills can be taught to the client during the course of PST. But first they should be identified.

Some clients, however, can experience difficulty implementing the solution alternatives that are necessary to solve the problems even if they are able to generate them. For instance, a client who knows that solving the problem of being unable to express oneself by saying "no" to the demands of others may have difficulty implementing it, that is saying "no." In this case, through role playing the therapist can help the individual learn how to say no by providing assertiveness training. Thus, identifying the client's deficiency has crucial importance in developing and implementing the right helping strategies.

Assessment with Self-Report Instruments

Self-report instruments are important for the assessment of problem-solving skills of clients who seek problem-solving treatment. These instruments constitute an important part of the clinical assessment. Different from the assessment through clinical interview methods, assessment through self-reports gives a quantitative and objective value. Data obtained through self-report instruments make it possible to compare the measurements across different people and within the same individual.

Two self-report measuring instruments that are widely used in measuring and assessing problem-solving skills will be presented below. These are Problem-Solving Inventory (PSI) and Social Problem-Solving Inventory Revised (SPSI-R).

Problem-Solving Inventory

The kind of problem-solving skills individuals display when they are faced with problems and the way they view themselves with respect to these skills are important. The view that problem-solving skills play an important role in the onset of psychological problems has been emphasized in recent years and this view has been supported with empirical evidence. Problem-solving skills are one of the important coping resources of an individual. Problem behaviors of the patients have traditionally been the primary focus in the psychiatric assessment and personal resources that ease their adaptation have not been emphasized. However, emphasizing, during the psychological assessment, the personal resources that ease the individual's adaptation can provide both the clinician and the patient with new insights. Knowing the level and the quality of the individual's problem-solving skills will make important contributions to assessment.

The importance of measuring instruments that will meet the requirements stated in the previous paragraph is apparent. The assessment of problem-solving skills aims to explore the individual's level of self-confidence, feelings of control, and the way they approach problems. A self-report tool called PSI was developed by Heppner and Petersen (1982) in order to assess these skills. This measurement tool has been translated into a number of languages and its psychometric characteristics have been tested.

PSI measures the way individuals perceive their own problem-solving skills rather than measurement from an outside perspective. The instrument evaluates the individuals' thoughts on their own levels of problem-solving skills. For this reason, it is more appropriate to define this measurement tool as an instrument that measures the individuals' perceptions of their own problem-solving skills rather than a tool that measures problem-solving skills themselves.

PSI is comprised of 35 items. However, three items are not included in the scoring. Therefore, 32 items are being used in calculating the PSI scores. Individuals filling out the PSI are being asked about the frequency with which they display the problem-solving behavior described in each item. The individual evaluates the items on a 6-point Likert scale ranging from "Always" to "Never." The instrument can be applied to adolescents and adults and the scores obtained range from 32 to 192. High scores indicate low confidence in his or her problem-solving abilities.

Both the internal consistency and the test/retest reliability of the instrument were found to be strong. The internal consistency coefficient for the instrument as a whole was found to be 0.90 and the coefficients for subscales were found to be between 0.72 and 0.85. The item total correlation coefficients ranged between 0.25 and 0.75. The test/retest reliability coefficient for subscales was found to range between 0.83 and 0.89. PSI was found to have a sufficient level of criterion validity. The factor analysis revealed that PSI consisted of three distinct dimensions. These are:

- *Problem-solving confidence*: This dimension evaluates the extent to which the individual trusts his or her abilities to deal with and solve the problems.
- *Approach/avoidance*: This subdimension evaluates the individual's behavioral characteristics when he or she faces problems. Does the individual try to solve the problems when they arise or does he or she avoid or ignore them?
- *Personal control*: This dimension evaluates the individual's subjective sense of control when faced with any kind of problem situation. Individuals who have a high sense of control will be able to engage in efforts to solve the problems. Individuals with a low sense of control may show the tendency to avoid problems.

Social Problem-Solving Inventory Revised

The most frequently used self-report assessment instrument in the literature on problem solving is the Social Problem-Solving Inventory (SPSI) (Maydeu-Olivares & D'Zurilla, 1995, 1996). The revised version of the instrument has been used in recent years (SPSI-R) (D'Zurilla, Nezu, & Maydeu-Olivares, 2002). The SPSI-R measures the social problem-solving skills of individuals described in the social problem-solving process by D'Zurilla et al. (2004). There is a long and a short form of SPSI-R. The long form is comprised of 52 items and the short form is comprised of 25 items. The individual responds to items of the SPSI-R on a 4-point Likert scale ranging from "Not at all true of me" to "Extremely true of me."

The SPSI-R measures two main problem-solving dimensions. They are: (1) problem orientation and (2) problem-solving styles. The problem orientation dimension is made up of one functional and one dysfunctional orientation. The problem-solving style consists of three styles. They are avoidant, impulsive/careless, and rational problem-solving styles. Thus, five subscale scores and a total scale score are obtained from the SPSI-R.

Problem Orientation

Problem orientation defines the way the individual reacts to problems they encounter in living and the way they think and feel in dealing with and solving them. The SPSI-R assumes that some people approach problems in a positive way whereas some display a negative approach. With this assumption, it measures positive and negative problem orientation styles. The problem orientation is defined as the individual's affective and cognitive reactions when faced with a problem. The two problem orientation scales of the SPSI-R are briefly defined below.

Negative Problem Orientation Subscale

Negative problem orientation means the individual affectively shows negative reactions and makes negative self-evaluations in the face of problems. Individuals possessing negative problem orientation perceive the problems they encounter as a threat.

That is why their emotional reactions are also negative. Another characteristic of individuals with negative problem orientation is their lack of confidence in their problem-solving skills and abilities. The long version of SPSI-R measures the negative problem orientation on a 10-item scale. Therefore, the raw scores that can be obtained from the negative problem orientation subscale in SPSI-R range from 0 to 40. The negative problem orientation in the short version of SPSI-R negative problem orientation is composed of five items and the scores range from 0 to 20.

Positive Problem Orientation Subscale

Contrary to the individuals possessing a negative problem orientation, individuals with positive problem orientation are optimistic about their ability to solve life's problems and difficulties. As mentioned earlier, individuals with positive problem orientation see problems when they arise and, contrary to individuals with negative problem orientation, they believe they can solve them. These individuals see the problems as opportunities that can add to their self-development rather than seeing them as threats. Such individuals believe they are able to solve the problems they face in living. The long and short versions of SPSI-R assess the positive problem orientation by five scales. Raw score that can be obtained from the subscales can range from 0 to 20.

Problem-Solving Styles

Whereas problem orientation describes the affective and cognitive characteristics of individuals when they face of problems, problem-solving styles define peoples' behavioral and cognitive characteristics when faced with problems. A negative problem orientation may prevent the individual from making use of rational problem-solving processes. Individuals who have negative problem orientation have a dysfunctional style of approaching the problems. Dysfunctional style means that the individual's way of dealing with or solving the problems is not compatible with the requirements of personal goals and adaptation.

Dysfunctional Problem-Solving Styles

The social problem-solving model presumes that individuals may basically have two problem-solving styles: functional and dysfunctional. The functional problem-solving styles, defined as rational problem solving, will be explained later. The model assumes that individuals may possess two types of dysfunctional problem-solving styles. The two dysfunctional problem-solving styles assessed by SPSI-R are: (1) impulsive/careless problem-solving style and (2) avoidant problem-solving style. Two SPSI-R subscales measuring the dysfunctional problem-solving styles and the subscale measuring the rational problem-solving style are presented as follows.

Impulsive/Careless Problem-Solving Style

Individuals displaying impulsive/careless styles in the face of problems act without taking the subsequent consequences into consideration. Individuals with this problem-solving style behave with the first idea that comes to their minds when faced with a problem. It is apparent that this type of approach itself will result in another problem in the future or will trigger the emergence of new problems. As was indicated in Chapter 3, individuals who adopt such a style act with the first solution that comes to their minds, cannot think about the possible consequences of the solution alternatives, and do not possess metacognitive skills to evaluate and correct their problem-solving processes.

The long version of the revised social problem-solving inventory measures the individual's impulsive/careless problem-solving styles with 10 items. The raw score that can be obtained from the impulsive/careless problem-solving style subscale range from 0 to 40. The short version of the SPSI-R contains five items measuring the impulsive/careless problem-solving style with score range of 0–20.

Avoidant Problem-Solving Style

The attitude of the individuals who avoid the problems they encounter in life rather than attempting to solve them is not functional. The avoidant problem-solving style, just like the impulsive/careless problem-solving style, leads to the emergence of new problems for the individual. Individuals who deal with problems in an avoidant way display behavioral characteristics such as ignoring them when they emerge, pretending that problems do not exist, and postponing the solution.

The long version of the SPSI-R contains seven items to assess the avoidant problem-solving styles of the individuals. The raw scores that can be obtained from this subscale range from 0 to 28. The short version of the SPSI-R contains seven items that measure the problem-solving style with score range of 0–20.

Functional–Rational Problem-Solving Style

The revised social problem-solving inventory describes a series of functional operational steps which are used by the individuals with positive problem orientation when they successfully solve their problems. The SPSI-R defines four rational problem-solving steps. They are: (1) defining and formulating the problem, (2) generating solution alternatives, (3) decision making, and (4) implementing the chosen solution and verification. The rational problem-solving subscale of the long form of the SPSI-R contains 20 items. The possible scores range from 0 to 80. The short SPSI-R contains five items with scores ranging from 0 to 20.

Defining and Formulating the Problem

The first step in the rational problem-solving style is defining and formulating the problem. What is important here is defining and identifying the source of the problem situation in a clear way. The SPSI-R uses five items to determine the skill level the individual can display in defining and determining the problems they encounter. The scores that can be obtained from this subscale range from 0 to 20.

Generating the Solution Alternatives

The second step of rational problem solving is generating solutions to the problems identified in the first step. At this step, the individual generates certain solution alternatives that are compatible with the problem-solving goal. In the SPSI-R, five items have been designed to measure the individual's ability to generate solution alternatives in relation to the problem defined. The scores that can be obtained from this subscale range from 0 to 20.

Decision Making

The third step in rational problem solving is decision making. The individual at this step decides on the alternative solution that will solve the problem and take him or her to the defined goal. This stage in rational problem solving is also defined as identifying the most appropriate solution alternative. There are five items in the SPSI-R in relation to the individual's decision making about the appropriate solution alternative. The scores to be obtained from this subscale range from 0 to 20.

Implementing the Solution and Verification

The last step in rational problem-solving style is the implementation and verification of the solution. Here, the individual realizes two steps. In the first step, the individual implements the solution alternative that he or she has chosen in order to solve the problem defined in the previous step. In the second, the individual evaluates certain issues by analyzing whether or not the implemented solution took him/her to the goal he or she had defined, the things that changed and the things that stayed the same and the extent to which the changes were satisfying for him/her.

The long version of the revised social problem-solving inventory contains a total of five items that measure the individual's skills in relation to the implementation of the chosen solution. The scores to be obtained from this subscale range from 0 to 20. The items designed to measure the individual's skills at the assessment stage focus generally on the individual's assessment of the implementation and the experiences that he or she gained during this process.

Conclusion

Assessment is the complementary element of today's psychotherapy practices. Two factors play a role here. The first factor is the fact that the process of psychotherapy turned into an academic field of research. As indicated earlier, the practice of psychotherapy is not an activity taking place behind closed doors anymore; rather, it is an academic subject in which scientific investigations explore the effects of therapeutic environments and change processes. The second factor is that various sections of the society started to follow and understand the psychotherapy practices. The economic and legal importance of the consequences of the psychological treatment played a role here. The social security institutions and insurance companies that finance health-related expenses started to raise concerns about the types of psychotherapies that have been proven scientifically effective and that can be compensated. Therefore, the importance of assessment in the practice of psychotherapy increased.

This chapter presented the importance of assessment, the way it will be implemented, the things to take into account, and the factors to consider in deciding on the measurement instruments based on self-reports and two self-report instruments used in the measurement of the individual's problem-solving skills. One can talk about two main goals in the assessment of the PST. The first goal is assessing the current situation and the second is evaluating the process of the treatment. Assessing the current situation is important for planning and implementing the treatment. For the assessment of the therapy, it is important to assess objectively whether or not the methods implemented were effective and whether or not the client's complaints diminished.

It is suggested that assessment be considered as a complementary and inseparable part in planning and implementing the PST. It is necessary to give due importance to assessment if PST will be planned and implemented as an activity based on empirical evidence. Identifying whether the client has a deficiency in problem-solving skills or whether he or she experiences problems in implementing them is of critical importance here. One should not forget that the identification of these situations is only possible through a healthy process of assessment.

10 Processes and Sessions of Problem-Solving Therapy

Introduction

This chapter describes the processes and stages of PST in a session-by-session fashion. It is suggested here that the PST be organized around eight sessions. The first is the assessment and providing rationale session and the second is the problem orientation training session. The other six sessions are sessions in which rational problem-solving steps are taught. The sessions of the PST suggested in this book are as follows:

1. Assessment and providing rationale
2. Problem orientation training
3. Defining problems
4. Goal setting
5. Generating solution alternatives
6. Choosing the appropriate solution
7. Solution implementation
8. Assessing the implementation.

This chapter emphasizes conceiving PST as a process. The process of problem solving was explained earlier in chapter 4 where theoretical approaches to problem solving were discussed. The process can be repeated for each specific problem. The aim here is to allow the client to use the problem-solving skills he or she learned during therapy in solving other problems. Rather than solving each and every problem of the client during therapy, PST aims to give the client the opportunity to learn how to solve problems. In other words, PST aims to teach the client "how to fish."

What is the purpose of PST? What are the problem-solving aspects of a client that need to be increased or decreased? In other words, what makes for effective and ineffective problem solving? Effective problem solving means that the individual possesses a positive problem orientation and the ability to use rational problem-solving steps or skills. Ineffective problem-solving, on the other hand, means that the individual possesses a negative problem orientation, uses impulsive/careless or avoidant problem-solving styles in dealing with problems, and is unable to use the rational problem-solving steps or skills. Thus, the aim of the PST is to decrease the impulsive/careless and avoidant problem-solving styles and to develop a

Problem Solving Therapy in the Clinical Practice. DOI: http://dx.doi.org/10.1016/B978-0-12-398455-5.00010-3

positive problem orientation and to improve a client's rational problem-solving steps or skills.

In practice, although it is recommended to plan 30- to 45-minute meetings for each session, the problem-solving therapist may increase or decrease this time according to a particular client's needs. However, one should not forget that this is related to the characteristics of the client or the nature of the problems. As discussed earlier, this is in fact one of the basic skills and approaches of psychotherapy, defined as *tailoring* which means adapting the therapy to the needs of the client.

What happens and what needs to be done practically at each session during the PST will be emphasized in the following sections. The topics to be covered in each session and the way they will be taught to the client will form the backbone of this chapter. Structuring the session is important in cognitive–behavioral psychotherapy practices. Therefore, the way a problem-solving session will be structured and the content of PST sessions are presented as follows.

Structuring the PST Session

The most important characteristic of cognitive–behavioral therapy is the structured nature of its sessions. Structuring the sessions is important for both the therapist and the client. Structured sessions decrease the therapists' anxiety and help them focus on the therapeutic affairs. Knowing beforehand the order in which things will be done in a therapy session decreases the anxiety and the feeling of confusion especially for the beginning therapists. This in turn makes it possible for the therapist to concentrate on the therapeutic endeavors. The anxiety and the confusion experienced by a therapist will reduce his or her likelihood of being helpful to the client.

A patient who has made the decision to seek psychotherapy has various questions in his or her mind. It may be difficult for the patient to understand the things he or she is expected to do, the rules he or she is supposed to follow during psychotherapy. This difficulty confuses the patient and increases his or her anxiety. The confusion and anxiety prevent patients from correctly perceiving what is expected of them and the level of the effort they need to make. All these factors decrease the client's motivation in relation to the PST. A patient who has lost his or her motivation will not be willing and eager to make the effort to meet the expectations in a psychotherapy session.

The problem-solving therapist should inform the client about the structure of the sessions. Clients who have not been sufficiently informed will experience difficulty conforming to the structure of the sessions. Problem-solving therapists have an important responsibility in this respect. The therapist should inform the client about the advantages of conforming to the structure of the therapy sessions. For instance, the clients should be informed that sessions similar in tone to daily conversations will not be helpful in overcoming the difficulties they experience, that they can always have these conversations with friends, and that in the therapy setting, simple conversations would be a waste of time and effort.

What should the structure of a session be in PST? What should be done, and in which order should things be done? The structure of a typical PST session should be as follows:

- *Greeting, meeting*: Greeting and meeting are especially important for the first session. Like in other cognitive–behavioral therapies, a trusting relationship between the patient and the therapist is extremely important in PST. A trusting patient–therapist relationship will help the client feel secure in the therapy and will add to the formation of cooperation that is expected of the patient during therapy. The client who feels that a trusting relationship exists between him- or herself and the therapist will be encouraged and motivated to do the therapeutic assignments during and outside the therapy. It should be kept in mind that psychotherapy is an encounter between two human beings.
- *Mood check*: Identifying the patient's mood during PST sessions with four simple parameters will provide the therapist with important clues about the client's psychological state. The mood check can be done by asking the patient to rate him- or herself on: (1) personal happiness, (2) self-love, (3) self-knowledge, and (4) self-confidence. These assessments will provide the therapist with information on the distress the patient experiences in certain situations and the patient's psychological state. This information can also be assessed as a subject matter to work on during that session.
- *Review of the previous session*: Except in the first session, at each PST session, it is important to remember the topics covered in a previous session in order to allow for the continuity of the therapeutic process in the patient's mind.
- *Homework control*: Like all cognitive–behavioral psychotherapy approaches, PST expects that patients actively participate in the therapeutic process. In all of the PST sessions, the therapist must enforce the completion of assigned homework. Has the patient done his or her homework? If the patient has not done or was not able to do the homework, the reasons for that should be explored so that PST can be effective. If homework is not enforced, the patient may feel like homework is not important and his or her time is being wasted.
- *Setting the agenda*: Setting the session's agenda by taking the patient's opinion into account is important in the practice of the PST. In PST, the agenda is the topic to work on at a given session. Identifying it by a mutual agreement offers some advantages. First of all, setting the agenda together with the client increases the client's motivation to participate in the therapeutic process. And second, there may be a topic that the patient would like to discuss urgently during that session. Making such a situation part of the agenda evokes the feeling that the patient is valued and understood by the therapist.
- *Working on the agenda*: After the therapist and the client set the agenda together they may start working on it. The agenda can be an important subject that the patient would like to discuss during that session or content-related work about the session. For instance, although the first session's agenda is assessing the patient and introducing the PST model, the agenda in the second session is transforming dysfunctional problem orientation of a client into a functional problem orientation. In addition, a distressful situation that the patient experienced can be included in the agenda.
- *Assigning homework*: Homework has an important role in the practice of cognitive–behavioral psychotherapies (Addis & Jacobson, 2000; Thase & Callan, 2006). Investigating the attitudes of psychologists toward homework, Kazantzis, Lampropoulos, and Deane (2005) found out that those who practiced cognitive–behavioral psychotherapy

displayed the most positive attitude. Scientific studies indicate that completing the assignments during cognitive–behavioral therapy is related to recovery (Burns & Spangler, 2000; Kazantzis, Deane & Ronan, 2000; Schmidt & Woolaway-Bickel, 2000). Assigning homework in PST is also effective in helping the patient actively participate in the treatment under the supervision of the therapist. For this reason, in the practice of PST, the therapist should assign homework to patients. Certain factors need to be kept in mind while assigning homework. The purpose of the homework and what exactly is expected from the patient should clearly be explained. Neglecting to explain the rationale behind the homework and what it entails in a clear way decreases the patient's motivation to complete the homework and demoralizes him or her.

- *Summarizing and finishing the session*: At the end of the PST, the topics covered during the session are summarized and the session is terminated. In the first few sessions, the summary is completed by the therapist, but the patient may be asked to do it in subsequent sessions. Asking the patient to do the summary results in the active participation of the patient to the therapeutic process.

Sessions of PST

Session I: Assessment and Providing Rationale

The first session of the PST should be reserved for understanding and assessing the client and the difficulties he or she is experiencing. As is known, assessment is the indispensable part of the practice of psychotherapy. If the practice of psychotherapy is planned as a scientific activity based on evidence, the current situation, whether or not interventions result in changes and whether or not the acquired gains are maintained, should be assessed objectively. The following topics should take place in the assessment and providing rationale session, which is the first session in the PST.

As it is the case in other psychotherapies, the first thing to accomplish in the initial session is to establish a good relationship with the client. Like other cognitive–behavioral psychotherapies, PST is a practice based on cooperation. This means the client will be actively working during the sessions of therapy. Establishing and developing a good client–therapist relationship during the PST sessions will have a positive impact on the whole process. Such cooperation will motivate the client to work actively during the therapy. Otherwise, the client either will get disconnected from the therapy or will not be motivated to work actively during therapy. In either case, PST will not accomplish the expected result.

The consideration of the client's psychological state and behavioral characteristics forms the backbone of the assessment in PST. The individual gets affected by the problems he or she experiences. Such an impact results from certain deficiencies in dealing with the problem situations. During the assessment session, both the psychological distress showing the degree to which the client is affected by problems and the problem-solving skill levels contributing to the experience of problems need to be identified. In this first session, these situations need to be evaluated. This kind of evaluation is important for the identification of the initial situation, the planning of the treatment, and the assessment of the progress and the results of the treatment in the future sessions. (The way in which assessment is carried out in the PST was explained in the previous chapter.)

Another important point in this session is informing the client about the rationale of the therapy and the nature of the steps involved in PST. The client should be informed here about the nature and the development of the psychological problems and the importance and the role of the PST approaches in the treatment of mental health problems. Such information is the prerequisite for the active and voluntary participation of the client to the activities in the therapy. Individuals have the right to know about the processes they will go through during therapy and about the impact of these processes. For this reason, it is important and essential to inform the clients about the steps in the problem-solving treatment and what is expected of them at each step.

Informing the clients about the number and the duration of the sessions is as important as informing them about the nature and the content of the therapy sessions. How many sessions will the PST contain? What is the budget and the amount of time the client needs to allocate to the therapy? The open and humanitarian psychotherapy practices of today stress the importance of informing the client about these subjects right at the beginning of the process. Therefore, the problem-solving therapist should inform the client about the content and the duration of the treatment during the first session. One should not forget that this is an indispensable ethical issue in modern psychotherapy practice.

Session II: Problem Orientation Training

The success of an individual in solving a problem situation depends upon a positive problem orientation—this is the combination of some behavioral, cognitive, and affective characteristics in the face of the problem. Positive problem orientation means the individual displays a functional attitude and behaviors toward the problem he or she encounters. The individual should be ready to face the problems encountered with the help of positive problem orientation training. The characteristics and the nature of the problem orientation may have a facilitating or inhibiting influence on the individual's behaviors during the process of problem solving. A major aim of problem orientation training is to make the individual ready to take action for resolving problems.

Developing a positive problem orientation consists of two basic perceptual processes. The first is being aware of the problems, and the second is the motivational orientation involving the ability to look at the problems in a positive way. In order to be able to approach a problem in a positive way, to see the problem not as a threat but as an opportunity for self-improvement, the individual should first see and be aware of the problem situations encountered during the journey of life. Only then can we discuss whether or not the individual's problem orientation is positive or not. The two perceptual processes will be discussed in the following section.

Being Aware of the Problems

If an individual experiences distress, it means that there is a problem causing this distress. The relationship between problem and distress can be defined as a cause and effect relationship. While the problem is the cause, the result is the distress. Problem and distress are often being confused in daily living. For instance, a client complains her voice trembles and she confuses words she has to speak in public. Initially, a trembling voice and confusion of words seem like a problem; however, a detailed analysis shows that the real problem is the individual's extreme anxiety in relation to public speaking and the belief that she will make a bad presentation. As a result of this anxiety and belief, the individual experiences the complaints that she describes. It can be easily understood that without coping with the anxiety and the belief in a bad presentation, the individual will not be able to get out of a trembling voice and fear of a bad presentation; she will only get stuck in the vicious cycle. The only way to get out of the vicious cycle is to identify the situations creating the problem.

Being aware of a problem situation is an important step toward solving the problem. English author and essayist G. K. Chesterton noted that for many people, recognizing problems and challenges is more difficult than finding a solution to problems. Accordingly, Chesterton said, "It's not that they can't see the solution, it's that they can't see the problem." This quote emphasizes that seeing the problem is indispensable for determining the solution. As long as we cannot see the problem, we cannot get rid of our troubles. If the initiatives that we undertake as a solution result in failures, we move away from solving the problem and create new problems instead. This only deepens the vicious cycle and we get stuck in a web of problems. However, when we are aware of the problems, we have the chance to see in advance which solutions will be effective in taking us away from our problems and which will increase our problems. This keeps us from creating new problems and helps us move one more step toward the solution.

The individual may not be seen or be able to see the problems or troubles he or she is experiencing for various reasons. He or she may not want to see the problems because seeing them may be perceived as a threat. For instance, the individual may not see the problems because of the fear of looking like a problematic individual or because of other underlying psychological needs. If the individual does not want to see a problem situation consciously, then the situation does not present a problem anyway. If the individual does not see a problem unconsciously, then we can talk about the existence of some unconscious psychological mechanisms. For instance, when the question of "What is the problem?" is asked of individuals seeking therapy due to psychological problems, clients might respond by saying: "Actually, I don't have any problems." The clients may not want to look problematic or may not want to see themselves as the source of any problems.

Cognitive distortions may be one of the reasons underlying some individuals' inability to perceive or see the troubles they are experiencing. Cognitive distortions may prevent the individual from perceiving the problems in an accurate way. For example, a perfectionist who thinks in terms of shoulds and should-nots may think as if he or she should not have any problems. Similarly a person with a tunnel vision may not notice the real problem since he or she will only see the things he or she wants to see.

Developing a Positive Orientation to Problems

Positive problem orientation—which can be defined as developing a positive orientation to problems—has basically two functions. The first function is to make sure the client is positively motivated toward the problems. Developing a positive orientation to problems means the individual is able to look at the problems he or she encounters, or may possibly encounter, in a positive way, and is able to perceive them as opportunities for self-improvement instead of threats. The second function is to decrease dysfunctional problem-solving styles by developing a positive problem orientation. As mentioned earlier, the impulsive/careless and avoidant problem-solving styles themselves present problems. It is also assumed that with positive problem orientation such styles will be minimized. Thus, an overall goal of problem orientation training is to minimize clients' negative problem orientation and increase positive problem orientation characteristics as described by Nezu and Nezu (2001) and D'Zurilla et al. (2004).

After the individual becomes aware of the problem, necessary help is provided so that the client transforms the negative outlook into a positive one. The aim is for the individual to develop a positive outlook in the face of problems he or she encounters in living. The individual who approaches the problems in a negative way and who sees problems as threats will have difficulty in being motivated and making the effort to solve the problems.

As a problem-solving therapist, it is important to know the kind of attitude the individuals need to display when they are faced with problems in order to be able to help them develop a positive outlook. Motivational characteristics that individuals need to possess in order to develop a positive orientation and examples of techniques that can be used to develop them are discussed as follows.

Seeing Problems as Natural Elements of Life

An individual who adopts the idea that problems are indispensable elements of life has gone a long way toward perceiving and being aware of the problem situations. An individual who sees problems as a part of life has already adopted a positive attitude toward them.

Certain points can be elaborated upon here, such as the client's views and evaluations about the problems and the way he or she perceives them. An individual who seeks out help from a mental health professional is fed up with the fact that he or she has had to deal with many problems. At this stage, the therapist should try to establish an emphatic relationship by assuring the client that he or she is able to understand and see the difficulty of the situation the client is in. An individual who constantly struggles with problems wishes a life free of problems. This is a natural human attitude. The client who feels that this is understood by the therapist will be ready to go into the next stage.

A client who feels understood will be willing and ready to discuss and reflect on the possibility that problems can be part of life. At this stage, the therapist can help the client see that other people also have problems in their lives by asking the client to make comparisons between his or her life and the lives of others. As a result of this comparison, the client may be inclined to accept that problems are natural. The aim here is to raise in the client the feeling that he or she is not the only one to experience problems.

On the other hand, the individual who learns, as a result of social comparison, that problems are a natural part of life should somehow be able to feel that problems are natural elements of life. The therapist at this stage can ask the client to imagine different lifestyles and ask which styles can possibly be realistic. After different lifestyles have been compared, the therapist can discuss the positive and negative ways and the authenticity of a life that includes a few problems and a problem-free life. The purpose of such an intervention is to raise the feeling that a problem-free life may not be realistic and that problems are necessary for the individual's development.

Being Able to Think That Problems Can Be Solved

After problems have been recognized and seen as a part of life, the individual stays face-to-face with them. In this case, the individual may think in two ways. The first way is the thought of "I can solve the problem." And the second is the exact opposite, "I cannot solve this problem." The second way of thinking increases the probability of a failure in dealing with problems to a great extent. The self-fulfilling prophecy may operate here; in other words, as the individual thinks that if he or she is not be able to do something at first, he or she may become incapable of doing it in the future. The thought of being able to solve the problem comforts and relaxes the individual. This increases the probability of solving the problem.

The ability of the client to see a problem situation as solvable depends on certain personal factors. A person's thoughts about a problem depend on his or her behavioral characteristics. For instance, an individual who is faced with a problem may automatically think "I cannot solve this," or "I don't have the power to solve this, I can't do it." In such situations, the individual stays away from the efforts to solve the problem and hence cannot solve the problem. This kind of thinking or reacting to problems lowers a person's sense of self-efficacy. A lowered sense of self-efficacy is a demotivating factor for the individual.

The aforementioned thoughts or reactions may also be conceived as automatic thoughts. These sorts of thoughts about a problem prevent the person from thinking that problems can be solved. In this case, therapeutic interventions should focus on the elimination or the reduction of the effects of such thoughts. The therapist should help the client replace the dysfunctional automatic thoughts with functional ones. After the validity of these automatic thoughts is checked, the extent to which the individual believes in them and the possible effects of this way of thinking are investigated, the client is taught how to develop the functional thoughts. Nezu et al. (1999) define these automatic thoughts in the PST practice as the individual's negative self-statements. Discovering them, discussing, or disputing them will contribute to the individual's belief that problems can be solved.

A client with a low sense of self-efficacy may never see him- or herself as a person who can solve the problems. In this case, the individual will see him- or herself as a hopeless and incompetent person. He or she may not even imagine him- or herself as capable of solving problems. In the case of these clients, it is necessary to help them feel self-competent at the experiential level. In order to accomplish this, Nezu et al. (1999) suggest a visualization technique. They point out that this technique is suitable especially for depressed patients who feel helpless. According to this, the problem-solving therapist should ask the patient to imagine him- or herself as solving a problem. Then the patient should be asked to imagine the way he or she would feel, the things that would change, and the things that would stay the same after he or she solves the problem.

According to Nezu, Nezu, and Perri (1990), another therapeutic technique that would help the client develop a positive orientation to their problems is the reverse advocacy role-play strategy. In this technique, the therapist selects one of the extreme behaviors and attitudes that can be displayed toward problems and role-plays it. The therapist asks the client to provide arguments against the therapist's position and to provide reasons why the therapist's view is irrational and illogical. For instance, to a client who feels that experiencing a problem is irrational and sees him- or herself as unfortunate, the problem-solving therapist may assert statements such as "problems are not common to everyone" or "if I have a problem, that means I'm crazy," and ask the patient to generate arguments against these beliefs and think about why these may be irrational.

Not Escaping the Problems

As indicated in the previous chapters, one of the characteristics of individuals who are not successful at problem solving is the tendency to escape problem situations even if they see or perceive the situations as problems. These people possess avoidant problem-solving styles. Individuals with an avoidant problem-solving style escape the problems and consciously or unconsciously ignore the existence of problems. It is likely that individuals who possess this style of coping with their problems will be faced with other kinds of problems as a result of unresolved issues.

When people think that problems are unsolvable, the first thing they do is try to escape them. Escape may seem to be very useful at decreasing the individual's anxiety at that moment. However, since escaping does not mean that problems will be resolved and since the trouble caused by the problems will continue to exist, the anxiety eventually comes back and in some situations it even increases and troubles become unbearable. The thought that problems cannot be solved causes unbearable trouble at that moment, and this may lead to the perception that escaping problems is the most logical behavior. Many people may have felt this way at certain points in their lives. The right thing to do in that situation is to stop and think about the problem.

Various reasons lie behind the avoidance of problems. The first reason is related to the individual's views, thoughts, and feelings about the problems. The individual may think that problems cannot be solved. Or the individual may think that he or she will not be able to solve the problems he or she faces. In either case, the individual will not have the necessary motivation and willingness to deal with and solve the problem situations. In other words, such thoughts and feelings will hinder the individual from being interested in the problem situation and will make him or her feel incompetent in the face of problems. In the end, the individual will have the tendency to escape the problems he or she encounters.

Now that we have seen that views, thoughts, and feelings about the problems are factors effective in causing an individual to seek escape from problems, we can start questioning the things we can do in order to overcome them and minimize their effects. How can an individual fight with the problems without avoiding them? First of all, the individual's thoughts about, feelings about, and interpretations of a problem situation can be handled with the previously discussed methods. And second, individuals may be asked to visualize the things that will change and the things that will stay the same in their lives when they solve the problems versus when they avoid them. As a result of these exercises, it is expected that the individuals' tendency to avoid problems will be minimized.

Not Acting Without Thinking

As is known, acting without thinking is a characteristic of the ineffective impulsive/careless problem-solving style. Individuals with this problem-solving style act with the first idea that comes to their mind and have no foresight about the consequences of their behaviors. These are in fact the main characteristics of impulsiveness. Individuals who act impulsively in the face of problems and who do not think about the consequences of their behaviors cannot be successful in solving their problems even if they want to.

One of the main characteristics of individuals who adopt the impulsive-careless problem-solving style is their inability to think about the possible consequences of their acts or actions. For instance, because these individuals do not or cannot think about the consequences of their behaviors, or the effects that their statements may have on other people, they experience deep relationship problems, not to mention difficulty solving other types of problems.

How can we help those individuals who act without thinking in the face of problems and who cannot solve the problems in the way they desire? The therapeutic technique that can be used with this type of client is the *stop-and-think* method. According to this method (Nezu et al., 1999), the client may be asked not to act immediately and to stop and think about the issue for a while. The client may be taught to take deep breaths while he or she stops. And the client can be asked to think either when he or she stops or while he or she is breathing. The client can be asked to think about the problem, his or her aims or goals, and the possible consequences of his or her actions. These exercises can be practiced in the therapist's office if necessary.

During the stop-and-think technique, the individual is taught to think about possible consequences of his or her behaviors. The possible consequences of the individual's behaviors and the effects of these consequences on the individual, his or her environment, and his or her future should be evaluated. The common characteristic of impulsive individuals is their focus on short-term gains without being able to consider long-term effects. Discussing the consequences of the problem-solving interventions to be carried out, and the consequences of their timing, may lead to a decrease in such tendencies.

Session III: Defining Problems

The client who is able to notice the problem and who is able to display a positive attitude toward it should be able to define the problem in order to start a successful problem-solving process. People encounter various problem situations in daily living. Perceiving them as problems and having a positive problem orientation are necessary conditions for a successful problem resolution, but these alone are insufficient. For effective problem solving, the individual should be able to use rational problem-solving style or steps. Defining problems is the first step in PST. As stated earlier, identifying and defining a problem indicate that the problem is half way for solution. Defining a problem involves a number of interrelated cognitive and behavioral processes.

Individuals who seek psychological help bring certain symptoms or complaints to therapy. Most of the time, the clients' complaints are not the problems to work on. Problems can be perceived as the cause for the client's distress and complaints as the effects of these causes. The following chart may be helpful to the problem-solving therapist in the problem-definition session. The problem-solving therapist can help the client differentiate between complaints and the problems causing these complaints by showing the chart in Figure 10.1 to the client.

Upon seeking therapy, the client's complaints are very important for sure, and they need to be dealt with during therapy. However, the problem-solving therapist aims to solve the problems causing the complaints and not the distresses themselves. The problems and their causes need to be differentiated using the chart in Figure 10.1.

The chart should also be used to teach the client to differentiate between problems and their causes. Similar to the one described by Gath and Mynors-Wallis (2000), defining and clarifying a client's problems in PST is composed of four subprocesses. These are: (1) identifying and defining emotional symptoms (complaints, distress), (2) formulating the problems, (3) making connections between the emotional symptoms and the problems, and (4) defining the problems. Each of the four processes will be explained separately as follows.

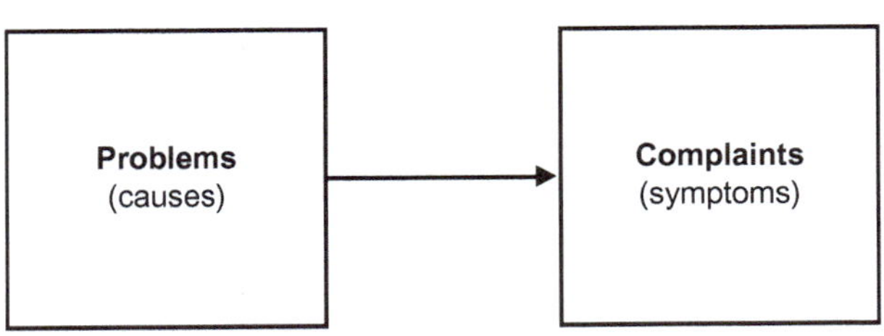

Figure 10.1 Differentiating between problems and complaints.

Identifying and Defining the Emotional Symptoms

Here, detailed information is gathered on the client's symptoms and complaints. The most common complaints of the clients applying to institutions for psychological help is the feeling of hopelessness, meaninglessness, boredom, willingness to escape, agitation, impulsiveness, anger, difficulty concentrating, etc. In certain cases, emotional symptoms may show themselves as physical or vegetative complaints such as stomach upset, headache, loss of appetite, sleeplessness, loss of sexual desire. Here, the client's emotional symptoms are being explored and listed in detail. This process of exploration is carried out with the cooperation of the client and the therapist.

Table 10.1 aims to identify complaints and their causes and is used to list the client's emotional symptoms. In this table, the client's complaints are noted in

Table 10.1 Identifying Complaints and Their Causes

Causes (Problems)	Emotional Symptoms (Complaints)
1.	1.
2.	2.
3.	3.
4.	4.
5.	5.
6.	6.
7.	7.
8.	8.
9.	9.
10.	10.
11.	11.
12.	12.
13.	13.
14.	14.
15.	15.
16.	16.
17.	17.
18.	18.
19.	19.
20.	20.

the column to the right under "Emotional Symptoms." Emotional symptoms should be explored and listed here. Sometimes the difficulties that the client experiences in interpersonal relations and in displaying or maintaining a specific behavior can be listed here as well.

Formulating the Problems

Those problems that the client has difficulty coping with and solving need to be explored here. What are the events that the client perceives as problems and that cause the client to experience psychological distress? Why does the individual feel unhappy? What are the reasons for this unhappiness? For instance, in the case of suicide, what are the problems that drive the individual to end his or her life? What are the apparent reasons for this behavior; in other words, what triggers this type of behavior? Problems can be personal, relational, material, work related, etc. The problems causing distress are emphasized at this stage. If the client is unable or unmotivated to define these problems, the therapist can urge the client to investigate the problems during the session.

The problems that make the client experience emotional symptoms are likely related to interpersonal relationships, work life, material things, and housing, health, and leisure time activities. The reasons for the client's complaints or symptoms should be written down in the left column of Table 10.1. The therapist should encourage the client to complete the chart.

There are some methods or techniques that can be used in differentiating and identifying the problems. The first method is determining the problem situations, the second is the screening method, the third is the stop-and-think method, and the fourth is the Lazarus technique. The problem-solving therapist should help the client identify the problems by using these techniques. The methods are shortly discussed in the following lines.

Identifying the problem situations: Problem solving starts with defining the problem situation. Defining problems in an accurate way may be the beginning of a process taking the individual to the correct target. That is why we have to analyze this stage very carefully. If we go back to the example of the individual who experiences problems in public speaking, we can see that the anxiety about making a bad presentation lies beneath the distress. The individual may be asked to keep a record of the situations in which the distress starts and intensifies. Such a record can reveal the circumstances in which the individual's mood changes and the disturbing affects appear.

The second method that can be used in identifying the problems is the *screening method*. In this method, different aspects of an individual's life cycle are reviewed and the therapist tries to assess the areas in which problems or distress has been experienced. Since a screening process on the life areas and stages will help the clients analyze and review their life in a systematic way, it will give them the opportunity to see the problems and distress that they experienced in various areas of life. For instance, problems and difficulties in marriage, private life, work life, relationships, material issues or carrier can be reviewed here.

The third technique that can be used to determine the problems or the problem situations is the *stop-and-think* technique. Here, the therapist teaches the client to use his or her emotions as signals. The client investigates the circumstances in which a sudden change in his or her own emotions takes place. The record-keeping system can be used here. By noticing the change in his or her emotions, the client investigates the circumstances in which negative affect expresses itself. As a result, the client perceives the situations in which emotions become negative as problem situations.

Finally, in the *Lazarus technique* (Lazarus, 1981), the therapist asks the client to describe the problem with one word. Then the therapist asks the client to use that word in a sentence that can describe his or her problem. This method is like an association method. For instance, a person who is about to divorce but has difficulty making a decision in that direction can say "divorce" in such a situation. This client can then use this word in a sentence such as "I cannot decide whether I should divorce or not." Here it will be clear that the client's problem is not the divorce but the difficulty he or she is experiencing in relation to the decision of divorce. The Lazarus technique can help clients free themselves of the effects of certain inhibitions.

The client–therapist collaboration is important for the individual's motivation during the problem identification stage. The client will not feel motivated to solve a problem that has been defined by somebody else. This is not a healthy practice in psychotherapy. In order to be motivated, the client should be able to see him- or herself as part of the process and be in a good relationship with his or her therapist.

One should pay attention to two points in defining problems. The first point is identifying clear and concrete problems. The client's problems need to be identified. This is done by the client and the therapist. It is appropriate here for the client to verbalize the problem in his or her own words. When problems are identified, one needs to be as clear as possible. Realities and assumptions need to be differentiated. One should stay away from the problems based on the client's assumptions. These subjective assumptions can be discussed as problems if necessary. The following questions can lead the patient to identify the problems in a clear and concrete way:

- What is the problem?
- When does the problem occur?
- What is the frequency of its occurrence?
- Where does the problem occur?
- Who is the problem related with?
- How serious is the problem?
- What is the problem's likelihood of being solved?

The second point is breaking the complex and general problems into smaller components. The client can talk about a general problem. It is difficult to deal with general and complex problems. In case such problems are brought up, the therapist should explain to the client in a simple way that dealing with them as they are will be difficult and unrealistic as far as therapeutic goals are concerned. That is why breaking them into smaller components to be discussed and solved during therapy is more appropriate. The therapist should guide the patient in that direction. For example, the patient can tell that the problem is his or her marriage. Here, the therapist, together with the client, should explore and identify the areas of the marriage that constitute a problem. Is the problem related to the spouse, to the kids, or to him- or herself? Is there a communication problem with the spouse? Is the problem related to his or her sex life? As can easily be understood, the problem of "marriage" is too complex and general to be worked on during therapy. Therefore, the general problems should be broken down into its smaller components.

At the stage of formulating the problems, the identified problems should be listed in the chart shown in Table 10.1 under the "Causes" column on the left. Up to this point, the affective symptoms of the client (complaints) and the problems causing them have been listed. Now it is the time to establish connections between the two.

Making Connections Between the Emotional Symptoms and the Problems

At this stage, a connection should be established between the clients' complaints and their causes (the problems). It should be explained to the client that their complaints are the emotional reactions they display to their problems. Examples should be used to help explain that their complaints will disappear when they are able to find solutions to the problems and are able to solve them. In order for the complaints to disappear, one should be able to find effective solutions to the problems. For instance, individuals who kill themselves see suicide as a solution. The individual should be encouraged to find effective solutions to their problems causing feelings of hopelessness.

The main goal here is to make connections between emotional symptoms and the problems. For various reasons, the client may be unable to see the problem or problems. The patient may perceive the emotional symptom or complaint as problems. In this case, the therapist should be able to see the real reason lying behind the patient's complaints and should be able to show it to the patient. The client should be informed that the real problem is not the symptoms/complaints but that another problem exists and that these symptoms are caused by that other problem. The therapist should go beyond the phenomenon, see the reasons behind the complaints, and both motivate and train the client to see it.

For example, a 14-year-old female client had to change her school because her family moved to another location within the same city. After the academic year started, the client started crying at school, which bothered the school administration and her peers. The client, who was brought to the therapy by her father, described the problem as "crying." She stated that her problems would be over when she stopped crying at school. The affective symptom and the complaint that the client brings to the therapy is "crying." During the process of PST, the client's inability to make friends at her new school appeared to be the reason behind her crying. The inability to make friends was identified as the problem and the therapy proceeded in that direction.

Finally, the emotional symptoms and the problem/causes should be associated and matched with each other. For this, the symptoms and the problems listed on the form should be matched with each other. The matching of the complaints with their underlying problems/causes listed on the form can easily be done with the help of a pen. This process should be done during the session by the client with the guidance of the therapist. This is a good exercise for the client to learn logic underlying clarification of complaints and their causes.

Defining the Problems

Up until now the client has learned that the things that bother him or her are symptoms or complaints and there are some factors or causes that bring them up. In the last stage of the problem-definition session, it is now the time to identify the problems that will be worked on. The process will be accomplished in three steps. First of all, the causes that have previously been listed in the form of identifying and differentiating the complaints and the causes should be written on the chart in Table 10.2 under the "Problems" column. Second, the problem candidates placed on the table should be scored. In the third stage, the problem candidates should be listed according to the scores they get.

After placing the problem candidates to the first column in Table 10.2, the problems should be scored. The problem candidates will be scored in two ways: according to their share in the emergence of the distress and the complaints and according to the extent to which they will decrease the complaints when they disappear (are resolved).

Scoring can be done between 0 ("Not at all") and 6 ("Too much"). If the problem candidate is thought to contribute too much to the emergence of the complaints and distress, a score of 6 should be written down next to it in the "Contribution" column. If it is thought to contribute at a moderate level, it should be given a score of 3, and if it is thought not to contribute at all, a score of 0 should be written down next to it. Similarly, in the "Decrease" column, if it is believed that the client's complaints will not decrease at all when the problem candidate disappears or solved, the problem should get a score of 0; if it is thought to decrease the complaint at a moderate level, it should get a score of 3; and if it is thought that the complaints will totally decrease when the problem disappears, the problem should get a score of 6.

At the final stage, scores are summed and the total scores are written down under the Score column. The problems are listed according to their scores in a descending order, from highest scoring to lowest scoring problems. The highest scoring one or two problems get selected by the client and the therapist. The selection may not be done based on the size of the scores. More creative methods can be used as well. Scoring is only one of the methods to which one can refer in identifying the problem. The suggestions of the therapist may sometimes be more important in the identification of the real problem. However, the client's views on the issue should be seen as very important. After all, it should be remembered that this is the client's therapy and he or she is the one who must work for it.

Table 10.2 Problem Identification Table

Problems	**Contribution**	**Decrease**	**Score**
1.			
2.			
3.			
4.			
5.			
6.			
7.			
8.			
9.			
10.			
11.			
12.			
13.			
14.			
15.			
16.			
17.			
18.			
19.			
20.			

Session IV: Goal Setting

The client comes to the PST with a problem or an agenda. There is a problem that needs to be resolved or a situation that needs to be dealt with in his or her own mind. He or she previously tried to solve or deal with the problem by him- or herself but has been unsuccessful at it. That is the reason for the use of PST. For healthy human functioning, goals are necessary. As the great philosopher Seneca says, "If one does not know to which port it is sailing, no wind is favorable." In order to benefit from the power of the wind, the ship needs to know the port she is sailing to.

Being able to set goals in life is important not only for those who seek psychological help but for the healthy development and functioning of all the individuals. If we take the words of Seneca into account, we can replace the ship with the individual, the port with the goal, and the wind with the opportunities and possibilities that life offers. The individual should identify a goal for him- or herself in order to take advantage of the possibilities and opportunities that life offers. In the process of psychotherapy, goals are the driving force for clients. Locke and Latham (1984) indicate that in the process of psychological help, goal setting has four important functions. Accordingly:

1. *Goals allow the clients to direct their attention and behavior toward a single point*: The clients who are able to set a goal by themselves or with the help of the therapist will concentrate their attention, energy, and behavior on the identified goal. This concentration will prevent them from wandering around in an aimless, scattered way, without knowing what to do, and will lead them toward a single desired direction.
2. *Goals activate the client's energy and efforts*: In a treatment process where goals are not set, the client will be wandering from one place to another without knowing what to do. Because he or she does not know which port he or she will be going to, the client will be enslaved by the wind and will not be able to improve. However, the ship that has a clear destination will be able to take advantage of the wind. Clearly identified therapeutic goals will activate both the client's and the therapist's energy and efforts.
3. *Goals motivate the clients to find ways to attain them*: The captain and the crew will be motivated to find the necessary ways to reach the port if the ship knows which port it will go to. A client who is able to set a therapeutic goal should be willing to search for the ways to attain that goal. A client who is willing to attain the goals will be open to change.
4. *Clearly set goals increase persistence*: Specific goals will help the client understand and grasp them in a clear way. It is important that the client understands the specific therapeutic goals during the process of psychotherapy. If the client understands the goals correctly, he or she will show the determination to attain them.

Now that we have discussed shortly the advantages of goal setting, we can talk about what the goals should be in PST. What kind of goals should we set? Do goals change according to the circumstances? Goals can be specified in two ways in PST. Similar to coping types described by Lazarus and Folkman (1984), the goals to attain by solving the problems defined in PST can be *problem-* or *emotion focused*. The difference and the relationship between these goals are beautifully stated in the following serenity prayer: "God grant me the serenity to accept the things I cannot change, the courage to change the things I can, and the wisdom to know the difference." Let us see now what these two goals are and under what circumstances they are being set.

Problem-Focused Goals

Problem-focused goals are those that necessitate an objective change in the problem situation. Problem-oriented goals are suitable for situations that can be changed. For instance, the goal to be set for an individual who cannot speak in public because of the fear of making mistakes, or for an individual who avoids relationships with other people, will be problem oriented. With certain therapeutic interventions, the client will be able to make changes in the problem situation as set by the problem-focused goal.

Emotion-Focused Goals

Emotion-focused goals are goals that aim to decrease the distress caused by a problem situation that cannot actively be changed. Let us take the case of a cancer patient as an example. It is apparent that cancer cannot be cured by PST. The goal to set for this patient can be to decrease the negative effect that the cancer diagnosis may have on the patient's psychology. However, the goal of the PST can be problem focused for a cancer patient who stops the chemotherapy or radiotherapy because of the adverse side effects. Because in this case, making changes in the problem situation is possible.

In the session for goal setting, the situation that the client wishes to attain needs to be determined. The client comes to the therapy with a problem. What does the client want to do with the problem, and what will the solution to the problem mean to the client? The point to be attained is in a sense the goal in problem solving. What does the therapy aim to do by solving the problem? Not every client knows where to go and how a problem can be solved in the best possible way. In case in which a client is confused and does not know what to do with the problem, the therapist can help and guide the client to clarify and identify the goal in a systematic way by asking the following questions:

- What does a better future look like?
- What will the resolution of your problem mean to you?
- What can be done in order to save you from the problems that bother you?

After the problems have clearly been identified, it is time for the therapist and the client to identify realistic and attainable goals for the therapeutic process. Treatment without a goal is not possible and psychotherapy is not an exception to this. The success of the psychotherapy depends largely on the identification of attainable goals. Otherwise after a while the client's ineffective cycle starts pulling the therapist into its own rhythm and puts the therapy into danger. In psychotherapy, it is important to occasionally review the goals with the client. In order for the PST to reach the desired outcome, the identified goals should be

- objective and goal oriented,
- defined in behavioral terms,
- attainable and realistic.

Certain resources are necessary to reach these goals. As is known, the client him- or herself possesses the necessary resources to attain the goals. If not enough, PST should aim at developing the client's resources for the attainment of goals. For this reason, it is important to know these resources. The problem should not be seen in a negative sense. Problems are inherent in life. Problems, in a sense, are strings that connect the individual to life. We should be concerned with when and how problems cause distress. Individuals seek psychological help when they do not have the necessary coping resources. That is why individuals' resources are extremely important. Personal resources are also important to reach the goals that have been identified during therapy. What lead the individual to the goal are the resources he or she possesses.

To give an example, since the individuals who have suicide problems are of perfectionist nature, they can identify difficult-to-reach goals for their treatment. The therapist can help the client set attainable and realistic goals. For this reason, the client–therapist collaboration is important. The client's resources that he or she may use in order to cope with the problems are important. These resources were discussed in detail in Chapter 9. Short reviews of the resources that can be taken into account in identifying goals are as follows:

- *Identifying the client's strengths and resources*: Every individual has strengths. Traditionally, clinical practices have focused on illnesses. This is apparently important but not complete. To be able to see the client as a human being and discover and bring his or her strengths and weaknesses out is an important clinical skill. Knowing the client's strengths and weaknesses will increase the reality of the goals within the specific conditions.
- *Identifying educational, spare time, and material resources*: Identifying these resources will increase the realness of the goals and will ease the therapeutic process. Otherwise, the identified goals will be nothing but assumptions and best wishes.
- *Identifying people who can provide social support*: As is known, social support is one of the most important resources assisting the individual through life's ups and downs. For this reason, the therapist should investigate the existence, the quality, or the lack of the client's social resources. If social support does not exist, then the reasons for this can be discussed within the context of problem-solving therapy.
- *Knowing of self-help groups that can help clients cope with their problems*: Identifying self-help groups and methods is an important step toward the resolution of problems. For instance, self-help groups such as Alcoholics Anonymous and Friends of Schizophrenics Association and information about them need to be reviewed. Knowing such information or characteristics will increase the reality and the applicability of the goals.

After identifying the type and the quality of the goals, the problem-solving therapist should help the client record the identified problem and goal(s) on the chart shown in Table 10.3. This can be seen as a simple process. However, taking the educational aspect of the psychotherapy into consideration, one will see that this is an important learning opportunity for the client. The identified problems and goals should be recorded on this chart.

Table 10.3 Goal Record Table

Problem: ....
Goal: ....
Goal: ....

Session V: Generating Possible Solution Alternatives

In this session, the therapist helps the client generate solution alternatives in the direction of the identified problems. Relevance of solutions to the defined problem is an important issue. Here, the therapist supports and helps the client. The generated solution alternatives should be listed on the chart shown in Table 10.4. These solutions may not be perfect. Here the client should be encouraged to generate as many solution alternatives as possible regardless of their nature. The aim in generating as many solution alternatives as possible is to have a sufficient number of potential solutions when a solution will be selected.

Table 10.4 Solution Alternatives

No.	Solution Alternative
1.	
2.	
3.	
4.	
5.	
6.	
7.	
8.	
9.	
10.	
11.	
12.	
13.	
14.	
15.	
16.	
17.	
18.	
19.	
20.	

As mentioned in the previous chapters, one of the common characteristics of inefficient problem solvers and those prone to develop psychopathology is *cognitive rigidity*. Persons who are cognitively rigid see the world and themselves through tunnel vision. Such individuals can display the behavioral characteristic of acting with the first idea that comes to their mind. Generating more than one solution to a problem helps the client alter or decrease this cognitive characteristic.

For the solution of the identified problem, clients can experience inhibitions in generating solution alternatives for various reasons. For this reason, some methods or techniques are used to facilitate the process of generating solutions. The following are five techniques that are commonly used.

Brainstorming Method

In this technique, the patient is encouraged to make the effort to generate as many solution alternatives as possible in relation to the problem. Here the individual is asked and encouraged to talk about every solution alternative that comes to his or her mind. The client is asked to generate as many alternatives as possible without making any judgments and without assessing their contribution to the solution. In other words, in this method the client is asked to tell and write down every single alternative that he or she can think of that can possibly solve the problem.

Reframing Method

Here the problem is reframed as a situation that can be dealt with and solved by the patient. With method reframing, the individual starts seeing events in a different way. For this reason, reframing may be of motivational character for the patient, in addition to the ability to generate solution alternatives. This method is similar to cognitive restructuring methods. It aims to stop the individuals' inhibitions that prevent them from generating solution alternatives by changing the client's frame of perspective. In this way, the clients are freed from their internal barriers and are motivated to generate alternative solutions. For instance, reframing a problem as an opportunity, unkindness as lack of understanding, etc., changes the meaning surrounding these events in the mind of a client.

Advising a Friend Method

This method is implemented by using the empty chair technique utilized in Gestalt therapy. Two chairs are placed facing one another. The client sits on one of them and is asked to pretend that a friend who experiences a similar problem sits on the other. The client is asked to offer solution alternatives that can solve the problem. The advantage of such an approach is that it allows for the client to be able to put some distance between him- or herself and the problem and thus be able to see the problem from a distance. Being able to put distance between oneself and the problem will save the individual from the internal inhibitions and this will liberate the individual. This liberation can help the client generate more solution alternatives.

Being a Hero Method

In this technique, after a short reminder on the characteristics of heroes, the client is asked to imagine him- or herself as a hero. Heroes are fearless and they possess the ability to do anything. The hero is reminded of the identified problem and is asked to generate as many solutions as possible. This method can be useful to help a patient get out of a problem when he or she is stuck. Internal inhibitions may prevent some clients to think of different ways of seeing, approaching, and handling situations deemed difficult. This method may especially prove useful for clients who are imaginative but have inhibitions.

Therapist's Advice

If the client is still not able to generate desired number of solution alternatives after all these facilitating techniques have been used, the therapist can offer some alternatives. One should not stick to the rule that solution alternatives must only come from the client. It is a good thing if the client can generate alternatives, but if he or she got stuck and is not able to do so, the therapist can offer his or her suggestions. The important point here is to make sure that the suggestions offered make sense to the client. Another point to keep in mind is that this therapy is for the client and he or she is the one to decide on the alternatives to be included in the list.

Some clients may be ineffective in generating solution alternatives and this may create emotional difficulty for them. In order to prevent this, the therapist should encourage the client in a constructive way. There are certain rules or principles that facilitate the generation of solution alternatives (Nezu et al., 1999). In using the techniques for the generation of solution alternatives, there are some rules that the client and the therapist must follow in order to prevent the client from getting stuck in the process. These rules are as follows:

- *No judging rule*: Do not judge the solution alternatives. The solution alternatives that come to the client's mind should not be judged as good or bad. These judgments can evoke anxiety in clients and can cause them to become stuck. The goal is to help clients become open to all the alternatives that they can think of.
- *Quantity rule*: According to this rule, the client should generate as many alternatives as possible. The aim is to be able to generate many alternatives. Here the goal should be to generate useful alternatives for the solution of the client's problem. The client is encouraged to generate a high number of solution alternatives and the process should be facilitated by the therapist.
- *Variety rule*: One should try to be original in generating alternatives. For this, the client should be able to use his or her imagination freely, without inhibitions. Contrary to the quantity rule, it is important here to generate various alternatives so that different aspects of the client's problem can be evaluated.
- *Nondichotomous thinking rule*: The client should be advised to avoid *black-and-white*, *all-or-nothing* type of judgments in generating alternatives. This type of thinking can present itself as a clinical problem.

Session VI: Choosing the Appropriate Solution

In this session, the therapeutic task is to choose the most appropriate solution from among the solution alternatives generated in the previous session. The client will soon take action to solve the identified problem to reach the goal he or she set for his or her treatment. In the problem-solving literature, this stage is also known as the decision-making stage. A decision will be made here about the most appropriate alternative for the resolution of the problem. Making the decision should be a collaboration between the client and the therapist. One should not forget that the client is the one who has the best information about his or her own life. The goal of this stage is to decide on the most appropriate solution alternative on the list.

How will one decide on the most appropriate solution alternative? According to which standards will the decision be made? Who will be able to know which alternative is the most appropriate? The golden rule when deciding on the most appropriate alternative is, "The appropriate solution alternative should both solve the problem and realize the goal." Is a solution that can solve the problem but cannot realize the goal an appropriate solution? The answer to this question is without any doubt "no."

What the golden rule will be like and how it will work is illustrated in the following example. A 17-year-old male client who was treated by the author wanted to tell his parents that he was homosexual but he was not able to express it. He ran away from home to another city with all the money that he secretly got from his parents. The client was found in that city by the police. During PST, it was agreed that the client had the problem of "not being able to express himself and to say no" and the goal was set as "being able to express his thoughts and to say no." During the meetings, the client indicated that even though he did not want to go out with his friends he had to do so because he was unable to say no to his friends. He then indicated that the most appropriate solution when his friends came over to ask him out was "to make his mother tell his friends that he was not home even though he was." The client thought that this would solve his problem. However, when he was asked whether or not this chosen solution would be able to meet the goal, he had identified for himself, he was able to see that the chosen solution alternative was not appropriate.

After discussing the golden rule for choosing the most appropriate solution, it is now the time to go over and evaluate the solution alternatives listed in the previous session. The evaluation of the solution alternatives is done in two ways. These are qualitative and quantitative evaluations. Qualitative evaluation can lay the groundwork for the qualitative evaluation, or can be used by itself in the decision making. In other words, both of the evaluations can be used by themselves or in a complementary way. The following processes need to be used for the quantitative evaluation:

- *A cost–benefit analysis is conducted for each alternative*: The advantages and disadvantages of each solution alternative are discussed. What the benefit and the cost of each solution alternative might be for the client and his or her close environment is emphasized.

- *Solution alternatives are compared with one another*: The advantages and disadvantages of each solution alternative are comparatively analyzed. These comparisons may provide the client with information on the relative advantages and disadvantages of the solutions and help him or her identify the alternatives better.
- *The client's personal and social resources are evaluated*: The compatibility of each solution alternative with the client's resources is reviewed here. This review may give the client some clues about the applicability of the solution alternatives. A solution alternative beyond the client's personal or social resources will lead to failure and will decrease his or her motivation to a great extent.

After the qualitative evaluation, solution alternatives are quantitatively evaluated; a numeric value facilitates the choice of the appropriate solution. Deciding on the best choice to reach the defined goal based on a numeric value may simplify the client's task. We can assume that the quantitative evaluation will be less affected by factors such as the client's blind spots, cognitive distortions, personal characteristics, social desirability, and the like.

The quantitative evaluation can be carried out by using the chart provided in Table 10.5. The quantitative evaluation is done in two steps. In the first, the solution alternatives from the solution alternative record table (Table 10.4) should be copied to Table 10.5. In the second, each solution alternative is scored using the following four criteria. Similar criteria were also suggested by Nezu et al. (1999). Each item is scored from 1 to 5, with 1 being "the lowest" and 5 being "the highest." Then for each solution, scores obtained from four criteria are summed and written under the Total Score column. Consequently, the score for each alternative will be the combination of four criteria. Therefore, the lowest score for each alternative will be 4 and the highest score will be 20. Then solution alternatives are ranked from the highest to the lowest scoring solutions. Taking the information obtained from the qualitative evaluation into account, the client and the therapist reviews this ranking and they make the decision of the most appropriate alternative. The criteria that can be used for the quantitative evaluation are the following.

The Alternative's Ability to Solve the Problem

The extent to which each solution alternative will solve the defined problem gets evaluated here. For instance, the alternatives that will solve the client's problem of self-expression are those that will be helpful in overcoming the situation defined in the problem. It is clear that writing poems will not solve this client's problem of self-expression. This, in a sense, is the relevancy of the solution alternatives to the problem.

The Solution's Congruence with the Goal

As stated earlier, the appropriate solution alternative will both solve the problem and meet the identified goal. The solution alternative's congruence with the goal and the extent to which it will meet the goal is evaluated by this criterion. The appropriate solutions for a client who has a problem with self-expression should be able to solve the problem and should satisfy the goal of self-expression.

Table 10.5 Evaluation of the Solution Alternatives

Solution Alternative	Solving Problem					Congruence with the Goal					Applicability					Acceptability					Total Score
	1	2	3	4	5	1	2	3	4	5	1	2	3	4	5	1	2	3	4	5	

The Solution's Applicability

Whether or not a solution alternative can practically be applied is evaluated by this criterion. A solution alternative should be able to solve the problem, meet the goal, and at the same time be applicable in order to be considered as an appropriate solution. An alternative with a low likelihood of being applied cannot be considered as an appropriate solution. When the applicability of a solution is being assessed within the specific circumstances of a client, it may not be appropriate to use a single criterion that generally applies to every client. In other words, while the applicability of a solution alternative may be high under certain life circumstances, it may be low under another circumstance, and moderate in some others. An important criterion that can be used in assessing the applicability of a given solution alternative can be "congruence with the client's resources." An alternative can be an appropriate solution; however, if the client's personal and social resources are insufficient, the applicability of that solution will be low. In this case, one way could be to increase the clients' resources.

The Solution's Acceptability

Solution alternatives should be evaluated in terms of their acceptability for the client and his or her social environment. A solution alternative can solve the problem and can meet the goal; however, its acceptability in terms of the individual's social status, moral values, and social relationships can be low. Its implementation can result in the emergence of other problems for the client.

At end of this session when the qualitative and quantitative evaluations are carried out, the three solution alternatives that are thought to solve the problem and meet the goal to higher extent than others should be recorded on the chart shown in Table 10.6. The implementation should start with the first solution alternative that is thought to be the most appropriate.

Session VII: Solution Implementation

In PST, after the appropriate solution alternatives are chosen from among the alternatives that will solve the defined problem and meet the identified goal, it is time for implementing the solution. This is the action stage. For instance, for the client who has the problem of "being unable to say no," the solution alternative chosen that will

Table 10.6 Appropriate Solution Alternative Record

No.	Appropriate Solution Alternatives
1	
2	
3	

meet the goal of saying no will be implemented in real life. There are certain processes and topics that should be accomplished and followed during the implementation stage.

The first thing to do during therapy before implementing the solution alternative is to discuss and deal with the client's fears. Some clients may find the solution alternative complex and may be intimidated by it. That is why the implementation stage should be designed in such a way that will motivate the client. Implementing a solution means the client makes certain changes in him- or herself. A change that will be implemented on a personal level contains some risks and fears. Therefore, the therapist should focus on the client's fears and on perceived risks during the implementation stage. One should not forget that the perceived risks may cause the client to become passive. Certain topics such as fears, the kinds of risks these fears may carry, the extent to which these fears are realistic, and how they will affect the realization of the solution should be discussed.

A client's motivation is important for the success of the therapeutic processes. Motivation fuels change. A proverb says "It is not the towering sail, but the unseen wind that moves the ship." Here, the unseen wind is the motivation. That is why motivating the client before the implementation stage is the prerequisite for a successful implementation. Being part of the treatment and assuming responsibility play an important role in clients' motivation. An important principle in relation to being behaviorally motivated is assuming responsibility. A client who assumes responsibility will be motivated in terms of therapeutic practices or processes.

Another important point to keep in mind in the implementation stage is the readiness of the client. Waiting for the client to feel ready for the implementation of the solution will increase the likelihood of getting positive results. In other words, the client should be ready for change. The role of the problem-solving therapist in this respect is to wait and make the steps that will help the client feel ready for the implementation, without forcing the client and without any rush. Rushing and forcing the client when the client does not feel ready does not comply with the principles of psychotherapy and this will result in failure. The client should feel ready for the implementation. Unless people feel mentally ready for doing something they keep away from doing it.

Another thing that should be done at this point is to evaluate, assess, and identify the client's behavioral characteristics and tendencies. Knowing the kinds of behavioral characteristics the client displays in the face of problems will help the therapist guide the client in a safe way. For instance, does the client act with the first idea that comes to his or her mind when faced with a problem situation? Or does he or she have the tendency to ignore the problems? We have seen earlier that impulsive/careless and avoidant problem-solving styles are ineffective ways of dealing with problems. It will be helpful to discuss these behavioral tendencies at the implementation stage even though the interventions to decrease these behavioral characteristics have been discussed at the problem orientation training stage.

Before engaging in an important act, people often calculate the pros and cons. If the pros are heavier than cons, they choose to do or engage in that thing. Accordingly, one thing that can be done to motivate the client is to ask the client to list the positive and negative consequences of implementing a solution. Similarly, the client can also be asked to list the positive and negative consequences of not being able to implement a solution. Another technique would be asking the client to imagine the future in case he or she is or is not able to implement a given solution. The chart in Table 10.7 should be used when implementing these methods.

One of the things that should be done before implementing the solution alternative is to identify the client's skill level in relation to the implementation. For

Table 10.7 Evaluating the Consequences of Implementing and Not Implementing the Solution

Positive Consequences of Implementing the Solution
1.
2.
3.
4.
5.
Negative Consequences of Implementing the Solution
1.
2.
3.
4.
5.
Positive Consequences of Not Implementing the Solution
1.
2.
3.
4.
5.
Negative Consequences of Not Implementing the Solution
1.
2.
3.
4.
5.

instance, a client who will try to say "no" to others may not know how to do it or may confuse it with aggressive behaviors. In that case, what "saying no" is and how it will be done may be shown in the comfort and privacy of the therapist's office. For instance, let us say the goal of "expressing oneself appropriately" is chosen as a solution for the treatment of the client who experiences physical and mental health problems as a result of self-expression difficulties. The efforts in this direction may first be taught to the client through the use of role-play exercises in the client's office. Here the therapist, via role-play, shows how the client will be able to express him- or herself in an appropriate way. The problem-solving therapist prepares the client for the implementation of the solution by discussing the problems that can possibly appear during these processes.

Finally, it is time to identify how the implementation will be carried out in real life. Client–therapist cooperation plays an important role in creating an action plan that will be prepared for the client's practice implementation of the solution. At this stage, the way this implementation will be carried out can be designed as a homework assignment. One should pay attention here to plan and design the implementation in such a way that will solve the problem and meet the goal. Taking into account the specific life circumstances such as the client's personal and social resources, socioeconomic status, and moral values will be important for the implementation to reach the goal and for the formation and preservation of the therapeutic principle and cooperation. The next step following the implementation in the PST is the assessment of the implementation.

Session VIII: Assessing the Implementation

For a client seeking PST to display a positive approach to his or her problems, problem orientation training has been delivered, the problem(s) causing distress have been defined, the treatment goal has been set, solution alternatives have been generated, the appropriate solution has been chosen, and the chosen solution alternative has been implemented. After all these process, it is now the time to evaluate the implementation, which is the last session in PST. The goal of this last session is to identify and evaluate how the implementation went. Here, the client and the therapist evaluate and assess the results of the implementation and that of the therapy in general. In this session two points are being emphasized. The first is the evaluation of the implementation of the solution and the second one is the evaluation of the treatment in general.

Evaluating the Implementation

In order to be able to evaluate the implementation, the client and the therapist discuss the extent to which the therapeutic goals have been reached. It will be useful to look for the answers to the following questions during the implementation. Has the implementation of the chosen solution alternative been successful? What are the results of the implementation? Has the identified problem been solved with the implementation? Has the identified therapeutic goal been met by the implementation of the solution? Has there been a decrease in the client's complaints? Will the client be able to implement similar practices by him- or herself for other problems? If the answers to these questions are positive, the client and the therapist may decide to end the problem-solving treatment or to deal with another problem.

In evaluating the implementation of the chosen solution, the answers to be given to the third and fourth questions in the preceding paragraph are important. If the problem has not been solved and the goal has not been met, answers to the following questions must be sought:

- Does the logic behind the PST make sense to the client?
- Has the problem been accurately defined?
- Have the goals been clearly identified?
- Are the goals realistic?
- Have a sufficient number of solution alternatives been generated?
- Has the appropriate solution alternative been chosen?
- Has the solution been implemented in an appropriate way?
- Is the implementation of the solution difficult? If it is, what is the reason?

If the implementation has not been successful, the therapist and the client try to determine where during the problem-solving process there has been a problem. For instance, if the problem has not been accurately defined, one should go back to the problem-definition stage and restart from there. If the goal has not been accurately identified, one should go to the goal-setting session and restart from there.

Evaluating the Therapy in General

At this stage, the therapeutic process as a whole should be evaluated, no matter whether the therapy has been successful or not. If the therapy has been successful, the therapist should make explorations on the kinds of practices that the client thinks have been effective or ineffective. The results from this exploration give important clues to both the client and the therapist. Based on the results, the therapist can find new opportunities in the practices of PST. And the client finds the opportunity to review the whole process and think about the processes implemented during therapy. This kind of review will give the client the opportunity to store the information and the skills acquired during the problem-solving process as metacognitions in his or her memory and make use of them in the future.

The metacognitive component of problem solving was discussed in Chapter 3. Metacognitive skills include the general framework about the rules and knowledge to follow in implementing a work and the way in which it is being carried out. The metacognitive components of problem solving include information on the way the problem-solving process will be carried out. One should not forget that evaluating the therapy as a whole will create the opportunity for both the client and the therapist to better understand the treatment process.

Conclusion and Suggestions

This chapter outlined eight sessions of PST lasting 30–45 minutes each. However, the time can be extended or shortened depending on the circumstances. Although eight sessions have been suggested here for the treatment of a client, the number of sessions can also be increased depending on the situational demands. Changing the number of sessions and the duration of each session depending on the circumstances is important for the adaptation of the treatment to the needs of a specific client.

It is important to emphasize what should and should not be done in implementing the PST. How should PST be conceived? What should one pay attention to during its practice? D'Zurilla and Nezu (2003) emphasize eight points that should and should not be done during the practice of PST accordingly.

PST Is Not a Mechanical Practice

The human factor should be taken into account during the practice of PST. One should not forget that warmth and positive relationships are as important as technique in psychotherapy. As mentioned earlier, psychotherapy is a journey that the client and the therapist embark upon together. Since this journey belongs to two individuals, it is impossible to think of it in isolation from human feelings. The problem-solving therapist should acknowledge the fact that feelings give life its color and depth, should give feelings their due importance during treatment, and should see them as materials to work on. Including the feelings in the therapy will contribute to the formation of a positive therapeutic environment. A positive therapeutic environment and client–therapist relationship will have a positive influence on the therapy and will make the therapeutic activity meaningful for the client and the therapist.

PST Should Be Relevant to the Client

The therapist should adapt the PST to the client's needs. As is known, in psychotherapy, the client and the problems are more important than the therapy and its techniques. That is why, implementing a therapy without adapting it to the needs of a specific client may decrease the therapeutic effect of the psychotherapy, and it may even be detrimental.

In the practice of psychotherapy, adapting the therapy to the client's needs and to the nature of the problem is called tailoring. The problem-solving therapist should conduct the therapy by taking the nature of the problem and the client's needs into consideration. One should always keep in mind that just as it is impossible to have psychotherapy without human beings, it is impossible to implement despite human beings. Psychotherapy can only take place in an environment in which the client and the therapist cooperate.

Homework Assignments Should Be Used

Successful PST, like other cognitive–behavioral approaches to psychotherapy, should not be carried out without assigning homework. That is why the therapist should not forget to assign homework. Homework assigned between the sessions will give the client the opportunity to review and learn by him- or herself. And this will help the client develop self-competency. One can infer the importance of homework from the fact that the ultimate goal in cognitive–behavioral therapies is to make the client become his or her own therapist.

PST Should Be Client Centered

In order for the therapy to be successful, it should be implemented in the right way; however, the human factor should never be forgotten. The real focus for the problem-solving therapist should be the client as much as the therapy itself. One should not forget that the therapy is for the client, and without the client the therapy loses all its meaning. A PST that forgets about the client and focuses on the technique may formally be a perfect therapy; however, it will not be a successful one. What will make it a successful implementation is its ability to focus on the client and his or her problems.

The Therapy Should Not Focus Solely on Superficial Problems

The problem-solving therapist, using his or her professional competence, should be able to know and identify the client's most important problems that need to be dealt with rationally. The therapist should waste neither his nor her own nor the client's time and energy by focusing on superficial problems.

The Therapist Should Focus on the Implementation of the Solution

After the solution alternatives have been identified, the client should be encouraged to make the effort to implement the chosen alternative. The essence of the PST is the implementation of the chosen solution that has been thought to meet the identified goal. Emphasizing the way in which the implementation will be carried out, the obstacles before it, and the facilitating factors—and then dealing with them during the therapeutic process—will help the therapist focus on the implementation of the solution.

Feelings Should Not Be Ignored During PST

Emotions are important in human behaviors and they can be the source of distress as well as happiness. For this reason, PST should focus on emotion-focused goals as well as problem-focused goals. PST can be conceived as an implementation with certain stages and processes. But this is not true. Emotions, which add beauty and color to life, should be within the range of the PST just as the rational aspects of life are. Experienced problem-solving therapists should include the client's emotional world into the therapeutic process, should work with them, and should know how to make use of the client's emotional world in the direction of the therapeutic goals.

Printed Material Should Be Used During Therapy

Such materials are extremely important for the clients and the therapist. The printed material should be prepared in such a way that will be able to deal with the clients and the problems. This material will increase the efficacy and the strength of the therapy. Printed material is not for the use of the therapist only. Problem-solving therapists can make the treatment more effective by giving this educational printed material to their clients. The printed material can include the importance and the nature of problem-solving process.

11 An Example of a PST Application

Case History and Formulation

Referral

The patient's mother applied to the author, Dr. Mehmet Eskin, indicating that her daughter wanted to get help. Dr. Eskin referred the patient to Canan Celik Ozden, one of his graduate students in clinical psychology who, at that time, saw patients under Dr. Eskin's supervision. The first appointment was made by the patient's mother.

Description of the Patient

The patient is a 16-year-old girl. She looks older for her age because of her advanced physical development. She styles the front part of her hair in such a way that it covers her eyebrows and a significant part of her eyes. She always wears a leather jacket.

The patient attended the 10th grade when she started the therapy; however, upon the fourth session, she indicated that she had suspended her registration at school. The patient lives in a medium-sized city located in the southwestern region of Turkey with her mother, a younger sister 2 years her junior, and her stepfather.

The patient's biological father lives in a large city on the Mediterranean coast with his second wife and a new baby. He sees the patient once or twice a year, and they have telephone conversations a few times a month. The patient indicated that she never called her father, and that they talked whenever the father called her.

She describes her stepfather as a calm person who does not interfere in her life unless her mother provokes him, who regularly drinks one to two glasses of alcohol every night, and who supports her when necessary.

She describes her mother as an irate person who does not care about her, who has made many mistakes (mainly her mother's extramarital affairs), and who cannot be tolerated for more than a few minutes in the same environment.

She describes her sister as a much more harmonious person compared to herself, who gets along much better with her father and mother, and who does not experience any problems at school. She thinks that her sister is favored by her mother. She associates her sister's harmonious character to her not witnessing her mother's mistakes.

Problem Solving Therapy in the Clinical Practice. DOI: http://dx.doi.org/10.1016/B978-0-12-398455-5.00011-5

Primary Complaints

The patient's primary complaints are the following: getting easily irritable, attacking and damaging things and people around her when she gets angry (physical violence), experiencing intense fights with family members at home and with peers at school (she cut some people's face with a razor blade at school), her belief in not being cared by her mother, and the sorrow that this creates for her.

History of Complaints

Starting at 11 years old, the patient witnessed her mother's extramarital affairs and her parents' fighting. She started to live with her mother after her parents divorced. She stated that she never approved of her mother's life and that she has always been angry with her.

She said that her complaints about being irritable and her fights with her mother started 2 years ago after her mother came home and slapped her while she was sitting at home with her boyfriend, insulted her, and took her to the physician for virginity control. (Although this practice has been illegal in Turkey since 2005, incidents such as this still occur in traditional segments of the population.) This state of irritability increased gradually and became prevalent.

History of Treatment

In the last 2 years, the patient has told her mother on various occasions that she wanted to get psychological help; however, she was unable to convince her mother. She indicated that she had insisted upon it a lot recently and finally convinced her mother to set an appointment. She does not have a prior history of therapy. During the sessions, no treatment method was implemented in addition to psychotherapy.

Psychological Assessment

Assessment Instruments Administered

The patient was administered Beck Depression Inventory (BDI), Beck Anxiety Inventory (BAI), Rotter Sentence Completion Test (RSCT), Minnesota Multiphasic Personality Inventory (MMPI), and Social Problem-Solving Inventory Revised (SPSI-R).

Findings Obtained from the First Measurements

BDI and BAI: The patient got 22 from BDI and 53 from BAI. These scores are significantly above the cutoff scores of the scales and point out that the patient experiences depression and anxiety at an intense level.

RSCT: The most frequently repeated themes in the RSCT include the desire to get rid of problems with family, the desire to move away from the family, and the uneasiness felt from being easily irritable. The patient indicated that she sometimes cried secretly, had difficulty falling asleep at night, experienced conflict with the other female students at school, and that is why she was seen as a dangerous person from the people around. Even though she stated that she was hopeful for the future, themes indicating the patient's belief that her mother did not sufficiently care about her and her sorrow about that were detected.

MMPI: The fact that the patient was an adolescent was taken into account and corrected for in evaluating the MMPI profile. The evaluations of the clinical and validity scales were evaluated accordingly. The configuration of the validity scales showed that the patient acknowledged her personal and emotional difficulties and that, being unable to cope with her problems, she asked for help. The elevated F subscale suggested that the patient wanted urgent help by exaggerating her problems.

According to MMPI clinical scales, anger, resentment, being sulky, extreme sensitivity to criticism and to others' requests, and blaming others are the main characteristics of the patient. The patient might have felt easily rejected and criticized. With very few data at hand and very little forethought, the patient might have reached the opinion that she was neglected and that others were at fault. Since the particular patient, Zeynep will rarely think about the role she has in experiencing troubles, it is not surprising that she experiences problems with close relations and social relationships. Lack of insight and impulsivity might be the main characteristics of the patient. Drug abuse can be expected. Academic failures might be related to the adaptation problems caused by impulse-control problems.

DSM-IV Diagnosis

Decrease in the patient's frustration threshold and signs of irritability and discomfort have emerged increasingly within the last 2 years. She has difficulty falling asleep. She usually spends 1–2 hours in bed before she sleeps. She occasionally cries by herself, she thinks she is not cared for enough, and she carries feelings of worthlessness. Even though she has not made any suicide attempts, she expresses that she has thought of it. Hurting herself with a razor blade and using physical violence against her environment are frequently encountered situations. Her academic success has gradually decreased and her adaptation problems at school increased; finally, she dropped out.

Axis I: Major depressive disorder
Axis II: None
Axis III: None
Axis IV: Family, peer, and academic problems
Axis V: Global Assessment of Functioning, current 55%.

Treatment

PST was applied based on the contents of the sessions outlined in Chapter 10. The first meeting was held on October 21, 2010, and the subsequent meetings were held once a week. The duration of the sessions ranged between 30 and 45 minutes.

The solution implementation was carried out in two sessions. Consequently, except for the follow-up sessions, nine sessions of PST were implemented with this patient. Besides PST sessions, the patient was given a problem-solving skills book for clients titled *I Can Solve My Problems* (Eskin, 2010).

In addition to weekly PST sessions provided to the client, two counseling sessions were offered to the patient's mother. In the first counseling session, effective parental behaviors such as rules, setting boundaries, and distinguishing between being a parent and a friend to children were covered. In the second, a general evaluation of the treatment process was done. Since the mother is known to the psychiatry department as a former patient with a borderline personality disorder, her own treatment needs and compliance with the treatment recommendations were discussed in this session as well.

Ethical Issues

Before the sessions, the need to get voice recordings for supervision had been explained to the patient and her mother; when they both approved, a written approval form was signed. The patient and her mother were told that voice recordings during the sessions would be acquired for the purpose of supervision.

The confidentiality principle was explained to the patient in the first session, and because she was not yet at the age of adulthood, she was reminded that in situations where she had the likelihood of (a) problems with the law, (b) using drugs, (c) seriously hurting herself or another person would be shared with her family, and her approval was obtained on this issue.

Pre- and Posttreatment Measurements

Following the end of the patient's treatment, the SPSI-R, BDI, and BAI that had been administered before the onset of the treatment were repeated and the results were compared with those obtained from the first administration. Pre- and posttreatment scores are provided in the following table. According to this, it was found that the patient's depression score, which was 22 before the treatment, dropped to 10; her anxiety score dropped from 53 to 20, and the SPSI-R total score increased from 12.3 to 16.3. The scores obtained from these scales are an indication that the patient made considerable improvement in terms of the signs of depression and anxiety, and social problem solving.

Measurement Instruments	Pretreatment	Posttreatment
Social Problem-Solving Inventory Revised (SPSI-R)	12.3	16.3
Beck Depression Inventory (BDI)	22	10
Beck Anxiety Inventory (BAI)	53	20

Patient's Views on the Therapy

During the "Assessing the Implementation" session, the patient indicated that at the beginning of the therapy she believed that it would be difficult for her to control her anger and comply with the requirements of therapy and that she thought that she had a very low likelihood of being successful. However, as the therapy proceeded, her thoughts gradually changed. The patient expressed this with the following sentences: "Actually, when I first learned about it, it seemed like a very difficult thing to do. However, when I started implementing it, I realized it was easy. I thought I wouldn't be able to control my anger but I was wrong."

She said that she felt relief for the first time in the goal-setting session, and after she identified a goal to be reached during therapy, her self-confidence and her trust in the therapy increased. On the other hand, she indicated that some of the techniques that she learned had been very useful and that they helped her notice certain things she had never been aware of. She also indicated that she made considerable improvement on controlling herself and behaving in an appropriate manner. The patient expressed this with the following sentences: "Especially after I set the goal, I was deeply relieved, I said I could do it. What impressed me the most was the question of 'How come?' I was hurting people badly. But now I don't have to hurt anybody after I ask this question. I am calm as well. I always ask to make sure, 'how come?' "

Termination of the Treatment

The first appointment given after the last session of the PST was for 2 weeks later. Later on, monthly meetings were planned until school started. During the meeting 2 weeks after the completion of PST, it was found that gains were maintained and that the patient started working as a staff member at a gym. The patient was called before the appointment for the following month, and the patient reported that she would not be able to make it for the appointment because she was working hard, but that she was doing well.

Session I: Assessment and Providing Rationale

Synopsis of the session: *Meeting the patient, becoming familiar with her distress, providing information on the content, rationale, and the format of the therapy, and filling out the self-report measurement instruments with the purpose of making the initial evaluations of the patient were actualized in this session.*

Canan: Welcome, Zeynep. My name is Canan. I am a graduate student in clinical psychology. I would like to repeat what I have just asked you before, for the records, because my supervisor would like to hear it. I would like to record our conversations if you don't mind. We will listen to them together with Professor Eskin. This is something that will help us conduct your therapy. What do you think about it?

Zeynep: OK. No problem.

Canan: OK, thank you. Zeynep, your mother called us to make an appointment. First of all, did you need this appointment? Did you ask for it?

Zeynep: I needed help 2 years ago. My mother postponed, postponed, and postponed it. Finally, I insisted a lot and she made this appointment.

Canan: OK, then you are the one who wanted this appointment the most.

Zeynep: Yes.

Canan: Good, because what we will be accomplishing here is not something that will be possible if you don't want it. It is important that you feel the need; it is not sufficient that your mother needs it only. I am glad that you are willing as well. Do you have any idea about what we will be doing here? Have you ever been in such a meeting before?

Zeynep: No, I haven't.

Canan: Here, I would like to learn about your needs primarily. I mean, why did you need to come here? What happened within the last 2 years that made you feel you needed this meeting? We will first talk about that. While we talk, sometimes I may be the one who listens more, and sometimes you may be the one who listens more. We will listen to the problems you are telling, and we will try to solve them, define them, and understand them so that we can overcome them. Each of our meetings will last for about 45 minutes. But sometimes we may need to extend or shorten it; we may be flexible in certain situations. We will keep meeting by fixing an appointment every week. Do you have any questions?

Zeynep: But everything will stay here right? I mean, my mother will not know about anything.

Canan: Of course, you can be sure about it. But I would like to remind you that my supervisor will know about our conversations since there will be a voice recording here. Since you are a minor there are three exceptions to this rule: If I notice that you have the potential to hurt yourself or somebody else seriously, that you are in trouble with the laws, and that you are using illegal substances, I may have to share this with your family or another legal person in charge in order to protect you, but never without informing you.

Zeynep: Let me put it this way: I will tell things that will upset my mother here. I don't want her to get upset.

Canan: I understand.

Zeynep: Otherwise, you can tell everything you want, it doesn't matter.

Canan: OK, we made a deal then. Could you please tell me now why you needed such a meeting? What is the problem that brings you here?

Zeynep: Let me tell you: My mother. I have been subject to very bad events ever since I was 11 years old. My mother's suicide attempts, my parents' divorce, my father beating my mother... and I know a lot about my mother. How should I tell this, I know things that will make me hate my mother, but I don't hate her? For example, I saw my mother having an affair with somebody else when she was married with my father. I saw it with my own eyes. I heard them getting into a relationship, I saw them. I saw it and heard it in every way. My mother used to leave us alone at home, at 3, 4 o'clock in the morning, or leave us at the neighbor's, and go next to that man. I mean, I knew everything. But I was young at that time, I was 10, 11 years old, I wasn't thinking about it. I wanted my mother to be happy but I had never thought this would hurt me in the future.

Canan: OK, can you answer this for me please: What kind of problems did the things that you saw and experienced create in you?

Zeynep: We fight a lot with my mother. We usually fight every day. And I think I have a nerve sickness, I don't know but I get mad to the tiniest things. I either break everything or I hurt the girls outside. My mother knows about it, I once chopped up a girl's face with a razor blade, I mean I cut. My mother, my sister, they all know about it. For example, my sister says, there is a fight, come and save me, I go immediately. Sometimes I even feel like beating up my mother. I mean, I am that angry. My mother values my sister more. She always neglects me. For example, she buys more clothes for her, she buys telephone, she does this to her and I stay aside. This upsets me, what can I say?

Canan: OK, to wrap up a little bit: You are telling that you are quick-tempered; you get angry at the tiniest things. You fight with the people at home or in the surrounding. And you also have the feeling of not being cared for enough, as far as I understand.

Zeynep: But this is true, my aunt knows it as well.

Canan: And this upsets you.

Zeynep: Yes. We went to Ankara [the capital of Turkey]. I was born in Ankara. My mother is married now, maybe you know it. There was a man called [name withheld] who she used to see there. And I did not want them to see each other, let me tell you frankly. She was married, and who knows what others would say when she met with another man. And she has two daughters. She goes and sees this man, she calls us with her. She had a fight with my aunt, and I know my mother is guilty, that's why I did not go with her, I stayed with my aunt in Ankara. My aunt started to tell me what is right and what is wrong. Meanwhile, I cry of course, I have nervous breakdown, I mean I am bad. One thing that my mother had done really upset me. My father, my sister's and my biological father, put 9000 liras in a bank account for our future. And my mother spent this money freely with other men in here and there. I know all this, and my aunt knows it also, I mean we know everything. I could have studied in a better school. My mother has lots of credit card debts. She could have paid off her debts. There was going to be lots of money there, money that was reserved many years ago. We would not have been in trouble. My mental state would not be that bad. Why do you spend that money with men? I got very angry when I heard it. I know lots of other things, that she lost her virginity when she was 17 years old, that she had one-night stands many times, I know lots of other things.

Canan: Fine, how do you witness all these things Zeynep? How do you hear? How do you learn about these?

Zeynep: There is a terrace in my aunt's house in Ankara. My aunt and my cousin talk there. My cousin is older; I mean she is in her thirties. I go inside telling them that I feel sleepy, I am curious about what they will talk about. Then, I start listening to them, and finally I no longer stand it and I go into the room.

I tell them that they should tell me everything. I told them I wanted to know everything. They did not deny anything. They told me everything.

Canan: Was it the first time you heard about them?

Zeynep: Yes.

Canan: How old were you at that time?

Zeynep: This happened this year, but I had witnessed everything earlier anyway, but I did not know about their consequences.

Canan: OK Zeynep, you talked about consequences, you said you were often fighting, that you were easily irritated, that you were sad, and I can see it as well now as you tell. When did your sadness and irritability start in the first place, as far as you can remember?

Zeynep: Two years ago.

Canan: Two years ago. OK, do you remember how it started? Do you remember how these things became evident?

Zeynep: I remember of course. One day, I was sitting home with my boyfriend. Of course, we were doing nothing; we were just sitting, drinking Coke. He was not a kind of boy who would make sexual demands, even if he did, I know already what is right and what is wrong, I would not do it. One day, my mother hears about it, comes home, she knocks on the door. We actually met with this boy before, and my mother knew it. I go and open the door, my mother slaps me but I don't feel it. She comes and tells lots of things to my boyfriend and to me. She takes me to the doctor to see whether I am virgin or not. She beats me up. Ever since that day, I cannot control my anger. I get suddenly angry. We have a fight at home, for example, I must go out and beat somebody up, I must discharge my anger. Otherwise I cannot discharge my anger.

Canan: How often do these fights at home take place?

Zeynep: Let me tell you this, my mother and I cannot stay in the same room for more than an hour.

Canan: Fights happen every day then?

Zeynep: Yes, they do. She pushes my stepfather to beat me up, can you believe, I feel very bad when I hear these things. I wanted to go next to my biological father. But then I said, I got used to my environment here. How can I leave my friends, especially my sister, and go? I could not leave my sister and my friends and go. I took the bus that night and was going to, but my sister and my friends came and picked me up. I could not go. How can I leave them and go?

Canan: I would actually like to listen to these in more detail. I would like to know about the kind of environment you live in, your circle of friends, and your biological father. These are important so that I can get to know you much better before we start the therapy, and that we can generate more realistic solutions to your problems. Let's start with your family if you like. Can you talk about the people at home?

Zeynep: There are three people at home: my mother, my stepfather, and my sister. I already told you about how we are with my mother. She really cares more for my sister. Sometimes she tells me that. She says: Your sister doesn't do like you. Well, but my sister did not see what I saw, did not hear what I heard.

Canan: How old is your sister?

Zeynep: She is 14.

Canan: How do you get along with your stepfather?

Zeynep: He is nice. We don't have many problems with him. Of course, unless my mother pushes him to beat me up.

Canan: You told me that your biological father lived in Antalya. How often do you see each other?

Zeynep: We see each other once or twice a year. I mean we see each other that often face-to-face. But he calls me when he wants to. He calls me once a week or once in 2 weeks.

Canan: Don't you ever call him at all?

Zeynep: No. He never call, neither my sister nor me. He is married as well. I have a younger brother from that marriage.

Canan: I understand that your friends are important for you. You told me that you would not be able to leave them. Can you talk about them a little bit?

Zeynep: Yes, they matter a lot to me. My mother also says the same thing; she says you care about them more than you do about me.

Canan: How do you spend time with your friends?

Zeynep: I am a big fan of Aydin Sports soccer team. We never miss any of its games. We don't quite leave Aydin, only for away games. There is a serious dislike between Aydin Sports fans and Goztepe Sports [a local soccer team in Izmir] fans. For example, if someone is wearing a Goztepe scarf, we beat him or her up. For example, I once took a scarf from around a girl's neck. The girl did not do anything, but she brought her sisters in the following day. They beat me up very bad. They pushed me down and kicked me at the stomach. After a while, I saw the same scarf on the same girl. There was a police standing there, but I went and took the scarf out again anyway. The girl had tears in her eyes. Apparently, her father gave these scarves to her as a present. Then, even though I was considering burning those scarves, I returned them to the girl. I mean, we are big fans of Aydin Sports team.

Canan: Which school were you attending?

Zeynep: [name withheld] High School, 10th grade.

Canan: These friends you were talking about, are they from that high school?

Zeynep: No. I am at odds with almost everybody at school. Nobody at school likes me. Except one girl, who is one of my friends from the neighborhood, the café circle. We go to the parks, the cafés together. We sit down and have chats, eat sunflower seeds. She supports me when I feel blue.

Cana: I think you are lucky in this respect. I can tell you care a lot about your friends, but I think they also care about you as well.

Zeynep: Yes, that's right.

Canan: Do you have habits like smoking?

Zeynep: Yes I do smoke. I smoke one to two packages a day.

Canan: Have you ever drunk alcohol?

Zeynep: It's not like cigarette. My stepfather drinks every day. There is always alcohol at home, but I only drink occasionally or when people at home tell me: "Come and have a drink."

Canan: When was the last time you had a drink?

Zeynep: For example, a few days ago my mother gave me some money. She told me to buy some raki [Turkish national drink with 45% alcohol content] for herself and my stepfather, and a beer for myself. I bought it and drank it that day.

Canan: Are there any problems at home because of your [step]father's drinking?

Zeynep: No. My [step]father comes home every day having had drinks, but he is a calm, silent person. He drinks raki. Sometimes my mother drinks with him as well.

Canan: How are your studies going?

Zeynep: This is one of the problems we have with my mother. There is something wrong with me; I never want to stay home. I get very bored at home. I want to go out and be with my friends. My mother insistently tells me that I am not studying. However, I do study, but not at home. For example, I do my homework during my free time at school, or in the parks, at the cafés after school when I do have homework. I am not a bad student. My grades are not bad either.

Canan: Are there times when you do not attend school?

Zeynep: Not much. I only have 3 to 4 days of absenteeism.

Canan: Do you have issues other than school that you cannot agree on with your mother?

Zeynep: Yes, there is also a permission issue. I don't ask for permission to go out. Because I know that she will not give permission, I just go out. I told you, I don't want to stay home. I get off school at 1:30 pm, but I come home at 5 or 6 o'clock pm. I sometimes tell small lies. For example, Aydin Sports has a game in Denizli [an industrial city next to Aydin] this weekend, but I will not tell her that the game will be there. Of course I won't say that it will be in Aydin, but I might say it will be in Kusadasi [a small tourist town at the Aegean coast]. If I tell her that it will be in Denizli she won't let me, but I have to go. There are such things as well.

Canan: To wrap things up, Zeynep, first of all, you have been experiencing certain things for the last 2 years that made you come here and ask for help. Initially you mentioned that you had experienced conflicts leading up to fights because of getting easily irritable and angry. After we get to know you well enough we may perhaps start working from there. On the other hand, you mentioned the issues that you felt sorrow for your distress in relation to your family. Your openness about all these was very important for our cooperation. In addition, as far as I understand you have a group of friends that support you and that you feel comfortable in their presence. I think this is also an important source of power.

Zeynep: Yes, that's true but sometimes it is not enough.

Canan: Yes, I bet, since you asked for professional help. I would like to inform you shortly about the problem-solving therapy that we will be working through here. In this treatment method, first we identify problems, and we analyze the way in which you see those problems, try to cope with them, and the extent to which these methods actually solve them. Next, we reflect together on some other ways in which these problems can be dealt with or approached. I think this therapy is important not only in solving the problems you are experiencing at this stage, but in affecting the way we deal with our problems in general, at every stage in our lives. Your participation in the therapy is very important, but your level of contribution today is promising. This method of therapy has been investigated in terms of a lot of problems of different sorts and it has been found effective in solving the problems that young people like you experience. As I told you before, I think we will be able to complete this therapy in about eight to nine sessions, by meeting once a week. I have a few things that I would like to learn about you. We will continue with those, next week. I will also ask you to fill out some forms. Is there anything that you would like to ask or tell me?

Zeynep: I am pleased to meet you.

Canan: Thank you, likewise. See you....

Session II: Problem-Orientation Training

Synopsis of the session: *In this session, the client's attitudes toward problems, the things she does, and the way she thinks and feels about problems have been primarily identified. Next, her attitudes toward problems have been described and the characteristics of the problem orientation have been explained to the client. Then, the way different kinds of problem orientations can make us feel, think, and approach the problems have been shown and exercises for developing positive problem orientation skills have been provided to the client.*

Canan: Welcome again, Zeynep. How have you been doing since we last met?

Zeynep: I am fine, I mean not bad.

Canan: What did we do last week?

Zeynep: We talked.

Canan: I actually tried to get to know you, didn't I? I tried to learn a little bit about your distress. I tried to understand the kind of family environment you live in. And you talked in detail about the problems you were experiencing and about your family members. In short, we talked about the reasons and the problems that brought you here. I will tell you what we will be doing today, but before that I would like to ask you: How you are doing? How did you spend this past week? Did you have other problems?

Zeynep: Yes, I did. I have had a lot of problems.

Canan: Did you? Can you talk a little bit about them?

Zeynep: I told you that I had a boyfriend. I had an Ankaragucu Sports team [a local soccer team] scarf that I gave to a friend of mine; he had told me he would have his picture taken with it. I mean it's a precious scarf for me. I went by him in the evening to take it back. We argued for 2 hours, he did not want to give it back to me.

Canan: This is not your boyfriend, right?

Zeynep: No he is not, he is just a friend. And he (my boyfriend) learned about it. He was quite mad. We even sent each other a lot of messages, we argued. Then something happened one day, you know we go to games, those of Aydin Sports. Apparently those girls that I had a fight with were going to come to the game.

Canan: Is this the game over the weekend?

Zeynep: Yes, the one on Saturday. Seven to eight girls were going to come to that game apparently. Of course, I got really mad when I heard about it. I went home, I burst from rage to my mother, I argued with her. I argued with my sister, I argued with my [step]father. Problems such as these happened. And problems also happened at school. I have a very bad cough that never stops, I have had difficulty breathing. Teachers kicked me out of the classes, I stayed free.

Canan: What do you mean by kicking out?

Zeynep: I mean, they told me to get out; they wrote me down as absent.

Canan: Why did that happen?

Zeynep: Because I was coughing a lot; so that others don't catch it. That's why; they took me out of the class. I got behind in the classes, and I could not catch up.

Canan: Is coughing the only reason?

Zeynep: Yes, that's the only reason. Also, teachers at school annoyed me, I mean some of them.

Canan: Did you get annoyed from another reason?

Zeynep: The same reason. I mean, when I coughed my hair clip fell off. I coughed toward the floor, and the clip fell off. The teacher started saying that my hair is messy and so forth. And I raved against the teacher. He tried to take me out of the classroom, but I didn't leave. We had quite a lot of arguments. He took me to the principal. There have been quite a lot of things, I mean at school, with friends as well. They again annoyed me. I was going to beat them up, but I could hardly detain myself, I also had a razor blade with me. I was almost going to cut people into pieces, I was that mad.

Canan: Zeynep, do you carry a razor blade with you all the time?

Zeynep: No, not all the time. We picked up tangerine from the garden that day. We couldn't cut it, we didn't have anything to cut with. We bought a razor blade from the grocery, that's why. These are what happened. I was quite mad. There is nothing else, these are what I remember.

Canan: I understand. Then, this past week, you had some problems with your boyfriend, members in your family, your teachers, and some other friends. The people that you have been mad at, are they people that you like, from your group of friends?

Zeynep: No, they are not. They are people whom I don't like, who get irritated by me.

Canan: They are the ones you already have conflicts with, in a sense?

Zeynep: Yes, the ones who look for small scars.

Canan: Then Zeynep, within this past week new problems emerged in relation to the problems related to irritability, fighting that you had mentioned last week.

Zeynep: Yes, unfortunately.

Canan: Ok, now at the beginning of each session I may ask you some questions. I would like to learn about your mood state, each week. Because, you may be happier, in better spirits some days, unhappy and in a bad mood in some others. For example, today, how happy do you feel? Think about it please, if you are very happy, say 100, if you are not happy at all, say 0, and if you are in the middle, neither too happy nor too unhappy, say 50. What would your happiness score be?

Zeynep: Today 0.

Canan: Today your happiness score is 0. OK, how much do you love yourself today?

Zeynep: None.

Canan: Then, your love for yourself is also 0.

Zeynep: Yes.

Canan: Is it so low?

Zeynep: For today, yes.

Canan: Today that's it. OK, your self-confidence?

Zeynep: Today 50.

Canan: OK, can you think of a reason why your happiness and love for yourself is so low?

Zeynep: Because my boyfriend annoyed me terribly.

Canan: Because of the problems you experienced with your boyfriend. I think you told me that you have sent messages to each other up until now. This is because of the Ankaragucu scarf, isn't it?

Zeynep: Yes, because of that. And also we experienced problems with teachers. These teachers hate me, I know that already.

Canan: Up until this time today you have experienced two problems that bothered you then, one with your boyfriend and the other with your teachers. Both of them irritated you quite a bit. Therefore, both your happiness and your love for yourself are low right now.

Zeynep: Yes.

Canan: OK. In fact maybe things just coincided. Today, I would like to talk about something like this with you: You are experiencing certain problems now. These problems are problems that are related to you being furious, in other words.... As I told you last week, we will conduct a therapy with you about solving problems, that's why first I would like to know about your style of approach when you face problems, troubles, and what you do at those times. I want this to be the topic of today's session, is that fine by you?

Zeynep: Fine.

Canan: What does Zeynep do when she faces problems, which happens almost every day, how does she approach them?

Zeynep: When I face a problem, I generally become very angry. I must either beat somebody up, hurt myself, or I will break other things up. But if I have very close friends with me, I don't damage other things in order not to hurt them, I don't want to hurt myself either, I prefer to sit by myself until I calm down. And this is not easy of course; it takes 1 or 2 hours. If not, I cut my arms with a razor blade. Or I beat up the first girl that I come across with. I get rid of my anger this way.

Canan: Can you tell me the first thing that comes to your mind?

Zeynep: To beat up a girl....

Canan: Are there people that you pick up especially for that?

Zeynep: Whoever comes up that can irritate me?

Canan: Let's say you were mad at your boyfriend. Then....

Zeynep: If there is nobody around to irritate me I sit by myself. Let's say there is such a person. I don't attack her verbally unless she does. I glare at her. I go and attack her verbally. If she does the same, I beat her up.

Canan: The second option is you sit by yourself if you do not come across someone, but meanwhile. . ..

Zeynep: I hurt myself. If I'm home breaking things, throwing things relaxes me. And also crying, that relaxes me as well.

Canan: Then the third option is damaging goods, and the fourth option is crying. Is there anything else?

Zeynep: I cannot think of anything else.

Canan: Let's try to think as broadly as possible. Teachers, friends, sister, your mother, other problems. . ..

Zeynep: I actually sleep sometimes, I listen to music. These relax me as well.

Canan: Can you do these, right at the problem situation, or do you sleep and listen to music after you give harm?

Zeynep: Right at that moment. For example, I sometimes think, when I'm angry, if I break things up now I will not earn anything, I say let me go to my room at least, I say let me sleep, listen to music, but when I am furious this is not possible, sleeping, et cetera, does not relax me.

Canan: Shall I get it this way then; your state of anger has levels, and different behaviors happen depending on those levels.

Zeynep: Yes, absolutely.

Canan: Shall we do it this way then? Think about it as a feeling thermometer. Or let's say first that this is an anger/furiousness thermometer.

Zeynep: OK.

Canan: Here your anger is 100 degrees. I mean it is at the top. And here your anger is 0 degree. We can say that you don't have any anger at all. You are too calm. And here let's say you have an anger of 50 degrees. But these have intervals you know, like 60, 70, and 80, and so on. [The therapist shows the thermometer by drawing it on paper.] Now tell me how do teachers, friends, mother, sister, boyfriend, and friends make you angry? Is there anybody else?

Zeynep: No.

Canan: OK, let's place each of them somewhere along the thermometer by thinking about the level of anger you experience with them. Which one would you like to start with?

Zeynep: I would like to start with my mother, she is generally 100.

Canan: When you experience problems with your mother your anger is here [showing the spot on the thermometer].

Zeynep: And also with my sister.

Canan: OK, let's write that down as well.

Zeynep: Let's write my boyfriend to 80 and my friends to 90.

Canan: These friends are not your best friends, are they?

Zeynep: They are. Sometimes I get very angry at them.

Canan: Shall we call them close friends then?

Zeynep: OK, it will be best if we also add the external environment.

Canan: Who are in this external environment?

Zeynep: Those girls, let's also say 100 to them and 60 to the teachers.

Canan: OK. This thermometer shows that there are times when you get very angry, and those when you get less angry. What do you do when you get angry at 100 degrees?

Zeynep: If I'm out I beat up girls, if I'm home I damage stuff. If there is no one I can burst into tears and hurt myself.

Canan: At 90 degrees you have your close friends, what do you do when you get mad at them?

Zeynep: I sit by myself.

Canan: What do you think about at that time?

Zeynep: Not good thoughts generally. I listen to music, I cry by myself.

Canan: At 80?

Zeynep: There is my boyfriend there, isn't there? I generally think about attacking his house. I want to report to his mother. When I get angry at my boyfriend I want to take it out on my family, my friends. I yell at them. There are times when I throw glasses at them.

Canan: Insult?

Zeynep: Oh! That's the most frequent.

Canan: Then insults exist in other cases as well.

Zeynep: Yes, quite a lot. When I have problems with teachers I leave school without even looking back.

Canan: Does it matter if you are in the middle of a class, or if you have an important exam?

Zeynep: It doesn't matter if I have an exam; I get a doctor's report. I don't think I can participate in an exam with that anger anyway.

Canan: What do you do when you leave?

Zeynep: I go to quiet places, places where I can have peace of mind, for example I go to the stadium over there. Usually there is nobody there. I am by myself, which relaxes me. If I'm very upset I cry. But if it's not something that bad, especially if it's teachers, I don't cry at all.

Canan: Then, if we look now, 100 is the highest but 90, 80 is not that low. What I infer from the things I wrote down, you do whatever comes first to your mind when you get very angry.

Zeynep: Yes, exactly.

Canan: Whatever comes to your mind then, you do it without looking back as if you say "I have to do that."

Zeynep: Yes.

Canan: The first things you can think of, that you cannot resist at that time are what we just wrote down.

Zeynep: Today, I again remembered, I wanted to hurt myself but I couldn't find something that I could hurt myself with, therefore I sat down.

Canan: Now, I would like you to choose what bothers you the most, what you would like to solve the most. Then, let's talk about the thing you chose in more detail. Because, I want to know Zeynep in those situations very well, I want to visualize it.

Zeynep: Let me choose my mother and my sister, since they are the ones whom I have the most problems with.

Canan: Now let's think together about an important distressful moment that you experience with your mother. Can you tell me how it started?

Zeynep: The most important: We were in Ankara. I love Ankara a lot, and they forced me to come here, to Aydin.

Canan: Yes, you told me last week a little bit about it, your aunts were also there right?

Zeynep: Yes, I also have an aunt in Cine [a small town next to Aydin], we went there together. The following day, my mother wanted to meet with a boyfriend. Of course, I don't let her; I don't want something like that to happen. How can a married woman possibly have a boyfriend, I mean people will get it wrong. But my mother took both my sister and me. She also took my grandmother.

Canan: All four of you went together then.

Zeynep: Yes, we went to Bolu [a large city in the Western Black Sea region] altogether. We went to Lake Abant. What I got mad at there was the man proposing to my mother. He asked my mother out from my grandmother. I got mad, I yelled. I said, get up we are going. Of course, my sister was young, she probably thought it was a joke, but even if it were a joke, it was bad.

Canan: It can be a joke but ultimately this annoyed you.

Zeynep: Yes, and a lot. We were sitting by the lake, I even felt like throwing everybody into the lake. My grandmother also got mad when she heard this, but she didn't show it. Anyway, she dropped us home. When I came home, I told it to my aunt. My aunt got very mad, because there had been certain things that happened when I was young. I mean, like cheating on my biological father, with a lot of men. They started telling that my mother will never get wiser. Of course, I get angrier as they talk. I am a guest I cannot damage anywhere there. Anyway, they started talking to my mother, I am also talking, and I'm there. My aunts talk mostly, I stay quiet, I look forward to getting more irritated and blowing up. I expect that my mother will get wiser when I blow up.

Canan: I would like to intervene for just one second here. Let's not forget where we are but this is important, before you blow up you have the following thoughts on your mind: Now if I give a very strong reaction, if I blow up....

Zeynep: My mother will get wiser. Of course if she hears it from me....

Canan: If she hears it from me she will get wiser.

Zeynep: Yes, I thought like that, but I didn't say anything. There they started talking about my biological father. I told you in the previous session, 9000 liras, etc. Of course, when I heard that she took our future away I got even angrier. My hands and feet are shaking. I feel like bursting into tears. My mouth gets dry. I feel like throwing up but I can't. Strange things happen to my heart. I get angrier. Finally I said I loved my father. And my mother could not bear it. She started thinking like I didn't love her and I loved my father. My father did something like that for us, and you took our future away. I yell of course. I am angry, extremely angry. My mother started packing our stuff, she said we were leaving. I said I wouldn't come, that I was happy there. They left. The following day she called my aunt. She said: "We are in Ankara, pick Zeynep up and come to us." I said: "I don't want to come by you." I called my father that day. I told him I would like to come by him. The processes started. Registration, transfers, etc. I passed to Cıne from there. I will get my bus ticket and leave in the evening. As I was just getting on the bus my friends came in. They wouldn't let me go. My mother came in, she was crying but I didn't care. I hug my friends. My sister is crying, I think about her. I couldn't go, leaving my sister with my mother. I just could not do it.

Canan: Now, when I look at this example, I can see that this is something that made you really upset and angry at the same time. You had crying attacks, you insulted people as far as I understand, then your mother went away, you made a decision, you wanted to go to your father. What I notice in this example is you feel the need to hold on to the first thing that comes to your mind when you are very angry or upset, I mean when you are face-to-face with a distressful situation. This is sometimes hurting someone, sometimes leaving or other similar things. I would like to know this then: I made you state an example on purpose, so that we can go back to it together, remember Zeynep's thoughts and feelings and understand how Zeynep sees problems at that time. How does Zeynep perceive the problems in those times? Are they things that cannot be solved? Is it something difficult? Is it something to escape or something else that I cannot think of right now?

Zeynep: I see it as a problem that cannot be solved no matter what you do.

Canan: No matter what you do!

Zeynep: Yes. Because my mother will be the same whether I move to my father or I stay here. Nothing will change.

Canan: When you say it is unsolvable, do you mean that nobody can solve it or that you cannot solve it?

Zeynep: Nobody can solve it because a person proceeds the way she continues her life. You cannot teach an old dog a new trick, in short.

Canan: Ok, and then let me ask you this: What do you understand by solution? When you say you cannot teach an old dog a new trick I feel like you think that there are some people who create the problem, and if they behave in this way rather than that way the solution will come true.

Zeynep: Yes, but the solution is to cover the problems, continue to live, something like that, I find it hard to explain.

Canan: Let's make an effort together please. Let me try to help you. You said to cover?

Zeynep: Pretend it doesn't exist, you know.

Canan: Ignore it you mean?

Zeynep: Yes, ignore it.

Canan: OK, why are you here then?

Zeynep: Because I cannot ignore it.

Canan: That's what I thought as well. It means that is not a solution for you. Look, I have sensed for the last two sessions that you have a strength. Even older people prefer to skip problems when they occur but you do not. In fact maybe all of us do that sometimes. And you speak as if "the solution is to do something but you are not able to do it, but on the other hand you say, no there is a problem there, I want it to be solved, I cannot ignore it that's why I have been telling my mom to bring me here." Then it's as if you were looking for other solutions out there somewhere. Is there anything you can think of?

Zeynep: Like a solution?

Canan: No, no. Let's not try to find a solution today. I just noticed an important thing in trying to look for the things that give you a hard time in approaching the problems. You said you perceived them as things that cannot be solved no matter what you do. How do you perceive yourself within these problems?

Zeynep: Got stuck in the middle. Shall she go to her father or to her mother? Shall she stay with her aunt? Who is right, who is wrong? A Zeynep who got stuck in the middle. She doesn't know who to believe, who is right.

Canan: Then there is a Zeynep who tries to make sense out of the situation, who tries to make a decision.

Zeynep: Yes, if I know who is right and who is wrong then I will decide on what I have to do.

Canan: Then, if you are going to decide on what to do, imagine that one day let's say you see who is right and who is wrong. When you see it you will be able to do something about it right?

Zeynep: Yes.

Canan: Then Zeynep, these are not problems that cannot be acted on?

Zeynep: In fact I found a solution. My English is good. I will take exams and so forth. If I pass them, I will go abroad, away from everybody.

Canan: Escape then.

Zeynep: Yes.

Canan: Can we say then that when you face problems your way of approaching them is to escape them?

Zeynep: Yes. I already ran away from home one day. I went to Cesme [a tourist town near the Aegean coast], next to my friends. I was going to have peace of mind, I was going to sit by the sea, et cetera. My mother called the police. And the police were very "helpful." Of course I got very mad when I heard about the police. I told her in fact: "Leave me alone for 1 day, I will come back the next day." If I had been caught by the police, they would find my friends guilty, as if I had been kidnapped. And plus I would have been found guilty. My mother is inconsistent, unstable; she doesn't know what she is doing. I mean yes, I ran away once.

Canan: Now listen, when problems are experienced, some people show a positive approach to the problems and some others have a negative approach. Those with a positive way of approaching problems think as follows: I have a problem but who doesn't experience problems, everybody does and this in a sense is an opportunity for me to improve myself.

Zeynep: Experience you mean.

Canan: Yes, experience. They can say that if they managed to overcome this problem nothing else can hurt them easily anymore. And the other group of people say the problems will never end, I got tired of them, there is nothing I can do about it, I wish I had no problems at all.

Zeynep: Yes, I say so.

Canan: Do you ever say "I wish I had no problems"?

Zeynep: I say it 5 or 6 hours a day.

Canan: Do you know someone who doesn't have any problems?

Zeynep: In fact, no. Yes, in fact, a girl. Her family is rich, she studies in a private school, and she gets everything she wants. She doesn't have any problems with her teachers, her friends. She doesn't have problems at school. This is my view as an outsider. I don't know her very well, we only say hi to each other, that's all. This is the way she looks from the outside.

Canan: Think about the people that you know better.

Zeynep: Yes, they also have problems. I have Ali, a very close friend of mine. He had a trial today; we all went to the court to support him. There is somebody else who has lots of problems as well; he will join the army in February. I have another friend Ege. He is at odds with his family. He stays at another friend's house. There is Ezel, she doesn't have any problems. She is busy with a party; she is trying to sell tickets for it.

Canan: She seems to have no problems but in general people around you have problems then. How would a life without any difficulties, problems be like? Let a miracle happen that could solve all the problems. How would your life be like?

Zeynep: Happy, peaceful. But boring by the way.

Canan: Why boring?

Zeynep: Problems sometimes are fun, they make us laugh. They can make people laugh at unexpected times. But I would be happier and more peaceful. At least I would not need such a treatment.

Canan: You would be better off psychologically, but your life would be boring.

Zeynep: Yes, it would probably be boring. I would sit home a lot, not going out means getting bored, I don't know.

Canan: Let's think about your current life now.

Zeynep: Now there is a girl who likes to go out a lot. Who has problems, who lives in Aydin. A bad girl I mean. According to her family a girl who is using drugs.

Canan: Of course, when you look at these two lives you choose the second one, don't you?

Zeynep: Yes.

Canan: Then knowing about these problems well and eliminating them is important for you. If these problems cannot be solved and eliminated and new ones are being added on top, do you think it's because they are unsolvable or because the ways followed are not appropriate? Up until now you have tried and used some ways to solve them. It is important for me to know whether you are eager to learn about trying new ways.

Zeynep: I am, that's why I came to a psychologist.

Canan: Good. Then I think we can find solutions with the new ways. You know another characteristic of those people who have a positive approach to problems is not giving up. Look, let's say you saw a problem. You did certain things to solve it. When you look back, you see that the problem is there as it is. If you have a negative approach, you say "See, I cannot solve it, this is not going to be solved anyway," but if you have a positive approach you say "I did something wrong somewhere." Then what happens?

Zeynep: I go back and correct it.

Canan: Which one seems to be taking us to the solution?

Zeynep: Not being pessimistic of course.

Canan: Where do you see yourself in this respect?

Zeynep: I used to see myself in the pessimistic side in the beginning but if I can still survive despite problems that means I not that much pessimistic.

Canan: And if you are here.

Zeynep: Yes, if I'm here it means I'm not that pessimistic.

Canan: OK, what do you see as the source of these problems?

Zeynep: My mother, my family, the external environment.

Canan: That is, situations, people, external factors. What you are saying conforms to what you just told me. You told me a while ago that you thought solution would involve change in certain people, naturally you see these people as the source.

Zeynep: Yes.

Canan: OK, we said that there are people who look at the problems in a positive and negative way.

Zeynep: Yes, there were positives and negatives.

Canan: We talked about the negatives but we didn't talk too much about the positives. I prepared a list about the characteristics of those positive people. Let's read it if you like Zeynep. [She starts reading the characteristics of people with positive problem orientation from the therapist's manual.]

Canan: OK, which one of these do you see in yourself?

Zeynep: Um, they don't ignore the problem and they say there is a problem, they have self-confidence, and also they think problems are inescapable. These suit me.

Canan: Do you have these, and also...

Zeynep: I said optimism.

Canan: Yes, you were pessimistic at the beginning but then optimism and pessimism went side by side.

Zeynep: Yes.

Canan: Let's keep that also in mind. I will read you a story now. Let's discuss what this story will make you think, what you will find in this story in relation to what we have just discussed, OK?

Zeynep: OK, alright.

[The therapist reads a fictive story about a girl named Ayse who has positive problem orientation.]

Canan: Now what kind of problem orientation does the main character in the story possess?

Zeynep: A positive one, the girl who doesn't give up.

Canan: [Looking at a list of characteristics of people with a positive problem orientation.] When you look at this list, which of these characteristics do you see in Ayse?

Zeynep: Ayse is optimistic, gifted, she doesn't wait for automatic solution, she herself can solve the problem, she knows that and she looks for various ways to solve it. In fact, shortly, everything on the list is there.

Canan: OK, if we look a little bit at Zeynep considering Ayse's behaviors as well, how does your problem orientation look like?

Zeynep: It looks violent.

Canan: It sure includes violence. It's as if there are some negative sides. You used to do two things when you faced problems. What were they?

Zeynep: I do the first thing that comes to my mind, and also, what was it?

Canan: Escape. . ..

Zeynep: Oh yes, I also wanted to escape right away.

Canan: OK Zeynep, I learned two important things about you today. One of them is doing the first thing that comes to your mind or your willingness to leave. This is your way of approaching the problems, your way of solving the problems. And the second is that you relate the onset of problems to some conditions and some people. Problems and the solutions are external to you, are they?

Zeynep: They are, but we will solve them.

Canan: Then, can I think that you slowly started seeing them as solvable things?

Zeynep: Yes. Being pessimistic all the time is bad, I mean getting angry all the time, crying, not being able to withhold yourself, beating up girls, et cetera, these are bad things. That's why. . .

Canan: I see hope. Since we have a Zeynep who put pressure on her mother for 2 years [to come to psychotherapy] she must have some hope, but she seems to be covering this hope. Besides, pessimism and hope are like two contestants who compete with each other, and at the beginning of this session pessimism was kind of on the front. How is it now?

Zeynep: They are equal.

Canan: OK Zeynep, it is very nice. How about if I ask you to keep a list for the next week?

Zeynep: What kind of a list?

[The therapist asks the patient to keep a list of what problems she experiences and what kinds of thoughts and feelings these problems give rise to.]

Canan: Is there anything you don't understand about this homework?

Zeynep: No.

Canan: OK then. We clarified the problems that we had started talking about last week. We talked about what you did at those times when you face problems and we rated your anger on a thermometer. This rating was very important. I also gave you this homework now. If you come to the next session having done this homework, you will be contributing a lot to the therapy and I will be very happy.

Zeynep: Of course, I will do it.

Canan: See you, Zeynep. Is there anything you would like to ask or say to me?

Zeynep: There isn't.

Canan: OK, let's schedule your next appointment then.

Session III: Defining Problems

Synopsis of the session: *In this session, the client's complaints and their underlying causes are identified initially. Then the contribution of the identified causes and problems to the existing situation are scored and the problems to work on are identified. Tables in relation to these studies are given in the text of the session.*

Canan: Hello Zeynep, welcome.

Zeynep: Hi, Miss Canan. [puts her homework on the table right away]

Canan: It looks like we will first have a look on your homework?

Zeynep: I did my homework. Let's have a look at it together.

Canan: OK, thank you.

Zeynep: It is a bit small and complicated but that's OK.

Canan: On the contrary, it is so neat, congratulations. Let's have a look at it, but first let's remember why we gave it to you, what we talked about last week.

Zeynep: We talked about solutions.

Canan: Yes we talked about solutions but do you remember what our main goal was? We talked about the kinds of reactions you displayed when you were faced with a problem.

Zeynep: Yes, that was what we talked about mainly.

Canan: And then I gave you this homework. Let's see what is there, I am curious about it.

Zeynep: We did these first two together last week. I did the following.

Canan: Yes. We did the problem you experienced with your teacher and the one about your boyfriend together. And you did the rest of it.

Zeynep: Yes.

Canan: Now, what is the first problem here?

Zeynep: Quarreling with a girl.

Canan: What happened before that? You went out in the break time. What did you think?

Zeynep: I thought: She is a popular girl, I must turn her water off, but I am at school.

Canan: OK, this was what you had in mind.

Zeynep: Yes.

Canan: Good, it is very important to notice it. What did you feel?

Zeynep: I got angry. I was happy but suddenly I changed.

Canan: Good Zeynep. Then comes this?

Zeynep: Yes. I had a nervous breakdown. My hands started shaking. I threw up. I didn't do anything, I took a sedative.

Canan: You took some medicine then. Where did you find it?

Zeynep: My mother had it, Xanax. I used that once, it works.

Canan: Then the reason you used it is the one over here.

Zeynep: Yes.

Canan: OK, while you were sitting at the park with your friends you had a fight with your boyfriend. You thought you loved him, and he loved you, that it shouldn't go on like that. You got unhappy and you felt a chest pain. Then you left the place and cried.

Zeynep: Yes, I left.

Canan: We talked about that last week, when you experienced problems with the people that you loved you would move away and start crying.

Zeynep: Yes. Then I was sitting at Kipa [shopping mall] with my girlfriends.

Canan: Your girlfriend told you that she liked your boyfriend.

Zeynep: Yes, she did.

Canan: You thought: "You're dead girl!" You got mad; you pushed the girl down and started kicking her. Where were you at that time?

Zeynep: I was at Kipa.

Canan: You beat the girl at Kipa then?

Zeynep: Yes.

Canan: Then you had a dispute with your mom while you were watching TV. You thought "I hate my mom; I wish I could move away from home a little bit." You got angry and became cranky. Then you slammed the doors, you punched and kicked.

Zeynep: Yes, unfortunately.

Canan: Then you had another fight with your mother. You thought: "Idiot, either I am going to die one day or she is." You were almost getting out of your mind. You hung up on her. You took a sedative.

Zeynep: Yes. Then I was home. I was going to go to a movie. We had a fight again with my mother. I thought I was almost about leaving home.

Canan: You got angry and you almost lost control. Then you went out. And also, you were going to stay at a friend's house, you asked for a cigarette, that's why you had another dispute with your mother.

Zeynep: I wished to die and break free. I got very angry and I left home.

Canan: You stayed at your friend's house. What did your mother do about that?

Zeynep: She shouted: Get out! She is only too glad to send me away.

Canan: I understand. Now I would like to say this first: You did wonderfully. Normally, before I assign such homework I give training on what thoughts are and what feelings are. I didn't give you such training, I only made two examples together but you could differentiate between your thoughts and feelings very successfully. I think this is also a skill. This is the second skill that I noticed in you, strength of you. Last week, we talked about your skills on realizing the problems if you remember. From what I understand from this homework, you are also aware of what you think, how you feel, and even what kind of changes happen in your body. We will use today's homework on various occasions. Now let's talk about what we will be doing today. You came here with certain complaints. You have certain symptoms that you would have liked changed in you, like irritability. The things that we have been talking about for the last 2 weeks. Now we will try to clarify these complaints and symptoms and what lies behind them. We will try to make a discovery today in other words. But before that let me ask you my usual questions. Do you remember the feeling thermometer?

Zeynep: Yes, I remember.

Canan: Last week, your happiness score was 0. What is it this week?

Zeynep: 50%.

Canan: It went up, how nice. OK, your self-confidence?

Zeynep: 100%. It doesn't go down if my mother doesn't irritate me.

Canan: I hope after this therapy it continues to be at 100% even when you are angry. What is your score for your love for yourself?

Zeynep: That is 50% as well.

Canan: There has been an increase in all of them. But when I asked you last week why these scores were so low you told me that you had problems before you came in. It means you feel better when problems are a little bit behind. When problems happen at a more recent time these scores go down. This is probably related to how you approach the problem.

Zeynep: Probably. I hope I won't have any problems today.

Canan: OK, I brought a list with me today (Table 11.1 from Chapter 10). There is a section here where we can write about your complaints. We will first list them. Then, we will try to find the underlying causes of these complaints. [Meanwhile the table is shown and presented.] Let's talk about the psychological symptoms one by one. What are the symptoms that you experienced in your body or in your mind and emotionally?

Zeynep: My hands shaking, feeling cold.

Canan: Do these happen together; shall I write them next to each other?

Zeynep: Yes. Nausea, fainting.

Canan: OK, we wrote that down as the first item. There is also getting easily angry.

Zeynep: Yes, these happen in my body.

Canan: Getting easily angry. What else?

Zeynep: Getting upset very quickly. Being too emotional.

Canan: Yes, but when? What kind of emotionality? How can I write this down in your own words here?

Zeynep: Getting quickly upset when I'm faced with a problem.

Table 11.1 Identifying Complaints and their Causes

Causes (Problems)	Emotional Symptoms (Complaints)
1. Not sharing my family problems with anybody	1. Getting angry easily
2. Not being able to control my anger	2. Changes in my body such as my hands shaking, feeling cold, nausea, blacking out
3. Not being able to control my sorrow	3. Getting angry especially at girls and beating them up
4. Having the feeling of being neglected	4. Feeling angry at my mother
5. Thinking that girls try to challenge me	5. Willingness to escape and run away
	6. Wanting to die sometimes
	7. Hurting myself and damaging goods
	8. Emotional breakdown/sorrow
	9. Not feeling love toward anybody but my friends

Canan: Shall we call it emotional breakdown?

Zeynep: OK. There are girls in Aydin. Let's call them "interesting" girls.

Canan: But this is not a symptom. We will write down the emotional symptoms that these so-called interesting girls create in you.

Zeynep: Getting angry at the girls and beating them up.

Canan: What else?

Zeynep: Fights with friends or people in the external environment. There is my mother. My biggest complaint is the problems I have with my mother.

Canan: Shall we describe it a little bit? How can we write it down as a symptom here?

Zeynep: Can we say the things my mother does?

Canan: What do the things that your mother does create in you?

Zeynep: Hatred. They create the feeling of hatred in me. And also there is something like this: I don't have feelings. Neither mercy nor pity. Even if the girl cries in front of me I feel no pity at all.

Canan: How shall we call it?

Zeynep: Lacking in the feeling of pity.

Canan: You define very well.

Zeynep: We can also add not feeling love toward anybody except my friends. Even toward my boyfriend.

Canan: But you said the opposite here.

Zeynep: It used to be that way then, but it is different now. What he did aroused hatred in me.

Canan: Think about as many areas of your life as possible please.

Zeynep: It can also be finding classes difficult.

Canan: Like not being able to succeed or understand?

Zeynep: Yes, and also having low grades on the exams.

Canan: We wrote down a bodily complaint. We wrote down "easily getting angry," "quick emotional breakdown," "getting angry at the girls, beating up" as the main complaints. The feeling of hatred caused by the things your mother does, failure in classes. OK, what can you say about the willingness to escape? Let's get some help from your homework?

Zeynep: I still want to escape. How can we define it?

Canan: Whichever way you feel like, I want you to define the symptom/complaint.

Zeynep: Willingness to escape, running away and even to die. But let's write it down separately. I tried it once [suicide attempt].

Canan: How did you try?

Zeynep: Three weeks ago. I tried to cut my wrist with a glass. But my friend did not let me do it.

Canan: Did you think about it at all afterwards?

Zeynep: For example, I thought about it today.

Canan: When did you think about it?

Zeynep: I was listening to music, I felt bad. But I didn't do it.

Canan: How were you able to restrain yourself?

Zeynep: There was no razor blade.

Canan: Could it be that an inside voice told you to stop?

Zeynep: That's not possible because it never did.

Canan: I get it. OK, now tell me a word thinking about one of the problems.

Zeynep: My mother.

Canan: Now, use this word in a sentence.

Zeynep: I hate my mother.

Canan: Then the anger you feel toward your mother is one of the problems.

Zeynep: Yes. By the way, you will see my mother after me today. She will not see these, right?

Canan: Of course not, don't worry.

Zeynep: Because she will drive me crazy if she sees them. The second word is sister.

Canan: Use it in a sentence.

Zeynep: My sister's behaviors drive me crazy.

Canan: What kind of behaviors are they?

Zeynep: She shouts out loud, she puts the music's volume high, she doesn't study, et cetera.

Canan: They make you...

Zeynep: Angry.

Canan: Let's get some more help from your homework. This willingness to escape shows itself as running away from the classroom sometimes.

Zeynep: Yes.

Canan: How can we define it?

Zeynep: Let's say running away.

Canan: We already wrote it down. We didn't talk about hurting yourself or damaging stuff.

Zeynep: Let's write it down as hurting myself and damaging goods. My mother is here, I can hear her.

Canan: Your mother will have to wait; it's your turn now.

Zeynep: There is also willingness to escape the problems.

Canan: What does that mean?

Zeynep: I sometimes wish to escape problems without solving them.

Canan: When does this happen?

Zeynep: When I think that problems are unsolvable. In fact problems are not unsolvable things but sometimes I get pessimistic.

Canan: What happens when problems seem to be unsolvable?

Zeynep: Willingness to leave, and escape without solving.

Canan: This is something that you would like to change then. Is there anything else that you can think of?

Zeynep: No, there isn't.

Canan: We can always add to the list when there is. We don't have to write everything down now and finish right away. What can you see as the underlying causes of your complaints? What do you think lies behind the complaints in general? What are your explanations about them?

Zeynep: What I have been through since I was 10 years old. The reason I'm that angry maybe the things I have been collecting.

Canan: How can we define it?

Zeynep: The problems I have been experiencing since I was younger.

Canan: This has been very general. Let's open it up a little bit.

Zeynep: The bad moments I have been experiencing since I was younger have been accumulated and they explode today. I have not shared them up until this age. Let's also add not sharing with anyone. My parents' divorce, bad things my mother did. Let's say not sharing the family problems in short.

Canan: You didn't share them even with any of your close friends?

Zeynep: No, I shared with my aunt this year and with you. Nobody else knows about them.

Canan: What else?

Zeynep: My [biological] father's aggressive nature.

Canan: What did you mean by that? What kind of cause can that be?

Zeynep: I mean my father beat my mother up in front of me. I may be aggressive because of that.

Canan: Was this something frequent?

Zeynep: No, it happened only once.

Canan: What did that make you feel?

Zeynep: I was curious. I wanted to know why he beat her up.

Canan: Do you have an explanation for that?

Zeynep: I didn't have it until this year. I had it this year. Because this year I learned about what happened.

Canan: What does this explanation make you feel?

Zeynep: Hatred.

Canan: Let's say here "Your father beating up your mother once."

Zeynep: And based on that, taking my father as a role model.

Canan: You said something else also; the explanation you made created hatred in you.

Zeynep: Yes, that also.

Canan: What else?

Zeynep: My mother's silliness.

Canan: What does that mean?

Zeynep: The insults and the words my mother used for me. Especially the ones that have sexual contents.

Canan: I noticed the following: You saw a popular girl and you thought that you had to turn her water off.

Zeynep: Yes.

Canan: This way of thinking leads to fights as well I think.

Zeynep: These girls want to hang out with my girlfriends. How can they want to hang out with them? I mean these girls wanting to hang out with the friends that I see as my sisters.

Canan: That's OK but how do you interpret this? Do you see it as a challenge, as a vanity, or as the act of stealing your friends from you?

Zeynep: Both a challenge and vanity.

Canan: How should we write it then?

Zeynep: The challenge and vanity of some girls, for example, their willingness to hang out with the girls who are with me.

Canan: This means challenge to you, it has such a meaning for you.

Zeynep: When I'm with my boyfriend there is also the stealing aspect. When you think about it, they also bother me when I'm studying.

Canan: If we would focus on your sadness. . .. If we were to look on the moment where you felt unhappy [using the homework]. How do you feel when you experience such moments?

Zeynep: Unhappy, heartbroken.

Canan: Do you also feel neglected?

Zeynep: Yes, I do.

Canan: Which one is more dominant?

Zeynep: Mostly unhappiness. Let's say being unhappy after the fight with the boyfriend.

Canan: You also said something important. You told me that when your mother did things like that you felt neglected.

Zeynep: I still feel it that way.

Canan: How shall we write that down?

Zeynep: The feeling of being neglected is above all the other feelings.

Canan: You define it so well, Zeynep.

Zeynep: It must be because I do reading a lot. Also, I think using cigarettes and drinking are other symptoms.

Canan: That's right. We can write that down as well.

Zeynep: I know the reason for this, my mother and father drink and smoke and I follow their example.

Canan: We will match these complaints and the reasons. In other words, we will find the specific cause of each consequence.

Zeynep: I would like to do that myself. [She takes the pen and puts the marks and she handed the list back to the therapist.]

Canan: Let's see how you matched the complaints and their causes.

Zeynep: I wrote it here.

Canan: You matched "hurting yourself and damaging goods" with "not sharing the family problems with anybody." You also said "following my father's example of beating up my mother in front of me."

Zeynep: I matched "being angry with the girls and beating" with "their attempts to steal my boyfriend from me" and "not sharing the family problems with anybody."

Canan: OK, let's see what you wrote down as the cause of the fights with people in the external environment; you said "your mother's words especially the ones with sexual contents, her insults" and again "the girls' attempts to steal your boyfriend." You matched "not having the feeling of pity" with "the feeling of being neglected being above all the other feelings." Meanwhile, you matched "not feeling love toward anybody" with "your mother's actions creating the feeling of hatred in you." You wrote you wanted to die because you thought you were being neglected. You wrote you wanted to escape and run away because of what you have been through because of your mother. You said you wanted to hurt yourself and damage goods because of the pressure you felt on yourself. And at the same time you wrote you wanted to run away without solving the problems again because of this pressure. You matched "anger toward your mother" with "her insults and what she made you experience ever since you were 10 years old."

Canan: How about if we group these and reduce the number of items?

Zeynep: Let's do it.

Canan: OK then, let's see what we wrote down as causes or problems. Not sharing my problems with anybody, not being able to control my anger, not being able to control my sorrow, feeling neglected and my belief that some girls challenge me. We grouped them into five problems then. Now we have to identify which one to start with. We will do a scoring in relation to that. We will think about each of these problems/causes. How much each of them contribute to your complaints, to the reason you applied here, and maybe to the fact that you dropped out of school and the problems you experience with your mother? Let's rate them on a scale of 6 points (Table 11.2 from Chapter 10).

Zeynep: 6 will be the most this time.

Canan: Yes, exactly. 6 is the most, 0 is not at all, 3 quite, 4 considerably, 5 a lot, 2 a little, 1 not much.

Zeynep: Not sharing my problems is 4, considerable level. Not being able to control my anger is 6. Not being able to control my sorrow is 4, feeling neglected can be 3, and the girls can be 5.

Canan: OK, my second question is this, if you solved these problems how much would your complaints go down? (Table 11.2 from Chapter 10) If we add up the scores, it looks like not being able to control your anger gets the highest score and that we should solve that first. But you have the right to say that another one is more important for me. Would you like to start from here or from somewhere else?

Zeynep: No, this is fine.

Canan: It means we will set goals in relation to this one. We will identify how a Zeynep who solved her problems would want to look like, where would she like to come. Then, we will identify the way in which we will reach that goal. OK, can you summarize what we did today?

Table 11.2 Problem Identification Table

Problems	Contribution	Decrease	Score
1. Not sharing my family problems with anybody	4	3	7
2. Not being able to control my anger	6	3	9
3. Not being able to control my sorrow	4	2	6
4. Having the feeling of being neglected	3	2	5
5. Thinking that girls try to challenge me	5	3	8

Zeynep: Today, we worked a lot. We reviewed the complaints for why I came here and we tried to find their causes. Then we grouped them, reduced their number, and we scored them so that we could find the most distressing problem. We chose my inability to control my anger as the starting point.

Canan: Now Zeynep, I will ask one more thing from you this week. Was this recording difficult for you?

Zeynep: No, not at all.

Canan: Can you continue doing it for one more week? We will see if anything new comes up. We can also look at the number of occurrence and see if it increased or decreased compared to this week.

Zeynep: How many complaints are there now, 9.

Canan: I will assign you a new homework. I will ask you to think a little bit and write down what you would like to add here. And then I will ask you to match them with each other using another color of pen. I mean, I want you to look at the reason lying behind each complaint.

Zeynep: Alright.

Canan: OK, let this be your second homework.

Zeynep: OK.

Canan: Is there anything you would like to ask me?

Zeynep: No, thank you.

Canan: See you then.

Session IV: Goal Setting

Synopsis of the session: *In this session the therapeutic task is to set goals. The desired goal for solving the problem previously identified with the patient is set at this session. The table containing the problem and the goals is given in the text of this session.*

Canan: Welcome back Zeynep. How are you, are you OK?

Zeynep: I'm good, very good.

Canan: You are good, how nice.

Zeynep: Ankaragucu team won yesterday, that's why I'm happy.

Canan: I don't understand Zeynep, do you support the Aydinspor or the Ankaragucu team?

Zeynep: Both of them. In fact I support Ankaragucu but since I cannot go to their games I support Aydinspor.

Canan: OK, you settle for Aydinspor.

Zeynep: Yes, what else can I do?

Canan: OK [pulls out her homework]. You did your homework, very well.

Zeynep: Yes, I brought everything. This is last week's homework. And this is the rest of the previous homework.

Canan: Congratulations, very good.

Zeynep: But, I don't do homework at school.

Canan: [Laughs.] Let's look at the homework first if you like, let's compare it with last week's. You wrote 9 complaints last week.

Zeynep: Today they are 7, I counted them.

Canan: There is a decrease I guess.

Zeynep: In fact there has been another problem today, I didn't write it down yet. I had a dispute with a girl a short while ago. There is nothing else other than that.

Canan: Yes, there are lots of fights in here.

Zeynep: Yes.

Canan: [Reading patient's homework.] You held yourself back even though you got angry here. Oh no, sorry, this is anger toward your mother. You were already able to hold back toward your mother. You hit when it happened with your friend though.

Zeynep: Well, I don't feel pity. When I get angry, my mother starts saying: "Hit me, you can't have my blessing otherwise," etc. I get angrier but I cannot hit.

Canan: OK, let's also look at the second homework. We tried to find the complaints that appeared last week and their underlying causes and we made this list, right?

Zeynep: Yes, but I couldn't find anything to add here. I think we wrote everything down already.

Canan: OK, there are a few things on this list that I would like to discuss in more detail, but first how would you rate your happiness today?

Zeynep: I would give 100.

Canan: Oh really! Each time it goes up a little bit higher.

Zeynep: Let Ankaragucu win all the time, I get happy all the time.

Canan: Good. Ankaragucu made you very happy then. I told you last week, as good things happen and problems stay behind, your happiness ratings go up.

Zeynep: Yes. I would give 100 to the others today.

Canan: To all of them! Your self-confidence is 100 today! What was the other one?

Zeynep: Self-love. That is 100 as well.

Canan: What are we going to relate these to?

Zeynep: Self-confidence is also related to Ankaragucu. For example they won; I was watching the game and browsing on Facebook. I felt very confident against the comments and everything. I also relate self-love to it; it may be related to my happiness I mean.

Canan: Let's put it this way, Zeynep. I understand the happiness. But I don't understand the connection between loving oneself and Ankaragucu winning the game.

Zeynep: I got happy when Ankaragucu won. And when I got happy I loved myself more.

Canan: Then it goes like this: When you are happy, you are able to love yourself more.

Zeynep: Yes, I think.

Zeynep: We get along very well with my mother by the way.

Canan: I'm very happy to hear that. You are also wearing your Ankaragucu T-shirt. How are you now? What did you try to do and what could you do, can you tell me that first?

Zeynep: We tried to solve the school problem. We went to school, we met with teachers, but the absenteeism had been a problem. I had 40 days of absenteeism. Twelve days were excused absences; I mean we took a doctor's report. I had 8 unexcused days. We tried to get a report from private doctors for those 8 days but we couldn't. That's why I suspended my registration for this year. We are planning on moving to Kusadasi anyway with my mother, a better life.... I mean that's my mother's idea. I said OK.

Canan: Wait a minute, when you say I suspended, I couldn't understand that part....

Zeynep: I am not studying right now.

Canan: You are not going to school you mean?

Zeynep: I am not because I failed this year.

Canan: How about if you went to school even if you failed.

Zeynep: I don't think it's a good idea.

Canan: It's not. OK. This is the decision you made with your mother as far as I understand.

Zeynep: Yes, we made this decision with my mom and dad together. I am thinking about working. One of my friends will come, I will study with him. I will study better; I will get prepared for the next year. It's going to be better, I mean.

Canan: I understand. Can you tell me a little bit about your decision-making process, the three of you made this decision? You made this decision with your mom and dad I mean.

Zeynep: I actually wanted to study but this year I didn't feel like studying. One day we were having breakfast with my parents. My mother told me to think for a while. "Do you want to study or not? We will respect every decision you make. But I think you should study," she said. She said: "If you don't study this year it will be even more difficult next year." She gave examples from her own life. She said: "At work, we take breaks but then we don't want to go back. It will be the same for you." I think there is something like this. You are able to finish high school in 3 years. There will be a new law about that next year. My dad said you can finish high school in 3 years. I made my decision then, I said I will study but not here, I will go to [name withheld] High School. I have my aunts there; it would be good for me. We talked with the school quite a bit.

Canan: With [name withheld] High School?

Zeynep: No, with my school about absenteeism. I had my reports, we took them there. I also did something like this, it's a fraud, but I changed the date on one of the reports. I changed it so that I don't fail. We took them there, but they didn't accept it. They said it was apparent that we changed the date. Then my mom and dad went to private doctors but none of them accepted to give false reports. I failed because of 10 days. So I am not going.

Canan: I didn't understand this; you said you wanted to go to [name withheld] High School. How did that become not going to school at all?

Zeynep: Like this. My absenteeism went from 40 to 30 days. When they didn't accept my report for 10 days I failed. I said this is better for me, therefore I am not going.

Canan: When you failed you said, "Why bother?"

Zeynep: My mother said: "We will find you a job. Your friend is coming next year, you will study together, it will be good, and you won't have difficulty."

Canan: Your mother supported your decision then. Your [step]father as well. What are you doing now, how do you spend your time?

Zeynep: I generally clean the house these days. I cleaned the kitchen one day, another room the other day, and so on. I clean everywhere so that my mother can relax when she comes home. Then I sit by the computer, watch TV, I usually sleep. I don't have to wake up early in the morning, that's good.

Canan: You also talked about applying to a study center. You said you were going to study with your friend.

Zeynep: I was planning to go to a study center. I was already registered there, but I wasn't attending. It was difficult. Having six classes there after school was too much for me. There are classes over the weekends as well. I was getting very angry. I spoke to my mother and I gave up. But I still have the chance to go there, I may register again.

Canan: Have you talked to your friend about that?

Zeynep: Yes, he called me yesterday, he is coming tomorrow.

Canan: He is coming from where?

Zeynep: From the Aegean University, Electronics Department.

Canan: What's his goal?

Zeynep: He found his classes difficult. He wants to transfer to another department. The classes we had in high school are nothing compared to these classes he said. My grades used to be higher than his grades. I will help him here.

Canan: You are confident that you will be helpful, as far as I understand.

Zeynep: Yes.

Canan: This is a final decision I guess. How many days have you been away from school now?

Zeynep: I didn't go at all this week.

Canan: What were your friends' reactions?

Zeynep: My friends hugged me when I went to school. The ones who love me of course, not the others. Some others tried to irritate me, but I didn't care. When I first went in, my friends were having their gym classes. We played volleyball together, we had quite fun. Actually, I was going to wait in the car. When I saw my friends I decided to play with them. They were quite happy to see me. I saw other friends on my way out. They hugged me as well. They missed me a lot, but others didn't.

Canan: OK, Zeynep, I wish that this will be the best for you. Since you made a decision and you don't want to go back, and you haven't been at school for 1 week. I hope this is the best for you.

Canan: OK, do you remember what we did last week?

Zeynep: Last week, we decided on the topic to work on.

Canan: Yes, we...

Zeynep: Decreased the number of topics by grouping them. Then we picked up the one to start with.

Canan: What were these five things that we grouped?

Zeynep: They are the problems in my life.

Canan: Right. In fact, when you came here you didn't tell me for example "I'm not sharing my problems with anybody." You didn't say in the beginning "I cannot control my anger." Or "I think some girls challenge me." In our first meeting you told me about other complaints. Do you remember what they were?

Zeynep: Yes, I said I get easily angry. I wasn't able to control my anger.

Canan: Yes we found this out together right. What did you say about this the first day?

Zeynep: Oh yes, I said I was fighting of course.

Canan: Things like, I am beating up girls, I am fighting a lot with my mother, and I am hurting myself. But we talked for weeks with you, we thought about them and we finally decided on the reasons why they happened.

Zeynep: Yes these five were those reasons.

Canan: Then we decided to start with not being able to control your anger. We will leave the topic of what to do to control the anger for next week. I want to do the following this week: Let's pretend we solved this problem. This problem doesn't exist in your life anymore. I would like to think about what Zeynep would be like. I mean, when we get over with the therapy, when you are be able to control your anger, what are the things that you will be doing and those that you will not be doing? What is our goal? Let's imagine that we start drawing a picture. What will the picture look like when we are done?

Zeynep: I see.

Canan: What do we call it?

Zeynep: The goal?

Canan: Yes, we will identify goals for ourselves. In order to decide on which way to go we will first have to decide on where to go. Is this clear?

Zeynep: Yes, very clear.

Canan: OK, in a previous session you said that there were changes happening in your life, that you wanted to be less angry. You said you were thinking about another Zeynep all the time. You said you were imagining yourself as a very different person. And now I say that you may start with your dreams, your wishes. You said you were making comparisons, you may start with them, where do you want to lead to?

Zeynep: My goal is to be a well-behaved girl, a girl who gets angry but who can control her anger.

Canan: What kind of Zeynep are we going to see when she will be able to control her anger?

Zeynep: A calm Zeynep, who doesn't get angry easily, who can solve her problems by talking through, who doesn't have a pessimistic approach to events.

Canan: Does this pessimism lead to irritability?

Zeynep: Yes, it does.

Canan: I didn't understand what you meant by being calm.

Zeynep: For example, not getting angry easily when something happens, keeping my cool, not shouting, and not yelling.

Canan: What kind of events, for example?

Zeynep: For example, when I fight with my mother, when there is a big dispute. If I don't yell, and if I keep my cool I become a calm person.

Canan: What does Zeynep do if she doesn't yell?

Zeynep: She speaks, she says OK.

Canan: By speaking, do you mean a Zeynep who says: "OK, mom"?

Zeynep: Yes.

Canan: Do you want to be able to say OK more frequently?

Zeynep: I don't want to say OK to everything.

Canan: For example?

Zeynep: I don't want to say OK when my mom tells me not to go out, for example. By the way, my mother wants to see you. I don't want to say OK when she tells me to stop using the computer. But I may say OK when she asks me to clean up my room.

Canan: We better focus on the moments when you get angry. Think about the moments you get angry, for example. You shout and yell at those times. You sometimes insult people. You hurt yourself. You hurt other people. What will Zeynep do instead of these? Will she say OK to everything? Should that be our goal?

Zeynep: No, of course not. This cannot be the solution anyway.

Canan: But something attracted my attention: a Zeynep who can solve her problem by talking through.

Zeynep: Yes. I mean without fighting.

Canan: Good. Let's work on it a little bit more. You can solve problems by talking through then?

Zeynep: I mean, let's say there comes a girl who flirts with my boyfriend. I may tell her that he is my boyfriend instead of beating her up. I can solve without fighting, by talking through without getting angry.

Canan: Actually, getting angry is sometimes a very natural feeling. Can you claim that you will never get angry and that you will always be like an angel?

Zeynep: No I can't.

Canan: Do you want to get rid of your anger completely?

Zeynep: This is certainly not possible.

Canan: Sometimes some people may irritate us, some situations may irritate us. Since we cannot control everything it's not possible to avoid getting angry. What do you do normally when you see the problem?

Zeynep: I beat up.

Canan: Now?

Zeynep: I want to solve it, by talking through. I think I can get rid of the problem by saying things like "he is my boyfriend, don't flirt with him."

Canan: Can we say "expressing yourself in an appropriate way when you get angry," for example?

Zeynep: Yes, it's nice.

Canan: Then let's write this down on our list. This is a list where we will write down the goals in relation to the problem we had decided to solve (Table 11.3 from Chapter 10). Let's write the problem part: the problem was "not being able to control your anger." Then your first goal is to express yourself in an appropriate way when you get angry. By "appropriate way" we mean talking through, expressing your thoughts as you said.

Zeynep: Yes, not hurrying.

Canan: Yes, we said expressing your anger in a more appropriate way, expressing your thoughts, talking through. In addition to expressing your anger in a more appropriate way, you would also like not to get angry easily.

Zeynep: I don't want to get angry at the tiniest things.

Canan: What can the tiniest thing be?

Zeynep: For example, my sister wearing my gloves is a tiny event. I don't want to get angry there, for example. Or people waking me up by poking me. It happened yesterday morning, for example. They woke me up so that I prepare the breakfast. I get angry. My mother retired, it got even worse.

Canan: Your mother will be at home then from now on.

Zeynep: Yes.

Canan: What shall we say about these tiny events?

Zeynep: Not getting angry.

Canan: You also said not being pessimistic. I couldn't make the connection between not getting angry and not being pessimistic, Zeynep.

Zeynep: For example, when I fight with my mother, being pessimistic and thinking that it will never end makes me angrier.

Canan: What would you want to be like instead?

Zeynep: If I can be optimistic at those times. If I can say: "I can fight with my mother then I can make peace with her," and I don't get angry.

Canan: Are you sure the feeling that comes about when you think these will never end is anger?

Zeynep: Yes.

Canan: How is that possible? Can you tell me?

Zeynep: I think: "How can this go on like that, what if it never gets solved, and how I can live in the same house with my mother?" And these make me angrier.

Canan: I see. These make you angrier. Then you want to change your way of thinking. When you get angry, instead of thinking it's unsolvable....

Table 11.3 Goal Record Table

Problem: Inability to control my anger, hurting myself or others when I get angry.
Goal: To be able to express my anger in a more appropriate way (e.g., conveying what I have in mind).
Goal: To change the pessimism that comes about when I get angry, my perception of what the other person is trying to do (challenge, humiliation), and to be able to cool off.
Goal: To manage not to get angry at the tiny and unimportant events.

Zeynep: It's better if we call it pessimism.

Canan: How about if we say: "to be able to comfort myself instead of having a pessimistic outlook when I get angry...."

Zeynep: OK.

Canan: Tell me if you can think of anything else. If you solve this problem, Zeynep who can control her anger, will first be able to express her anger by talking it through, second, she will manage not to worry about tiny things, third, she will manage to say that the situation can be solved and will be able to comfort her. In this way, she will be able to control her anger and manage not to hurt herself and the others. How do you find these goals?

Zeynep: I think they are good.

Canan: Do you think we will solve the problems by reaching these goals?

Zeynep: Yes.

Canan: Zeynep, do you know what one of your strengths is? There have been times when you were not able to control your anger, or you hurt yourself and the others, but you are able to look back and criticize your behaviors. You can say "I wish I could do like this." Keeping this in mind, is there anything else you would like to add to this list?

Zeynep: [silence] No.

Canan: OK, great. I would also like to tell you this: After you solve the first problem you can set the goals for the second and third problems on the list. Let's not get in there in order not to be confused. Is there anything you would like to ask me?

Zeynep: No.

Canan: OK, Zeynep. How do you spend your time when you don't go to school?

Zeynep: Sometimes when I want to go out my mother tells me to stay home because I am a "house girl," I get angry at her, but she lets me anyway, she is just joking. And sometimes just as I am reading a book she tells me to go and clean the kitchen. I get irritated.

Canan: Is there a feeling other than being irritated there?

Zeynep: No. There is not much anger either, I mean a little bit. Actually my mother likes to joke about these things.

Canan: I thought maybe you would get upset. You have been a student up until now. And plus you say that you have been a good student. Actually you are a smart student. I think you are smart in other areas as well. I can see the same thing in our studies here, you pick up very easily.

Zeynep: I miss school sometimes, yes. I miss school but not that school particularly.

Canan: You mean being at school?

Zeynep: Yes. But staying home and sleeping are not bad either.

Canan: In fact you didn't have many alternatives I know. You would either continue even though you failed, or you would quit. You chose the second one. After I spoke with you here I realized that I got sorry for you. Let me tell you how I felt. I also got scared.

Zeynep: For what Miss Canan?

Canan: What if you don't go back to school?

Zeynep: There is no such thing. I will go back. I have dreams. For example, Ankara University's translation and language department. Not going back to school is not a choice.

Canan: You also talked about working. I also got worried about that.

Zeynep: Working?

Canan: You said you might start working. Work life is very different from being a student. It's difficult to earn money.

Zeynep: I worked, Miss Canan. I worked as a waitress at a café. I want a similar job. If I find it, I'll work. If not, I won't.

Canan: The first thing that came to my mind was this: You will feel alienated from school after you enter the adult life; you are a young girl. . ..

Zeynep: I will study because I am a young girl. I will make myself a career. I will not depend on my husband in the future. I will have my own career. I will have my own money.

Canan: It's nice to hear these. We see lots of women around, who are dependent on their husbands and their children, who are unhappy, who feel incapable, don't we? We have such patients here. I don't mean to tell you that you will become like one of them if you don't make a career, but you get worried when you think about it. I think it's important that girls study in countries such as ours. Especially girls like you.

Zeynep: Let me tell you the truth, in fact I also think sometimes, what if I find this life easy, what if I get used to it. But I know that things will be bad then. I will start school, I will certainly start. I don't have the option of not starting I mean. I checked the entrance requirements of the Ankara University the other day, that of the language department.

Canan: But you are not in the language department at high school.

Zeynep: I want to transfer to the language department. And my father will register me to a private English language course.

Canan: Will he? When?

Zeynep: I don't know, but he will, in the near future.

Canan: You are planning to make such investments then.

Zeynep: Yes.

Canan: You know what? The topic of our session today is about this. I mean we talk about controlling your anger, not getting angry. Let's think like this: Let there be a power within you, let it be inside your chest, a power that supports you, that makes you stand up, shall I call it the willpower that will help you control your anger.

Zeynep: I think willpower is what you just described.

Canan: OK, but sometimes that is not enough by itself, it is necessary to have certain things that can provide support from the front, the back, and the sides. What are the supports that a person of your age can have? It is a friend. I felt like the second support might be a language course.

Zeynep: I also talked about it to my father. I will go to an English course now. I will spend my time there this year. When it's over it can be another language.

I like French as well. I am already willing to learn English and so on. I was going to represent my school in the Czech Republic last year. I was successful at English. But then I had problems with my father, I couldn't go. I was going to go to Germany this year, but I quit school.

Canan: You were also planning to go to a study center; this could also be a support for you.

Zeynep: When my friend comes, we will register ourselves there.

Canan: I am also happy about that.

Zeynep: I mean I will read books, go to the study center and the language course. I looked at the courses at the Youth Center the other day. All of them are booked out. I think there are lots of people who like English like me. I will also have to register to a study center in order to get ready for the university entrance exam. You know, Miss Canan, I read small story books in English. My English teacher recommended them to me when I was in the 8th grade. My 8th grade teacher would take the time to work with me after school. She used to tell me to study at home. I used to do what she had told me.

Canan: Your teacher must have discovered your skill in this area. By the way, it's good that you are reading books in your spare time.

Zeynep: A book is something quite different. I get very excited. For example, I read the book *Twilight* before it was in theaters.

Canan: I also notice that you keep seeing your friends.

Zeynep: Yes, you already met one of them, the boy with pine tree head.

Canan: Ok, that's good.

Zeynep: Also high school will be 3 years only instead of 4; this is also going to be very good for me.

Canan: You are not over with the school idea as far as I can see.

Zeynep: No I am not. I studied yesterday, geography and literature.

Canan: You are telling me not to get worried then.

Zeynep: Yes.

Canan: OK then, can you summarize today's agenda for me please?

Zeynep: I always do the closure every day.

Canan: Let's divide the work and let this be your share, OK?

Zeynep: OK then. Actually we set goals today.

Canan: We set, clarified three goals, right?

Zeynep: Yes.

Canan: OK, is there anything you would like to ask me?

Zeynep: No, but I would be happy if you could see my mother.

Canan: Don't worry, I will. Let's set the appointment.

Session V: Generating Solution Alternatives

Synopsis of the session: *Solution alternatives that are thought to solve the previously identified problem are generated in this session. Methods such as* *brainstorming, reframing, and advice to a friend are used for that purpose. The table containing the solution alternatives is given in the text of this session.*

Canan: Welcome Zeynep, how are you?

Zeynep: I'm fine Miss Canan, how are you?

Canan: I'm fine, thank you. How was your week?

Zeynep: I had a very fun week. I went to Kusadasi to be with my friends. We had fun. We ate and drank, et cetera. Other than that I read books at home. I went out in the evenings with my friends. I didn't go to games. I don't want to go to the games anymore. I will go to Ankaragucu's game in İzmir on January 16, hopefully. That's it.

Canan: OK, good. You said you were going to look for an English course.

Zeynep: I am still looking for [it]. I found one in Youth Center but that one was full. There is one at the Adnan Menderes University.

Canan: At the university? Do they accept high school students there?

Zeynep: Yes, they do, apparently.

Canan: How is the price and everything?

Zeynep: It is 75 Turkish liras. I am expecting to get alimony from my father. He hasn't been paying it for 4 months. I will get registered as soon as I get it. I spoke to him, he says he will send it but he doesn't.

Canan: I see. OK. What will your happiness score be today?

Zeynep: I would say 100%. I was with my boyfriend before I came here.

Canan: Your boyfriend?

Zeynep: I started to go out again with the old one. I didn't find a new boyfriend I mean.

Canan: Oh really? What is your self-love score?

Zeynep: That's 100% as well. Everything is 100%.

Canan: I forgot the other one again, what was it?

Zeynep: There is also self-confidence. You always forget that [laughing]. That is 100 as well. By the way I like your bracelets, they are shiny.

Canan: Thank you. I usually don't wear these things but I did today. You are very attentive. OK, Zeynep, what did we do in our last session, do you remember?

Zeynep: We identified goals.

Canan: That's right. What did we identify as a goal?

Zeynep: It was controlling my anger.

Canan: Yes, our goal was to be able to control our anger, and not to hurt right? I gave you some hints last week about what we would be doing today, do you remember that?

Zeynep: We were going to start, I guess.

Canan: Yes, we will start generating solution alternatives today. I am excited about today because I think it will be a very active and fun session.

Zeynep: Hopefully, but I haven't been angry this week.

Canan: Really? Has your irritability decreased?

Zeynep: Yes, it did.

Canan: Your mother said the same thing when I spoke to her. She was happy as well.

Zeynep: It would have been better if she had done this 2 years ago though. Anyway, it was meant to be today.

Canan: Sorry, I didn't understand. What would have been better 2 years ago?

Zeynep: If she had brought me to a psychologist. I told her many times, anyway, it was meant to be today. Do you know, Miss Canan, my mother cried when she got home?

Canan: Really, why?

Zeynep: "I know that you thought I didn't love you," she said. She said: "You thought so." She hugged me. She said: "How can I not love you?" et cetera.

Canan: But this is not something that I told your mother....

Zeynep: I know, she realized it herself.

Canan: How did you feel about it?

Zeynep: I laughed, I don't know. I mean good.

Canan: Didn't you get angry at anything this week?

Zeynep: I got angry at small stuff, that's all.

Canan: But not getting angry at small stuff was one of our goals I think?

Zeynep: Yes, but I didn't get very angry at them either.

Canan: I see, it wasn't a destructive anger.

Zeynep: Yes.

Canan: OK. Look, we will be using this list today (Table 11.4 from Chapter 10). This is our new list. I come with a new list every week. How many items are there here? Look carefully.

Zeynep: 20.

Canan: If this were a bigger piece of paper there would be more items, as many as possible. I would like to do the following today: We identified our goal. We set the goal of "a Zeynep who can control her anger even if she gets angry, who manages not to get angry at small stuff, who can communicate without fighting, who can solve problems by talking them through." In order to reach this goal, we will generate as many solution alternatives as possible with you today. OK?

Zeynep: OK.

Canan: But let's make a deal. Our goal today is not to find the best way. We are not thinking about the best way, the right way, or the most appropriate way.

Zeynep: You ask me to say whatever I can think of.

Canan: It can be silly, funny, not very useful, anything. Our task is to generate as many alternatives as possible. I will help you on that. We can play games about it. We can even start with a game if you like.

Zeynep: OK.

Canan: Zeynep, I know you are better now, right? Please, don't think, like, "It will be silly, or inappropriate if I say this," OK? Let's give today's work a name if you like: Let it be brainstorming.

Zeynep: OK.

Canan: What did "brainstorming" make you think?

Zeynep: Whatever I can think of.... It can be silly things.

Table 11.4 Solution Alternatives

Solution Alternatives
1. To be able to say comforting words (e.g., to be able to say "There are lots of other boys out there, etc., when I have a fight with my boyfriend").
2. Not using the "you language." Expressing yourself using the "I language."
3. Give up, break up, leave.
4. Engaging in relaxing activities such as listening to music.
5. Thinking about things that will make me laugh (e.g., Fenerbahce team losing, etc.).
6. Daydreaming about pleasurable moments.
7. Thinking about the things I will do the following day.
8. Thinking about the therapy, the therapist. Thinking about the distance covered in the therapy.
9. Stopping to talk with the person. Suggesting talking after cooling off.
10. Cracking a joke. Using humor.
11. Conveying my thoughts about fighting, my intention not to fight.
12. Doing breathing exercises.
13. Suggesting an activity that will decrease the tension when I notice a tense moment (saying let's have some tea together to my mom).
14. Finding a password and repeating it when I'm angry (e.g., meatball).
15. Apologizing when I'm wrong.
16. Saying the true feelings and thoughts that I actually would like to say (e.g., I love you but you are pushing too much, etc.).
17. Asking the other person what she meant and clarifying the message.

Canan: Yes, as long as you can generate ideas. Let's start with a game. Get up. Let's put this chair here, can you please bring the other one? First, I would like you to sit here. I called this a game but this is in fact a technique. Its name is the empty-chair technique. Let's call it the empty-chair game if you like. Pretend you have across you a chair that is not empty but...

Zeynep: Will I pretend somebody is sitting there?

Canan: Yes, pretend you have a friend sitting across you please. But I think it shouldn't be anybody. It must be somebody who gets easily angry just like you.

Zeynep: Let it be Ece [a friend].

Canan: OK. I want you to imagine Ece. Let's imagine a situation. Ece is angry. What kind of a situation can that be?

Zeynep: She had a fight with her boyfriend. Her boyfriend hung up on her.

Canan: He hung up the phone. Wow! Then?

Zeynep: Besides, he is sitting with girls at a café.

Canan: Wow! She had a fight with her boyfriend. He hung up the phone and is sitting with other girls at a café. How is Ece?

Zeynep: Furious, she is crying.

Canan: This is possible. This is the first scenario. What other things can Ece be angry at?

Zeynep: She gets angry when she fights with her mother.

Canan: She might have had a fight with her mother. What else?

Zeynep: She might have had low grades at school. And also her shoelace might have been broken.

Canan: Ece is a girl who can get angry in more than one area.

Zeynep: Yes.

Canan: I see. Now you are a friend of hers who is aware of her anger, who observes this anger and who wants you to help her reduce her anger. I want you to pretend that Ece is sitting on that chair, and I want you to give her some advice. What can she do in order to control her anger? Talk to her please.

Zeynep: There are lots of other boys in the world. He is not the only one. He is not worth anyone's love anyway. I can tell her that she can stay at our house tonight, because she had a fight with her mother. Never mind, we will get another shoelace. We can go there and make him leave the place; we can help you make it up. We can change your shoe. We can straighten things up with your mom. I can't think of anything else, Miss Canan.

Canan: You are doing great. Do you know what I noticed? Correct me if I'm wrong please. You say things like: "Never mind, we will fix things. If your shoelace is broken we will buy a new one. If you had a fight with your mother, stay with us, you will calm down. If your boyfriend doesn't answer your calls. . .." Are you trying to tell Ece that she should tell herself things that will comfort her, that will lower her anger?

Zeynep: Yes.

Canan: Is it what you are trying to tell her?

Zeynep: Yes.

Canan: OK, if you were to adapt it to yourself, how should you write it down as a solution alternative?

Zeynep: The same things, there are lots of other boys in the world. He is not the only one. Let's say I had a fight with my mom, never mind, we fight every day, it will always happen and it will never end. I may say I have to calm down. If my shoelace were broken, I would wear another shoe, or buy another lace.

Canan: Then, one of your ways of controlling your anger is to tell yourself certain things that will comfort you. Is this the first way?

Zeynep: Yes.

Canan: OK, this can be one way. What else?

Zeynep: Other than that?

Canan: You may think of anything; don't forget, it's brainstorming.

Zeynep: Breaking up with my boyfriend. This can be another way, I can calm down.

Canan: Don't think about your boyfriend only. Think about other things, other situations where you get angry. Breaking up. Shall we call it standing up against somebody, how would you apply it to your mother?

Zeynep: I will never stand up against my mother. I will go and find things that will relax me. I will listen to music, that's for sure.

Canan: Engaging in relaxing activities, like listening to music. I am writing this down as well. What else?

Zeynep: For example, I'm fighting with girls. What can I do at that time? I can think of silly things, things that will cheer me up.

Canan: For example?

Zeynep: It can be Fenerbahce team losing.

Canan: This was something that I thought about as well, daydreaming. Good. What kind of dreams can they be?

Zeynep: I may lie down at the beach. I am having good food. I am sitting, there is a relaxing music. I wish it were true.

Canan: Not only fun but also cheerful dreams, for example, the beach. We can also decide on a dream afterwards.

Zeynep: I had a fight with my mother, for example.

Canan: Wait a minute; we are trying to relax before you fight.

Zeynep: Yes, that's right.

Canan: You got angry,

Zeynep: Oh, OK. I can think about what I will do with my friends when I meet them tomorrow. I can think about how we will have fun together.

Canan: Good, what else?

Zeynep: What else?

Canan: I thought about something. You told me that what makes you angry, what makes you pessimistic, is the thought that things will never end. What can be done about that for example?

Zeynep: I shouldn't think that it will never end.

Canan: How are you going to be able to do that? If you could, you would. Imagine that you are arguing...

Zeynep: With a girl...

Canan: Or with your mom. You think you are quite good in anger management. You can control yourself much better. But then one day, you get really angry at a girl, you want to beat her up, you say: "Damn, I will never get to solve anything, I am angry again, this fight...."

Zeynep: I may say: "I wasn't supposed to behave like this in the therapies, I will not beat this girl up, I will not fight with her, I will not even talk to her, I will keep going." I mean I will think about here.

Canan: OK, thinking about here and me. Let's say to think about the therapy. OK, I remembered something. Can you pick up on one thought there? Shall I tell you what I have in mind?

Zeynep: Stop Miss Canan, don't tell me, I want to find it.

Canan: You are great. Go ahead.

Zeynep: I am having an argument. "I think I will never get better, I will never change. I will always stay angry. I will never be able to control my anger." I will probably think like that.

Canan: We picked up on that way of thinking there. Do I remember correctly, Zeynep? Last week, you told me that you would get angrier when you thought like that?

Zeynep: Yes.

Canan: I agree that what makes you angrier is your way of thinking. The thought that "It will never end."

Zeynep: I guess I will have to change my way of thinking.

Canan: What can it be?

Zeynep: It can be "This will finally come to an end, I will control my anger."

Canan: I don't know why, but this didn't satisfy me. What would you like to say right there and then?

Zeynep: I would like to curse. I would like to shout and yell, I mean. But I have to work things out.

Canan: OK, I will get there but before that, this curse, this beating, what do they represent?

Zeynep: They are the representations of pessimism.

Canan: Meaning?

Zeynep: The thought that it will never end.

Canan: What is the message that you convey to the other person when you hit and yell?

Zeynep: I am telling her that I am stronger.

Canan: Good, what else?

Zeynep: I mean I can beat you up in every way.

Canan: This is what you would really like to show.

Zeynep: Yes, it is.

Canan: OK, how are you seen in this picture?

Zeynep: Powerless.

Canan: Why?

Zeynep: Because when people see me beating up a girl they think that I have been helpless.

Canan: What do you think I would think if I saw you in that situation?

Zeynep: You would probably think that I couldn't work things out.

Canan: That's exactly how I would think. I would probably think that you looked a little bit weak there. What could another way of showing your strength be?

Zeynep: Another way would be talking.

Canan: How?

Zeynep: Calmly.

Canan: She wouldn't listen, she is angry.

Zeynep: Then I would say, come back when you relax. There is nothing else I can do about it.

Canan: Does this relax you?

Zeynep: I mean, when I give her the time to calm down I will calm down as well. I will speak comfortably then.

Canan: OK, I am writing this down. Proposing to see each other after calming down. There was another way that you had suggested earlier. We said that if you made jokes, you would lighten the atmosphere.

Zeynep: Yes, I can make a joke there [laughs]. The problem disappears.

Canan: You just said that you wanted to use your power. There are other ways in which you can use your power. Humor can be one of them.

Zeynep: I think it can also be the way of thinking.

Canan: How is that?

Zeynep: I mean I think like this: For example, if a girl comes and understands that I have no intention of fighting, and if she says: "This girl doesn't want to fight, it's good!," this way of thinking would please me. Because that's what I would think about the girl. For example, I get very angry. The girl says she is sorry, I think: "She doesn't want to fight, it's good." It means she doesn't like to fight, she likes to solve by talking through.

Canan: What do you do when you are faced with somebody who behaves in this way?

Zeynep: I don't do anything. When the other person doesn't want to fight I don't touch her. Then saying, "I don't want to fight, let's solve things by talking through" might be a solution, Miss Canan.

Canan: Very good. This can also be one of the ways. OK, let's say that you were not able to calm her down. Let's say you are home. There is a tension between you and your mom. Your mother is not in a good mood, and you are tense. You got angry at something and you have a conflict.

Zeynep: Yes, that's possible.

Canan: How do you feel in that situation, what are the changes that take place in your body? Are you able to follow your physical reactions?

Zeynep: Yes, my hands and feet are shaking. I have tears in my eyes. I feel nauseated, I have a stomach ache.

Canan: Do these happen frequently?

Zeynep: Yes, of course.

Canan: Would decreasing these symptoms lower your anger?

Zeynep: In fact, these can be under control if there is less anger.

Canan: I suggest the opposite. Would you forget about your anger if you focused on eliminating these physical symptoms?

Zeynep: I probably would.

Canan: You may have heard about this. If you count to ten and take deep breaths when you get angry, you can calm down.

Zeynep: Oh yes.

Canan: Let's write this as "making breathing exercises" here, shall we?

Zeynep: OK.

Canan: What else?

Zeynep: I have something like this in mind: Let's say my mother is not in a good mood, I'm not either. We are quarreling. I may say: Let's drink some tea together, and talk quietly.

Canan: Do you mean talking about the same topic or about something else?

Zeynep: We can talk about other things, things that will cheer us up.

Canan: There is no fight yet. You are tense and you see that your mother is tense as well. You are saying that you would do things that will decrease the tension.

Zeynep: Yes.

Canan: I think that's a great idea. How shall we put it?

Zeynep: We can say: "Doing things that will decrease the tension."

Canan: Let's call it making a suggestion, for example. It is 11 pm already. Let me tell you something that somebody had suggested.

Zeynep: What is it?

Canan: When this person got angry, especially at somebody that she was not able to oppose, for example her teachers, she would silently call this person "meatball."

Zeynep: [laughing] How weird.

Canan: But you laughed when I said "meatball," didn't you? She said that in fact she was relieved when she was silently making fun of the other person. I want to give you another example. I found this one on the Internet: People who practice karate say: "The sun is warm, the grass is green" when they get angry.

Zeynep: And this relieves them as well.

Canan: I mean this is like a password. Did you notice that my friend's example was like a password?

Zeynep: Yes, I did. She is about to curse but she is using this password instead.

Canan: What happens there?

Zeynep: She calms down.

Canan: I also have a similar password you know? I would like to share it with you.

Zeynep: I am curious about it.

Canan: I feel nauseated very easily. If I smell something bad, if I see a dirty place, I immediately throw up. I secretly say muffin-cake-pastry. I say these words by thinking about a beautiful chocolate cake. Then suddenly I don't feel nauseated anymore. What do you think is the common point of these three words?

Zeynep: Finding a password and relaxing.

Canan: Shall we write this down?

Zeynep: Let's do it.

Canan: What else, Zeynep? More storm, please. I think I am stuck. You have been more successful at generating solutions.

Zeynep: I am in the middle of a dispute with my mother. I can apologize if I'm wrong. I can calm down.

Canan: What if she is wrong?

Zeynep: I wait for an apology. Then I forget about it

Canan: Can this be a solution alternative? To forget about it.

Zeynep: What can I do if she doesn't apologize?

Canan: OK, let's say that your mother needs to apologize. You started quarreling. And tensions start rising. You see that you are not wrong. What do you do in that situation? Be careful, I am not asking you what you should do but what do you do?

Zeynep: I get angry but I cannot control it. There is nothing I can do about it. I expect her to accept her fault and to apologize.

Canan: What lies behind this expectation? Why do you have this expectation?

Zeynep: I would probably think: I am not stupid, why would I apologize? She will.

Canan: I am not wrong, she is, then. . . .

Zeynep: Let her apologize and let's get over with it. Then the tension disappears.

Canan: OK, let's say she doesn't apologize. She just doesn't.

Zeynep: Then? I don't know!

Canan: What should we do then?

Zeynep: Focusing on the TV might be an option.

Canan: I noticed something. You mostly thought about shifting your thoughts to somewhere else as solution alternatives. Our discussion about who is right and who is wrong made me think about the following: Do you ever reach such a point? This may happen when you are angry at small stuff; you are so angry that you end up behaving in a completely different way. The words that come out of your mouth are not the things that you would actually like to say. Do you have such examples?

Zeynep: No.

Canan: Have you not said things that you regretted afterwards?

Zeynep: Oh yes.

Canan: That's what I am asking.

Zeynep: I once told my mom that I hated her. I told her that I would go and live with my father, that I would be happier there. I also yelled at my sister. I told her that I hated her, that I hated everybody.

Canan: At what point did you say that?

Zeynep: At a point where I couldn't control my anger.

Canan: That was a critical point I guess.

Zeynep: Yes.

Canan: What did you actually mean to say there?

Zeynep: "Don't treat me like that, I actually love you but you are pushing too much."

Canan: OK. Now let them be the ones who are sitting on the chair. Tell them what you actually mean to say when you tell them you hate them, and that you want to leave.

Zeynep: These problems can actually be solved. But you need to change. You are pushing too much.

Canan: You also said something else: "Don't treat me like that." OK, what if you stopped and said exactly what you actually wanted to say when you were very angry?

Zeynep: If I could say.

Canan: Look, your face looked like that [face shown] when you said you hated. You were much softer when you said: "But I actually love you but don't treat me like that." This may be another solution.

Zeynep: Yes.

Canan: We'll talk about how to do that later. We are writing this down as well. Look, I remembered something else. There is an "I language" and a "you language," have you ever heard of it?

Zeynep: I don't think I know it.

Canan: OK, let's try this out. Let's sit down here. Now, I will tell you some serious things, and you will tell me how you feel, OK?

Zeynep: OK.

Canan: But I'm not me now. Pretend, for example, that I am a friend who is pissing you off. "You are very aggressive. You are always shouting at people. You pull girls' hair and knock them down. It is difficult to get along with you because you are always fighting. You are stubborn. You are messy. You are such a person." [silence] How do you feel?

Zeynep: I think she is right. She is telling the truth.

Canan: Let's not talk about what's rational. Tell me about your true feelings please.

Zeynep: If somebody were to say these to me, I would be angry and also upset. She is openly saying these to my face.

Canan: Like a slap in the face. OK, what if I told you in this way: "Fighting with you makes me sad. I want to trust you. I want to be good friends with you. But I am always scared that you will get angry at me. I feel like you will shout at me. I have such feelings I mean. That's why I'm scared a little bit." [Silence.] How do you feel now?

Zeynep: I don't get angry at this one.

Canan: What is the difference between these two languages?

Zeynep: You are angry in one of them and calm in the other one.

Canan: Also, I said you are like this, you are like that, I was finger pointing, and in the other one I said I was sorry.

Zeynep: You accused me in one of them and you accused yourself in the other one.

Canan: Good. I accused you in the first case. And I described how I felt in the second one. Can you see the difference in the feelings between the two? Look at my finger. When I use the "you language" my index finger is pointing at you all the time. Can we write this down as a solution alternative? How shall we write that down?

Zeynep: How can it be? It can be "expressing in the you language."

Canan: We wrote 16 solution alternatives down. Isn't it too much?

Zeynep: Yes. I think it's enough.

Canan: I think so too. I think we thought about almost everything that we could think of [laughing]. But I would still like to give you an assignment. If you can think of other ways.

Zeynep: Shall I write them down?

Canan: Yes. You can write them down. Because today we mostly concentrated on the things that irritated you. But there is also smaller stuff that you come across in daily living. If you can focus on them and think of anything new you can bring them to me, OK?

Zeynep: OK.

Canan: We had a distribution of tasks last week, if you remember. This section of the session is yours. What did we do today?

Zeynep: We found solutions. In fact that's it.

Canan: Did you understand why we found them?

Zeynep: So that I can control my anger.

Canan: Where are we heading to, do you have any idea?

Zeynep: I don't know.

Canan: We will choose from among them.

Zeynep: Are we going to group them again?

Canan: That's why we tried to generate as many solutions as possible. Maybe, we will choose one and try, but then maybe you will say this is not for me. We will be implementing mostly from now on. OK, is there anything you would like to say?

Zeynep: No.

Canan: OK, see you then, Zeynep.

Session VI: Choosing the Appropriate Solution Alternative

Synopsis of the session: *In this session, solution alternatives generated in the previous session are evaluated based on certain criteria such as the ability to solve the problem, compatibility with the identified goal, applicability, and acceptability. Each criterion has been rated on a scale of 5 points and a solution has been chosen for the implementation. The table is presented in the text of the section.*

Canan: Welcome again, Zeynep. I'm sorry to hear that you got sick on Wednesday. Are you OK now?

Zeynep: I'm not bad but I still feel weak, Miss Canan. We went out with friends the other day. Nobody had an umbrella, so we got all wet. I got sick the next day.

Canan: Yes, you still look sick. Or are you sleepy? I called you early today.

Zeynep: No, I'm not sleepy. I woke up at 10 o'clock, and then I stayed in bed a little bit more.

Canan: That's what we call sleepy [laughing]. OK, how are you feeling?

Zeynep: Fine, I mean not bad. By the way Miss Canan, next Sunday is January 16. right?

Canan: Let's see, today is the 7th, and yes next week is the 16th. What is special about that day?

Zeynep: Ankaragucu's game.

Canan: Yes, I remember it from last week. You were planning to go to that game, right?

Zeynep: Yes.

Canan: How have you been last week?

Zeynep: I had a good week, it was fun. There hasn't been much of a problem.

Canan: OK, did you have a dispute or a fight?

Zeynep: No, nothing happened. I would like to ask you something, Miss Canan. My friend Ece has the same problem as me; she is in the same situation as I was before I came in here. Can you see her one day?

Canan: Of course I can, but I have a very busy schedule these days because I am working in a new department. But what I can do is this: We are soon going to end our sessions with you unless we feel the need to work on another problem. In a few sessions, we will be finishing what we had aimed to do for your therapy. Then, I can start seeing Ece. Or I can ask if another colleague of mine who works in this department would be available. OK?

Zeynep: OK.

Canan: Now, if we check up on your mood as we do every week, how would you rate your self-love today?

Zeynep: 100%. In fact, all of them are 100%. Happiness and self-confidence are also 100.

Canan: Very good. What did we do in our last session?

Zeynep: We found solution alternatives together. We played a game.

Canan: We got into different shapes in trying to find solution alternatives, didn't we?

Zeynep: [laughing] Yes. You also gave me an assignment. And I wrote it down into my sister's notebook. Since she is at school I couldn't bring it.

Canan: Do you remember if you have been able to find different solution alternatives?

Zeynep: I think I had four.

Canan: You found four new alternatives, great. What were they?

Zeynep: I don't remember what they were, it's been a while.

Canan: OK, no problem. You can bring them next week. Do you remember, last week we talked about the ways to decrease your anger especially against provocations, but we said that we could also work on the exaggerated reactions you gave to minor things. I wrote these down on this list before you came in here. In fact I think that the methods that we wrote down can be used in every situation no matter if they are big or small.

Zeynep: Yes, I agree. I can use them in every situation.

Canan: We found 17 solution alternatives last week. We had set a goal previously; we said we would solve the problem of not being able to control your anger. We talked about a Zeynep who was able to control her anger, calm herself down, and bring her feelings a little bit down.

Zeynep: Yes.

Canan: And we found out some solution alternative candidates that could possibly help you reach your goal. Today we are going to do this: I brought you this table today (Table 11.5 from Chapter 10). We numbered the alternatives last week if you remember. We will write the numbers here. These are our solution candidates. Let's think like this: Today we will make a selection or decision. We will rate each candidate, OK?

Table 11.5 Evaluation of the Solution Alternatives

Solution Alternative	Ability to Solve the Problem					Compatibility with the Goal					Applicability					Acceptability					Total
	1	2	3	4	5	1	2	3	4	5	1	2	3	4	5	1	2	3	4	5	
1			x				x							x					x		13
2				x				x					x						x		14
3	x					x					x					x					4
4				x				x							x			x			15
5				x				x							x				x		16
6			x				x					x						x			10
7	x					x								x					x		10
8	x					x								x					x		10
9		x					x							x				x			11
10				x					x				x						x		15
11					x					x				x					x		18
12				x						x					x			x			17
13			x					x						x						x	15
14		x						x						x					x		13
15		x					x							x					x		12
16				x					x				x						x		15
17				x					x						x				x		17

Zeynep: OK.

Canan: We will use the following criteria in making this selection (showing Table 11.5): How much does this candidate solve our problem? How compatible is it with your goal? Or how applicable and acceptable is it? For example, you can say this about a candidate: Miss Canan, this is compatible with my goal, I mean I can really control my anger if I do this, I agree, but I also know myself, or I did try that before, I cannot do it (Table 11.6).

Zeynep: OK, I got it.

Canan: You can think about its applicability in the following way, for example. Let's pretend you did it. Is this something acceptable by the people around you? For example, let's look at one of them on the list, standing up against, breaking up, and leaving. This is a solution candidate, right?

Zeynep: But it doesn't quite solve the problem and it won't be accepted either.

Canan: Yes, do others accept it? Do you understand what we are going to be doing for today?

Zeynep: Yes, I understand very well.

Canan: OK then, we will write the scores in these tiny boxes, but I will also ask this, let's not just write the scores and quickly be over with it. I mean let's think a little bit.

Zeynep: OK, of course.

Canan: We will rate them over 5 points. For example, if we were to rate them, 1 would be very little, 2 little, 3...

Zeynep: We said moderate to 3 previously.

Canan: Yes we can call it moderate, or we can say "quite" on a scale of 5, like it solves the problem quite a bit. Let 4 be good and 5 very good or definitely. Let's name them like this, and keep them in mind for reference.

Zeynep: The first solution candidate is saying things that will calm me down in relation to the issue that makes me angry.

Canan: Do you remember what we talked about, the examples we gave last week?

Zeynep: We already wrote them here. If I had a fight with my boyfriend, I can say never mind, there are lots of other boys out there. If I had a fight with my mom I can say don't bother, you will meet with your friends tomorrow, et cetera.

Canan: Yes, making sentences that start with "never mind" calms you down. If we call it our first candidate, how much do you think it solves your problem?

Zeynep: Let's give it 3.

Table 11.6 Appropriate Solution Alternative Record

No.	Appropriate Solution Alternatives
1	Telling what I actually want to say
2	Making breathing exercises
3	Clarifying the message

Canan: Moderate level you mean. It means if you do this you can control your anger quite a bit, this will comfort you at a moderate level.

Zeynep: Yes.

Canan: Is this a way that will take you to the goal we had identified?

Zeynep: I think it's 2.

Canan: A little bit. OK, can you do it? For example, think about it, pretend you are about to fight with your mom, or your boyfriend, you are getting angry. Can you tell yourself sentences that start with "never mind!"?

Zeynep: I actually do this sometimes. I would give 4 to it. Let's give 4 to its acceptability as well. It is possible I mean.

Canan: OK. Let's look at the second candidate. Not using the "you language." Expressing yourself with sentences that start with "I." Do you remember this; this was one of the games we played last week.

Zeynep: Yes, we sat on these chairs when we played this game. You accused the other person in one and you expressed yourself in the other.

Canan: I notice that you have a good memory. You remember almost everything we talk about.

Zeynep: I don't know. I think I only remember what happens here.

Canan: OK, do you think this solves the problem?

Zeynep: It does, it is 4.

Canan: Is this a method that will take us to your goal?

Zeynep: Let's give it 3.

Canan: Is this something you can do? Because when we are very angry we may choose not to do it. We may want to irritate the other person even more. Does this happen to you, are there times when you don't want to control your anger.

Zeynep: When you look at this in this way, let's give 3 to its applicability.

Canan: Would it be accepted by others around you? How would that affect the other person?

Zeynep: Let it be 4. I actually liked this technique.

Canan: OK.

Zeynep: The other is standing up against, breaking up, leaving. Let's not do this at all, Miss Canan.

Canan: No, I think we have to rate it just like others. Let's see what score it gets.

Zeynep: Then 1, let's give 1 to all of them. The other one is, engaging in relaxing activities like listening to music.

Canan: Let's think about it like this please, you are at home. Let's pretend you are about to fight. The other person may be doing lots of things that upset you. Let's say you are starting to get angry. You can feel that your anger starts to mount. We are talking about leaving everything and listening to music. Actually, we made a few exercises before. We had tried a few things in fact, like looking at the Ankaragucu uniform, looking at the picture of a cat we found on the Internet. Do you think this method can solve the problem?

Zeynep: I would give it 4. I would give 3 to its compatibility with the goal, and 5 to its applicability. Also I don't think I would receive a negative reaction from others, it is 4.

Canan: Do you think your mother would let you do it in that situation, or would the environment be suitable for it, let's say, when you are with your boyfriend?

Zeynep: My boyfriend wouldn't let me but my mother would. Let's say 3 to its acceptability. One other thing was thinking about funny things.

Canan: Does this help you control your anger, does it calm you down?

Zeynep: Yes, 4.

Canan: OK, is it compatible with your goal? Can we say we are on the right track when we use this method?

Zeynep: Let it be 3. I can do it 5. Let's give 5 to its acceptability, there is no problem there.

Canan: What is our sixth solution candidate?

Zeynep: Daydreaming about pleasurable moments.

Canan: You had a very nice dream about it last week, what was it?

Zeynep: I was lying down at the beach. I can't remember it very well but there was a beach, a calm and silent environment.

Canan: Yes. Then you were lying at a sun bed. There were people serving you.

Zeynep: [laughing]

Canan: Dreaming about such things. But Zeynep look, there are certain things we have to be careful about. Don't forget that the situation that you are in at that time is very different from the one you are right now. We wrote these things so that you can control your anger at a moment where your anger starts to mount. Let's start with the applicability in that situation. What would your likelihood of applying this when you can't take it anymore?

Zeynep: Let's give it a 2, Miss Canan.

Canan: Is this valid for thinking about funny things?

Zeynep: No, that is easier, 2 is for pleasurable dreams.

Canan: OK. Does this solve the problem if you can apply it?

Zeynep: 3.

Canan: Then, this is not something that can definitely solve.

Zeynep: Yes. Let's give 2 and 3 to the others. Another candidate is thinking about the things I will do the following day.

Canan: Let's imagine for example a situation that you experienced. For example, your sister wore something that belonged to you. What was it?

Zeynep: Gloves.

Canan: Let's go back to that situation, for example. Can you apply this in such a situation?

Zeynep: I can do it. I give it a 4 for acceptability and 4 for applicability, but solving the problem and compatibility with the goal are both 1.

Canan: The other alternative was thinking about the therapy and the things we accomplished in the therapy. But you will again tell me to think about that moment.

Zeynep: Can I think of it right at that time I wonder?

Canan: Yes, we can assign a low grade to its applicability if you think it is difficult. OK, let's say we were able to do it. Do you think this is a good solution for your problem of being unable to control your anger?

Zeynep: Solving my problem and compatibility with my goal are both 1 and the others are 4, Miss Canan. To stop to talk with the other person, or proposing to talk after we calm down. Was this what I told you about suggesting my mom to have some tea together in order to relax?

Canan: No, this is not it, we wrote it down as a separate item. Look we wrote it down over here. How can proposing someone to talk later be for example?

Zeynep: Let's say we are having an argument with my boyfriend. I can say, we are angry now, we can hurt each other's feelings, let's talk later.

Canan: What would you give to its applicability?

Zeynep: I would give it a 4.

Canan: Would the other person accept it, is it acceptable?

Zeynep: Of course, I would give 3.

Canan: OK, would your problem of not being able to control your anger be solved if you did this?

Zeynep: In fact, I am not sure if this would relax me. Even if I can do it I mean.

Canan: Do you say that you can say let's discuss it later, but you may blow up later on?

Zeynep: Yes. Let's give it 2 for solving problem and compatibility with the goal. I mean I can do it. He will accept it but we may still keep fighting. I may blow up. That's why. The other alternative was cracking jokes.

Canan: You had given a very good example about that actually?

Zeynep: What did I say?

Canan: If, for example, girls came and looked as if they wanted to have fights with you....

Zeynep: And I cracked a joke and laughed altogether.

Canan: Yes. You said that you would lighten up the atmosphere and there would be no reason for you to fight.

Zeynep: Yes, the example of "You haven't been a champion even once." I remember it.

Canan: Is using humor a candidate for solving the anger problem?

Zeynep: It is. It worked once. One of my friends used to crack a joke when I was furious, and I would relax. Let's give it 4.

Canan: This works when your friend does it. But can you do it?

Zeynep: Let it be 3. Let its acceptability and compatibility both be 4. Expressing my thoughts about fighting, my intention of not fighting.

Canan: You also expressed this very well last week.

Zeynep: Solving by talking through, yes.

Canan: You said something like this: When a girl tells me she doesn't want to fight, I say "Wow! Look at that girl!"

Zeynep: This solves the problem. Let's give it 5. It is also compatible with the goal, 5. I would give 4 to its applicability. And its acceptability would also be 4. You also said doing breathing exercises.

Canan: You actually don't know how to do that. I mean we didn't practice it together.

Zeynep: Yes, I heard about it, but I have never done it.

Canan: We are not in the implementation stage yet but I will make a small demonstration so that you have an idea about what that is. You can't evaluate something that you don't know. Let's get seated here on that couch [where relaxation exercises are practiced].

Zeynep: Where did you get this couch from Miss Canan, it's beautiful.

Canan: You liked it, ha!

Zeynep: It's wonderful.

Canan: Are you comfortable now?

Zeynep: Yes.

Canan: I will soon ask you to close your eyes.

Zeynep: Then I will fall asleep, right?

Canan: [laughing] Let's imagine a moment when you are angry and then try the breathing exercises. Let's see how it goes. OK?

Zeynep: OK, let's give it a try.

Canan: Now close your eyes please. Try to do what I tell you to do. Now try to remember a moment that upsets you, that makes you burst out.

Zeynep: Do you remember the fight that I had with my mom in Ankara, Miss Canan?

Canan: OK, you remembered that moment right away. How were you feeling?

Zeynep: Furious, about to blow up.

Canan: What happened to your body?

Zeynep: I threw up once. I had a stomach ache. I was trembling.

Canan: How was your breathing?

Zeynep: Very difficult.

Canan: Try to remember what you said to your mother, what you wanted to tell her.

Zeynep: I wanted to tell her that she was pushing too much, but I couldn't. I had insulted her instead.

Canan: You insulted her. You were that tense. Can you visualize that tension for some time please? Now pretend you have a balloon in your stomach. Take a deep breathe through your nose as if you were going to blow the balloon, hold it for 1–2 seconds. Now exhale. Again.... [repeated it a few times]. OK, how did you feel?

Zeynep: It was very good.

Canan: OK, this was an example to give you an idea about it. Now stand up. Let's rate it for the angry instances. We will use this method in order for you to control your anger in those angry instances. Do you think you can use it suddenly when you are very angry?

Zeynep: I can. I will give it 4. I would give 5 to its compatibility and 4 to its ability to solve.

Canan: Would you receive a negative reaction if you did this? How should we rate its acceptability?

Zeynep: Let's give it 3, because if people make fun of me I can be mad.

Canan: But we can talk about how to use it secretly, and the situations in which we can use it, if we choose to use this method.

Zeynep: OK. Suggesting an activity that will ease the tension when I notice that I am tense, like suggesting having some tea to my mom. Yes, I can do it.

Canan: Does this solve the problem?

Zeynep: 3, 3, 4, 5. My mom would accept it I mean.

Canan: This is a positive aspect of your mom then?

Zeynep: Yes. Finding a password and repeating it when I'm angry. Like "meatball" or "the sun is warm, the grass is green." Oh, and you told me about what you did when you felt nauseated, Miss Canan, I remember it.

Canan: Its ability to solve [not audible].

Zeynep: I would give 2 for solving the problem and 3 for compatibility and 4 for applicability.

Canan: Do you think this is unacceptable?

Zeynep: No, that would be 4. There is also apologizing if I'm wrong.

Canan: Does this solve your anger problem?

Zeynep: This can only be 2, 2 for the goal, 4 for the applicability, and 4 for its acceptability. There is also this. Saying what I actually want to say. For example, saying that I love them but that they are pushing too much. We did that with a game.

Canan: Yes. We used the empty chair.

Zeynep: 4, 4, 3. Let this be 4.

Canan: Finally, Zeynep, we have written down asking the other person what she meant and clarifying the message. How would you rate this alternative?

Zeynep: Miss Canan I would give 4 to solving problem, compatibility, and acceptability, and 5 to its applicability.

Canan: Very good Zeynep. What do you think we will do now?

Zeynep: What? Oh, we will add the scores probably.

Canan: Yes, that's right [tallying scores]. There is one 18 and two 17s. The solution alternatives "telling what actually you want to say, doing breathing exercises, and clarifying the message" got the highest ratings. It seems that they give you the opportunity to make you stop and think about or do things that will help you calm down and those that will make you aware of your anger. Does that make sense for you?

Zeynep: Yes Miss Canan, it does.

Canan: In fact that's what we had intended for today. Can you summarize what we did?

Zeynep: We scored. We did that to be able to decide on the most helpful solution alternatives.

Canan: Yes, there were all candidates. We selected the strong candidates. We will move to the implementation next week. Zeynep, I would like to ask you one final thing today. When you think about the process that we have been through, up until today, have you been able to understand what we are doing in this therapy?

Zeynep: In fact looking at it from the outside, it seemed like a very difficult thing to do. But I realized that it was easy as I started practicing it.

Canan: Which part looked difficult?

Zeynep: I had thought I would never be able to control my anger, but it's not so.

Canan: At which point did you understand that you would be able to control your anger?

Zeynep: I don't know.

Canan: I mean, at which point did you start to find it easy?

Zeynep: What do you mean by point?

Canan: I mean at which stage in this therapy?

Zeynep: Where we identified a goal.

Canan: Oh I see, it means you felt like it was going to be easy once we identified what we were doing, where we were going to. But it is important for you to realize this, because it shows that you were part of every stage in the therapy. Is there anything you would like to ask me?

Zeynep: No, thank you.

Canan: OK, see you then in the next session.

Session VII: Solution Implementation

Synopsis of the session: *In this session, attempts are made to show the client how to implement the solutions chosen in the previous session. Demonstrations in terms of role-plays are done and homework is assigned.*

Canan: How have you been since we last met, Zeynep?

Zeynep: I'm good, Miss Canan.

Canan: Are you a bit sleepy, or tired?

Zeynep: No, I'm not sleepy. I have a little bit of headache.

Canan: You looked tired in our last meeting as well, I wonder why?

Zeynep: No, Miss Canan. I was sick last week, you know that.

Canan: You look calm and too quiet. How have you been lately?

Zeynep: I have been feeling angry lately.

Canan: You are angry. I can feel it. What is this anger about?

Zeynep: I quarrel a lot with girls.

Canan: Which girls?

Zeynep: We will move to the Kusadasi, Miss Canan. I have friends there but all of them are boys that I have met during games. They want to introduce me to some girls. Girls send me friend requests on Facebook.

Canan: These are the girls from Kusadasi, right?

Zeynep: Yes. Friends there tell them to add me as their friends. They say talk to her. She is a nice girl, et cetera. Yesterday, one girl did something, she said: "You can't stay alive here." Of course I got mad; I gave her the necessary answer. I said: "I will come on Sunday, we'll see who is going to stay alive." I got very angry. And today, the girl apologized.

Canan: I want to listen to this dialogue in detail in a while. We had said that we would start implementing the solution today. It's been a good coincidence. We can use this case as an example. Do you remember what we did last week?

Zeynep: Yes, we made a selection from among the solution alternatives. We scored them.

Canan: OK, do you remember what we chose, what we decided to do?

Zeynep: No, I can't remember that.

Canan: OK, let's see then.

Zeynep: Miss Canan, shall I rate my self-confidence, et cetera, as we do every week?

Canan: [laughing] Yes, please. We used to do that, right? We jumped up to what we had done last week.

Zeynep: Self-confidence is 50%, self-love and happiness are 50% as well for today.

Canan: Do you think it is related to something specific?

Zeynep: I don't know, somehow I feel different today.

Canan: Can it be because of that dispute?

Zeynep: It may be.

Canan: When did this incidence happen?

Zeynep: Last night.

Canan: How did you sleep, I mean how did you feel before you felt asleep?

Zeynep: I took some pills I guess. Yes, I took a sedative.

Canan: Did you? You must have gotten very angry then. Have you ever thought of trying one of the things we discussed here?

Zeynep: No, I haven't.

Canan: But you might have after this session.

Zeynep: But Miss Canan, something like this happened, I don't remember which day it was, I think it was 2 days ago. My friends came from the Kusadasi. There is somebody that I call brother, his name is Eren. He pulled my scarf and said: "You will take this out. You can't wear this in Aydin." I got mad. I did the breathing exercise.

Canan: Really, did it work?

Zeynep: Yes, it absolutely did.

Canan: How did you decide to do it?

Zeynep: I suddenly got breathless. I remembered it right away.

Canan: Then what happened?

Zeynep: I relaxed. We went to work with my friends. I didn't have a nervous breakdown or anything like that.

Canan: I am very happy to hear that, because this is an important step toward our goal. Let's go back to the dispute over the Facebook [comment]. Why did you have such a dialogue? Why did that girl tell you such a thing all of a sudden?

Zeynep: I told her that I would go there to study the following year, and that I didn't want any girl fights. I said I wanted to stay away from fights. And she said: "But you can't stay alive in this place. People here are very aggressive, including myself." Then, I said I wouldn't stop. I said: "When somebody does something to me I give the necessary response." She said OK, we'll see. I said OK, let's see each other when I get there on Sunday. And I have a friend called Eken, today he did quite a lot of things in Kusadasi. And that girl apologized. She said: "If you are like a sister to Eken, then you are my sister as well." But the fact that she is a year younger than me really pissed me off.

Canan: OK, Zeynep. What were we working on here? What do we see in this Facebook example? Did I understand correctly; you said "I don't want any fights." You tried to say: "I have nothing to do with these things."

Zeynep: Yes, exactly.

Canan: And the girl didn't tell you anything personal. She said it was hard to stay out of trouble there.

Zeynep: Yes. And she also said I wouldn't be able to stay alive there.

Canan: And she told you wouldn't be alive there.

Zeynep: Yes.

Canan: OK, how did this make you feel?

Zeynep: I got mad. I perceived it as a threat.

Canan: You perceived it as a threat. That is, what she told you sounded like a threat to you.

Zeynep: Yes, of course. And the anger started to mount, to put it in your own words.

Canan: OK, then what happened? Did you do anything to stop that anger?

Zeynep: I spoke to one of my friends. We laughed. Then I thought she was younger than me, that she spoke like a child, there was nothing she could do about it. I didn't care at all.

Canan: I am observing something, Zeynep. We emphasized the same thing while we were doing the scorings last week. There is a situation you are successful in, and a situation you are unsuccessful in [taking a sheet of paper, dividing it in two]. Shall we write the successful or the unsuccessful one first?

Zeynep: Let's write the successful one.

Canan: OK. Let's write the successful one first. What you are successful at is this: If we follow this last example, in fact we talked about many other similar examples, you got mad, you gave a response, and that turned into a battle of words. You are successful at calming yourself down after this quarrel or fight is over. You are able to say to yourself things like, "OK, calm down, I will not care, talk to your friend," et cetera. You are successful at not maintaining it. But what are we trying to do with you here?

Zeynep: We are trying to stop the anger at the time of the conflict.

Canan: Aren't we? What we are trying to do is to prevent the dispute, the fight or the battle of words before they take place.

Zeynep: Yes we were going to eliminate them.

Canan: Now we know what you are not successful at. This is the reason why we are working together here. If we look at this example, where should you tell yourself to stop?

Zeynep: At the time of the dispute.

Canan: Which moment is that?

Zeynep: The moment where the girl said: "You can't stay alive here."

Canan: You said you perceived it as a threat. What did you feel? Can you describe it for me please?

Zeynep: I got mad. I didn't want to write anything on the computer. I was about to break the computer. I thought: "Why is this girl talking to me like that? How dare she talk to me like that?"

Canan: Can you recognize your anger there? Does it always happen in the same way?

Zeynep: Actually, it always happens in the same way.

Canan: That's what we have to catch. We have to find a clue in order to catch it, either in your body or in your thoughts. And we have to use the technique that we decided on as soon as we catch it. We are again in the same situation, Zeynep, how are we going to determine how to work things out?

Zeynep: [silence] I can't think of anything when I'm angry Miss Canan.

Canan: That's what I'm trying to say. You are right, you can't think of using a particular technique when you are angry. That's why I am saying that we should catch the state where you are usually in. But, how are you going to catch it? You are not going to catch it by thinking through it, that's for sure. It can be, for example, the moment where you start trembling, the moment where you feel noxious. What is usually happening?

Zeynep: I start trembling. I feel nauseated.

Canan: Did you start trembling there?

Zeynep: I did.

Canan: Which part of your body trembled?

Zeynep: My hands.

Canan: Can you make me visualize that moment? You are in front of the computer.

Zeynep: I'm in front of the computer. I want to write something but I can't. I remember something then I forget. My hands are shaking, I can't write.

Canan: What kind of moment is that? What shall we call it?

Zeynep: The moment where I cannot work things out.

Canan: Yes, anger starts to mount more and more. OK, do trembling hands happen all the time?

Zeynep: Yes, all the time.

Canan: Can we use it as a sign, I wonder?

Zeynep: Maybe.

Canan: You said you weren't able to write, your hands were trembling. Can you feel at that moment that you are again in the same state?

Zeynep: Yes, it's impossible not to feel it.

Canan: We decided on what to do right at that moment last week. We will in fact start implementing it this week. Do you remember what we chose last week?

Zeynep: I don't remember.

Canan: Let's see. They were these, weren't they?

Canan: We talked about the decrease in your self-confidence a while ago, right? I remembered something about that. We decided to implement it last week [reading the item]. Can you be angry at yourself because you were not able to implement it, I wonder?

Zeynep: Maybe.

Canan: But we said that could be possible. You have been unable to work things out up until today. That's what you are learning here. I told you last week that we would choose one of these methods, start with it, and change it if we see that it doesn't work. We are not saying that this is the best method; you are going to be great when you use it [laughing]. Please do not get discouraged. We are going to start the implementation this week; we didn't implement what we have talked about until now.

Zeynep: But I made an implementation, Miss Canan.

Canan: Oh yes, you are right, you made a successful implementation all by yourself. Good for you. I wasn't expecting you to implement the breathing exercises this week, because it was only a brief demonstration just to introduce it to you. You did a good thing, congratulations. That's why it's not something that should discourage you. There may be times when you are able to control and times when you can't. We will try hard together, OK?

Zeynep: OK, Miss Canan, thank you.

Canan: As you know, we worked on this list last week and decided that telling what actually you want to say, doing breathing exercises, and clarifying the message would be good for you. Now we will start working on them. Let's do this: Lie down here again [on the couch].

Zeynep: OK, let me lie down.

Canan: You liked this couch, didn't you?

Zeynep: Yes, I did.

Canan: Are you comfortable?

Zeynep: Yes.

Canan: Now close your eyes and imagine that situation. Was it the first time you met that girl that night?

Zeynep: Yes, it was.

Canan: How did the conversation start?

Zeynep: She wrote: "Hi, who are you?" I wrote: "This is Zeynep." We asked each other where we were from, and we met. I asked her which team she was supporting. She said Kusadasi Sports. She asked about my team. I said Ankaragucu. And we went on and on. We have a common friend whose name is Batu. I told her that my friend Batu went there and that I was going to get there as well. She said, "OK, come, we'll hang out together." [Pause.] There is a school there called [name withheld] High School. I asked her if that school had a language department. She said yes. She said she was kicked out of school. Apparently, she lied to me. I got even angrier when I learned about that. I asked her if there were fights there and told her that I didn't want to fight. "You can't stay alive here," she said. Then I said, "I will react to whoever reacts to me." And she said, "We'll see." I said, "OK, we'll see on Sunday." That's it.

Canan: Let's go back to the moment in the conversation where you said you didn't want to fight. That is in fact a moment where you were not angry, right?

Zeynep: Yes.

Canan: Let's keep imagining please. You are having a normal conversation, in fact. Knowing about your anger, you think that you don't want to experience the same problems. That's why you ask the girl who knows the place: "How is the situation there? I don't want to get into fights." It is actually a very friendly situation where you want to know about her opinion. Because she knows that environment.

Because you have never been there and you are planning to go there with the hope of not getting into fights. And she is telling you that you can't stay alive there. How does this make you feel?

Zeynep: I got angry.

Canan: Yes you did.

Zeynep: It's mounting.

Canan: Yes, from where to where?

Zeynep: I first felt it in my feet. They started to get cold. I started shivering. Then my hands started trembling. The girl might have said it with a different purpose but I perceived it as a threat.

Canan: Stop right there. Be aware of the state you are in there. Be aware of the changes that take place in your body. Try to notice that you are going from a normal state to another one. Feel your feet getting cold, and your hands trembling. I want to think about that right there: Wait a minute, I was speaking normally, but suddenly I had some changes, my hands started trembling. What are trembling hands the sign of?

Zeynep: My anger.

Canan: OK, where does this anger go to, if you don't stop it?

Zeynep: It's mounting.

Canan: What happens when it mounts?

Zeynep: I do the first thing that comes to my mind.

Canan: Good for you. OK, what did we decide to do with you? What is the goal we set?

Zeynep: Controlling my anger.

Canan: We identified three ways of controlling your anger. What were they?

Zeynep: Telling what I actually want to say, doing the breathing exercises, and clarifying the message.

Canan: Yes, there was also thinking about funny things. Yes. Now, you are at the stage where you start getting angry. You got a threatening response to your friendly question. Which one of these would you like to try when your hands start trembling?

Zeynep: The breathing exercises.

Canan: OK, let me see how you do it. [Zeynep starts doing the breathing exercises.] Good, the balloon expanded tremendously. You did very well. Imagine that all your anger is leaving your body when you exhale, please. Concentrate on your breathing. Feel how much you are relaxed. Let everything go. How are you?

Zeynep: Good, quite good.

Canan: OK, now if you were to write this girl an answer in your imagination after you controlled and stopped the anger, by the way, are your hands still shaking?

Zeynep: A little bit.

Canan: A little bit, you are under control then. How would you answer this girl now?

Zeynep: I would say: "Then I won't stay in the same environment with them, I would go next to my friends."

Canan: I want to ask you again, Zeynep, what are we going to use as a sign?

Zeynep: My hands trembling.

Canan: We have to use the changes that happen in your body. What is evident in you is your hands trembling. For example, my hands never tremble. My heart beats so fast that I feel like it will get out of my body. And when I notice it, I tell myself to calm down. OK, then we will use this as a sign, the sign of relaxation. Does that make sense to you?

Zeynep: Yes, it does.

Canan: There is something that I noticed, Zeynep, that I would like to share with you. How is this girl?

Zeynep: What do you mean?

Canan: What is the impression you have about this girl?

Zeynep: I have the impression that this girl will go through what I have been through.

Canan: That is?

Zeynep: She is at the very beginning. She doesn't know that fighting is bad. I can say that.

Canan: I feel like she doesn't know any other ways of handling things, her challenging style, and all that.

Zeynep: Yes, definitely.

Canan: Did you notice what you said; you said she was younger than you. And you also said you felt like she was going through what you have been through. Then, where are you, compared to her?

Zeynep: I mean I'm in a situation where I have had enough with the fights, where I want to lead a normal life.

Canan: Why do you communicate with these girls then?

Zeynep: I don't have any communication with them.

Canan: But you communicated with them.

Zeynep: I mean yes, we had a communication in a fight format.

Canan: Why that girl? Do you consider establishing a relationship with that girl later on?

Zeynep: No, I don't.

Canan: We are talking about controlling your anger, but there is such a truth, wait a minute, how should I explain this, I want to give you a good example, give me some time to think about it, please. [Pause.] Think about this, you say you don't want to smell a bad thing, you don't want to see a nasty scene and you don't want to be in a dirty environment. You say you want to be in a healthy, clean, nice-smelling environment but you wander around in the garbage.

Zeynep: Yes! I talked with that girl. Why did I talk to her instead of avoiding her? I remember now what I was supposed to do. I was going to delete her as soon as she spoke to me like that.

Canan: Or you don't have to be bad and make an enemy, but wouldn't saying: "Thank you, I now have an idea about that place" and leaving it there be an option? You have to be able to make this distinction, Zeynep. That place is garbage, but you don't want to be in the garbage, therefore you will get out of there or you will stay there and keep going.

Zeynep: Yes, that's right.

Canan: There are two important things here. One of them is finding a sign in your body and start using the method that we chose in order to work things out. And the second is staying away from the people and the places that will not help you control your anger if your goal is to control it. [Zeynep takes a deep breath.]

Canan: [laughing.] Are you relieved?

Zeynep: Yes. By the way did you change your voice recorder?

Canan: No I did not. There has been a problem with mine, so I exchanged it with my colleague's. By the way, I wonder why you preferred the breathing exercise over others.

Zeynep: Because I may not be able to think about a funny thing at that time.

Canan: You found it more useful to engage in a behavior then, ha?

Zeynep: Yes.

Canan: OK, I want to give you another example, but let's exchange the roles this time. Let you be the therapist and me the patient. I was looking forward to sitting on that chair. Now I'm the one who has the anger control problem. OK, let's do it.

Zeynep: When do you get angry Miss Canan?

Canan: [Silence.] I get very angry about injustice.

Zeynep: OK, let's pretend you are faced with an injustice. You start getting angry. What do you do to relax?

Canan: Let me think about a time when I get very angry. For example, I worked really hard to do my homework. And I shared it with a friend of mine. I told her that I had such and such an idea, and that I would show it to my instructor. She went in to the instructor's office and told him about my ideas as if they were her own and the professor was congratulating her. And I see this and hear all about it. I am looking at my friend, I can't believe it. My heart starts beating very fast. My hands start shaking.

Zeynep: OK, Miss Canan, what do you do to calm you down?

Canan: Actually, I can calm down in my thoughts but first I have to calm my trembling body down because if I start talking in that situation my voice will tremble as well. That's why I do the breathing exercises, I guess.

Zeynep: OK, Miss Canan. You know how to do it. Start doing it. OK, let's say your body calmed down, how can you get calm in your thoughts?

Canan: Let me first catch what I have in mind. I caught the things that happened in my body. First of all I would think that she was a thief. That she stole my ideas. I won't feel relaxed unless I tell her that. But I would choose a place where nobody is in. I would tell her that she hasn't been honest, and that I wouldn't be able to trust her anymore. I would tell her that we cannot be close friends anymore.

Zeynep: OK, you shared your thoughts and your feelings with her. Did you get relaxed?

Canan: I get relaxed because I have been able to tell directly what I had in mind and because I haven't been out of control. Telling these make me feel good. And then, I wouldn't care about that person anymore, to tell you the truth.

Zeynep: You are out of the garbage then.

Canan: Yes, absolutely. Oh! I feel good. You would make a good therapist.

Zeynep: I had the therapist's experience. What are we doing now?

Canan: In fact, we have done almost everything we could do today. Now I will ask you to do something for next week. This week you brought a case where you were able to control and a case where you were not able to control your anger. I want you to collect such cases again for the next week; it can be an example over the Internet, face-to-face, with friends or with other people. OK?

Zeynep: Of course.

Canan: It will be nice if you can bring examples of being able to control, but bring the ones where you were unable to control your anger as well, so that we can talk about that, OK?

Zeynep: OK.

Canan: This was the first one. As a second task, I will ask you to take the time to write an essay. You know that we have a goal. I want you to think about the things that keep us away from the goal. This can be within the circle of friends, or on your mind.

Zeynep: Can it be in my environment?

Canan: Yes. It can be anything you can think of. OK, can you please summarize what we did today?

Zeynep: We talked about an example. And we also found out the sign of my hands trembling. I want to ask you something, Miss Canan. The example that you gave, you really experienced it, didn't you?

Canan: How could you tell?

Zeynep: From the way you told it. Do you see this person?

Canan: Yes, but by keeping a distance. We have the right to accept or not to accept people in our lives. You also have such a right; I mean the right to choose.

Zeynep: Thank you, Miss Canan. See you.

Session VIII: Solution Implementation

Synopsis of the session: *In this session solution implementation is continued. Attempts are made to show the client how to implement the solutions chosen in the previous session. Demonstrations in terms of role-plays are done.*

Canan: How are you, Zeynep?

Zeynep: I'm good, Miss Canan. I woke up and came in here.

Canan: You got here as soon as you opened your eyes then.

Zeynep: I stayed up late to watch movies.

Canan: Which movies did you watch?

Zeynep: There was a horror movie called *Poison*. There was *Gomeda*.

Canan: Did you watch *Gomeda*? How was it?

Zeynep: Very silly. I didn't understand anything from that movie, did you, Miss Canan?

Canan: I didn't either.

Zeynep: What is the movie about?

Canan: I felt the same when I was watching that movie. OK, Zeynep. How have you been last week?

Zeynep: Not bad. I mean half good, half not.

Canan: Is the not-so-good part related to anger?

Zeynep: Yes it is.

Canan: That means you came in with an example.

Zeynep: Yes, I came in with two examples.

Canan: Good. We'll talk about them. First of all, I would like to hear about your state of mood. How do you grade your happiness today?

Zeynep: What day is it today?

Canan: It's Wednesday.

Zeynep: I'll give 100%. Tomorrow there is the Ankaragucu game.

Canan: Your self-confidence?

Zeynep: That is 100%. Love is 50%. I always feel this way when I wake up.

Canan: How?

Zeynep: I don't like myself. I feel ugly when I look at the mirror.

Canan: On the contrary. It's the first time I've seen you without make-up on. I think you have a beautiful face. I remember giving you two assignments last week.

Zeynep: Yes, I was supposed to write an essay. Here it is.

Canan: What was this essay about? What did you write?

Zeynep: What can I do to be better? How did I feel when I first started the therapy, and how do I feel now? I wrote down everything.

Canan: OK, would you like to read it?

Zeynep: Can you read it, Miss Canan?

Canan: OK [reading]. Ever since we started out therapy I have been thinking and telling you that you have a great motivation. And this has been like a written proof of it.

Zeynep: These are the things that I could think of.

Canan: Good job, Zeynep. I noticed this, here: If you remember, I assigned you this homework because we had talked about the things that make it harder for you to control your anger.

Zeynep: Yes, that's why I wrote "wicked environment."

Canan: Yes, I noticed that. I see two things that make your life difficult. There are even three of them. I think we started dealing with one of them already. One of them is the circle of friends you hang out with. You said your anger started mounting and you had difficulty controlling your anger because of that.

Zeynep: Yes.

Canan: And second, you said you used to find it hard to manage the physical symptoms before, but now, you were able to control them. And third, the thoughts and the words...

Zeynep: Yes, my thoughts.

Canan: Yes we partly talked about these. In fact you must be more or less aware of them since you said that you will be successful at it with time. It means we will have to work a little bit more on it with you. You have found three things. That's good. Congratulations again. Is there anything in here that will make it easier for you to control your anger?

Zeynep: I don't think so.

Canan: I think there is your determination and perseverance. And there is also the fact that you understand easily. These are what will help you control your anger. And your circle of friends, your thoughts, and the physical symptoms are what make things difficult. OK, you have done your homework. You were also going to collect examples.

Zeynep: I did that as well. I brought in two examples, but I forgot one of them.

Canan: Didn't you write it down?

Zeynep: I kept in mind. I remember one of them very well, because I got mad.

Canan: I am curious about this example.

Zeynep: It's a silly state of being angry but anyway. I was going to watch the Ankaragucu game on TV. And my sister took the remote control and said she wouldn't let me watch the game. She turned off the TV.

Canan: Why did she do that?

Zeynep: On purpose. She said she wouldn't let me. I got very angry, and started trembling. I could tell it from my hands. I did the breathing exercises but it didn't work. And then suddenly I found myself squeezing my sister's throat. Then I went to the kitchen and started crying. I calmed down there a little bit.

Canan: OK, we will talk about that in detail. How is your second example? Let's talk about that.

Zeynep: My friend's boyfriend didn't want her to talk with me. That's why she didn't want to talk to me. I got very angry there, but I was able to control myself there. I was able to control my anger by thinking about other things, by saying "There are other friends in this world."

Canan: OK. It means you struggled with your own thoughts. OK, we are again at the implementation stage today. We will go over the homework. We have two examples at hand. Let's go over the one with your sister. You wanted to watch the game on TV.

Zeynep: Yes, and she didn't let me.

Canan: But how did that happen? Did you turn the channel on?

Zeynep: I did.

Canan: Then?

Zeynep: I went to the kitchen to pour myself some tea. When I came back I saw that she switched to another channel.

Canan: OK.

Zeynep: I told her that the game was about to start and asked her to switch back to that channel. She said no. She cursed. She really spoke harshly with me. And I got quite mad. I thought about controlling, because my hands were shaking. I tried but I couldn't.

Canan: Do you remember what you were thinking when your hands started shaking?

Zeynep: I said: It started again.

Canan: What started?

Zeynep: It started mounting.

Canan: The anger started mounting you mean, right?

Zeynep: Then I thought I had to do the breathing exercises. And I did. I was able to relax.

Canan: Can you tell me how you did it?

Zeynep: I was sitting at the couch. I inflated my stomach, I exhaled.

Canan: What did your sister do?

Zeynep: She was sitting next to me. She was watching TV. I did the exercise for 5 minutes. Then my sister kept talking to me. Then I couldn't do it. She spoke very badly. And I squeezed her throat. I took the remote. My sister had difficulty breathing. I saw it. I went to the kitchen and I cried. Then she gave me the remote. She said: "Take it, you can watch." I woke my mother up. I told her what happened. And that's it.

Canan: OK, the breathing exercises that we practiced here didn't work. I thought about a few things. Let me ask you this first: You are trying to do the breathing exercises. What is the purpose of doing that?

Zeynep: Relaxing me.

Canan: The person who upsets you is also in the environment where you are trying to relax. And how is she behaving?

Zeynep: She is mean.

Canan: Yes. And she is also provoking you. I wonder how much you can relax when you are in the same environment as the person you are angry at. How much could you relax?

Zeynep: Not much.

Canan: How else could it be?

Zeynep: If I went to the kitchen and did it there maybe.

Canan: What would you do if you relaxed? Let's pretend that you relaxed.

Zeynep: I would calmly ask her to give me the remote and watch TV. She could have gone to a friend's house to watch it. I would tell her that I wanted to watch the game.

Canan: Would it work?

Zeynep: It wouldn't.

Canan: What could the solution be? You finally got what you wanted. You have been able to watch the game. How do you think that happened?

Zeynep: I cried. My sister couldn't stand it. She brought me the remote.

Canan: Then what do you think works with your sister?

Zeynep: I have to be emotional toward her.

Canan: [Silence.] How else can this emotionality be shown I wonder?

Zeynep: [Silence.] I don't know.

Canan: Is crying the only way to show the emotion?

Zeynep: Of course not by crying only. I don't know. I have never thought about it.

Canan: Let's write this aside as a question? [Silence.] Let's think about what you thought at that time.

Zeynep: When I'm angry?

Canan: Yes. What were you thinking at the point where you were not able to control your anger?

Zeynep: I thought it wasn't working.

Canan: What did you think was not working?

Zeynep: Breathing exercises.

Canan: You thought these breathing exercises didn't work. Let's go back to where the anger started to mount. What did you think about your sister, or about not being able to watch the game?

Zeynep: I thought I would be very upset if I weren't able to watch the game. I watch all the games and I didn't want to miss this one. I thought my sister could go to our downstairs neighbor's to watch TV.

Canan: But I think this is very selfish.

Zeynep: Why?

Canan: Why don't you go to the neighbor's to watch the game, or watch it on the Internet? Why do you expect your sister to do that?

Zeynep: I tried watching it on the Internet. But it wasn't on it. And our downstairs neighbor doesn't like to watch the games. And I didn't have the permission to go out that day. If I could leave the house, I would go out and watch the game with my friends at the café anyway. I wasn't allowed.

Canan: Why were you not allowed?

Zeynep: I was forbidden to leave the house for one day because I was going out a lot.

Canan: I see. You didn't have any other choice; you had to watch it at home. And you thought you wouldn't be able to watch the game when your sister turned another channel on. I understand all that. Let's think about this, how else could you have behaved? You didn't want to miss the game. You got upset, you got worried and you attacked. You made an effort, and then you attacked. How else would you be able to show what you wanted?

Zeynep: I told about that to my mother. But she was sleeping. My mother told my sister to give the remote to me and let me watch. In fact I had told my mom in the morning when we went out shopping that I wanted to watch the game in the evening. And she had said yes. I told her that my sister created problems but she didn't understand anything because she was half asleep. I had to solve it.

Canan: Let's look at what we did. We had solution alternatives if you remember. They were too many. We identified telling what actually you want to say, doing breathing exercises and clarifying the message as the highest scoring alternative. There are times when it's up to us to get or not to get angry at someone. I mean we need to manage to control ourselves, calm down, and not attack the other person. We can call them the times when the other party is passive. But there are other times when the other person has control over the situation. For example, in this example, you want a channel and your sister wants another channel. There is nothing to do other than making an agreement. I think you could have expressed yourself, your wishes, and your feelings.

Zeynep: I said: "Let me watch the game and you can watch what you want when there is a break." And she said: "Let's make the opposite. Let me watch the movie, and you can watch the game during the ads."

Canan: Did you talk about its importance for you?

Zeynep: No.

Canan: What is the significance of Ankaragucu for you?

Zeynep: It's important, very important. It is the only source of fun for me.

Canan: Does your sister have such a thing?

Zeynep: We can say Internet.

Canan: OK. Talk to your sister. Try to tell her the situation; try to make her understand your situation.

Zeynep: How?

Canan: Try to explain the situation. So that she can understand you.

Zeynep: This game is the only source of fun for me. It is important for me. I want to watch it. You go and surf on the Internet. You can watch the reruns anyway.

Canan: What would she say to this?

Zeynep: She wouldn't mind.

Canan: This didn't work. I don't think your sister understood it very well.

Zeynep: The games take the stress out of me. I like the supporters. I can see my friends on TV when they show the spectators on the screen. Let's watch it today, and you will watch another day.

Canan: What would she say to this?

Zeynep: She would probably say: "Take the remote, it's yours."

Canan: Would she?

Zeynep: She would.

Canan: How is this different, what is in there?

Zeynep: I have friends that I missed among them that I haven't seen for a long time.

Canan: Is there emotion?

Zeynep: Yes.

Canan: What kind of behavior works with your sister then?

Zeynep: Being emotional.

Canan: And explaining I guess.

Zeynep: Yes.

Canan: I think that's what missing in you, to be honest!

Zeynep: I think so, too.

Canan: You jumped up right away. You don't explain the situation to the other person; you don't talk about its importance to you.

Zeynep: I never do that.

Canan: This is important. Let's see if we will find the same thing, can you tell me what happened with your friend?

Zeynep: I have a very close friend. We see each other every day. Her boyfriend didn't want her to see me. And he asked her to make a choice between him and me. And she chose him. She told me not to talk to each other, not to text each other. I got upset but I thought: "There are other friends in this world." Then I said "OK."

Canan: What did you actually feel there?

Zeynep: I got sorry, for her boyfriend. Her boyfriend will go away one day, but I will always stay with her. There is an end in every relationship. I got sorry. But yesterday, she said she regretted it and she apologized.

Canan: You didn't talk about your feelings there either.

Zeynep: Actually, I didn't want to say it, but I did yesterday. "I used to love you very much; I have never thought that you would sacrifice me for a boyfriend. I said you know that your boyfriend will go away one day. We are going to stay with you as your friends." She said she doesn't have the heart to talk to me. Yesterday we met with friends. I went by her and said hello. We had a conversation.

Canan: Did you have anger before this talk, or just sorrow?

Zeynep: I had a little bit of anger.

Canan: How did you feel when you expressed your thoughts and your feelings?

Zeynep: I felt good.

Canan: Did you get the message from the things we talked about until now?

Zeynep: Jumping up to the conclusion doesn't work. I have to be able to express what I have in mind and in my heart.

Canan: Do you remember we put two chairs over here? You sat in one of them.

Zeynep: Yes, we played a game.

Canan: Yes, we pretended your family was sitting there. When you shout at them, when you curse...

Zeynep: You told me to tell them what I have in mind.

Canan: Yes, I told you to stop cursing and express what you actually want to say. I told you to stop and think about what you have in mind. Do you remember what you said?

Zeynep: A little bit.

Canan: I remember very well. You said: "I actually love you but you are pushing too much. I don't know what to do."

Zeynep: I remembered.

Canan: Then I had a hope. Because when you stop and think you are able to find what you have in mind. The only thing left is to express it. And I think it works.

Zeynep: Yes, it does.

Canan: This was the first thing. There is another thing I would like to talk about. But can you first summarize what you remember from what we have talked about?

Zeynep: I mean telling what I have in mind can work for me.

Canan: I think we had "saying what you actually want to say" as a solution alternative. Let's see what score it got. That is 18 points. It looks like this solution will work for you. Do you remember in the example you brought in last week, breathing exercises worked. What is the difference between this case and that of the last week? Because it worked in one of them and it did not work in the other.

Zeynep: That example was about my sister. I couldn't control there. Trying it next to my sister didn't work I guess. It didn't work when my sister was there talking. But last week, I did it when I was by myself and it worked.

Canan: Oh OK, last week you didn't do it next to that person. Then we have to make this in two stages: stopping where you feel the anger is mounting and doing the breathing exercises but then saying what you actually wish to say.

Zeynep: Let me save this to my phone so that I don't forget them, Miss Canan.

Canan: OK, alright.

Zeynep: I will ask you something irrelevant, Miss Canan.

Canan: Of course.

Zeynep: Have you ever been in Kusadasi?

Canan: Yes.

Zeynep: There is a wishing tree in the Pigeon Island, within the castle. Do you know that place?

Canan: I have never paid attention.

Zeynep: It is apparently a sacred tree. Your wishes become true when you hang them on it. I wrote two wishes and put it up there.

Canan: Can I ask you what they are, if you don't mind?

Zeynep: I wrote "I wish Ankaragucu never gets demoted." And I also wished to be able to continue studying.

Canan: Both of them seem possible.

Zeynep: Yes. Ankaragucu had debts. And after I made that wish the debts were paid off.

Canan: It's good. Shall I go there as well? [laughing.] I want to ask you another thing, Zeynep.

Zeynep: OK.

Canan: When I was listening to the conversation we had last week I noticed something. You get a message while you talk to someone. But is this message right or wrong?

Zeynep: I can't tell, right?

Canan: I feel like you don't even care if it's right or wrong?

Zeynep: How is that, Miss Canan?

Canan: You were chatting with that girl over the Internet.

Zeynep: Oh yes, I got it.

Canan: What did you understand?

Zeynep: I mean you will tell me that the girl might have had good intentions. She might have tried to tell me that girls over here are aggressive.

Canan: You asked her about the school and the school environment. Did she try to warn you and tell you to be careful or did she want to threaten you? Do we know that?

Zeynep: No. That is, we have to think whether it's right or wrong.

Canan: There is a name for it, did you know that?

Zeynep: What is it?

Canan: It's called: "Clarifying the message you get." That is to say, clarifying whether the message you got is right or wrong. You know it was one of the solutions that obtained a high rating. How would you be able to do that?

Zeynep: I could have asked. I could have asked her why she said that.

Canan: Yes. "What do you mean?" It's that simple. I am doing it very often here with you if you have noticed. You tell me something. I actually understand something but I always ask you, how is that, what does that mean, what do you mean.

Zeynep: Yes, you do.

Canan: I don't hear it very often from you. Do you know when you actually do that? When you don't really understand what the other person say.

Zeynep: Yes, I know.

Canan: This was the second point I thought was important.

Zeynep: I see.

Canan: Let's think about how you could use these two during the incident you had with your sister, and also the breathing exercise.

Zeynep: How am I going to use them, Miss Canan?

Canan: Think for a while. [Silence.] What is the message she gave you with her behavior, and how did you interpret it?

Zeynep: I got the message that she wouldn't let me watch it.

Canan: Is that right or wrong?

Zeynep: I must have gotten it right.

Canan: But how would you clarify it if I asked you to do so? Let's play a game again.

Zeynep: I could ask: "Won't you let me watch the game?"

Canan: "I won't, because I have my own movie, go and watch it somewhere else."

Zeynep: I can't leave the house. I would have watched it if I could leave. Why don't you go to the downstairs neighbor to watch the movie there?

Canan: OK, now you practice the first stage.

Zeynep: "Look, this game is important for me. It is my only source of fun, I want to watch it. You hang out on the Internet, your source of fun. But please let me watch this game."

Canan: You said please!

Zeynep: Yes, I said it the other day as well, but it didn't work.

Canan: It didn't work.

Zeynep: But I insisted too much and she insisted too much. But we were both very angry.

Canan: Good. How did you insist?

Zeynep: I said I was going to watch. She said she wouldn't let me.

Canan: From the very beginning?

Zeynep: No, not from the beginning. She took the remote. And I said: "I will watch the game, just so you know."

Canan: And she said: "No, I'll watch the movie." Look, let this be a triangle [drawing a triangle]. You start climbing from this side. And she starts climbing from the other side. You will bump into each other at the top. There is no other way. The real problem is there I guess. We are faced with the challenging issue again, did you notice?

Zeynep: Yes, I did.

Canan: You also thought that the girl on the Internet was challenging you.

Zeynep: Yes.

Canan: You thought that your sister was challenging you as well.

Zeynep: It means I have to use the second.

Canan: Where do you think you need to use it exactly?

Zeynep: Where I don't quite understand what she means.

Canan: But sometimes you are very sure about what she means.

Zeynep: That's OK. I can still ask.

Canan: I think you have to ask when you are very angry. What was your sign of anger?

Zeynep: My hands shaking.

Canan: What do you infer from your hands shaking?

Zeynep: That my anger is mounting.

Canan: Yes. My hands are shaking equals: my anger starts mounting. What does this signal?

Zeynep: To calm myself down.

Canan: Breathing exercises were one of the things you could do about that. Today, we figured something else out. What was it?

Zeynep: Clarifying the message I get.

Canan: I have to ask just to make sure I understand correctly.

Zeynep: I wonder if I can I remember it at that time.

Canan: In fact, you may not. But we found a sign that would remind it to you, your hands shaking, didn't we? What are the two things at that time?

Zeynep: One of them is the breathing exercises. And the other thing is the question of: "Do I understand it correctly?"

Canan: Let's do a few exercises about that: tell me what you understand now for example, but say the first thing that you can think of. "Go away immediately."

Zeynep: I understand that you are chasing me.

Canan: You thought I was chasing you. What if I say: "There is a bomb inside, hurry up and go away!"

Zeynep: I would think that you were trying to protect me.

Canan: You can't do with that boy.

Zeynep: You are interested in that boy.

Canan: "He is an errant. He is not good enough for you."

Zeynep: You were again trying to protect me.

Canan: The friends that you hang out with are not friends.

Zeynep: You heard or saw something about them and you are trying to warn me.

Canan: "I hope she leaves them and starts hanging out with me."

Zeynep: And then...

Canan: Can you see that what you hear may not be the same as the intention behind it.

Zeynep: Yes.

Canan: It looks like you got it.

Zeynep: Yes, I got it, Miss Canan.

Canan: OK, can you summarize what we did in this session?

Zeynep: Two things can help me when I try to control my anger. Saying what I am thinking, and understanding whether or not I got the right message. We gave examples about them, and we made a few exercises.

Canan: What does this therapy trying to teach you?

Zeynep: To control my anger.

Canan: Our goal is clear. How are we trying to do these?

Zeynep: I have my breathing exercises. My hands shaking are my signs. I think about what I have to do at that time and I try to do it.

Canan: Then, the responsibility is mostly...

Zeynep: Mine.

Canan: Yes, it gives you the responsibility; it makes you work, doesn't it?

Zeynep: Yes.

Canan: How do you see yourself?

Zeynep: I believe I will be successful.

Canan: Good. Do you ever get successful? Can you give such examples like: I used to do this here before, but I would do this now?

Zeynep: No, I can't say that but fights do not happen very often anymore except some small disputes. I get angry less frequently.

Canan: Yes, I notice that. We also need to work on this challenge issue I think. Did you talk to that girl again?

Zeynep: Yes, I did. She said: "I wasn't trying to be mean. I was trying to tell you about the environment here. Come, we'll hang out together."

Canan: [laughing] Are we all set, then?

Zeynep: Yes.

Canan: I will give you an assignment now. I expect you to come to the next session having tried the things we talked about [telling what actually you want to say, doing breathing exercises, and clarifying the message] at least twice and having succeeded.

Zeynep: OK.

Canan: You may have a few unsuccessful trials. But I want to see that you have succeeded at least twice.

Zeynep: OK, Miss Canan. I will try my best.

Canan: See you then.

Zeynep: See you, Miss Canan.

Session IX: Assessing the Implementation

Synopsis of the session: *In this session an assessment of the solution implementation and the problem-solving treatment is accomplished.*

Canan: Welcome, Zeynep. We haven't seen each other for 2 weeks. How have you been?

Zeynep: I was very sick, Miss Canan. That's why I couldn't come last week. First, my mom got sick, and then I got sick. But I'm OK now.

Canan: I am sorry about that!

Zeynep: Thank you.

Canan: What have you been doing in these last 2 weeks?

Zeynep: I had fun. It was great.

Canan: I am happy for you. Were you able to do the homework I assigned you?

Zeynep: You know I did the first homework you gave me. I made an implementation and I brought you an example. You asked me to bring other examples. But I have never been angry within the last 2 weeks. There was nothing bothering me. I always laughed and had fun. We always have fun with friends when we go out. There hasn't been anything that irritated me.

Canan: I see. You say that you are not getting easily angry anymore.

Zeynep: Yes, my friends said the same thing.

Canan: But have you not experienced any incident where you felt the anger was mounting, or you said "Calm down, Zeynep, ask if you understood it correctly"?

Zeynep: I will today.

Canan: How?

Zeynep: You have met one of my friends, Miss Canan. She used to have a boyfriend, and he happened to be my friend. Apparently, he started seeing his old girlfriend, I will see whether that's true or not. I may get mad if it's true.

Canan: Why are you going to be mad?

Zeynep: I can be mad because he is cheating on my friend. But I first need to ask if that's true.

Canan: Good, this shows that you want to confirm with the other person before you react. This was what we had intended to do in the first place, right? Are there any other examples?

Zeynep: No, there aren't.

Canan: What would your happiness score be today?

Zeynep: I would give 100 to all of them. There is nothing wrong.

Canan: We have been talking about a few things during the therapy: We defined the problems, set goals, found solution alternatives; we chose the ones that we thought would be appropriate solutions and we started implementing them. You brought two examples, one where you had been successful and one where you had been unsuccessful. Then I gave you an assignment. You were expected to implement them when you were faced with a problem situation. You didn't bring in a specific example but you are telling that you don't get angry very easily anymore. I think we solved this problem to a great extent.

Zeynep: Yes Miss Canan. We solved it quite a bit.

Canan: I have the following plan for today: We told you at the beginning of our sessions that our PST would last for about 8 or 10 weeks. This is our ninth session. I want to make an evaluation today. Have we been able to reach our goal? Did we find the right solution? How do you evaluate the things we have done here so far? I am planning to discuss these and make an evaluation session today.

Zeynep: You mean I won't get tired mentally today!

Canan: Yes not much. Then I think about slowly spacing our sessions out, for example, every other week instead of every week.

Zeynep: We are on the right track then.

Canan: That's what I think.

Zeynep: I also think the same way. Miss Canan, do you remember that you got worried when I told you that I was considering working.

Canan: Yes.

Zeynep: I started to work at the Internet café of a friend of mine but I don't want to earn money. I want to work just to keep myself busy.

Canan: It must be keeping you really busy.

Zeynep: It's better than doing nothing.

Canan: Yes. I also noticed that you never stop thinking about school.

Zeynep: Yes, I'm still thinking about school.

Canan: I am not as worried as I have been earlier.

Zeynep: Yes, I am already studying at home.

Canan: You are checking on the schools sometimes. I don't have question marks in my mind about that. I will get there at the end of our session. But today I would like to assess the extent to which you will be able to implement the things you have learned here when I am not seeing you, how useful have the sessions been for you, what did you get out of here, OK?

Zeynep: OK.

Canan: We had identified many solution alternatives with you. We said that we would use a few of them simultaneously. Can you remind me of them please?

Zeynep: There was the breathing exercise, telling what actually I want to say and understanding the right thing. I remember these.

Canan: But after what you have been through with your sister...

Zeynep: There was expressing myself in an appropriate way. There was getting what I want without yelling and shouting, like saying: "This is the only source of fun for me."

Canan: Good. We worked on expressing whatever you really wanted to say, didn't we?

Zeynep: Yes.

Canan: But we also talked about one last thing. Do you remember that?

Zeynep: Oh yes, also, checking whether or not I understood correctly.

Canan: Yes.

Zeynep: Did I get it right or wrong?

Canan: We called this clarifying the message, didn't we?

Zeynep: Yes.

Canan: We discussed in detail that we were going to use these solution alternatives when necessary. We said that you could do the breathing exercises in order to relax in a situation where you had to control yourself, or express yourself nicely when you had problems with other people.

Zeynep: Yes.

Canan: To what extent do these methods solve the problem we identified? How successful they are? How would you rate them over 100.

Zeynep: I can say 70%.

Canan: How is this percentage?

Zeynep: Quite good.

Canan: It solves the anger problem then. To what extent does this solution take you to your goal?

Zeynep: To a great extent.

Canan: Do you think we are reaching our goal?

Zeynep: We are.

Canan: Has there been a decrease in your complaints, your problems after this implementation?

Zeynep: Yes, a lot.

Canan: If we assume that your complaints used to be 100, what do you think it would be now?

Zeynep: We can say that it's 30% now.

Canan: Do you think you will be able to implement these methods by yourself when we are done? It is important that you give an honest answer to this one, because we are going to shape the future sessions accordingly. How much do you trust yourself in this respect?

Zeynep: I trust my own skills and I will try my best to do them by myself but I am not sure if I will be able to do it or not.

Canan: But nowadays?

Zeynep: I am able to do it.

Canan: What do you think can sidetrack you?

Zeynep: If there is a big problem.

Canan: Like what?

Zeynep: For example, if I had a big fight with my mom, she doesn't let me out, she took my phone away, she banned the computer, I'm at the home detention, I can't do it with such a problem.

Canan: But I want to remind you once again that our goal is not to be free of anger. You know that right?

Zeynep: This wouldn't be possible anyway.

Canan: But getting angry at small stuff was a problem, right? We talked a lot about how you expressed yourself when you got angry. You had quite a lot of problems with girls if you remember. It would suddenly go up, the dose was inappropriate. I think what you experienced over the Internet lately was a very important example. You...

Zeynep: I didn't ask the girl what she meant.

Canan: Yes, had you asked that question you wouldn't get angry at her? Our goal was to control the anger when it happened at an inappropriate place and in an inappropriate way, wasn't it?

Zeynep: Yes, when I think of it this way I think I can do it. If I get angry in an appropriate situation I can lower my anger, I won't have to get angry anyway. If I implement these I will understand what is right and what is wrong anyway.

Canan: Do you think we found the appropriate solution alternatives?

Zeynep: Yes I do. Since they worked...

Canan: Is it difficult to implement them?

Zeynep: It is sometimes getting harder. I may not be able to remember them when I'm very angry.

Canan: But we found a solution for this problem as well.

Zeynep: Yes my hands trembling.

Canan: Yes we even put things in order. When there is a sign...

Zeynep: I was going to do the breathing exercises. Then getting the right message.

Canan: Yes we said that we were going to establish a good communication. OK. Can you also remind me of the stages we have been through during these nine sessions?

Zeynep: I was furious at the beginning. I was able to shout and yell and fight without understanding correctly. Slowly, my anger started to decrease. We found the right alternatives, the right solutions. We started to reach our goal.

Canan: Yes. We shouldn't skip the first stage I think. What was it?

Zeynep: What was that?

Canan: We talked about problem orientation, ways of approaching the problem.

Zeynep: I don't remember that.

Canan: We identified your style.

Zeynep: Yes, I remember. I was furious, fighting type.

Canan: We also discussed which one was healthier.

Zeynep: Yes, talking through...

Canan: We read a story, do you remember that?

Zeynep: Yes. Ayse.

Canan: Good, you even remember her name. What kind of style did Ayse have?

Zeynep: She wasn't pessimistic.

Canan: Her nonpessimistic way of thinking is what impressed you the most I think.

Zeynep: What impressed me the most was the question of "What do you mean?"

Canan: Was it? Can you tell me a little bit about that? What does that mean?

Zeynep: I was hurting people. But now that I ask this question, I don't have to hurt them anymore. I calm down.

Canan: Maybe that will be the most useful thing for you.

Zeynep: Yes.

Canan: I have the feeling that you can do it without me.

Zeynep: Yes, I can.

Canan: Because you got it.

Zeynep: I would have been very mad at my friend if I hadn't got that. I will ask now if there is such a thing, etc.

Canan: Pretend you asked this question and your friend told you that it was true. Then what?

Zeynep: Then I will say: "It's up to you" and get over with it. Because my girlfriend wasn't that upset about it. Both of them are my friends. I wouldn't want to hurt any of them. But I just want to know the truth.

Canan: I think this is an important point. There is no need to be Don Quixote when your friend wasn't even upset about that. You don't want to hurt neither of them. This reminded me of something. We talked about keeping the balance between being bad and eradicating everything and pretending that nothing happened.

Zeynep: Yes, we talked about not saying yes to everything.

Canan: OK, you remember all the solution alternatives, you remember our decisions, and you seem to have understood this way very well. I think your confidence in being able to apply it by yourself is not bad. Lastly, what do you think about being in a relationship with angry people?

Zeynep: No, Miss Canan; why would I be with them?

Canan: I think this will be important when you start going to a new school next year.

Zeynep: I have already said this to everybody. My friends tell me to ignore them. And also, yesterday my friends and I were walking together. We were making fun of people's outfits. Girls are looking at us angrily, but we can't get angry we are just laughing.

Canan: What stopped you from getting angry there?

Zeynep: I thought there was no need for me to get angry at those girls because I didn't even know them. I had fun.

Canan: Using humor, having fun was one of our solution alternatives, wasn't it?

Zeynep: Yes.

Canan: OK Zeynep, good. It looks like you understood and you are really able to practice.

Zeynep: Yes. Thank God I don't have any problems these days.

Canan: But don't forget this. Problems will happen. And there may be times when you get angry. There are times when I get angry, when everybody gets angry. Let's hope it doesn't happen for minor reasons, against everybody, and that it stays within certain limits if it happens. When we first met, you used to break people's head. What would you do if anything happened to one of them?

Zeynep: Yes, but they are over now.

Canan: Yes. I will now ask one last thing from you. I had asked you to fill out some questionnaires at the beginning of our sessions, if you remember. I will ask you to fill them out again. Because I want to see if there is a difference between the first ones and the ones you fill out today.

Zeynep: OK.

Canan: OK, let's schedule our meeting after 2 weeks from now. We can decide on what to do depending on the situation. Is there anything you would like to ask me?

Zeynep: No. I just want to thank you.

Canan: You are welcome. It has been a pleasure to work with you because you have always had a great motivation; you are smart and hard working. You worked on the problem with a great enthusiasm and I think you won. You may stop once in a while but I believe that you will always go forward. When you can't handle it you know that we will always be here....

Zeynep: Yes, I know. Thank you.

References

Ackerman, R. T., & Williams, J. W. (2002). Rational treatment choices for non-major depression in primary care. *Journal of General Internal Medicine*, *17*, 293–301.

Addis, M. E., & Jacobson, N. S. (2000). A closer look at the treatment rationale and homework compliance in cognitive–behavioral therapy for depression. *Cognitive Therapy and Research*, *24*, 313–326.

Aguilera, A., López, S. R., Breitborde, N. J. K., et al. (2010). Expressed emotion and sociocultural moderation in the course of schizophrenia. *Journal of Abnormal Psychology*, *119*, 875–885.

Alexopoulos, G. S., Raue, P. J., & Arean, P. (2003). Problem solving therapy versus supportive therapy in geriatric major depression with executive dysfunction. *The American Journal of Geriatric Psychiatry*, *11*, 46–52.

Alexopoulos, G. S., Raue, P. J., Kiosses, D. N., et al. (2011). Problem solving therapy and supportive therapy in older adults with major depression and executive dysfunction: Effect on disability. *Archives of General Psychiatry*, *68*, 33–41.

Allen, S. M., Shah, A. C., Nezu, A. M., et al. (2002). A problem-solving approach to stress reduction among younger women with breast carcinoma: A randomized controlled trial. *Cancer*, *94*, 3089–3100.

Allen, N., Whittemore, R., & Melkus, G. (2011). A continuous glucose monitoring and problem-solving intervention to change physical activity behavior in women with type 2 diabetes: A pilot study. *Diabetes Technology and Therapeutics*, *13*, 1091–1099.

American Psychiatric Association (1994). *Diagnostic and Statistical Manual of Mental Disorders (DSM-IV)*. Washington, DC: American Psychiatric Association.

American Psychological Association. 10 ways to build resilience. <www.APAHelpCenter.org/resilience/> Retrieved 12.05.07.

Anderson, J. R. (1982). Acquisition of cognitive skill. *Psychological Review*, *89*, 369–406.

Anderson, J. R. (1983). *The architecture of cognition*. Cambridge, MA: Harvard University Press.

Andreasen, N. C. (1985). Positive and negative schizophrenia: A critical evaluation. *Schizophrenia Bulletin*, *11*, 380–389.

Ang, R. P. (2003). Social problem-solving skills training: Does it really work? *Child Care in Practice*, *9*, 5–17.

Appley, M. H., & Trumbull, R. (1986). Development of the stress concept. In M. H. Appley, & R. Trumbull (Eds.), *Dynamics of stress* (pp. 3–18). New York, NY: Plenum Press.

Arean, P. A., Perri, M. G., Nezu, A. M., et al. (1993). Comparative effectiveness of social problem solving therapy and reminiscence therapy as treatments for depression in older adults. *Journal of Consulting and Clinical Psychology*, *61*, 1003–1010.

Arie, M., Apter, A., Orbach, I., et al. (2008). Autobiographical memory, interpersonal problem solving, and suicidal behavior in adolescent inpatients. *Comprehensive Psychiatry*, 22–29.

Atkinson, R. L., Atkinson, R. C., Smith, E. E., et al. *Psikolojiye giriş* [*Introduction to psychology, Turkish translation*]. Ankara: Arkadaş Yayınları.

Bandelow, B., Seidler-Brandler, U., Becker, A., et al. (2007). Meta-analysis of randomized controlled comparisons of psychopharmacological and psychological treatments for anxiety disorders. *The World Journal of Biological Psychiatry*, *8*, 175–187.

Bandura, A. (1977). Self-efficacy: Toward a unifying theory of behavioral change. *Psychological Review*, *84*, 191–215.

Bandura, A. (1986). *Social foundations of thought and action: A social cognitive theory*. Englewood Cliffs, NJ: Prentice-Hall.

Bannan, N. (2010). Group-based problem-solving therapy in self-poisoning females: A pilot study. *Counselling and Psychotherapy Research*, *10*, 201–213.

Barrett, J. E., Williams, J. W., Oxman, T. E., et al. (1999). The treatment effectiveness project: A comparison of the effectiveness of paroxetine, problem solving therapy and placebo in the treatment of minor depression and dysthymia in primary care patients: Background and research plan. *General Hospital Psychiatry*, *21*, 260–273.

Bass, J., Poudyal, B., Tol, W., et al. (2012). A controlled trial of problem-solving counseling for war-affected adults in Aceh, Indonesia. *Social Psychiatry and Psychiatric Epidemiology*, *47*, 279–291.

Bateson, M., Brilot, B., & Nettle, D. (2011). Anxiety: An evolutionary approach. *Canadian Journal of Psychiatry*, *56*, 707–715.

Baumgardner, A. H., Heppner, P. P., & Arkin, R. M. (1986). Role of causal attribution in personal problem solving. *Journal of Personality and Social Psychology*, *50*, 636–643.

Bauml, J., Frobose, T., Kraemer, S., et al. (2006). Psychoeducation: A basic psychotherapeutic intervention for patients with schizophrenia and their families. *Schizophrenia Bulletin*, *32*, 1–9.

Beardslee, W., & Gladstone, T. (2001). Prevention of childhood depression: Recent findings and future prospects. *Society of Biological Psychiatry*, *49*, 1101–1110.

Beautrais, A. L. (2002). A case control study of suicide and attempted suicide in older adults. *Suicide and Life-Threatening Behavior*, *32*, 1–9.

Becker-Weidman, E. G., Jacobs, R. H., Reinecke, M. A., et al. (2010). Social problem-solving among adolescents treated for depression. *Behaviour Research and Therapy*, *48*, 11–18.

Bedell, J., Lennox, S. S., Smith, A. D., & Rabinowicz, E. F. (1998). Evaluation of problem solving and communication skills of persons with schizophrenia. *Psychiatry Research*, *78*, 197–206.

Bell, A. C., & D'Zurilla, T. J. (2009a). Problem-solving therapy for depression: A meta-analysis. *Clinical Psychology Review*, *29*, 348–353.

Bell, A. C., & D'Zurilla, T. J. (2009b). The influence of social problem-solving ability on the relationship between daily stress and adjustment. *Cognitive Therapy and Research*, *33*, 439–448.

Bellack, A. S., Schooler, N. R., Marder, S. R., et al. (2004). Do clozapine and risperidone affect social competence and problem solving? *American Journal of Psychiatry*, *161*, 364–367.

Belzer, K. D., D'Zurilla, J. D., Maydeu-Olivares, A. (2002). Social problem solving and trait anxiety as predictors of worry in a college student population. *Personality and Individual Differences*, *33*, 573–585.

Berk, M. S., Jeglic, E., Brown, G. K., et al. (2007). Characteristics of recent suicide attempters with and without borderline personality disorder. *Archives of Suicide Research*, *11*, 91–104.

Bertolote, J. M., & Fleischmann, A. (2002). A global perspective in the epidemiology of suicide. *Suicidologi*, *7*, 6–8.

Biggam, F. H., & Power, K. G. (1999). A comparison of the problem solving abilities and psychological distress of suicidal, bullied, and protected prisoners. *Criminal Justice and Behavior*, *26*, 196–216.

Bijl, R. V., Ravelli, A., & van Zessen, G. (1998). Prevalence of psychiatric disorder in the general population: Results of The Netherlands Mental Health Survey and Incidence Study (NEMESIS). *Social Psychiatry and Psychiatric Epidemiology*, *33*, 587–595.

Blanchard, J. J., Sayers, S. L., Collins, L. M., & Bellack, A. S. (2004). Affectivity in the problem solving interactions of schizophrenia patients and their family members. *Schizophrenia Research*, *69*, 105–117.

Boeschoten, R. E., Nieuwenhuis, M. M., Oppen, P. V., et al. (2012). Feasibility and outcome of a web-based self-help intervention for depressive symptoms in patients with multiple sclerosis: A pilot study. *Journal of the Neurological Sciences*, *315*, 104–109.

Borkovec, T. D., & Castonguay, L. G. (1998). What is the scientific meaning of empirically supported therapy? *Journal of Consulting and Clinical Psychology*, *66*, 136–142.

Bourke, M. L., & Hasselt, V. B. V. (2001). Social problem-solving skills training for incarcerated offenders: A treatment manual. *Behavior Modification*, *25*, 163–188.

Bray, S., Barrowclough, C., & Lobban, F. (2007). The social problem-solving abilities of people with borderline personality disorder. *Behaviour Research and Therapy*, *45*, 1409–1417.

Burns, D. D., & Spangler, D. L. (2000). Does psychotherapy homework lead to improvements in depression in cognitive–behavioral therapy or does improvement lead to increased homework compliance? *Journal of Consulting and Clinical Psychology*, *68*, 46–56.

Bustini, M., Stratta, P., Daneluzzo, E., & Pollice, R. (1999). Tower of Hanoi and WCST performance in schizophrenia: Problem-solving capacity and clinical correlates. *Journal of Psychiatric Research*, *33*, 285–290.

Butler, A. C., Chapman, J. E., Forman, E. M., et al. (2006). The empirical status of cognitive–behavioral therapy: A review of meta-analysis. *Clinical Psychology Review*, *26*, 17–31.

Cameron, J. I., Shin, J. L., Williams, D., & Stewart, D. E. (2004). A brief problem-solving intervention for family caregivers to individuals with advanced cancer. *Journal of Psychosomatic Research*, *57*, 137–143.

Cannon, B., & Mulroy, R. (1999). Dysfunctional attitudes and problem solving skills predict hopelessness in major depression. *Journal of Affective Disorders*, *55*, 45–49.

Carlton, P. L., & Goldstein, L. (1987). Physiological determinants of pathological gambling. In T. Glaski (Ed.), *A handbook of pathological gambling* (pp. 657–663). Springfield, IL: Charles C. Thomas.

Carlton, P. L., & Manowitz, P. (1987). Physiological factors as determinants of pathological gambling. *Journal of Gambling Behavior*, *3*, 274–285.

Caselli, R. J., Reiman, E. M., Hentz, J. G., et al. (2004). A distinctive interaction between chronic anxiety and problem solving in asymptomatic APOE e4 homozygotes. *Journal of Neuropsychiatry and Neuroscience*, *16*, 320–329.

Chambers, E., & Belicki, K. (1998). Using sleep dysfunction to explore the nature of resilience in adult survivors of childhood abuse or trauma. *Child Abuse and Neglect*, *22*, 753–758.

Chan, R. C., Chen, E. Y., Cheung, E. F., et al. (2004). A study of sensitivity of the sustained attention to response task in patients with schizophrenia. *Clinical Neuropsychology*, *18*, 114–121.

Channon, S., Charman, T., Heap, J., et al. (2001). Real-life type problem-solving in Asperger's syndrome. *Journal of Autism and Developmental Disorders, 31*, 461–469.

Chen, S. Y., Jordan, C., & Thompson, S. (2006). The effect of cognitive behavioral therapy (CBT) on depression: The role of problem-solving appraisal. *Research on Social Work Practice, 16*, 500–510.

Cheng, S. K. (2001). Life stress, problem solving, perfectionism, and depressive symptoms in Chinese adolescents. *Cognitive Therapy and Research, 25*, 303–310.

Chibanda, D., Mesu, P., Kajawu, L., et al. (2011). Problem-solving therapy for depression and common mental disorders in Zimbabwe: Piloting a task-shifting primary mental health care intervention in a population with a high prevalence of people with HIV. *BMC Pubic Health, 11*, 828.

Chisholm, V., Atkinson, L., Donaldson, C., et al. (2010). Maternal communication style, problem-solving, and dietary adherence in young children with type I diabetes. *Clinical Child Psychology and Psychiatry, 16*, 443–458.

Clum, G. A., & Febbraro, G. A. A. (2004). Social problem solving and suicide risk. In E. C. Chang, T. J. D'Zurilla, & L. J. Sanna (Eds.), *Social roblem solving: Theory, research, and training* (pp. 67–82). Washington, DC: American Psychological Association.

Clum, G., Patsiokas, A., & Luscomb, R. (1979). Empirically based comprehensive treatment program for parasuicide. *Journal of Consulting and Clinical Psychology, 47*, 937–945.

Coche, E., & Flick, A. (1975). Problem solving training groups for hospitalized psychiatric patients. *The Journal of Psychology, 91*, 19–29.

Coid, J. (2003). Epidemiology, public health and the problem of personality disorder. *The British Journal of Psychiatry, 182*, 3–10.

Coid, J., Yang, M., Tyrer, P., et al. (2006). Prevalence of personality disorder in Great Britain. *British Journal of Psychiatry, 188*, 423–431.

Collishaw, S., Maughan, B., Goodman, R., & Pickles, A. (2004). Time trends in adolescent mental health. *Journal of Child Psychology and Psychiatry, 45*, 1350–1362.

Cook, S., Herold, K., Edidin, D. V., & Briars, R. (2002). Increasing problem solving in adolescents with type 1 diabetes: The Choices Diabetes Program. *The Diabetes Educator, 28*, 115–124.

Corey, G. (1996). *Theory and practice of counseling and psychotherapy*. Pacific Grove, CA: Brooks/Cole Publishing Company.

Coyne, J. C., Aldwin, C., & Lazarus, R. S. (1981). Depression and coping in stressful episodes. *Journal of Abnormal Psychology, 90*, 439–447.

Crawford, M. J. (2007). Can deficits in social-problem solving in people with personality disorder be reversed? *British Journal of Psychiatry, 190*, 283–284.

Cuijpers, P., van Straten, A., & Warmerdam, L. (2007). Problem solving therapies for depression: A meta-analysis. *European Psychiatry, 22*, 9–15.

Dekovic, M. (1999). Risk and protective factors in the development of problem behavior during adolescence. *Journal of Youth and Adolescence, 28*, 667–685.

Demirbas, H., Ilhan, I. O., & Dogan, Y. B. (2012). Ways of problem solving as predictors of relapse in alcohol dependent male patients. *Addictive Behaviors, 37*, 131–134.

Dereboy, C., Eskin, M., & Senyuva, H. S. (2007). *Aydın ili normal populasyonda kişilik bozukluklarının prevalens çalışması ve ilişkili parametrelerin çalışılması* [*Prevalence of and associated factors with personality disorders in community sample in the province of Aydin, Turkey, in Turkish*]. Ankara: Turkish Science Foundation. Project Number: SBAG G-HD-128 106S113.

Dereboy, C., Harlak, H., Gürel, S., et al. (2005). Teaching empathy in medical education. *Turkish Journal of Psychiatry, 16*, 83–89.

DeRubeis, R. J., Hollon, S. D., Amsterdam, J. D., et al. (2005). Cognitive therapy vs. medications in the treatment of moderate to severe depression. *Archives of General Psyhiatry*, *62*, 409–416.

Dixon, L. B., Dickerson, F., Bellack, A. S., et al. (2010). The 2009 schizophrenia PORT psychosocial treatment recommendations and summary statements. *Schizophrenia Bulletin*, *36*, 48–70.

Dixon, W. A., & Heppner, P. P. (1993). Distinguishing among antecedents, concomitants, and consequences of problem-solving appraisal and depressive symptoms. *Journal of Counseling Psychology*, *40*, 357–364.

Dixon, W. A., Heppner, P. P., & Rudd, M. D. (1994). Problem-solving appraisal, hopelessness, and suicide ideation: Evidence for a mediational model. *Journal of Consulting and Clinical Psychology*, *41*, 91–98.

Dodge, K. A., & Crick, N. R. (1990). Social information-processing bases of aggressive behavior in children. *Personality and Social Psychology Bulletin*, *15*, 8–22.

Dowrick, C., Dunn, G., Ayuso-Mateou, J. L., et al. (2000). Problem solving treatment and group psychoeducation for depression: Multicentre randomized controlled trial. *British Medical Journal*, *321*, 1450–1454.

Dowson, J., Bazanis, E., Rogers, R., et al. (2004). Impulsivity in patients with borderline personality disorder. *Comprehensive Psychiatry*, *45*, 29–36.

Dreer, L. E., Elliott, T. R., & Tucker, E. (2004). Social problem-solving abilities and health behaviors among persons with recent-onset spinal cord injury. *Journal of Clinical Psychology in Medical Settings*, *11*, 7–13.

Dugas, M. J., Ladouceur, R., Léger, E., et al. (2003). Group cognitive–behavioral therapy for generalized anxiety disorder: Treatment outcome and long-term follow-up. *Journal of Consulting and Clinical Psychology*, *71*, 821–825.

Dugas, M. J., Letarte, H., Rhéaume, J., Freeston, M. H., & Ladouceur, R. (1995). Worry and problem solving: Evidence of a specific relationship. *Cognitive Therapy and Research*, *19*, 109–120.

Dumont, M., & Provost, M. (1999). Resilience in adolescents: Protective role of social support coping strategies, self-esteem and social activities on experience of stress and depression. *Journal of Youth and Adolescence*, *28*, 343–363.

D'Zurilla, T. J., Chang, E. C., & Sanna, L. (2003). Self-esteem and social problem solving as predictors of aggression in college students. *Journal of Social and Clinical Psychology*, *22*, 424–440.

D'Zurilla, T. J., & Goldfried, M. R. (1971). Problem solving and behavior modification. *Journal of Abnormal Psychology*, *78*, 107–126.

D'Zurilla, T. J., & Nezu, A. M. (1982). Social problem solving in adults. In P. C. Kendall (Ed.), *Advances in cognitive–behavioral research and therapy* (pp. 202–274). New York, NY: Academic Press.

D'Zurilla, T. J., & Nezu, A. M. (1999). *Problem-solving therapy: A social competence approach to clinical intervention*. New York, NY: Springer.

D'Zurilla, T. J., & Nezu, A. M. (2003). Problem solving therapies. In K. S. Dobson (Ed.), *Handbook of cognitive–behavioral therapies* (pp. 211–245). New York, NY: The Guilford Press.

D'Zurilla, T. J., Nezu, A. M., & Maydeu-Olivares, A. (2002). *Manual for the Social Problem Solving Inventory-Revised (SPSI-R)*. North Tonawanda, NY: Multi-Health Systems.

D'Zurilla, T. J., Nezu, A. M., & Maydeu-Olivares, A. (2004). Social problem solving: Theory and assessment. In E. C. Chang, T. J. D'Zurilla, & L. J. Sanna (Eds.), *Social problem solving: Theory, research, and training* (pp. 3–27). Washington, DC: American Psychological Association.

Egan, G. (1998). *The skilled helper: A problem-management approach to helping*. Pacific Grove, CA: Brooks/Cole Publishing Company.

Elliott, T. R., Berry, J. W., & Grant, J. S. (2009). Problem-solving training for family caregivers of women with disabilities: A randomized clinical trial. *Behaviour Research and Therapy*, *47*, 548–558.

Elliott, T. R., & Shewchuk, R. M. (2003). Social problem solving abilities and distress among family members assuming a caregiving role. *British Journal of Health Psychology*, *8*, 149–163.

Elliott, T. R., Schewchuk, R. M., Miller, D. M., & Richards, S. (2001). Profiles in problem solving: Psychological well-being and distress among persons with diabetes mellitus. *Journal of Clinical Psychology in Medical Settings*, *8*, 283–291.

Ellis, T. E., & Rutherford, B. (2008). Cognition and suicide: Two decades of progress. *International Journal of Cognitive Therapy*, *1*, 47–68.

Eskin, M. (1995). Suicidal behavior as related to social support and assertiveness among Swedish and Turkish high school students: A cross-cultural investigation. *Journal of Clinical Psychology*, *51*, 158–172.

Eskin, M. (1996). Cross-cultural gender differences in the psychosocial correlates of current adolescent suicidal ideation. *Journal of Gender, Culture and Health*, *1*, 189–205.

Eskin, M. (1997). Cross-cultural tests of the gender-role consistency and stigma hypotheses of suicidal behavior. *Journal of Gender, Culture and Health*, *2*, 245–262.

Eskin, M. (1999). Gender and cultural differences in the 12-month prevalence of suicidal thoughts and attempts in Swedish and Turkish adolescents. *Journal of Gender, Culture and Health*, *4*, 187–200.

Eskin, M. (2007). İntiharda bilişsel davranışçı sağaltım yaklaşımları [Cognitive-behavioral treatment approaches to suicide, in Turkish]. *Turkish Journal of Crisis*, *15*, 15–35.

Eskin, M. (2010). *Sorunlarımı çözebilirim [I can solve my problems, in Turkish]*. Ankara: Hekimler Yayın Birliği.

Eskin, M. (2012). *İntihar: Açıklama, Değerlendirme, Tedavi, Önleme [Suicide: Explanation, assessment, treatment and prevention, in Turkish]*. Ankara: Hekimler Yayın Birliği.

Eskin., M., Akoglu, A., & Uygur, B. (2006). Traumatic life events and problem solving skills in psychiatric outpatients: Relationships with suicidal behavior. *Turkish Journal of Psychiatry*, *17*, 266–275.

Eskin, M., Ertekin, K., & Demir, H. (2008). Efficacy of a problem-solving therapy for depression and suicide potential in adolescents and young adults. *Cognitive Therapy and Research*, *32*, 227–245.

Eskin, M., Ertekin, K., Dereboy, C., & Demirkiran, F. (2007). Risk factors for and protective factors against adolescent suicidal behavior in Turkey. *Crisis: The Journal of Crisis Intervention and Suicide Prevention*, *28*, 131–139.

Eskin, M., Ertekin, K., Harlak, H., & Dereboy, Ç. (2008). Prevalence of and factors related to depression in high school students. *Turkish Journal of Psychiatry*, *19*, 382–389.

Eskin, M., Kaynak-Demir, H., & Demir, S. (2005). Same-sex sexual orientation, childhood sexual abuse, and suicidal behavior in university students in Turkey. *Archives of Sexual Behavior*, *34*, 185–195.

Esposito, C. L., & Clum, G. A. (2002). Social support and problem-solving as moderators of the relationship between childhood abuse and suicidality. Applications to a delinquent population. *Journal of Traumatic Stress*, *15*, 137–146.

Evans, E., Hawton, K., Rodham, K., & Deeks, J. (2005). The prevalence of suicidal phenomenon in adolescents: A systematic review of population-based studies. *Suicide and Life-Threatening Behavior, 35*, 239–250.

Falloon, I. R. H. (2000). Problem solving as a core strategy in the prevention of schizophrenia and other mental disorders. *Australian and New Zealand Journal of Psychiatry, 34*, 185–190.

Falloon, I. R. H., Barbieri, L., Boggian, I., & Lamonaca, D. (2007). Problem solving training for schizophrenia: Rationale and review. *Journal of Mental Health, 16*, 553–568.

Fitzpatrick, K. K., Witte, T. K., & Schmidt, N. B. (2005). Randomized controlled trial of a brief problem-orientation intervention for suicidal ideation. *Behavior Therapy, 36*, 323–333.

Folkman, S., & Lazarus, R. S. (1985). If it changes it must be a process: Study of emotion and coping during three stages of a college examination. *Journal of Personality and Social Psycholology, 48*, 150–170.

Folkman, S., & Lazarus, R. S. (1986). Stress process and depressive symptomatology. *Journal of Abnormal Psychology, 95*, 107–113.

Fossati, P., & Ergis, A. M. (2001). Problem solving abilities in unipolar depressed patients: Comparison of performance on the modified version of the Wisconsin and the California card sorting tests. *Psychiatry Research, 104*, 145–156.

Frese, M. (1986). Coping as a moderator between stress at work and psychosomatic complaints. In M. H. Appley, & R. Trumbull (Eds.), *Dynamics of stress* (pp. 183–206). New York, NY: Plenum Press.

Garcia-Vera, M. P., Sanz, J., & Labrador, F. J. (1998). Psychological changes accompanying and mediating stress-management training for essential hypertension. *Applied Psychophysiology and Biofeedback, 23*, 159–178.

Garland, A., & Harrington, J. (2000). A pilot study of the relationship between problem solving skills and outcome in major depressive disorder. *British Journal of Medical Psychology, 73*, 303–309.

Gath, D., & Mynors-Wallis, L. (2000). Problem-solving treatment in primary care. In D. M. Clark, & C. G. Fairburn (Eds.), *Science and practice of cognitive behaviour therapy* (pp. 415–431). Oxford: Oxford University Press.

Gellis, Z. D., & Bruce, M. L. (2010). Problem solving therapy for subthreshold depression in home healthcare patients with cardiovascular disease. *American Journal of Geriatric Psychiatry, 18*, 464–474.

Gellis, Z. D., & Kenaley, B. (2008). Problem-solving therapy for depression in adults: A systematic review. *Research on Social Work Practice, 18*, 117–131.

Ghahramanlou-Holloway, M., Bhar, S. S., Brown, G. K., et al. (2012). Changes in problem-solving appraisal after cognitive therapy for the prevention of suicide. *Psychological Medicine, 42*, 1185–1193.

Gotlib, I. H., & Asarnow, R. F. (1979). Interpersonal and impersonal problem solving skills in mildly and clinically depressed üniversity students. *Journal of Consulting and Clinical Psychology, 47*, 86–95.

Granholm, E., McQuaid, J. R., McClure, F. S., et al. (2005). A randomized controlled trial of cognitive behavioral social skills training for middle-aged and older outpatients with chronic schizophrenia. *American Journal of Psychiatry, 162*, 520–529.

Granholm, E., McQuaid, J. R., McClure, F. S., et al. (2007). Randomized controlled trial of cognitive behavioral social skills training for older people with schizophrenia: 12-month follow-up. *Journal of Clinical Psychiatry, 68*, 730–737.

Grant, J. S., Elliott, T. R., Weaver, M., et al. (2002). A telephone intervention with family caregivers of stroke survivors after rehabilitation. *Stroke*, *33*, 2060–2065.

Grant, J. S., Elliott, T. R., Weaver, M., et al. (2006). Social support, social problem-solving abilities, and adjustment of family caregivers of stroke survivors. *Archives of Physical Medicine and Rehabilitation*, *87*, 343–350.

Halder, S., & Mahato, A. K. (2009). Relationship between executive function and problem solving ability of schizophrenia patients. *Eastern Journal of Psychiatry*, *12*, 41–44.

Hamrin, V., & Pachler, M. C. (2005). Child and adolescent depression: Review of the latest evidence-based treatments. *Journal of Psychosocial Nursing and Mental Health Services*, *43*, 54–63.

Harley, R., Petersen, T., Scalia, M., et al. (2006). Problem-solving ability and comorbid personality disorders in depressed outpatients. *Depression and Anxiety*, *23*, 496–501.

Hassink-Franke, L. A. J., Hartman, T. C., Beek, M. M., et al. (2011). Problem-solving treatment in general practice residency: A focus group study of registrars' views. *Patient Education and Counseling*, *85*, 106–112.

Hatashita-Wong, M., Smith, T. E., Silverstein, S. M., Hull, J. W., & Willson, D. F. (2002). Cognitive functioning and social problem-solving skills in schizophrenia. *Cognitive Neuropsychiatry*, *7*, 81–95.

Hatcher, S., Coupe, N., Durie, M., et al. (2011). Te Ira Tangata: A Zelen randomized controlled trial of a treatment package including problem solving therapy compared to treatment as usual in Maori who present to hospital after self harm. *Trials*, *12*, 117.

Haverkamp, R., Arean, P., Hegel, M. T., & Unützer, J. (2004). Problem-solving treatment for complicated depression in late life: A case study in primary care. *Perspectives in Psychiatric Care*, *40*, 45–52.

Hawton, K. (2000). Attempted suicide. In D. M. Clark, & C. G. Fairburn (Eds.), *Science and practice of cognitive behaviour therapy* (pp. 285–312). Oxford: Oxford University Press.

Hawton, K., Arensman, E., Townsend, E., et al. (1998). Deliberate self harm: Systematic review of efficacy of psychosocial and pharmacological treatments in preventing repetition. *British Medical Journal*, *317*, 441–447.

Hay, J., Byrne, M., & Butler, C. (2000). Evaluation of a conflict-resolution and problem-solving programme to enhance adolescents' self concept. *British Journal of Guidance and Counselling*, *28*, 101–113.

Hegel, M. T., Barrett, J. E., & Oxman, T. E. (2000). Training therapists in problem-solving treatment of depressive disorders in primary care. *Families, Systems and Health: The Journal of Collaborative Family Health Care*, *18*, 423–436.

Hegel, M. T., Dietrich, A. J., Seville, J. L., & Jordan, C. B. (2004). Training residents in problem-solving treatment of depression: A pilot feasibility and impact study. *Family Medicine*, *36*, 204–208.

Hegel, M. T., Lyons, K. D., Hull, J. G., et al. (2011). Feasibility study of a randomized controlled trial of a telephone-delivered problem-solving-occupational therapy intervention to reduce participation restrictions in rural breast cancer survivors undergoing chemotherapy. *Psychooncology*, *20*, 1092–1101.

Heppner, P. P., & Anderson, W. P. (1985). The relationship between problem solving self-appraisal and psychological adjustment. *Cognitive Therapy and Research*, *9*, 415–427.

Heppner, P. P., & Krauskopf, C. J. (1987). An information-processing approach to personal problem solving. *The Counseling Psychologist*, *15*, 371–447.

Heppner, P. P., & Petersen, C. H. (1982). The development and implications of a personal problem solving inventory. *Journal of Counseling Psychology*, *29*, 66–75.

Hill-Briggs, F. (2003). Problem solving in diabetes self-management: A model of chronic illness self-management behavior. *Annals of Behavioral Medicine*, *25*, 182–193.

Hill-Briggs, F., Gary, T. L., Yeh, H.-C., et al. (2006). Association of social problem solving with glycemic control in a sample of urban African Americans with type 2 diabetes. *Journal of Behavioral Medicine*, *29*, 69–78.

Hill-Brigs, F., Lazo, M., Peyrot, M., et al. (2011). Effect of problem-solving-based diabetes self-management training on diabetes control in a low income patient sample. *Journal of General Internal Medicine*, *26*, 972–978.

Hoek, W., Schuurmans, J., Koor, H. M., & Cuijpers, P. (2009). Prevention of depression and anxiety in adolescents: A randomized controlled trial testing the efficacy and mechanisms of Internet-based self-help problem-solving therapy. *Trials*, *10*, 93.

Hof, E., Stein, D. J., Marks, I., et al. (2011). The effectiveness of problem solving therapy in deprived South African communities: Results from a pilot study. *BMC Psychiatry*, *11*, 156.

Hoge, C. W., Castro, C. A., Messer, S. C., et al. (2004). Combat duty in Iraq and Afghanistan, mental health problems, and barriers to care. *New England Journal of Medicine*, *351*, 13–22.

Hollon, S. D., DeRubeis, R. J., Shelton, R. C., et al. (2005). Prevention of relapse following cognitive therapy vs. medications in moderate to severe depression. *Archives of General Psyhiatry*, *62*, 417–422.

Hooley, J. M. (2007). Expressed emotion and relapse of psychopathology. *Annual Review of Clinical Psychology*, *3*, 329–352.

Hopko, D. R., Armento, M. E. A., Robertson, S. M. C., et al. (2011). Brief behavioral activation and problem-solving therapy for depressed breast cancer patients: Randomized trial. *Journal of Consulting and Clinical Psychology*, *79*, 834–849.

Horowitz, L. M. (1979). On the cognitive structure of interpersonal problems treated in psychotherapy. *Journal of Consulting and Clinical Psychology*, *47*, 5–15.

Huband, N., McMurran, M., Evans, C., & Duggan, C. (2007). Social problem-solving plus psychoeducation for adults with personality disorder: Pragmatic randomized controlled trial. *British Journal of Psychiatry*, *190*, 307–313.

Hughes, R. B., Nosek, M. A., Howland, C. A., et al. (2003). Health promotion for women with physical disabilities: A pilot study. *Rehabilitation Psychology*, *48*, 182–188.

Ijff, M. A., Huijbregts, K. M. L., Marvijk, H. W. J., et al. (2007). Cost-effectiveness of collaborative care including PST and an antidepressant treatment algorithm for the treatment of major depressive disorder in primary care: A randomized clinical trial. *BMC Health Services Research*, *7*, 34.

Jeglic, E. L., Sharp, J. R., Chapman, J. E., et al. (2005). History of family suicide behaviors and negative problem solving in multiple suicide attempters. *Archives of Suicide Research*, *9*, 135–146.

Johnson, G. R., Krug, E. G., & Potter, L. B. (2000). Suicide among adolescents and young adults: A cross-national comparison of 34 countries. *Suicide and Life-Threatening Behavior*, *30*, 74–82.

Karterud, S., & Urnes, O. (2004). Short-term day treatment programs for patients with personality disorders. What is the optimal composition? *Nordic Journal of Psychiatry*, *58*, 243–249.

Kazantzis, N., Deane, F. P., & Ronan, K. R. (2000). Homework assignments in cognitive and behavioral therapy: A meta-analysis. *Clinical Psychology: Science and Practice*, *7*, 189–202.

Kazantzis, N., Lampropoulos, G. K., & Deane, F. P. (2005). A national survey of practicing psychologists' use and attitudes toward homework in psychotherapy. *Journal of Consulting and Clinical Psychology*, *73*, 742–748.

Kazdin, A. E., Siegel, T. C., & Bass, D. (1992). Cognitive problem-solving skills training and parent management training in the treatment of antisocial behavior in children. *Journal of Consulting and Clinical Psychology*, *60*, 733–747.

Keltigangas-Jarvinen, L. (2001). Aggressive behavior and social problem-solving strategies: A review of the findings of a seven-year follow-up from childhood to late adolescence. *Criminal Behaviour and Mental Health*, *11*, 236–250.

Keltigangas-Jarvinen, L. (2002). Aggressive problem-solving strategies, aggressive behavior, and social acceptance in early and late adolescence. *Journal of Youth and Adolescence*, *31*, 279–287.

Keltigangas-Jarvinen, L., & Pakaslahti, L. (1999). Development of social problem-solving strategies and changes in aggressive behavior: A 7-year follow-up from childhood to late adolescence. *Aggressive Behavior*, *25*, 269–279.

Kern, R. S., Green, M. F., Mitchell, S., et al. (2005). Extensions of errorless learning for social problem-solving deficits in schizophrenia. *American Journal of Psychiatry*, *162*, 513–519.

Kim, H. Y. (2003). Correlation of mental health problems with psychological constructs in adolescence: Final results from a 2-year study. *International Journal of Nursing Studies*, *40*, 115–124.

Kinard, E. M. (1998). Methodological issues in assessing resilience in maltreated children. *Child Abuse and Neglect*, *22*, 669–680.

King, D. K., Glasgow, R. E., Toobert, D. J., et al. (2010). Self-efficacy, problem solving, and social-environmental support are associated with diabetes self-management behaviors. *Diabetes Care*, *33*, 751–753.

Kingdon, D. G., & Turkington, D. (2005). *Cognitive therapy of schizophrenia*. New York, NY: The Guilford Press.

Kizilbash, A. H., Vanderploeg, R. D., & Curtiss, G. (2002). The effects of depression and anxiety on memory performance. *Archives of Clinical Neuropsychology*, *17*, 57–67.

Klohnen, E. (1996). Conceptual analysis and measurement of the construct of ego-resiliency. *Journal of Personality and Social Psychology*, *70*, 1067–1079.

Klonsky, E. D., Oltmanns, T. F., & Turkheimer, E. (2002). Informant-reports of personality disorder: Relation to self-reports and future research directions. *Clinical Psychology: Science and Practice*, *9*, 300–311.

Krohne, H. W. (1986). Coping with stress. In M. H. Appley, & R. Trumbull (Eds.), *Dynamics of stress* (pp. 207–232). New York, NY: Plenum Press.

Kurylo, M., Elliott, T. R., DeVivo, L., & Dreer, L. E. (2004). Caregiver social problem solving abilities and family member adjustment following congestive heart failure. *Journal of Clinical Psychology in Medical Settings*, *11*, 151–157.

Ladouceur, R., Blais, F., Freeston, M. H., & Dugas, M. J. (1998). Problem solving and problem orientation in generalized anxiety disorder. *Journal of Anxiety Disorders*, *12*, 139–152.

Ladouceur, R., Léger, E., Dugas, M., & Freeston, M. H. (2004). Cognitive–behavioral treatment of generalized anxiety disorder (GAD) for older adults. *International Psychogeriatry*, *16*, 195–207.

Lang, A. J. (2004). Treating generalized anxiety disorder with cognitive–behavioral therapy. *Journal of Clinical Psychiatry*, *65*(Suppl. 13), 14–19.

Langhinrichsen-Rohling, J., Friend, J., & Powell, A. (2009). Adolescent suicide, gender, and culture: A rate and risk factor analysis. *Aggression and Violent Behavior, 14*, 402–414.

Lazarus, A. A. (1981). *The practice of multimodal therapy*. New York, NY: McGraw-Hill.

Lazarus, R. S. (1993). From psychological stress to the emotions: A history of changing outlooks. *Annual Review of Psychology, 44*, 1–21.

Lazarus, R. S., & Folkman, S. (1984). *Stress, appraisal, and coping*. New York, NY: Springer.

Leff, S. S., Gullan, R. L., Paskewich, B. S., et al. (2009). An initial evaluation of a culturally adapted social problem-solving and relational aggression prevention program for urban African-American relationally aggressive girls. *Journal of Prevention and Intervention in the Community, 37*, 260–274.

Lenzenweger, M. F. (2008). Epidemiology of personality disorders. *Psychiatric Clinics of North America, 31*, 395–403.

Lerner, M. S., & Clum, G. A. (1990). Treatment of suicide ideators: A problem-solving approach. *Behavior Therapy, 21*, 403–411.

Levenson, M., & Neuringer, C. (1971). Problem-solving behavior in suicidal adolescents. *Journal of Consulting and Clinical Psychology, 37*, 433–436.

Lewin, K. (1939). *A dynamic theory of personality*. New York, NY: McGraw-Hill.

Lewinsohn, P. M., Rohde, P., & Seeley, J. R. (1998). Major depressive disorders in older adolescents: Prevalence, risk factors, and clinical implications. *Clinical Psychology Review, 18*, 765–794.

Lindsay, W. R., Hamilton, C., Moulton, S., et al. (2011). Assessment and treatment of social problem solving in offenders with intellectual disability. *Psychology, Crime and Law, 17*, 181–197.

Linehan, M. M., Aamper, P., Chiles, J. A., et al. (1987). Interpersonal problem solving and parasuicide. *Cognitive Therapy and Research, 11*, 1–12.

Lochman, J. E., & Curry, J. F. (1986). Effects of social problem-solving training and self-instruction training with aggressive boys. *Journal of Clinical Child Psychology, 15*, 159–164.

Lochman, J. E., & Lenhart, L. A. (1993). Anger coping intervention for aggressive children: Conceptual models and outcome effects. *Clinical Psychology Review, 13*, 785–805.

Locke, E. A., & Latham, G. P. (1984). *Goal setting: A motivational technique that works*. Englewood Cliffs, NJ: Prentice Hall.

Lovett, B. J., & Sheffield, R. A. (2006). Affective empathy deficits in aggressive children and adolescents: A critical review. *Clinical Psychology Review, 1*, 1–13.

Luthar, S., Cicchetti, D., & Becker, B. (2000). The construct of resilience: A critical evaluation and guidelines for future work. *Child Development, 71*, 543–562.

Maat, S., Dekker, J., Schoevers, R., & De Jonghe, F. (2006). Relative efficacy of psychotherapy and pharmacotherapy in the treatment of depression: A meta-analysis. *Psychotherapy Research, 16*, 566–578.

Malcarne, V. L., Banthia, R., Varni, J. W., et al. (2002). Problem-solving skills and emotional distress in spouses of men with prostate cancer. *Journal of Cancer Education, 17*, 150–154.

Malhi, G. S., Adams, D., Porter, R., et al. (2009). Clinical practice recommendations for depression. *Acta Psychiatrica Scandinavica, 119*(Suppl. 439), 8–26.

Malouff, M. J., Thorsteinsson, E. B., & Schutte, N. S. (2007). The efficacy of problem solving therapy in reducing mental and physical health problems: A meta-analysis. *Clinical Psychology Review, 27*, 46–57.

Maluccio, A. (2002). Resilience: A many-splendored construct? *American Journal of Orthopsychiatry*, *72*, 596–599.

Marcotte, D., & Alain, M. (1999). Gender differences in adolescent depression: Gender-typed characteristics or problem-solving skills deficits? *Sex Roles*, *41*, 31–48.

Masten, A. S. (2001). Ordinary magic resilience processes in development. *American Psychologist*, *56*, 227–238.

Matthys, W., Cuperus, J. M., & Engeland, H. V. (1999). Deficient social problem-solving in boys with ODD/CD, with ADHD, and with both disorders. *Journal for the American Academy of Child and Adolescent Psychiatry*, *38*, 311–321.

Maydeu-Olivares, A., & D'Zurilla, T. J. (1995). A factor analysis of the social problem solving inventory using polychoric correlations. *European Journal of Psychological Assessment*, *11*, 98–107.

Maydeu-Olivares, A., & D'Zurilla, T. J. (1996). A factor analytic study of the social problem solving inventory: An integration of theory and data. *Cognitive Therapy and Research*, *20*, 115–133.

Mayer, R. E. (1998). Cognitive, metacognitive, and motivational aspects of problem solving. *Instructional Science*, *26*, 49–63.

McAuliffe, C., Keeley, H. S., & Corcoran, P. (2002). Problem solving and repetition of parasuicide. *Behavioral and Cognitive Psychotherapy*, *30*, 385–397.

McGuire, J. (2001). What is problem solving? A review of theory, research and applications. *Criminal Behaviour and Mental Health*, *11*, 210–235.

McGuire, J., & Hatcher, R. (2001). Offense-focused problem solving: Preliminary evaluation of a cognitive skills program. *Criminal Justice and Behavior*, *5*, 564–587.

McMurran, M., Fyffe, S., McCarthy, L., et al. (2001). "Stop and Think!": Social problem-solving therapy with personality disordered offenders. *Criminal Behaviour and Mental Health*, *11*, 273–285.

McMurran, M., Huband, N., & Duggan, C. (2008). A comparison of treatment completers and non-completers of an in-patient treatment programme for male personality-disordered offenders. *Psychology and Psychotherapy: Theory, Research and Practice*, *81*, 193–198.

McMurran, M., & Wilmington, R. (2007). A Delphi survey of the views of adult male patients with personality disorders on psychoeducation and social problem-solving therapy. *Criminal Behavior and Mental Health*, *17*, 293–299.

Medalia, A., Revheim, N., & Casey, M. (2002). Remediation of problem solving skills in schizophrenia: Evidence of persistent effect. *Schizophrenia Research*, *57*, 165–171.

Medalia, A., & Tysen, J. (2008). Insight into neurocognitive dysfunction in schizophrenia. *Schizophrenia Bulletin*, *34*, 1221–1230.

Morris, C. G., & Maisto, A. A. (1996). *Introduction to psychology* [Turkish translation]. Ankara: Turkish Psychological Association Publications.

Morris, S. E., Bellack, A. S., & Tenhula, W. N. (2004). Social problem solving and schizophrenia. In E. C. Chang, T. J. D'Zurilla, & L. J. Sanna (Eds.), *Social problem solving: Theory, research, and training* (pp. 83–98). Washington, DC: American Psychological Association.

Mraz, W., & Runco, M. A. (1994). Suicide ideation and creative problem solving. *Suicide and Life-Threatening Behavior*, *24*, 38–47.

Mulvaney, S. A., Rothman, R. L., Osborn, C. Y., et al. (2011). Self-management problem solving for adolescents with type 1 diabetes: Intervention processes associated with an Internet program. *Patient Education and Counseling*, *85*, 140–142.

Mynors-Wallis, L., Davies, I., Gray, A., et al. (1997). A randomized controlled trial and cost analysis of problem-solving treatment for emotional disorders given by community nurses in primary care. *British Journal of Psychiatry*, *170*, 113–119.

Mynors-Wallis, L., Gath, D., Day, A., & Baker, F. (2000). Randomized controlled trial of problem solving treatment, antidepressant medication, and combined treatment for major depression in primary care. *British Medical Journal*, *320*, 26–30.

Mynors-Wallis, L. M., Gath, D. H., Lloyd-Thomas, A. R., & Tomlinson, D. (1995). Randomised controlled trial comparing problem solving treatment with amitriptyline and placebo for major depression in primary care. *British Medical Journal*, *310*, 441–445.

Newman, T. B. (2004). A black-box warning for antidepressants in children? *New England Journal of Medicine*, *35*, 1595–1598.

Newton-Howes, G., Tyrer, P., Anagnostakis, K., et al. (2010). The prevalence of personality disorder, its comorbidity with mental state disorders, and its clinical significance in community mental health teams. *Social Psychiatry and Psychiatric Epidemiology*, *45*, 453–460.

Nezu, A. M. (2004). Problem solving and behavior therapy revisited. *Behavior Therapy*, *35*, 1–33.

Nezu, A. M. (1987). A problem-solving formulation of depression: A literature review and proposal of a pluralistic model. *Clinical Psychology Review*, *7*, 121–144.

Nezu, A. M. (1985). Differences in psychological distress between effective and ineffective problem solvers. *Journal of Counseling Psychology*, *32*, 135–138.

Nezu, A. M. (1986). Efficacy of a social problem-solving therapy approach for unipolar depression. *Journal of Consulting and Clinical Psychology*, *54*, 196–202.

Nezu, A. M., & Carnevale, G. J. (1987). Interpersonal problem solving and coping reactions of Vietnam veterans with posttraumatic stress disorder. *Journal of Abnormal Psychology*, *96*, 155–157.

Nezu, A. M., & Nezu, M. N. (2001). Problem-solving therapy. *Journal of Psychotherapy Integration*, *11*, 187–205.

Nezu, A. M., Nezu, C. M., Felgoise, S. H., et al. (2003). Project genesis: Assessing the efficacy of problem-solving therapy for distressed adult cancer patients. *Journal of Consulting and Clinical Psychology*, *71*, 1036–1048.

Nezu, A. M., Nezu, C. M., Friedman, S. H., et al. (1999). Cancer and psychological distress: Two investigations regarding the role of social problem-solving. In J. A. Bucher (Ed.), *The application of problem solving therapy to psychosocial oncology* (pp. 27–40). New York, NY: The Haworth Medical Press.

Nezu, A. M., Nezu, C. M., Houts, P. S., Friedman, S. H., & Faddis, S. (1999). Relevance of problem-solving therapy to psychosocial oncology. In J. A. Bucher (Ed.), *The application of problem solving therapy to psychosocial oncology* (pp. 5–26). New York, NY: The Haworth Medical Press.

Nezu, A. M., Nezu, C. M., & Perri, M. G. (1990). Psychotherapy for adults within a problem-solving framework: Focus on depression. *Journal of Cognitive Psychotherapy*, *4*, 247–256.

Nezu, A. M., & Perri, M. G. (1989). Social problem solving therapy for unipolar depression: An initial dismantling investigation. *Journal of Consulting and Clinical Psychology*, *57*, 408–413.

O'Brien, M. P., Zinberg, J. L., Ho, L., et al. (2009). Family problem solving interactions and 6-month symptomatic and functional outcomes in youth at ultra-high risk for psychosis and with recent onset psychotic symptoms: A longitudinal study. *Schizophrenia Research*, *107*, 198–205.

Oflaz, F., Hatipoglu, S., & Aydin, H. (2008). Effectiveness of psychoeducation intervention on post-traumatic stress disorder and coping styles of earthquake survivors. *Journal of Clinical Nursing*, *17*, 677–687.

Olexa, D. F., & Forman, S. G. (1984). Effects of social problem-solving training on classroom behavior of urban disadvantaged students. *Journal of School Psychology*, *22*, 165–175.

Olsson, C., Bond, L., & Burns, J. (2003). Adolescent resilience: A concept analysis. *Journal of Adolescence*, *26*, 1–11.

Orbach, I. (1986). The "unsolvable" a determinant in the dynamics of suicidal behavior in children. *American Journal of Psychotherapy*, *40*, 511–520.

Orbach, I. (1989). Familial and intrafamilial splits in suicidal adolescents. *American Journal of Psychotherapy*, *43*, 356–367.

Orbach, I., Mikulincer, M., Blumenson, R., et al. (1999). The subjective experience of problem solving irresolvability and suicidal behavior: Dynamics and measurement. *Suicide and Life-Threatening Behavior*, *29*, 150–164.

Orbach, I., Rosenheim, E., & Hary, E. (1987). Some aspects of cognitive functioning in suicidal children. *Journal of the American Academy of Child and Adolescent Psychiatry*, *25*, 181–185.

Pakaslahti, L. (2000). Children's and adolescents' aggressive behavior in context: The development and application of aggressive problem-solving strategies. *Aggression and Violent Behavior*, *5*, 467–490.

Paykel, E. S. (2007). Cognitive therapy in relapse prevention in depression. *International Journal of Neuropsychopharmacology*, *10*, 131–136.

Peterson, C., Buchanan, G. M., & Seligman, M. E. P. (1995). Explanatory style: History and evolution of the field. In G. M. Buchanan, & M. E. P. Seligman (Eds.), *Explanatory style* (pp. 1–20). Hillsdale, NJ: Lawrence Erlbaum Associates.

Peterson, C., & Seligman, M. E. P. (1984). Causal explanations as a risk factor for depression: Theory and evidence. *Psychological Review*, *91*, 347–374.

Pierce, D., & Gunn, J. (2007a). Using problem solving therapy in general practice. *Australian Family Physician*, *35*, 230–232.

Pierce, D., & Gunn, J. (2007b). GP's use of problem solving therapy for depression: A qualitative study of barriers to and enablers of evidence based care. *BMC Family Practice*, *8*, 1–8.

Pierce, D., & Gunn, J. (2011). Depression in general practice: Consultation duration and problem solving. *Australian Family Physician*, *40*, 334–336.

Platt, J. J., Siegel, J. M., & Spivack, G. (1975). Do psychiatric patients and normals see the same solutions as effective in solving interpersonal problems? *Journal of Consulting and Clinical Psychology*, *43*, 279.

Platt, J. J., & Spivack, G. (1972). Problem-solving thinking of psychiatric patients. *Journal of Consulting and Clinical Psychology*, *39*, 148–151.

Pollock, L. R., & Williams, J. M. (2004). Problem-solving in suicide attempters. *Psychological Medicine*, *34*, 163–167.

Pollock, L. R., & Williams, M. G. (1998). Problem solving and suicidal behavior. *Suicide and Life-Threatening Behavior*, *28*, 375–387.

Priester, M. J., & Clum, G. A. (1993). Perceived problem-solving ability as a predictor of depression, hopelessness, and suicide ideation in a college population. *Journal of Consulting Psychology*, *40*, 79–85.

Printz, B. L., & Shermis, M. D. (1999). Stress-buffering factors related to adolescent coping: A path analysis. *Adolescence*, *34*, 715–734.

Prochaska, J. O., & Norcross, J. C. (1984). *Systems of psychotherapy: A transtheoretical analysis*. Pacific Grove, CA: Brooks/Cole Publishing Company.

Raj, A. J., Kumaraiah, V., & Bhide, A. V. (2001). Cognitive–behavioural intervention in deliberate self-harm. *Acta Psychiatrica Scandinavica, 104*, 340–345.

Revheim, N., & Medalia, A. (2004). Verbal memory problem solving skills and community status in schizophrenia. *Schizophrenia Research, 68*, 149–158.

Richmond, T. K., & Rosen, D. S. (2005). The treatment of adolescent depression in the era of the black box warning. *Current Opinion in Pediatrics, 17*, 466–472.

Robichaud, M., & Dugas, M. J. (2005a). Negative problem orientation (Part I): Psychometric properties of a new measure. *Behaviour Research and Therapy, 43*, 391–401.

Robichaud, M., & Dugas, M. J. (2005b). Negative problem orientation (Part II): Construct validity and specificity to worry. *Behaviour Research and Therapy, 43*, 403–412.

Robinson, R. G., Jorge, R. E., Moser, D. J., et al. (2008). Escitalopram and problem-solving therapy for prevention of poststroke depression: A randomized controlled trial. *The Journal of the American Medical Association, 299*, 2391–2400.

Rodewald, K., Rentrop, M., Holt, D. V., et al. (2011). Planning and problem-solving training for patients with schizophrenia: A randomized controlled trial. *BMC Psychiatry, 11*, 73.

Rosen, D., Morse, J. Q., & Reynolds, C. F. (2010). Adapting problem-solving therapy for depressed older adults in methadone maintenance treatment. *Journal of Substance Abuse Treatment, 40*, 132–141.

Rotheram-Borus, M. J., Trautman, P. D., Dopkins, S. C., et al. (1990). Cognitive style and pleasant activities among female adolescent suicide attempters. *Journal of Consulting and Clinical Psychology, 58*, 554–561.

Rouse, K., Ingersoll, G., & Orr, D. (1998). Longitudinal health endangering behavior risk among resilient and nonresilient early adolescent. *Journal of Adolescent Health, 23*, 297–302.

Rushe, T. M., Morris, R. G., & Miotto, E. C. (1999). Problem solving and spatial working memory in patients with schizophrenia and with focal frontal and temporal lobe lesions. *Schizophrenia Research, 37*, 21–33.

Rutter, M. (1991). Nature, nurture and psychopathology: A new look at an old topic. *Development and Psychopathology, 3*, 125–136.

Ryan, N. (2005). Treatment of depression in children and adolescents. *The Lancet, 366*, 933–940.

Sahler, O. J., Fairclough, D. L., Phipps, S., et al. (2005). Using problem-solving skills training to reduce negative affectivity in mothers of children with newly diagnosed cancer: Report of a multisite randomized trial. *Journal of Consulting and Clinical Psychology, 73*, 272–283.

Sahler, O. J., Varni, J. W., Fairclough, D. L., et al. (2002). Problem-solving skills training for mothers of children with newly diagnosed cancer: A randomized trial. *Journal of Development and Behavioral Pediatrics, 23*, 77–86.

Salkovskis, P. M., Atha, C., & Storer, D. (1990). Cognitive–behavioural problem solving in the treatment of patients who repeatedly attempt suicide: A controlled trial. *British Journal of Psychiatry, 157*, 871–876.

Scheier, M. F., & Carver, C. S. (1987). Dispositional optimism and physical well-being: The influence of generalized outcome expectancies on health. *Journal of Personality, 55*, 169–210.

Schichor, A., Bernstein, B., & King, S. (1994). Self-reported depressive symptoms in inner-city adolescents seeking routine health care. *Adolescence, 29*, 379–388.

Schmidt, N. B., & Woolaway-Bickel, K. (2000). The effects of treatment compliance on outcome in cognitive–behavioral therapy for panic disorder: Quality versus quantity. *Journal of Consulting and Clinical Psychology, 68*, 13–18.

Schotte, D. E., & Clum, G. A. (1982). Suicide ideation in a college population: A test of a model. *Journal of Consulting and Clinical Psychology, 50*, 690–696.

Schotte, D. E., & Clum, G. A. (1987). Problem-solving skills in suicidal psychiatric patients. *Journal of Consulting and Clinical Psychology, 55*, 49–54.

Schotte, D. E., Cools, J., & Payvar, S. (1990). Problem-solving deficits in suicidal patients: Trait vulnerability or state phenomenon? *Journal of Consulting and Clinical Psychology, 58*, 562–564.

Schumann, K. P., Sutherlan, J. A., Majid, H. M., & Hill-Briggs, F. (2011). Evidence-based behavioral treatments for diabetes: problem-solving therapy. *Diabetes Spectrum, 24*, 64–69.

Seid, M., Varni, J. W., Gidwani, P., et al. (2010). Problem-solving skills training for vulnerable families of children with persistent asthma: Report of a randomized trial on health-related quality of life outcomes. *Journal of Pediatric Psychology, 35*, 1133–1143.

Selman, R. L. (1971). Taking another's perspective: Role taking development in early childhood. *Child Development, 42*, 1721–1734.

Selman, R. L. (1977). A structural-developmental model of social cognition: Implications for intervention research. *Counseling Psychologist, 6*, 3–6.

Sherwood, P., Given, B. A., Given, C. W., et al. (2005). A cognitive behavioral intervention for symptom management in patients with advanced cancer. *Oncological Nursing Forum, 32*, 1190–1198.

Silverstein, M., Feinberg, E., Cabral, H., et al. (2011). Problem-solving education to prevent depression among low-income mothers of preterm infants: A randomized controlled pilot trial. *Archives of Women's Mental Health, 14*, 317–324.

Siu, A. M. H., & Shek, D. T. L. (2005). Relationships between social problem solving and indicators of interpersonal and family well-being among Chinese adolescents in Hong Kong. *Social Indicators Research, 71*, 517–539.

Smith, R. E. (1993). *Psychology*. New York, NY: West Publishing Company.

Smokowski, P., Reynolds, A., & Bezruczko, N. (1999). Resilince and protective factors in adolescence: An autobiobiographical perspective from disadvantaged youth. *Journal of School Psychology, 37*, 425–448.

Spijker, B. A. J., Straten, A., & Kerkhof, J. F. M. (2010). The effectiveness of a web-based self-help intervention to reduce suicidal thoughts: A randomized controlled trial. *Trials, 11*, 25.

Spivack, G., Platt, J. J., & Shure, M. B. (1976). *The problem-solving approach to adjustment*. San Francisco, CA: Jossey-Bass.

Stanley, M. A., & Beck, J. G. (2000). Anxiety disorders. *Clinical Psychology Review, 20*, 731–754.

Steward, R. E., & Chambless, D. L. (2009). Cognitive–behavioral therapy for adult anxiety disorders in clinical practice: A meta-analysis of effectiveness studies. *Journal of Consulting and Clinical Psychology, 77*, 595–606.

Strecher, V. (2007). Internet methods for delivering behavioral and health-related interventions (eHealth). *Annual Review of Psychology, 3*, 53–76.

Sukhodolsky, D. G., Kassinove, H., & Gorman, B. S. (2004). Cognitive–behavioral therapy for anger in children and adolescence: A meta-analysis. *Aggression and Violent Behavior, 9*, 247–269.

Szasz, T. S. (1961). *The myth of mental illness*. New York, NY: Harper.

Takahashi, F., Koseki, S., & Shimada, H. (2009). Developmental trends in children's aggression and social problem-solving. *Journal of Applied Developmental Psychology*, *30*, 265–272.

Tarrier, N., Taylor, K., & Gooding, P. (2008). Cognitive–behavioral interventions to reduce suicide behavior: A systematic review and meta-analysis. *Behavior Modification*, *32*, 77–108.

Temple, S., & Ho, B. C. (2005). Cognitive therapy for persistent psychosis in schizophrenia: A case controlled clinical trial. *Schizophrenia Research*, *74*, 195–199.

Thase, M. E., & Callahan, J. A. (2006). The role of homework in cognitive behavior therapy for depression. *Journal of Psychotherapy Integration*, *16*, 162–177.

Townsend, E., Hawton, K., Altman, D. G., et al. (2001). The efficacy of problem-solving treatment after deliberate self-harm: Meta-analysis of randomized controlled trials with respect to depression, hopelessness and improvement in problems. *Psychological Medicine*, *31*, 979–988.

Trumbull, R., & Appley, M. H. (1986). A conceptual model for the examination of distress. In M. H. Appley, & R. Trumbull (Eds.), *Dynamics of stress* (pp. 21–45). New York, NY: Plenum Press.

Ucok, A., Cakır, S., Duman, Z. C., et al. (2006). Cognitive predictors of skill acquisition on social problem solving in patients with schizophrenia. *European Archives of Clinical Neuroscience*, *256*, 388–394.

Vaskinn, A., Sundet, K., Hultman, C. M., et al. (2009). Social problem-solving in high-functioning schizophrenia: Specific deficits in sending skills. *Psychiatry Research*, *165*, 215–223.

Vaughn, S. R., Ridley, C. A., & Bullock, D. D. (1984). Interpersonal problem-solving skills training with aggressive young children. *Journal of Applied Developmental Psychology*, *5*, 213–223.

Veltro, F., Mazza, M., Vendittelli, N., et al. (2011). A comparison of the effectiveness of problem solving training and of cognitive–emotional rehabilitation on neurocognition, social cognition, and social functioning in people with schizophrenia. *Clinical Practice and Epidemiology in Mental Health*, *7*, 123–132.

Wang, J., Zgibor, J., Matthews, J. T., et al. (2012). Self-monitoring of blood glucose is associated with problem-solving skills in hyperglycemia and hypoglycemia. *The Diabetes Educator*, *38*, 207–218.

Warmerdam, L., Straten, A., Jongsma, J., et al. (2010). Online cognitive behavioral therapy and problem-solving therapy for depressive symptoms: Exploring mechanisms of change. *Journal of Behavior Therapy and Experimental Psychiatry*, *41*, 64–70.

Wasbusch, D. A., Walsh, T. M., Andrade, B. F., King, S., & Carrey, N. J. (2007). Social problem solving, conduct problems, and callous-unintentional traits in children. *Child Psychiatry and Human Development*, *37*, 293–305.

Watkins, E., & Baracaia, S. (2002). Rumination and social problem solving in depression. *Behaviour Research and Therapy*, *40*, 1179–1189.

Webster-Stratton, C., Reid, J., & Hammond, M. (2001). Social skills and problem-solving training for children with early-onset conduct problems: Who benefits? *Journal of Child Psychology and Psychiatry*, *42*, 943–952.

Weiner, B. (1986). *An attribution theory of motivation and emotion*. New York, NY: Springer Verlag.

Weishaar, M. E. (1996). Cognitive risk factors in suicide. In P. M. Salkovskis (Ed.), *Frontiers of cognitive therapy* (pp. 226–249). New York, NY: Guilford Press.

Weissman, M. M., Verdeli, H., Gameroff, M. J., et al. (2006). National survey of psychotherapy training in psychiatry, psychology, and social work. *Archives of General Psychiatry*, *63*, 925–934.

Westen, D. (1999). *Psychology: Mind, brain and culture* (2nd ed.). New York, NY: Wiley.

White, J. L., Moffitt, T. E., Caspi, A., et al. (1994). Measuring impulsivity and examining its relationship to delinquency. *Journal of Abnormal Psychology*, *103*, 192–205.

Williams, J. M. G., & Broadbent, K. (1986). Autobiographical memory in suicide attempters. *Journal of Abnormal Psychology*, *95*, 144–149.

Williams, J. M. G., & Dritschel, B. H. (1988). Emotional disturbance and the specificity of autobiographical memory. *Cognition and Emotion*, *2*, 221–234.

Wilkinson, P., & Mynors-Wallis, L. (1994). Problem-solving therapy in the treatment of unexplained physical symptoms in primary care: A preliminary study. *Journal of Psychosomatic Research*, *38*, 591–598.

Wilson, C., & Hughes, C. (2011). Worry, beliefs about worry and problem solving in young children. *Behavioural and Cognitive Psychotherapy*, *39*, 507–521.

Wilson, K. G., Stelzer, J., Bergman, J. N., et al. (1995). Problem solving, stress, and coping in adolescent suicide attempts. *Suicide and Life-Threatening Behavior*, *25*, 241–251.

Winnicott, D. W. (1986). Transitional objects and transitional phenomena. In P. Buckley (Ed.), *Essential papers on object relations* (pp. 254–271). New York, NY: New York University Press.

Wohlfarth, T. D., Zwieten, B. J., Lekkerkerker, F. J., et al. (2006). Antidepressants use in children and adolescents and the risk of suicide. *European Neuropsychopharmacology*, *16*, 79–83.

Wolf, N. J., & Hopko, D. R. (2008). Psychosocial and pharmacological interventions for depressed adults in primary care: A critical review. *Clinical Psychology Review*, *28*, 131–161.

Wood, R., & Bandura, A. (1989). Social cognitive theory of organizational management. Special issue: Theory development forum. *Academy of Management Review*, *14*, 361–384.

World Health Organization (2004). *Prevention of mental disorders: Effective interventions and policy options*. Geneva: World Health Organization.

Xia, J., & Li, C. (2007). Problem solving skills for schizophrenia. *Cochrane Database Systematic Review,* 18, CD006365.

Yang, B., & Clum, G. A. (1994). Life stress, social support, and problem-solving skills predictive of depressive symptoms, hopelessness, and suicide ideation in an Asian student population: A test of a model. *Suicide and Life-Threatening Behavior*, *24*, 127–139.

Yamashita, C., Mizuno, M., Nemoto, T., & Kashima, H. (2005). Social cognitive problem-solving in schizophrenia: Associations with fluency and verbal memory. *Psychiatry Research*, *134*, 123–129.

Yang, C. H., Tsai, S. J., Chang, J. W., et al. (2001). Characteristics of Chinese suicide attempters admitted to a geropsychiatric unit. *International Journal of Geriatric Psychiatry*, *16*, 1033–1036.

Yerkes, R. M., & Dodson, J. D. (1908). The relation of strength of stimulus to rapidity of habit-formation. *Journal of Comparative Neurological Psychology*, *18*, 459–482.

Yetis, Ö. Y. (2010). *Üniversite öğrencilerinde kişilik bozukluğu yaygınlığı ve sorun çözme becerileri ile ilişkisinin incelenmesi* [*An investigation of the prevalence of personality disorder and its relationship with problem solving skills in university students, in Turkish*]. Master's thesis (unpublished). Maltepe University, Istanbul.

Zanello, A., Perrig, L., & Huguelet, P. (2006). Cognitive functions related to interpersonal problem-solving skills in schizophrenic patients compared with healthy subjects. *Psychiatry Research*, *142*, 67–78.

Zanis, D. A., Coviello, D., Alterman, A. I., & Appling, S. E. (2001). A community-based trial of vocational problem-solving to increase employment among methadone patients. *Journal of Substance Abuse Treatment*, *21*, 19–26.

Zoffmann, V., & Kirkevold, M. (2005). Life versus diabetes in difficult diabetes care: Conflicting perspectives disempower patients and professionals in problem solving. *Qualitative Health Research*, *15*, 750–765.

FSC
www.fsc.org
MIX
Papier | Fördert
gute Waldnutzung
FSC® C083411

Kolibri 360 GmbH
Ferdinand-Jühlke-Straße 7
99095 Erfurt, Deutschland
produktsicherheit@kolibri360.de